EVERY CATHOLIC'S GUIDE TO THE SACRED SCRIPTURES

EVERY CATHOLIC'S GUIDE TO THE SACRED SCRIPTURES

THOMAS NELSON PUBLISHERS
Nashville

Published in Nashville, Tennessee, by Thomas Nelson, Inc., and dis-
tributed in Canada by Lawson Falle, Ltd., Cambridge, Ontario.

Printed in the United States of America.

Scripture quotations are from The New Catholic Study Bible, St. Jerome
Edition. Copyright © 1975, Thomas Nelson, Inc., Publishers.

Library of Congress Cataloging-in-Publication Data

Every Catholic's guide to the Sacred Scripture.
    p.   cm.
  ISBN 0-8407-3186-8
  1. Bible—Introductions. 2. Catholic Church—Doctrines.
BS475.2.E92   1990
220.6'1'02422—dc20   90-39488
                                        CIP

CONTENTS

✠ ✠ ✠

PART I:
The Bible and Church Teachings

Church Teaching on Inspiration 13
The Bible and the Teaching Church 30
How the Bible Came About 38
The Bible and History 51
Literary Forms of the Bible 64
Biblical Themes 76

PART II:
Introduction to Bible Study

How to Study the Bible 93

PART III:
Introductions to the Books of the Bible

The Old Testament

Genesis . . . . Gen. 105
Exodus. . . . . Ex.. 109
Leviticus. . . . . Lev. 111
Numbers. . . . . Num. 114
Deuteronomy . . . . Deut. 117
Joshua . . . . Josh.. 119
Judges . . . . Judg. 123
Ruth . . . . Ruth. 125

First Samuel . . . . 1 Sam.. 128
Second Samuel . . . . 2 Sam.. 131
First Kings. . . . . 1 Kings 134
Second Kings . . . . 2 Kings 138
First Chronicles . . . . 1 Chron. 141
Second Chronicles. . . . . 2 Chron. 144
Ezra . . . . Ezra 147
Nehemiah . . . . Neh.. 150
Esther . . . . Est. 153
Job . . . . Job. 157
Psalms . . . . Ps. (Pss.) 160
Proverbs . . . . Prov. 164
Ecclesiastes . . . . Eccl. 168
Song of Songs . . . . Song. 171
Isaiah . . . . Isa. 174
Jeremiah . . . . Jer. 178
Lamentations . . . . Lam.. 181
Ezekiel . . . . Ezek. 184
Daniel . . . . Dan.. 188
Hosea . . . . Hos.. 192
Joel. . . . . Joel 195
Amos . . . . Amos 197
Obadiah . . . . Obad.. 199
Jonah . . . . Jonah 202
Micah . . . . Mic. 205
Nahum. . . . . Nah.. 208
Habakkuk . . . . Hab.. 211
Zephaniah . . . . Zeph. 214
Haggai . . . . Hag.. 217
Zechariah . . . . Zech. 221
Malachi . . . . Mal. 224

The Deuterocanonicals/Apocrypha

Tobit . . . . Tobit. 229
Judith . . . . Judith 233
Esther (Greek). . . . . Rest of Est. 235
Wisdom of Solomon . . . . Wisd. Sol.. 238

Sirach . . . . Si. 241
Baruch . . . . Bar. 245
Letter of Jeremiah . . . . Let. Jer. 249
Song of the Three Young Men . . S. of III Ch. 252
Susanna . . . . Sus. 253
Bel and the Dragon . . . . Bel. 254
First Maccabees . . . . 1 Macc. 256
Second Maccabees. . . . . 2 Macc. 260
Some Additional Books
First Esdras . . . . 1 Esd. 263
Second Esdras. . . . . 2 Esd. 267
The Prayer of Manasseh . . . . Pr. Man. 270

The New Testament

Matthew . . . . Matt. 272
Mark . . . . Mark 276
Luke . . . . Luke. 280
John . . . . John 284
Acts . . . . Acts 288
Romans . . . . Rom. 292
First Corinthians . . . . 1 Cor. 297
Second Corinthians . . . . 2 Cor. 301
Galatians. . . . . Gal. 305
Ephesians . . . . Eph. 308
Philippians . . . . Phil. 313
Colossians . . . . Col. 317
First Thessalonians . . . . 1 Thess. 321
Second Thessalonians. . . . . . 2 Thess. 325
First Timothy . . . . 1 Tim. 328
Second Timothy. . . . . 2 Tim. 331
Titus . . . . Titus. 335
Philemon . . . . Philem. 339
Hebrews. . . . . Heb. 342
James . . . . James 347
First Peter . . . . 1 Peter. 351
Second Peter. . . . . 2 Peter. 355
First John . . . . 1 John 358

CONTENTS

Second John. . . . . 2 John. 362
Third John. . . . . 3 John. 364
Jude . . . . Jude. 366
Revelation . . . . Rev. 370

PART IV:
Additional Study Helps

Part I

THE BIBLE AND CHURCH TEACHINGS

✠ ✠ ✠

CHURCH TEACHING ON INSPIRATION

Daniel A. Murray

The phrase "the inspiration of Scripture" means many things to different people. For a Roman Catholic, the inspiration of Scripture is an indisputable fact. It has been solemnly defined by the teaching authority of the Church.

How exactly inspiration works is another question. This is an open-ended issue and has been explained by many theories throughout the centuries. Scholars continue to develop and refine their theories today.

The Church, while never defining anything about the "how" of inspiration, has nevertheless responded to some theories on this subject and has laid down certain guidelines to follow.

This article has a very limited purpose. It stresses the Church's teaching on the "fact" of inspiration and the principles that are to guide scholars in their treatment of the "how" of inspiration and its consequence, the truth of Scripture.

Inspiration—The Fact

Surely, one of the most complex issues facing dogma and Scripture scholars today is "inspiration." The English term *inspiration* comes from St. Jerome's Vulgate translation of a word in Second Timothy 3:16: "All Scripture is inspired by God (Vulg., *divinitus inspirata* for the Gr., *theopneustos*—"God-breathed" or "the breath of God") and is useful for teaching the truth, rebuking error, correcting faults, and giving instruction for right living."

Biblical scholars recognize that there are many difficult problems with this verse. It is part of a larger passage, Second Timothy 3:10–17. The author is not speaking as a dogmatic theologian. Rather, he is exhorting his readers to be steadfast in faith and virtue. As part of his exhortation the author reminds the reader of a then commonly held truth: every passage of Scripture comes from God, or is the breath of God. The Fathers of the Church and most modern commentators understand the verse in this sense. If Sacred Scripture came from God or was God-breathed, it had a unique authority. The term *inspira-*

13

tion refers to the special authoritative character of the sacred writings we call the Bible.

Israel came to recognize the Bible's special authority even though nowhere in the Old Testament is a book said to be inspired by God.

What the Old Testament contains is Israel's belief that God revealed himself in history and that that history was guided by God's Spirit. The writers of the Old Testament teach that the "breath of God" came upon Moses, the Judges, Saul, David, the prophets, etc. These specially chosen persons, with the help of God's Spirit, interpreted Israel's history.

From this belief the scribes easily deduced that the same Spirit of God was with the sacred authors when they wrote their "books." It was the presence of God's Spirit that gave Scripture its authoritative character.

One easy way to understand this unique authority of Scripture is to remember the importance of the idea of covenant in the Bible. We know that covenants or treaties were one of the principal ways of establishing national and international contact and order in the societies of the ancient Near East. It should come as no surprise that the authors of Scripture conceived of God's relationship with Israel in this way too.

We speak of God's covenant with Adam, with Noah, with Abraham, with Moses, with David, etc. Since, however, God is the One who initiates this covenant, and since God sets the terms of the covenant relationship, then a unique authority is obviously present in these covenants that is not present in any other one. The covenant contains God's word. In a long and very complex history, that word was transmitted in oral and written forms. The community of Israel and the early Church community recognized that the Spirit of God was at work among them. Their traditions, oral and written, were God-breathed. Over the centuries the Spirit inspired a number of human authors to take these oral and written traditions (adding some of their own) and produce a series of books that witness to God's self-revelation through history. In addition God's Spirit inspired the faith communities of Israel and the Church to recognize that the covenant word, God's word, constituted them in being and contained their rule of faith and life. Israel and the Church recognized that Sacred Scripture was normative for them for all time. All aspects of Israel's and the Church's life, cult, and culture stood under the covenant rule. The covenant documents held and hold for believers an authoritative dimension that no other literature holds. It is to this dimension that we refer when we speak of the "inspiration of Scripture."

Inspiration, or the unique authority of Sacred Scripture, is a scriptural and dogmatic fact that few would deny. It was taught and held by the Fathers and Doctors of the Church. The papal encyclicals of Leo XIII (*Providentissimus Deus*), of Benedict XV (*Spiritus Paraclitus*), and of Pius XII (*Divino Afflante Spiritu*) affirm the fact of inspiration. The First Vatican Council solemnly teaches the fact of inspiration, and Vatican Council II affirms this teaching.

Inspiration—The Explanation

The fact of inspiration is one thing; the nature of it, or how it works, is another. Early Christian writers, such as Clement of Alexandria and Origen, borrowed biblical language when they called the Bible "holy writings," "sacred books," or "the divine word." However, some of the learned Fathers and Doctors of the Church, such as Ambrose and Augustine, went a step further. They began to say that God is the author of Sacred Scripture.

This phrase stuck and has become part of our scriptural, dogmatic, and conciliar vocabulary. On April 24, 1870, the Bishops at Vatican I approved the following statement:

> These (the books of the Old and New Testaments) the Church holds to be sacred and canonical, not because, having been carefully composed by mere human industry, they were afterwards approved by her authority, nor merely because they contain revelation with no admixture of error, but because, having been written by the inspiration of the Holy Spirit, *They have God for their author* and have been delivered as such to the Church herself. (*Dei Filius*)

Vatican II, on November 18, 1965, in its dogmatic constitution on revelation, *Dei Verbum*, repeated the formulation of Vatican I. This phrase, "God is the author of Sacred Scripture," has been at the center of all discussions on the nature of inspiration.

What complicated the discussion was the fact that now both God and man were being referred to as authors of Sacred Scripture. Were they authors in the same sense? Was God to be thought of as a literary author? Did God actually write down words? Did God dictate thoughts to a scribe who wrote them down? Or is God the "author" of Scripture in the sense that he is the authority or cause who called Israel and the Church into existence and in so doing willed that the Sacred Scriptures would constitute an essential element of their foundation?

By way of answer, the first thing we must remember is that we are dealing with a mystery. The Church has never put forth an official teaching which explained the nature of the divine-human collaboration that produced the Sacred Scriptures. The Church has officially discarded some explanations offered by scholars over the past centuries.

One theory rejected by the Church is *the mechanical dictation theory.* According to this theory, God alone is the author of Scripture. God dictated to a human being every noun, adjective, and verb; all syntax and punctuation. The human being was but a robot-like instrument who made no contribution to the written work other than write it down.

Pius XII in his encyclical letter *Divino Afflante Spiritu* discarded such an explanation when he encouraged interpreters to determine "the peculiar character and circumstances of the sacred writer, the age in which he lived, the sources written and oral to which he had recourse and the forms of expression he employed. Thus can he the better understand who was the inspired author, and what he wishes to express by his writings." Pius XII went on to say:

> Nevertheless no one, who has a correct idea of biblical inspiration, will be surprised to find, even in the Sacred Writers, as in other ancient authors, certain fixed ways of expounding and narrating, certain definite idioms, especially of a kind peculiar to the Semitic tongues, so-called approximations, and certain hyperbolical modes of expression, nay, at times, even paradoxical, which help to impress the ideas more deeply on the mind. For of the modes of expression which, among ancient peoples, and especially those of the East, human language used to express its thought, none is excluded from the Sacred Books, provided the way of speaking adopted in no wise contradicts the holiness and truth of God, as, with his customary wisdom, the Angelic Doctor already observed in these words: "In Scripture divine things are presented to us in the manner which is in common use amongst men." For as the substantial Word of God became like to men in all things, "except sin," so the words of God, expressed in human language, are made like to human speech in every respect, except error. In this consists that "condescension" of the God of providence, which St. John Chrysostom extolled with the highest praise and repeatedly declared to be found in the Sacred Books. (par. 37)

The Pontifical Biblical Commission likewise discarded a mechanical dictation theory of inspiration when on April 21, 1964, it published its "Instruction on the Historical Truth of the Gospels." In this document the Commission taught:

> The sacred authors, for the benefit of the churches, took this earliest body of instruction, which had been handed on orally at first and then in writing— for many soon set their hands to "drawing up a narrative" of matters concerning the Lord Jesus—and set it down in the four Gospels. In doing

this each of them followed a method suitable to the special purpose which he had in view. They selected certain things out of the many which had been handed on; some they synthesized, some they explained with an eye to the situation of the churches, painstakingly using every means of bringing home to their readers the solid truth of the things in which they had been instructed. For, out of the material which they had received, the sacred authors selected especially those items which were adapted to the varied circumstances of the faithful as well as to the end which they themselves wished to attain; these they recounted in a manner consonant with those circumstances and with that end. . . . The Holy Spirit distributes His gifts to each one according as He wills, therefore, too, for the sake of those Books which were to be set so high at the very summit of authority, He undoubtedly guided and controlled the minds of the holy writers in their recollection of what they were to write. (par. 2)

Vatican Council II also rejects the mechanical dictation theory of inspiration in its dogmatic constitution *Dei Verbum:*

Since God speaks in sacred Scripture through men in human fashion, the interpreter of sacred Scripture, in order to see clearly what God wanted to communicate to us, should carefully investigate what meaning the sacred writers really intended, and what God wanted to manifest by means of their words. Those who search out the intention of the sacred writers must, among other things, have regard for "literary forms." For truth is proposed and expressed in a variety of ways, depending on whether a text is history of one kind or another, or whether its form is that of prophecy, poetry, or some other type of speech. The interpreter must investigate what meaning the sacred writer intended to express and actually expressed in particular circumstances as he used contemporary literary forms in accordance with the situation of his own time and culture. For the correct understanding of what the sacred author wanted to assert, due attention must be paid to the customary and characteristic styles of perceiving, speaking, and narrating which prevailed at the time of the sacred writer, and to the customs men normally followed at that period in their everyday dealings with one another. (par. 12)

A second theory rejected by the Church is the one called *mere assistance.* This theory denied that there is any such thing as inspiration. Whereas the mechanical dictation theory states that God alone is the author of Scripture, this new theory teaches that the human author alone is responsible for the Sacred Writings. The Holy Spirit stirs the human author to write simply what he already knew, having learned it before, or understood it through his own perception. The Holy Spirit does not reveal directly to the human author what he should put into writing. The Spirit does, however, assist the author in such a way that he will choose to write only those things than conform to the truth. This assistance is what, according to this theory, we mean by inspiration.

This theory goes on to say that inspiration as it pertains to revelation is to be distinguished from inspiration as it pertains to Sacred Scripture. Inspiration in the first case is a positive influence. Through it God reveals a truth to a human being. Inspiration in the second case is a negative assistance. It provides the human author with no new information but simply prevents the writings from being contaminated by error.

According to this theory, Scripture is not really the Word of God. It is simply a textbook composed by a human author whose purpose is to edify the reader in faith and charity.

Vatican I explicitly condemned this theory by teaching:

> Those books are held to be sacred and canonical by the Church, not . . . merely because they contain revelation with no admixture of error, but because, having been written by the inspiration of the Holy Spirit, they have God for their author and have been delivered as such to the Church herself.

A third approach to inspiration rejected by the Church is that of *subsequent approbation.* According to this theory a book is written in a purely human manner. Sometime later this book is elevated, through reception into the Canon, to be an expression of divine communication to men. In this theory, inspiration is a concomitant influence and consists simply in the Church's acceptance of a book into its Canon. Inspiration does not involve any direct intervention in the spirit of the human author.

Vatican I expressly condemned this theory when it taught:

> Those books are held to be sacred and canonical by the Church, not because they were produced by mere human industry and afterwards approved by her authority—but because, having been written by the inspiration of the Holy Spirit, they have God for their author and have been delivered as such to the Church herself. (*Dei Filius*)

The Church has never officially adopted any one explanation of inspiration as her own. In conciliar and encyclical teachings, however, she has insisted that any theory that seeks to explain the nature of inspiration must contain two elements: (1) God is actively present in a unique manner in the composition of the Bible; that is, Scripture is the Word of God. (2) The human authors are free to make use of their own talents and resources, in cooperation with the Holy Spirit, in writing the books of the Bible; that is, Scripture is the Word of God in the words of men.

Critical scholarship today recognizes that an adequate theory of inspiration must take into account the action of God, the effect of God's action on the human author, and the written work itself.

1. The Action of God

The action of God is the most difficult to explain. As was stated earlier, this is part of a mystery that no human mind can unravel. Leo XIII in *Providentissimus Deus* spoke of God stimulating and moving the human author. Pius XII in *Divino Afflante Spiritu* endorses the analogy of instrumental causality as an effective way of explaining God's action. This theory has been refined by Catholic scholars and states that God is the principal cause who moves and elevates the human author (the instrumental cause), who thus produces an effect of an order higher than he could were he working on his own. The effect can thus be attributed to both God and man. In the process God respects the freedom and intelligence of the human author who speaks a particular language, lives at a particular time, and is the product of a particular age and culture.

2. The Effect of God's Action on the Human Author

The effect of God's action on the human author is still another part of the mystery. The Spirit guides the human author as he makes certain judgments and decisions about the truth God wants taught and what literary form to use in order to communicate that truth.

In discussing God's action and its effect on the human author in the process of inspiration, scholars today must take into account the results of recent scholarship on the question of biblical authorship.

Many of the traditions found in the Bible circulated for years, even centuries, in oral and/or written form. Many authors were responsible for the material which was created for, and received by, a believing community. It was in this dynamic social setting that the sacred traditions were developed, interpreted, and synthesized before they became a "book" of Scripture. The Pontifical Biblical Commission acknowledges that this is the case for the New Testament:

> The sacred authors, for the benefit of the Churches, took this earliest body of instruction, which had been handed on orally at first and then in writing

. . . and set it down in the four Gospels. (*Instruction on the Historical Truth of the Gospels*)

Certainly the same must be said for the Old Testament. This has led some scholars to speak of the social character of inspiration. This means that the communities of Israel and the Church, not just the final writer or editor of a particular "book" could well have possessed the charism of inspiration.

3. The Written Work Itself

Any integral consideration of the question of inspiration has to address the issue of the inspired text itself and its meaning. Most classical treatments of inspiration focus on the action of God and on the inspired author.

The meaning of a biblical text was arrived at in different ways throughout the history of interpretation. Jewish scholars had long recognized that the revealed word of God had many possible meanings. The lifetime task of the student of the Bible was to study ways to unlock the rich variety of meanings in a particular text.

Early Church Fathers shared the insight of the Jewish scholars and spoke of the historical and the allegorical meanings of a text. These were expanded by the Medieval exegetes who emphasized four meanings which could be given to any text. They spoke of the four senses of Scripture. There was the historical or literal, the allegorical or christological, the tropological or moral, and the anagogical or eschatological.

Early twentieth century biblical scholars spoke of the *literal sense* as the meaning directly intended by the human author. It is the meaning which his words convey. These scholars also spoke of the *fuller sense* of Scripture. This, they said, is the deeper meaning, intended by God, but not directly intended by the human author. They also spoke of a *typical sense* which is the deeper meaning that the persons, places, and events of Scripture possess because in the intention of God they foreshadow future things.

In his encyclical *Divino Afflante Spiritu*, Pius XII taught that interpreters of Scripture have as their foremost and greatest endeavor the duty of discerning and defining clearly "that sense of the biblical words which is called literal." He went on to say that scholars can determine the literal sense of a passage in Scripture by studying its context and by comparing it with similar passages, always using their knowledge of Hebrew and Greek. Pius XII also taught that in determining the literal meaning, scholars should take into account the explanations and declarations of the teaching authority of the Church as well as the interpretation given by the Fathers of the Church. (cf. par. 23)

The Pontifical Biblical Commission in its *Instruction on the Historical Truth of the Gospels* said that the Catholic exegete must make skillful use of the new aids to exegesis, especially those which the historical method has provided. The Instruction speaks of textual criticism, literary criticism, and linguistic studies. It also directs the scholar to come to grips with the character of Gospel testimony, of the religious life of the first churches, and of the significance and force of the apostolic tradition. The task of determining the literal sense is most important according to the Instruction:

> Unless the exegete, then, pays attention to all those factors which have a bearing on the origin and the composition of the Gospels, and makes due use of the acceptable findings of modern research, he will fail in his duty of ascertaining what the intentions of the sacred writers were, and what it is that they have actually said. (par. 2)

Later twentieth century scholars have seen the value of the historical-critical method for ascertaining the literal sense, the meaning intended by the inspired author. They also see its limitations in determining the meaning of the text itself. Distinctions have to be made in what the literal sense actually is. In many biblical books, for instance, scholars find that the original author's meaning has to be understood in the light of what a final editor has done to his composition. In addition, the final edition of a biblical "book" takes on added or new meaning when it becomes part of a collection of books (canon) and is thus handed on to a believing community by a believing community. Here it is important to remember that the object of the definition of inspiration in Vatican I is the books themselves. It is the books, not their authors, which have been entrusted to the Church.

Pius XII in *Divino Afflante Spiritu* taught that "the words of God, expressed in human language, are made like to human speech in every respect, except error." It is human language, therefore, with its laws and history that has been the instrument of divine communication.

Linguistic studies emphasize this in trying to determine what the text means today. Those who approach Scripture from this discipline point out that language has a force, a meaning, a life of its own independent of the one who uses it. They view a literary work as a precise system of words ordered to one another and having meaning. This being the case, the meaning of a biblical text cannot be limited to the literal sense.

The Church recognizes the importance of the literal sense and encourages scholars to use all sound scriptural aids to determine it. The historical-critical method, modern literary criticism, and linguistic studies will help scholars determine not only what a biblical passage meant but also what it means.

The Church issues a caution to Roman Catholic scholars who are engaged in the work of interpreting the Bible. Leo XIII has said in *Providentissimus Deus:*

> . . . it must be recognized that the sacred writings are wrapt in a certain religious obscurity, and that no one can enter into their interior without a guide. (Part II, Section C, par. 1)

He quotes from Vatican I and reminds scholars that

> in things of faith and morals, belonging to the building up of Christian doctrine, that is to be considered the true sense of Scripture which has been held and is held by our Holy Mother the Church, whose place it is to judge of the true sense and interpretation of the Scriptures. (Part II, Section C, par. 1a)

Vatican II in *Dei Verbum* echoes this teaching:

> The task of authentically interpreting the word of God, whether written or handed on, has been entrusted exclusively to the living teaching office of the Church, whose authority is exercised in the name of Jesus Christ. (Ch. 2, par. 10)

Inspiration—the Consequence I

Sacred Scripture teaches that God is rich in mercy and faithfulness. These two words, mercy and faithfulness (*hesed* and *'emeth* in Hebrew) can be called part of Israel's covenant vocabulary. The writers of the Old Testament reminded Israel that throughout her long history God was ever faithful. God was, is, and always will be true to his promises, true to his covenant word.

The New Testament writers shared this conviction. They saw Jesus Christ as the fulfillment of the promises and of the covenant God had made with Israel. Jesus Christ is the Way, the Truth, and the Life. He is the faithful and true Word of God.

The truth of the Bible was taken for granted. It was one of the presuppositions on which the faith of Israel and of the Church was based. No one ever thought to question the truth of Sacred Scripture.

Centuries after the close of the biblical era a shift begins to take place in theological reflection on the truth of Scripture. Instead of viewing the truth of Scripture in the sense of God's being true and faithful to his word, scholars began to speak of Scripture as being free from mistakes, errors, and contradictions, even in the smallest details. Wherever contradictions or errors were found, they were explained away by harmonization or by some other means.

When in 1543 the Polish churchman, Copernicus, published his thesis *De Revolutionibus Orbium Caelestium*, the scientific revolution began. A new context was born for the study of Scripture. Copernicus put forth a tentative hypothesis that the earth goes around the sun. He thus challenged the then uncritically accepted geocentric view of the universe. This was the view of Aristotle and was worked into a cosmological system by Ptolemy of Alexandria. The Aristotelian-Ptolomaic world view dominated the minds of educated people until the sixteenth century.

The Bible seemed to corroborate this geocentric world view. Everyone accepted the notion that Scripture was not just a sacred literature, but also a scientific one which gave information on such things as plant and animal life and the structure of the solar system.

Copernicus' hypothesis created a problem. If the Bible is proved wrong in its cosmology, perhaps it is wrong in other areas as well. The scientific revolution was seen in some quarters as an attack on the truth of the Bible.

An age of skepticism had arrived. Educated people began to ask critical questions of the Bible. The so-called historical revolution of the nineteenth century created newer problems. Historians came to see that historical facts were not something cold and objective. An essential part of writing history is the subjective interpretation of the author.

When these ideas were applied to Scripture as a historical document, the result was disastrous. It was discovered that there were historical errors of fact in Scripture. In addition, the Bible, from Genesis to Revelation, was filled with interpretation. To some minds this meant distortion. To others, it meant that it was impossible to ascertain any truth about the history of Israel or of the public ministry of Jesus.

Catholic scholars were clearly on the defensive. They tried to develop theories that would reconcile the findings of modern science with the notion that there were no errors in the Bible.

Some claimed it was enough to say that the Bible was inspired, or partially inspired, with no need for inerrancy. Others wanted to restrict inerrancy to doctrinal matters. Still others said that anything that wasn't part of the human author's primary purpose in writing was not covered by inerrancy.

Leo XIII repudiated these theories in his encyclical *Providentissimus Deus:*

> It is absolutely wrong and forbidden either to narrow inspiration to certain parts only of Holy Scripture or to admit that the sacred writer has erred. As to the system of those who, in order to rid themselves of these difficulties, do not hesitate to concede that divine inspiration regards the things of faith and morals, and nothing beyond, because (as they wrongly think) in a question of the truth or falsehood of a passage we should consider not so much what God has said as the reason and purpose which He had in mind in saying it—this system cannot be tolerated. . . . For all the books which the Church receives as sacred and canonical are written wholly and entirely, with all their parts, at the dictation of the Holy Spirit; and so far is it from being possible that any error can coexist with inspiration, that inspiration not only is essentially incompatible with error, but excludes and rejects it as absolutely and necessarily as it is impossible that God Himself, the supreme Truth, can utter that which is not true. . . . Hence, because the Holy Spirit employed men as His instruments, we cannot, therefore, say that it was these inspired instruments who, perchance, have fallen into error, and not the primary author. For, by supernatural power, He so moved and impelled them to write—He so assisted them when writing—that the things which He ordered, and those only, they, first, rightly understood, then willed faithfully to write down, and finally expressed in apt words and with infallible truth. (Part II, Section D, par. 2c)

While Leo XIII closed the door on these explanations he opened a window to future scholars when he treated the issue of the natural sciences. He said that the human authors of Scripture

> did not seek to penetrate the secrets of nature, but rather described and dealt with things in more or less figurative language, or in terms which were commonly used at the time, and which in many instances are daily used at this day, even by the most eminent men of science. Ordinary speech primarily and properly describes what comes under the senses; and somewhat in the same way the sacred writers—as the Angelic Doctor also reminds us—"went by what sensibly appeared," or put down what God, speaking to men, signified, in the way men could understand and were accustomed to. (Part II, Section D, par. 2b)

Pius XII in *Divino Afflante Spiritu* opened the window wider. He recognized that the human authors of Scripture did not always employ the forms of speech we use today. Rather, they used ones common to the men of their times and countries. Pius XII noted that the ancient authors had certain fixed ways of expounding and narrating, certain definite idioms and forms of expression which they used in poetic description, or in the formulation of laws or rules of life, or in recording the facts and events of history.

The Pope instructed Catholic commentators to demonstrate and prove Scripture's immunity from error by determining to what extent the manner of expression or the literary mode adopted by the human writer may lead to a correct or genuine interpretation:

> Not infrequently—to mention only one instance—when some persons reproachfully charge the Sacred Writers with some historical error or inaccuracy in the recording of facts, on closer examination it turns out to be nothing else than those customary modes of expression and narration peculiar to the ancients which used to be employed in the mutual dealings of social life and which in fact were sanctioned by common usage. When then such modes of expression are met with in the sacred text, which, being meant for men, is couched in human language, justice demands that they be no more taxed with error than when they occur in the ordinary intercourse of daily life. By this knowledge and exact appreciation of the modes of speaking and writing in use among the ancients can be solved many difficulties, which are raised against the veracity and historical value of the Divine Scriptures, and no less efficaciously does this study contribute to a fuller and more luminous understanding of the mind of the Sacred Writer. (Part II, Section 3, par. 38–39)

Taking advantage of the insights of Leo XIII and Pius XII, Catholic scholars came to realize that Scripture contains many different literary forms. They recognized too that human language, the instrument of divine communication in Scripture, has many functions: teaching, exhorting, impressing, etc. All of these are found in Sacred Scripture and must be taken into account when discussing the truth of the Bible.

Scripture is not principally a history book; nor is it a textbook on science, biology, cosmology, etc. Scripture is the faith document of a believing community. That document contains God's word in the words of men.

Vatican II recognized this when it said that the truth of Sacred Scripture is the truth that leads to salvation. In other words, the Bible isn't teaching every manner of truth (ontological, logical, scientific, etc.). It is teaching the truth which God wished to communicate for the sake of our salvation. That truth, the Council said, is expressed and proposed in a variety of ways.

The Council Fathers laid down what could be called three guiding principles that must be part of any explanation of the truth of Scripture (Constitution on Divine Revelation, *Dei Verbum*, Ch. III, par. 11–12).

1. The truth of Scripture is the truth that leads to salvation. The Bible isn't teaching every manner of truth:

> Since everything asserted by the inspired authors or sacred writers must be held to be asserted by the Holy Spirit, it follows that the books of Scripture must be acknowledged as teaching firmly, faithfully, and without error that truth which God wanted put into the sacred writings for the sake of our salvation.

2. The truth of Scripture is expressed in a variety of ways:

> Those who search out the intention of the sacred writers must, among other things, have regard for "literary forms." For truth is proposed and expressed in a variety of ways, depending on whether a text is history of one kind or another, or whether its form is that of prophecy, poetry, or some other type of speech. The interpreter must investigate what meaning the sacred writer intended to express and actually expressed in particular circumstances as he used contemporary literary forms in accordance with the situation of his own time and culture.

3. The truth of Scripture must be considered in the light of the content and unity of the whole of Scripture as well as in the light of the living tradition of the whole Church:

> But, since holy Scripture must be read and interpreted according to the same Spirit by whom it was written, no less serious attention must be given to the content and unity of the whole of Scripture, if the meaning of the sacred texts is to be correctly brought to light. The living tradition of the whole Church must be taken into account along with the harmony which exists between elements of the faith. It is the task of exegetes to work according to these rules toward a better understanding and explanation of the meaning of sacred Scripture, so that through preparatory study the judgment of the Church may mature. For all of what has been said about the way of interpreting Scripture is subject finally to the judgment of the Church, which carries out the divine commission and ministry of guarding and interpreting the word of God.

It is important that any student of the Bible appreciate all the problems facing scholars in trying to explain the very complex problems of inspiration. No human being will ever explain fully the process involved in the divine-human authorship of Scripture.

No matter how elusive the process may be, however, the fact of inspiration is an article of faith which must be accepted by Roman Catholics.

God has played a part in the composition of the Bible. These "books" contain God's word in human form. In the end all scholars and students of the Bible must submit to the mystery that "no prophetic message ever came just from the will of man, but men were under the control of the Holy Spirit as they spoke the message that came from God" (2 Peter 1:21).

Inspiration—the Consequence II

The Council of Trent solemnly defined as canonical those books of the Old and New Testaments which contain "the saving truth and rule of conduct" (Fourth Session, First Decree, 1546).

Vatican Council I expanded on this by solemnly teaching that the Church holds these books to be sacred and canonical "because having been written by the inspiration of the Holy Spirit, they have God for their author and have been delivered as such to the Church herself." According to Vatican Council I there is a very close connection between inspiration and canonicity. A book of Scripture is canonical because the Church recognizes that it is inspired; it has God for its author (*Dei Filius*, Chapter 2).

Vatican Council II reaffirmed this teaching:

> Holy Mother Church relying on the belief of the apostles, holds that the books of both the Old and New Testaments in their entirety, with all their parts, are sacred and canonical because, having been written under the inspiration of the Holy Spirit they have God as their author and have been handed on as such to the Church. (*Dei Verbum*, Ch. 3, par. 11)

Once again the close connection between inspiration and canonicity is affirmed. The books of Sacred Scripture are canonical because the Church recognizes that they are inspired; they have God as their author. The Canon then is that collection of inspired books received by the Church and thus recognized as the infallible rule of faith and morals because of divine origin.

An obvious question now comes to mind: Just how did the Church come to recognize a book as inspired? How did the Church make the judgment that a book contained the saving truth and rule of conduct? What were the criteria used in declaring a book canonical?

There are no easy answers to these questions. The history of Judaism and the Church reveals that the process of canonicity was a very fluid one. Rabbinic scholars did not always agree on which books of Scripture were to be considered canonical. The Essenes at Qumran had their own ideas. Palestinian and Alexandrian Jews had different lists of books.

For the early Church, Sacred Scripture meant only one thing: the Law, the Prophets, and the Writings; that is, the Hebrew Scriptures. It was in reaction to Marcion that the Church Fathers of the second century began to defend the idea of a closed collection of books. According to Marcion there was an irreconcilable opposition between the Old and New Testaments, between Law and Gospel. The Old Testament, he said, should be rejected outright by Christians. It was Justin Martyr in his *Dialogue with Trypho* who rejected this idea and defended the scriptural authority of the Old Testament for Christianity.

The Roman Catholic Church recognizes forty-six books of the Old Testament as sacred and canonical. The Jews recognize thirty-nine. The seven disputed books are Tobit, Judith, Wisdom of Solomon, Sirach, Baruch, First Maccabees, and Second Maccabees. Various theories have been proposed about the criteria used by the Jews and the Church in determining which books were canonical. None is totally satisfying. As was said earlier, the process was very fluid, and the definition of Trent settled the issue for Roman Catholics.

There is much more historical evidence for the process of canonization that produced the twenty-seven books now recognized as comprising the canon of the New Testament.

It would take some time before the Church recognized the writings of Paul as Scripture. Marcion again proved to be a catalyst in moving the Church to consider the question of a canon of New Testament books. Marcion taught that only Luke's Gospel and some letters of Paul should be recognized by the Church. In reaction to this the Church Fathers of the second and third centuries spoke of a four-Gospel canon. By the end of the fourth century there was general agreement in the Church as to what books constituted the New Testament. St. Athanasius' Easter letter, A.D. 367, has a list of twenty-seven books of the New Testament which are identical with the list contained in the definition of Trent in 1546.

Nothing certain can be said about the criteria used by the Church in determining which Christian writings should be considered canonical. Several of these writings might well have found their way into a fixed, definitive canon, but did not: the Letters of Clement of Rome, the Epistle of Barnabas, the Didache, the Letters of Ignatius of Antioch, and the Shepherd of Hermas.

By what criteria were these excluded while others were included in the canon? Scholars have suggested many theories. Some say that the Church, filled with the Holy Spirit, recognized something connatural with her own being in writings which had been handed down from the apostolic age. These writings gave life to the Church in the midst of crisis and became the vehicle for survival for the communities who molded their lives around them.

Others point to a criterion such as orthodox content. For a writing to be considered canonical, it had to contain the basic kerygma of the death and resurrection of Jesus. If a writing satisfied this criterion and also had its origin in a renowned Christian center such as Rome, Jerusalem, or Antioch, and was used in the liturgical life of the Church, then it was considered canonical.

All of these theories are being tested and revised in the light of newer studies and the discovery of ancient gnostic libraries. Obviously the practice and life of the believing and praying Church of the first few centuries were determining factors in the process of canonization. This is important because in Roman Catholic theology the ultimate reason why a book is or is not canonical is the decision of the Church. This makes sense in the context of an ecclesiology which states that the basic assurance that the books listed by Trent are sacred and canonical rests on faith that the Church, in making that decision, was guided by the Holy Spirit.

THE BIBLE AND THE TEACHING CHURCH

Thomas J. Herron

The Church has had a positive attitude toward the Scriptures during the two thousand years since her birth. This article will offer a brief sketch of a few key points in the Church's teaching as it developed over the centuries and then focus on the major recent documents of the Teaching Church which articulate the present position of the Roman Catholic Church regarding Sacred Scripture.

To put this discussion in context, one has at the outset to recall a few historical facts which have had a considerable influence on how the Church in the twentieth century comes to view the Scriptures. Initially, these facts may not seem to have any obvious connection to the teaching of the Church, but it should always be remembered that that teaching, assisted as it is by the power of the Holy Spirit, is nevertheless a combination, an "incarnation," of the divine and the human. It is true that God has revealed much about Himself in Sacred Scripture. That is why it is *sacred*. At the same time, the Church is a church of the very human followers of Jesus.

One of the biggest changes in history which directly affected the Church and the Bible was the invention of the printing press by Johannes Gutenburg in 1449–50. It was no accident that Gutenburg's first book was in fact the Bible itself. Prior to the invention of the press, each and every Bible had to be painstakingly copied by hand. A whole class of skilled workers called scribes was developed even in Old Testament times to perform the sacred work of preparing new copies of the Scriptures as old ones wore out. This task was a very important part of the life of Christian monks from earliest times. One unfortunate effect of this hand-copying was that Bibles were both rare and expensive. The faithful, unless they were very rich, could hardly afford any books at all, much less a copy of the very lengthy Bible. The consequence was that the reading and the studying of the Bible were largely left to the clergy and the scholars.

A comparison of the Church's attitude toward Scripture in the period prior to the fifteenth century with what she is teaching today will reveal two considerably contrasting views. In the time before mechanical printing, the Church's interest in and use of Scripture lay principally

30

in two areas: theology and liturgy. While there are many close bonds between the two, they are best treated separately.

Theology is reflection on the meaning of God. From her earliest days, the Church has meditated constantly on exactly what it was that God meant to tell us in Jesus. Gradually, she began to realize that Jesus was none other than the long-promised Messiah, the Anointed One, the Christ, for whom God's chosen Jewish people had been waiting. The dawning of the Church's faith, and the first expression of it, was helped enormously by the Old Testament. In fact it was the Old Testament which made it possible for the earliest believers to identify Jesus as *the* Christ.

A precious indication of the importance of the Scriptures for the early Church is found in Luke's Gospel, in the story of the two disciples on the road to Emmaus, in 24:13ff. The risen Jesus appeared to the disciples and "explained to them what was said about himself in all the Scriptures, beginning with the books of Moses and the writings of all the prophets" (v. 27). Later, those disciples ask, "Wasn't it like a fire burning in us when he talked to us on the road and explained the Scriptures to us?" (v. 32). It was the Scriptures, then, that led the disciples to realize that Jesus, despite his suffering and death, was none other than the One God had sent for their salvation.

As these disciples go on to write the books of the New Testament, their heavy use of the Hebrew Scriptures becomes more and more evident. The author of Second Timothy can say confidently, "You remember that ever since you were a child, you have known the Holy Scriptures, which are able to give you the wisdom that leads to salvation through faith in Christ Jesus. All Scripture is inspired by God and is useful for teaching the truth, rebuking error, correcting faults, and giving instruction for right living" (2 Tim. 3:15–17).

The Church made great use of Scripture in the *liturgy* as well. Although there was probably a great deal of indifference in local customs as the early community came together for worship, it is certain that the earliest liturgical format was heavily influenced by the well-known Jewish synagogal prayer service. This is not at all surprising since the first converts to Christianity, Jesus' own disciples, were Jewish. That service principally comprised readings and commentaries on Scripture, prayers, and hymns. So it was that the Church began what is now one of her most venerable customs, the "Liturgy of the Word." Here it was that Christians of every background and national origin, learned or illiterate, were nourished by the bread of wisdom, the written word of the Lord.

In the centuries prior to the invention of the printing press, the Liturgy provided Christians their main access to the Bible. Though they could not afford books of their own, and often could not even read, Christians had the Scriptures read to them at every Eucharist. In the Middle Ages, even the Church's architecture would reflect this fundamental bond between the liturgy and the Bible. Artists working on the European cathedrals fashioned numberless stained glass windows which told over and over again the scriptural stories which form the basis of Christian faith.

Throughout her long history the Church has prized the Scriptures as one of the major sources of her faith. The Bible has never been "optional" for the Church, but has been an indispensable aid in understanding and celebrating her faith. After the invention of the printing press the Church suffered through some dark times. This had an effect on the Church's attitude toward Scripture. The Bible was used as a weapon by Christian against Christian, each arguing that his own particular *interpretation* of the Bible's words was the only correct meaning.

This issue of interpretation is a key one because there is a difference between what the Bible *says* and what the Bible *means*. To read is to interpret, and many individuals have tried to interpret the Bible in a way contrary to what the Church taught at a particular time. The Bible in many ways became a source of division instead of unity. It is the Roman Catholic Church's position that the college of bishops in union with the bishop of Rome are the only authentic interpreters of the Bible.

The Catholic Church also teaches that, in addition to the Scriptures, there is a *tradition* from which she cannot deviate and which is also a source of truth for her. Vatican Council II teaches:

> The words of the holy Fathers witness to the living presence of this tradition, whose wealth is poured into the practice and life of the believing and praying Church. Through the same tradition the Church's full canon of the sacred books is known, and the sacred writings themselves are more profoundly understood and unceasingly made active in her; . . .
>
> Hence there exists a close connection and communication between sacred tradition and sacred Scripture. For both of them, flowing from the same divine well-spring, in a certain way merge into a unity and tend toward the same end. . . . Consequently, it is not from sacred Scripture alone that the Church draws her certainty about everything which has been revealed. Therefore both sacred tradition and sacred scripture are to be accepted and venerated with the same sense of devotion and reverence (Constitution on Revelation, ch. 2, par. 8–9).

Tradition, in its most fundamental meaning, implies that something was handed down. The Catholic Church affirms that still today she hands down the faith she first received from the Lord.

Sacred tradition and sacred Scripture form one sacred deposit of the word of God, which is committed to the Church. This teaching on tradition, however, has unfortunately given some the mistaken impression that the Church is somehow not entirely serious about the attention she gives to the Scriptures. Nothing could be farther from the truth. In fact, it is the Scriptures themselves which form an essential element in her tradition. Without them she would be impoverished beyond measure since they are God's gift to her.

Through many periods of struggle, internal and external, the Church gradually developed what should be seen as a characteristic of her general position regarding the Scriptures: they are the property of no individual, but belong to the whole Church. Thus, it is the community, the Church herself, and particularly those responsible for the community (the pastors or bishops of the Church), who have the responsibility of interpreting Scriptures. It is one of the most fundamental tasks of the Teaching Church or Magisterium to say what the Scriptures mean.

One very clear position taken by the Magisterium—which has often been underrated in its importance for relations between the Christians and Jews—is the fact that the Catholic Church has consistently taught that the Hebrew Bible, or the Old Testament, is fully a part of God's written word along with the New Testament. The Church has always believed in the very same and single God of Abraham and Moses.

The inspiration of both Old and New Testaments was solemnly affirmed by the Council of Trent in 1546. At the same time, the Council published a list of the inspired books of the Bible which then became normative for Catholics. It was the identical list compiled by St. Augustine in the fifth century and includes the familiar forty-six books of the Old Testament and the twenty-seven books of the New Testament.

The era immediately after the Council of Trent continued to be marred by fierce and bitter struggles of Catholics against Protestants and vice versa. It was some four hundred years after the close of Trent that Pius IX convened the First Vatican Council in 1869. The interim period between the Councils saw enormous political and philosophical changes which affected the entire western world and, with it, the Catholic Church (e.g., the colonization of the New World, the Post-Reformation reforms, the American and French Revolutions, the Industrial Revolution, the Enlightenment, and the Scientific Revolution).

There was a new emphasis on the autonomy of man and a denial of the importance of any supernatural authority. Pius IX's Council ended as Garibaldi invaded Rome in his struggle to unite Italy. This atmosphere, charged with revolutionary sentiment, understandably gave many people the impression that whatever was old should be

33

replaced, whether it was a government, an economic system, or a church. In fact, many eighteenth-century intellectuals felt that their "modern" world was held back from achieving full development by the whole idea of religion. The Catholic Church with its dogmatic structures and its clear condemnations of immorality came in for particularly bitter attack. These "modernists," as they were called, tried to show that the Christian Church was unscientific and based on many falsehoods, among which was the Bible. This they considered so completely primitive, contradictory, and repressive that they ridiculed it with special venom. Some of these modernists had in mind nothing less than the dismantling of Christianity in the West and replacing it with a naturalist religion whose only apparent goal was the full and free development of the human potential as they understood it.

The response to these attacks was swift on the part of the Catholic Church. Through a series of instructions from the "Holy Office" (or doctrinal office), the Holy See defended the traditional understanding of how the Bible was written and who wrote it. Convinced that the Bible was the word of the Lord, the Holy Office refused to entertain any theory which seemed to suggest that the Scriptures contained any error. These early instructions, which have been partially revised by subsequent official documents, have to be understood in the context of the times. The modernist threat was a real one. It attacked both Scripture and the Church in an attempt to undermine the faith of the people and the institutions of the Church. The modernists ridiculed the idea that the Pentateuch or the Gospels should be considered true and authentic history, asserting that there were many factual inconsistencies in these books which are incompatible with real history.

The modern crisis became a time for real progress in biblical studies however. Christians—Protestants first and Catholics later—began to reflect on the charges made against the Bible. They admitted that the idea that the Pentateuch and the Gospels were ordinary history was a presumption. They recognized that these works were principally theology, and that the manner of their composition, long since forgotten in the centuries since they were written, was much more complicated than had been recognized.

In the aftermath of the modernist crisis, more sober scholars began to make real contributions toward a better appreciation of the real worth of the Scriptures. These scholarly contributions highlighted the literary qualities of the Scriptures and completely changed the climate from one of attack upon the Church's beliefs, to one of defense of those beliefs through a more accurate understanding of the nature of the biblical literature.

It was in this new climate that Pope Pius XII issued what has been called the "Magna Carta" of Catholic biblical studies, his 1943 encyclical, *Divino Afflante Spiritu*.

With World War II still raging, and the revolutionary currents of modern society as strong as ever, Pius XII nevertheless judged that a new era for Catholic scriptural studies had begun. The modern discoveries of ancient manuscripts and new archeological finds had for some time been causing something of a sensation in the scholarly world. The Pope saw in these new discoveries not only something of interest to intellectuals, but also a symbol for the whole Church that there was much about the Bible which had yet to be discovered, and therefore to be understood or appreciated. In effect, he was calling for an end of the bias (that some Catholic theologians had expressed) which presumed that the Catholic Church was *already* in possession of a *complete* understanding of the biblical literature. He saw in the recent discoveries an opportunity to deepen the Church's understanding without sacrificing the rich appreciation and high value she already attached to God's written word.

The Pope went on record (par. 35–39) as promoting the study of *literary forms* or *genres* as a faithful approach to interpreting the Bible. And, although he consistently maintained the Church's right to interpret the Scriptures authoritatively for the whole community of believers, he called on priests to encourage a love for, and an appreciation of, the Bible among the laity. This official papal recognition of modern advances in biblical studies did not, at one sweep, vacate the cautious and negative judgments of the Holy Office, which dated from the prior period of the Modernist crisis. What it did, more than anything else, was encourage Catholic scholars to deepen the Catholic understanding of the Scriptures by taking into account modern developments in the field, especially regarding the literary nature of the Bible. *Divino Afflante Spiritu* signaled a new era for Catholic scriptural studies.

Implicitly the encyclical had an early effect on ecumenical relations as well, since the basic contributions to scriptural studies of the previous hundred years had been made essentially by Protestant scholars. Though the war and the post-war recovery postponed the practical implementation of the Pope's teaching, many would see *Divino Afflante Spiritu* as being at least partially responsible for making possible the subsequent Catholic scholarly developments, not only in biblical but also in theological circles, which later came to bear fruit in the Vatican Council II.

The Council (1962–65) was much more comprehensive and dealt with numerous aspects of Catholic life. Still, its Apostolic Constitution on Divine Revelation, *Dei Verbum*, is the single most important document of the Magisterium on Scripture in modern times. Of particular

35

interest in that decree is the official recognition it gave to what has been called the "three stages" of the development of the Gospels.

In its famous paragraph 19, *Dei Verbum* described the composition of the four canonical Gospels: *The first stage* was what Jesus "while living among men really did and taught for their eternal salvation." Important here is the notion that there was development in the composition of the Gospels. The decree acknowledged that what the Gospels would ultimately contain, when they later came to be written down, was *theology*, not history. The Gospels' focus is on what the Lord did "for our salvation." They are not a sterile record of dispassionate history.

The second stage was the period after the resurrection. The Apostles preached and taught the things which in actual fact the Lord had said and done. This they did in the light of that fuller understanding they enjoyed as a result of the Resurrection appearances and the Pentecost experience.

The third stage was the period of the written Gospels themselves. Thus a whole complex period of development came between the Lord's public ministry and the composition of the Gospels.

By concentrating on the developmental process which resulted in the Gospels as we know them, the decree abandons any notion of the so-called dictation theory of inspiration in which the Holy Spirit simply tells the author what to write, and he writes it. According to *Dei Verbum,* it is much more plausible to see the process of composition in three human stages. As the modern reader, then, reflects on the Gospels, he should not interpret them as a mere recital of historical words and deeds. Our belief that these are "the Word of the Lord" bids us to see in the Gospels a unique form of literature, sacred to the Church since they come from the Lord and are addressed by human beings to the whole human family.

Pope John Paul II in speaking to the Pontifical Biblical Commission acknowledged that biblical studies are becoming ever more specialized and complex. The Holy Father recognized that at all times God made use of human language and experience to communicate his wonders.

Part of the paradox of revelation, the Pope said, is that historical persons and events should convey a transcendent and unconditional message. The function of biblical science and its hermeneutical methods is to establish the distinction between what belongs only to a limited period of history and what must be of permanent validity. To make such a distinction requires a very keen sensitivity, not only in the scientific and theological sphere, but also and especially, in regard to the Church and to life itself (Address of Pope John Paul II to the Biblical Commission, April 26, 1979).

The Bible is the Church's book and the expression of her faith. In the Church, the sacred Scriptures have been cherished, preserved, and handed on. It is hoped that this article has demonstrated the Church's positive attitude toward Scripture and how, throughout the ages, she has encouraged the efforts of scholars and taken steps to promote reverence for Scripture among the people of God.

HOW THE BIBLE CAME ABOUT
Jerome Kodell, O.S.B.

Though the Bible may look like any other book on a desk or shelf, it is more like a library in itself than just another book. It is a collection of many different writings by several authors and produced over hundreds of years. As in a library, the books of the Bible are not simply stacked one after another in the order in which they were produced, but they are arranged carefully according to their topic. For instance, *Genesis* is placed first because it deals with the creation of the world and man's early history, not because it was the first Bible book to be written. *Revelation* is placed last because it deals with "last things"— the end of the world, the final judgment, and the heavenly reign at the end of time.

The individual books in the Bible are significantly different from books produced today. Most modern books are written by a single author within a period of a few weeks, months, or possibly years. Few of the biblical books, especially those in the Old Testament, came to us straight from the pen of an individual writer. Many of them were edited and reedited over the course of several generations. A prophet like Isaiah was more likely to speak the word of God than to write it down; he left the task of writing to his disciples. They, in turn, might have produced only random notes of what Isaiah said. Later followers organized those notes and put them into a smoother written style.

This participation of many different people, sometimes over a period of many years and in more than one place, in the production of a certain writing is a major characteristic of the Bible. With few exceptions, the authors of the Old and New Testament books did not think of themselves as professional writers. They were members of a community which felt itself to be especially chosen as the bearer of God's promise. Their writing was an expression of the community in action: it was the result of the process of listening to God's word in history and in the religious experience of the nation, of reflecting on that word, of telling the story, and of handing on the message to later generations of the community. Thus, the writings and the stories they tell are understood to be the property of the entire community, not just the author. It is no matter that the identity of the authors may be blurred; and there is no anxiety about preserving an individual writer's words intact. The Bible comes from the midst of the community of faith in order to serve the community of faith.

Old Testament

Earliest Writings. From the time of Abraham, the Israelites were a people on the move. The nomads of the Ancient Near East had little room for carrying written scrolls. They carried their library in their heads. The ancient Hebrews, like all people who depend on oral traditions instead of written documents to preserve their history, developed amazingly retentive memories. Their storytellers put the saga of their ancestors into poetic rhythms. Their songs of worship were easy to remember because they repeated the same ideas and phrases. For the first five hundred years of their existence as a people, the Israelites shared their history and passed along their traditions almost exclusively by word of mouth.

It was not until the nation became a settled kingdom under David and Solomon that a national written literature began to emerge, even though there are fragments of biblical writing that reach much further back in time. Some of the earliest parts of the Old Testament are snatches of the ancient Hebrew religious ballads and songs used in Israel's public worship. Several of these were originally battle hymns or victory hymns praising God. Considered among the oldest are the Song of Deborah in Judges 5, composed after the Israelites triumphed over the Canaanites at Taanach about 1125 B.C., and the Song of Miriam in Exodus 15, which may date from the Exodus from Egypt around 1280 B.C.

Some scholars think that the first community writing took place at Kadesh-barnea, the place the Israelites used as their main base during their years of wandering before they entered Canaan. Though Moses is not the actual author of the Pentateuch, the first five books of the Bible (his death is recorded in Deut. 34:5), he is the inspiration behind it. It is reasonable to think that he wrote down the basics of his teaching during this desert period.

Other early texts are blessings and oracles which cannot be clearly identified with any particular historical occasion. Examples are the boast of Lamech (Gen. 4:23), the blessing of Rebecca (Gen. 24:60), and the blessing of Isaac (Gen. 27:27–29).

Monarchy. The Israelites entered the world of writing when David established his capital in Jerusalem. Official documents had to be kept in the same manner as they were kept by the surrounding nations. These documents dealt with history, trade, land transfer, international affairs, and military matters. A central storage place for official documents, or national archives, was required to be established. We find references in the Bible to written historical sources used by the biblical writers such as, the "Book of the Lord's Battles" (Num. 21:14–15) and the "Book of Jashar" (Josh. 10:12–13; 2 Sam. 1:18–27).

David himself composed psalms and gave great impetus to the production of religious poetry and song. A talented writer of that period, drawing from his own eyewitness experience and using the various documents at his disposal, composed a colorful court history of the time. Part of this history is preserved in 2 Samuel 9–20 and 1 Kings 1–2. It traces how the royal crown passed from David to Solomon, in spite of intrigue, murder, and betrayal.

About the same time, perhaps during the reign of Solomon, another gifted author composed the first written account of Israel's development from the beginning. This writer is known as the "Yahwist" because he refers to God by the Hebrew name *Yahweh*, not merely after the revelation of that divine name to Moses (Ex. 3:14–15), but from the account of the Creation itself. There is no single biblical book which is said to have been written by this author, but much of the Pentateuch comes from his pen. We know now that this part of the Bible, which tells about the Creation and Fall, the Fathers, the Exodus, and the Wandering, is the product of a complex process which took several centuries to complete. The Pentateuch received its final written form after the Exile in the fifth century B.C. It is possible to see four major written sources or traditions that were woven together to produce a single narrative. They are called the "Yahwist," the "Elohist" (who referred to God by the Hebrew name *Elohim* before the revelation of God's name to Moses in Ex. 3:14), the "Deuteronomic" (which includes *Deuteronomy*, with its stresses on the needs for reform in social and religious law and justice), and the "Priestly" (which concentrates on rules about religious ritual, on religious covenants, and on genealogies).

The political unity and peace of the Israelite monarchy achieved under David gave the Yahwist and his contemporaries time to ponder the great religious questions: What kind of God is responsible for saving us and bringing us to the land? Is he more powerful than the gods of other nations? If this God is good, where did evil come from? What is the connection between God and nature? The Yahwist looked back to the origins of humanity with the eyes of his Hebrew faith. He saw the God who had saved his people in the Exodus already preparing them long before they ever went to Egypt.

40

Divided Kingdom. Fifty to a hundred years after the Yahwist, the Elohist author wrote under very different conditions in the northern part of the divided kingdom (ninth century B.C.). The Elohist expressed his faith in the constant love of God for his people in spite of their many infidelities by applying the idea of the covenant to the relationship between God and his people. In the Pentateuch, the Elohist tradition begins with the covenant God made with Abraham. It often parallels the work of the Yahwist in the stories about the Fathers and Moses. These two traditions (Yahwist and Elohist) were later combined by an unknown editor during the reign of King Hezekiah of Judah, just about the time that the Deuteronomic and Priestly traditions were beginning to form.

During the ninth century B.C. also, Elijah and his successor, Elisha, engaged in their prophetic work in the North (Israel). They were the first prophets to confront the king and national political and religious institutions. This kind of moral and religious confrontation marks the prophet's role down through history. In the eighth century B.C., the prophets Amos and Hosea, two more antiestablishment figures, spoke prophetic oracles which were the first ones to be written down. In the South (Judah) meantime, Isaiah of Jerusalem and Micah of Moresheth began their prophetic ministry. Because their disciples took notes, the tradition of writing down prophecy became well established.

Fall of Samaria. The intervention of foreigners into the national life of Israel and Judah profoundly affected the process by which the Bible was formed. This intervention would affect the Israelites for the next two hundred years. The first major disruption was the overthrow of Samaria, the royal city of Israel, by Assyria in 722 B.C. Many Israelites saw this event as the fulfillment of the warnings the prophets had made against the breakdown of moral standards and the mixture of pagan worship with the worship of God. Many priests who had descended from Levi and had been active at the northern sanctuaries escaped to Judah. They preserved the distinctive religious traditions of Israel. Their own experience prepared them well to support King Hezekiah's plan to destroy the places of Baal worship, reform worship as it was practiced in the Temple, and centralize worship in the Jerusalem Temple.

The teaching of these northern priests would have far-reaching influence on the composition of the Bible. It became the core of the Deuteronomic tradition, is found in the book of *Deuteronomy*, and is the work of the Deuteronomic historians who wrote *Joshua, Judges, 1* and *2 Samuel,* and *1* and *2 Kings.* This tradition insisted on a central sanctuary and on moral and religious reform. It also spoke warmly of God's love for his people and of his free choice of them to enter into a covenantal relationship with him. This tradition also emphasizes the present reality of this covenant in their lives.

The reform of Hezekiah, however, was not destined to endure. His son, Manasseh, has been called the worst king in Judah's history. He overturned the policy of the single sanctuary dedicated to God, and he encouraged the worship of false gods in the fertility cults of the "high places" on the hilltops (2 Kings 21:1–17). Manasseh's son Amon followed in his father's footsteps.

Josiah's Reform. A new burst of religious enthusiasm and literary activity came with the reign of Josiah. Promoted by the "people of Judah" (2 Kings 21:24), who were disgusted with the direction that the royal court had taken under Manasseh and Amon, Josiah repudiated the foreign gods of his father and grandfather. Then in 621 B.C. when the high priest Hilkiah found the "Book of the Law" in the Temple, Josiah inaugurated a full-scale religious reform. The scroll discovered by Hilkiah seems to have been the Deuteronomic Code written during the time of Hezekiah and set aside under Manasseh and Amon.

Several prophets proclaimed the divine message during this period (there are written records, for example, from Zephaniah, Nahum, and Habakkuk), but the great spokesman of the time was Jeremiah. He received his call in 627 B.C., during Josiah's early years, and was Israel's conscience until the Exile in 587 B.C. He cooperated with the reform of Josiah and later described this king as one who was "always just and fair and . . . gave the poor a fair trial" (Jer. 22:15–16). Jeremiah's secretary, Baruch, preserved much of Jeremiah's speaking and writing from loss or destruction on the eve of the deportation of the people to Babylon.

Exiles. In 587 B.C., the disaster came to pass which Jeremiah had been predicting. The Babylonian king, Nebuchadnezzar, destroyed Jerusalem and led the people into exile. This dark period of Israelite history turned out to be a particularly fruitful period of sacred writing. Although the exiles were isolated from the Temple, they kept alive the old prayers and songs (Ps. 137). The Psalter contains several new compositions from this period. Back in Jerusalem, meanwhile, some of the few who had not been deported wept over the ruins and the emptiness of the city. Their sorrow eventually produced the plaintive *Lamentations.* Priests in exile devoted themselves to collecting old traditions from the days of the desert wanderings and to setting down in order an account of the practices of worship in the days when the Temple was the center of worship in Jerusalem. Two prophets, Ezekiel and Second Isaiah (Isa. 40–55), gave new hope with oracles that proclaimed that one day the exiles would return and restore the nation. When the Israelites emerged from the Exile, they brought the core of the Hebrew Scriptures with them.

Restoration. The return to Jerusalem in 538 B.C. was not as glorious as the exiles had dreamed it would be. Tensions involved in rebuilding the city and the Temple can be sensed in the writings of Haggai and Zechariah 1 (Zech. 1–8); a more thorough story is told in the books of *Ezra* and *Nehemiah*, which along with *1* and *2 Chronicles*, show how the anonymous author we call the Chronicler understood history as the working out of God's will.

The priests continued their important editing work. Sometime in the fifth century these authors, whom we call all together "the Priestly tradition," put the Pentateuch into its final form. The book of *Deuteronomy*, which for a while had served as the introduction to the history continued in the books from *Joshua* through *Kings*, now became the concluding book of the Pentateuch. The writing of prophetic literature ceased about 400 B.C. with a glance to the past in Obadiah's cry for vengeance against the Edomites who harassed the returning exiles, visions of the future in promises of a perfect messianic sacrifice (Mal.), and a great Day of the Lord (Joel; Zech. 9–14). *Ruth* was also written in this time, as was *Jonah*, which, though listed with the prophetic books, is a satire on Judah's narrow nationalism.

Wisdom Literature. The largest single block of biblical writing associated with postexilic Judah is the group of books belonging to the wisdom tradition: *Job, Psalms, Proverbs, Qoheleth (Ecclesiastes), Song of Songs, Sirach (Ecclesiasticus),* and *Wisdom.* "Wisdom literature" is a broad category. It originated outside Israel in the court life of neighboring nations, particularly Egypt, and is full of instructive "words for wise living." These short, pointed sayings are found especially in *Proverbs* and *Sirach.* Wisdom literature also contains a collection of marriage songs (*Song of Songs*), a poetic masterpiece on the mystery of suffering (*Job*), and a meditation on the mystery of life itself (*Qoheleth*).

The wisdom literature of Israel is linked with the name of King Solomon, though little of it can actually go back to his time. He was famous as "the wisest of men" and, in the ancient world, books were often said to be written by great leaders in order to make sure that they survived and were circulated. Thus *Qoheleth, Song of Songs,* and *Wisdom,* all written after Israel returned from the Exile, were presented as though they had been written by Solomon. In the same way, Moses was given credit for writing the Pentateuch, and David the Psalms.

A new set of influences began to affect Judah after Alexander the Great conquered Syria and Palestine in 333 B.C. Greek ways became a threat to the worship of God in the traditional manner just as Baal worship had been in earlier times. Biblical writings of this period contain warnings against adopting Greek life-styles. Hellenizing remained subtle and indirect until the Syrian ruler, Antiochus IV Epiphanes, came to the throne. He was determined to crush the worship of God (Yahweh).

Severe religious persecution provoked the Maccabean Revolt of 167–164 B.C., described by two different historians about fifty years later (1 and 2 Maccabees). The book of Daniel, which used in part a form of writing then popular, was published during the years of persecution to encourage hope and faithfulness. Daniel uses a form of language and imagery called "apocalyptic." It concentrates on the "last days" of judgment and final victory. It makes its point by telling stories of beasts, of battles in the heavens, and of dreams and visions. Most of this book is written in Hebrew; but part of it, for an unknown reason, is in the Aramaic language. (A section of the Book of Ezra is also in Aramaic.) Other late Old Testament productions were in the "historical novel" tradition: Esther, Tobit, and Judith.

Old Testament Canon. The various writings collected to form the Old Testament grew out of a long and varied development. None of the authors thought of themselves as composing divinely inspired literature which would be used as a guide by succeeding generations. The prophets understood their spoken utterances as coming from God, but the written records of prophecy came only gradually to share such authority. How did a canon (or authorized collection) of inspired writings develop in Israel?

The first step in the canonizing process was the finding of the Deuteronomic Code in the Temple in 621 B.C. Because it was thought to be written by Moses, this book became the unquestioned word from God to guide King Josiah's reform. For the first time a writing was officially recognized as the word of God. Over the next two hundred years other writings expanded the "law given through Moses," including the narrative accounts of Israel's origins. By 400 B.C., the different strands of material had become the five books of the Pentateuch, which was published at this time as the "Torah," or Law, and very soon was accepted as the word of God written.

Meanwhile the Deuteronomic history of *Joshua, Judges, Samuel,* and *Kings* continued to enjoy popularity and grew in stature as a definitive record. Some of the prophetic collections were appearing: *Isaiah, Jeremiah, Ezekiel,* and the minor prophets. As the Jewish community used these books, they recognized the authentic message of faith they contained. By an unobtrusive process, by 200 B.C., these books came to be generally accepted as the part of the Bible called the "Prophets."

The wisdom literature and other books from the postexilic period were known as the "Writings," a convenient catch-all title for works not contained in the Law or the Prophets. At the time of Jesus there were still disputes over the canonicity (acceptance as a part of the Bible) of some of these books. Part of the hesitation was due to the fact that some of them were written in Greek instead of in Hebrew.

There are two main Jewish traditions in the matter, the Palestinian and the Alexandrian. The rabbis who met at Jamnia, a town west of Jerusalem, after A.D. 70 under Johanan ben Zakkai accepted thirty-nine books (which in the Jewish method of dividing them were counted as twenty-four). These thirty-nine books are called the Palestinian Canon. The attitude of Greek-speaking Jews who lived outside Palestine is seen in the practice of the rabbis in Alexandria. They accepted seven additional books (1 and 2 *Maccabees, Tobit, Judith, Sirach, Wisdom,* and *Baruch*) and some additional parts of *Daniel* and *Esther*. The Alexandrian Canon was translated into Greek by Jewish scholars and became the Scriptures commonly used by early Christian authors. Today Jews and most Protestants accept the Palestinian Canon as the Bible; Catholics follow the Alexandrian Canon, and thus include the additional books in the Bible. These additional books are sometimes called the *Deuterocanon*.

New Testament

The formation of a body of Christian writings into what we revere as the New Testament was a process comparable to the development of the Old Testament. Jesus left no written records. His Bible and that quoted by his disciples was the Old Testament. The first complete Christian document dates from twenty years after his time (1 *Thessalonians*); and it was another fifteen or so years before a Gospel (*Mark*) appeared. The New Testament literature, like that of the Old Testament, emerged within the community of believers according to their own needs and the guidance of the Spirit as they reflected on and responded to the drama of salvation in Christ.

In the first years after the resurrection, there was little thought given to writing down a Christian library. Some of this was undoubtedly due to the example of the Lord himself who, like the rabbis of the time, taught by the spoken word, which in turn was remembered and discussed by disciples. There was no need for writing while the apostles were still alive to clarify or verify anything uncertain. Because his followers expected Jesus to return soon, any permanent writing of his teachings seemed unnecessary, and perhaps even faithless.

There was, however, some writing going on in the Christian community in the earliest decades. As in Israel, the liturgy was the mixture of songs, creeds, psalms, and other prayers (Col. 3:16). Paul's writings contain excerpts from these sources (e.g., the hymns in Phil. 2:6–10 and Col. 1:15–20). Sayings of Jesus were being collected during the A.D. 30–40 period. They were eventually written to form a chain of episodes, appearing first probably in the Aramaic language, then in Greek. Parts of this document, now called "Q" from the German *Quelle*, "source," are traceable in *Matthew* and *Luke*. In addition to Q, there may have been other collections for the use of preachers: collections of parables, proof-texts from the Scriptures, and notes on various deeds of Jesus. There seems to have been an early written account of the Passion.

Paul. The first unified Christian writings to come down to us are the letters of Paul. They were attempts to bridge the distances as the apostle traveled from community to community in Asia Minor and Greece. Even in the earliest of these letters, *1* and *2 Thessalonians* (A.D. 50–51), he used a pattern of correction, encouragement, and instruction which he later used in all his letters. Paul's major doctrinal work appeared in the Great Letters between A.D. 54 and 59: *Galatians, 1* and *2 Corinthians,* and *Romans.* The Captivity Letters (*Philippians, Philemon, Colossians,* and *Ephesians*) were written while Paul was in prison at various times in Caesarea, Ephesus, or Rome. *Philippians,* the most affectionate of Paul's letters, is the first of this group. *Ephesians* is the last, and differences in style and vocabulary from Paul's earlier letters have made his authorship of this letter appear questionable. Since it is not addressed to any particular community ("To the Ephesians" is a note added later), this letter may have been composed by one of Paul's disciples as a summary of Paul's doctrine to be circulated among the churches in Asia Minor.

The Pastoral Letters (*1* and *2 Timothy, Titus*) give attention to the new situations that arose when Christian communities began to be settled and were more formally organized. The letter to the *Hebrews,* long thought to be written by Paul, is now recognized as the work of a later disciple. It presents an interpretation of Christ's priesthood which is unique in the New Testament.

Gospels. As Paul came to the end of his career, another development was underway which would produce the most distinctively Christian documents of the New Testament, the four Gospels. Because they are placed first in order among New Testament books in our Bibles and because they tell the story of Jesus, we tend to think the Gospels were the first Christian documents written. As we have seen, Paul's letters were the first Christian writings. In fact, Paul himself probably died before the first Gospel, *Mark*, was in circulation.

By the time Mark appeared, over thirty years had passed since Jesus' resurrection. The memory of Jesus' words and deeds was kept alive by preachers and storytellers in the various Christian communities. However, a traveler would have noticed differences in the memories of the various centers. A story was told with a different emphasis at Rome than at Jerusalem or Ephesus; Alexandria remembered incidents that had never been heard of at Corinth. There was a danger that some important material or the meaning of it all would be lost. Many of the new converts were asking for a systematic presentation of the story of Jesus.

Mark. The Gospel of *Mark* appeared on the scene around A.D. 65, just about the time that the great leaders, Peter and Paul, were martyred. It is difficult for us to appreciate the achievement that the writing of the first Gospel represents. Mark had to compose something for new Christians and for prospective converts that would tell the basic story, but not be too lengthy or heavy for the interested reader. By this time, information about Jesus' life and his teaching was complicated by inaccuracy and rumor. Theories about the meaning of God's saving act in Jesus needed to be sorted out and evaluated. As far as we know, Mark was the first writer of a life of Jesus, so he could not compare his work with that of others.

The story he told became the source of Gospel writers to follow. It became the standard by which they evaluated information about Jesus. *Mark* is not simply a biography of Jesus; many questions about Jesus' life are left unanswered. Nor is it merely a catechism nor a sermon about the meaning of Jesus. But in a way it is all these things. The essentials of Jesus' life and teaching are presented and interpreted simply and clearly. But Mark does not get wound up in details. He does not recite everything that Jesus did; he records little of the preaching. He keeps the eyes of the reader on the person of Jesus, the Messenger of God, the Healer, the Savior.

Matthew. Mark's Gospel probably originated in Rome. Non-Jewish Christians were its primary audience. The need for a Gospel written primarily for Jewish Christians developed. After the destruction of Jerusalem and its Temple in A.D. 70, the Jewish community had closed ranks behind the leadership of the rabbis. They saw the rise of Christianity as a challenge to their own religious traditions and identity. Some may have associated Christianity with the Roman threat.

47

This led to strict separation from Christians. A canon of Hebrew Scriptures was agreed to at Jamnia. Christians were banned from attending the synagogues. This caused much confusion and some bitterness on the part of Christian converts from Judaism. They felt alienated from their families. In some cases, they were cut off and even disowned. Up to this time many had doubtless thought of themselves still as Jews, but Jews who had discovered the full meaning and completion of the ancient promises. Even the apostles had continued to worship as Jews for a time (Acts 3:1). Now it seemed that the family and religious roots of Jewish Christians had been severed.

The Gospel of *Matthew* was written for these Jewish Christians in Palestine and Syria about A.D. 80. There is a tradition of a Gospel written in Aramaic much earlier by the Apostle Matthew, but the Gospel in our Bibles was written by a later disciple in Greek. Though Matthew used *Mark* as his framework, his work is almost twice as long as *Mark*. Much of the additional material comes out of his concern that Jewish converts understand Jesus' mission and their Christian faith as the fulfillment of the Old Testament promises. Matthew quotes the Old Testament Scriptures more than sixty times.

Luke and Acts. At about the same time that Matthew wrote his Gospel, but independently of Matthew, a Greek Christian convert of Asia Minor composed a two-volume work that would extend the story of Jesus into the story of the early Church. The Gospel of *Luke* and the *Acts of the Apostles* were directed to the Greek-speaking communities of the Roman Empire. Their concerns and needs were different from those of the Jewish converts of Matthew's community. Luke's readers did not need reassurance about the Old Testament (which they had probably never read), but they needed to know how their own Christian faith, which had come to them through missionary preachers, was based on the words and deeds of Jesus. They probably wondered about the Jewish traditions of the liturgy and asked about the Jewish origins of their faith. They would have been interested in knowing how a Jewish religion had become open to all people.

John. There is a strong feeling that the Apostle John eventually went to Ephesus in Asia Minor with Mary, the mother of Jesus. There the Christian community centered around John and the Mother of Jesus. He and his disciples had to counter false teachings that Jesus had not really become man. These false teachers said that Jesus only *seemed* to be human, but he had actually kept himself free from earthly contamination. The three *Letters of John* counteract these errors. One of them is a beautiful essay on the love of God revealed in Jesus (1 *John*); the other two seem to be letters to local communities written on some particular occasion.

The Gospel of *John* was the last of the four Gospels. It appeared about A.D. 90. It seems to have been worked over and reedited by John's community over a period of several years. There is practically no repetition (except in the Passion account) of material covered in the earlier Gospels. Jesus is presented as the Word who "became a human being" (John 1:14), who gives himself to his followers as the "bread of life" (John 6:35).

Catholic Epistles and Revelation. The New Testament letters outside the Pauline collection are often grouped together under the heading "Catholic Epistles," those addressed to the whole Church instead of to a particular community. *James* is an example of New Testament wisdom literature. It applies the gospel message to practical issues of Christian morality. *First Peter* is also concerned with the practice of the faith, but with much more interest in the doctrinal basis for Christian behavior. Some of its beautiful and memorable passages were influenced by an early baptismal liturgy. *Jude* and *2 Peter* were both written to combat errors that emerged in the last part of the first century.

The last book in the Bible is in a category by itself. It is known as the *Revelation*, or the *Apocalypse*. The apocalyptic form of writing was used in the Old Testament in books such as *Ezekiel* and *Daniel*. It was a very popular form from 200 B.C. to A.D. 200. It was crisis literature: that is, it was written to strengthen the faith and hope of a community in the midst of persecution and suffering. The occasion for *Daniel* was the persecution of the Jewish community by Antiochus IV; for *Revelation*, it was the Roman persecution of the Christian community.

New Testament Canon. Compared to the long process of canonization of the Old Testament books, acceptance of the writings of the apostles and gospel writers as inspired Scripture came rather quickly. Reference to New Testament books as the standard for faith and practice are found in writings as early as those by Clement of Rome and Ignatius of Antioch at the beginning of the second century. Tertullian, about A.D. 200, is the first to use the title "New Testament." The canonization process was hastened as a result of the rejection of the Old Testament and most of the New Testament by the Christian heretic, Marcion, about A.D. 150. Disputes about whether certain books should be in the New Testament continued for a while, especially *Hebrews, James, 2 Peter, 2* and *3 John,* and *Revelation.* On the other hand, some books no longer in the canon were considered inspired at different times by some: *1* and *2 Clement*, the *Didache*, and the *Shepherd of Hermas*. It was not until the fourth century that a New Testament canon was finally fixed.

How were the present New Testament books finally selected? There were various factors to be considered: apostolic origin, the importance of the community addressed, the centrality of the doctrine contained. In the final analysis, however, it was the Church's awareness, under the guidance of the Holy Spirit, that certain books were an authentic and necessary reflection of her own life of faith. The community of believers saw their own faith in these books as in a mirror. They have been the primary standard of Christian faith ever since.

THE BIBLE AND HISTORY
Paul Jurkowitz

On first turning the pages of the Bible, today's reader may be misled by what he or she sees. At first glance, the Bible seems to be a collection of books which tell the story of the world from Creation right through to the Second Coming of Jesus. More careful reading, however, shows that the Bible writers told their story to make certain important points about God and mankind. Therefore, they often emphasized certain events which historians might not mention, and sometimes they barely mentioned some events about which other historians would have written pages. The Bible is not just "history as it happened"—*it is the story of God in action*. The following outline will help the Bible reader to see the whole picture along with all its parts.

The Fathers (or the Patriarchs)

After setting the scene of the creation of the world and mankind in the opening chapters of *Genesis*, the Bible begins the history of the people of Israel with stories of the "Fathers" (often called *Patriarchs*— a term meaning "first or earliest fathers.") The people of Israel remembered that the Fathers had come to Canaan (Palestine) from Mesopotamia. That ancient center of civilization would influence Israelites throughout their history. The people of Israel lived midway between the two great centers of power of the ancient Near East—Mesopotamia to the east, and the valley of the Nile to the west. The people of Israel were deeply affected by each center. Their roots, however, were deeper in Mesopotamia.

The stories of the Fathers are arranged in order according to family relationships. *Abraham* and Sarah's son, *Isaac*, had two sons by Rebecca. Of these two sons, *Esau* and *Jacob*, God chose Jacob despite Jacob's less than ideal character. Jacob gave *his sons* by Leah and Rachel names which later would be identified with various tribes of the people of Israel. One of Jacob's sons, *Joseph*, had *two sons* whose names would also be carried by later tribes. Through Joseph, Jacob's clan entered Egypt, not to leave until *Moses* led them back to Palestine.

Although Israel's memory may have simplified more complex happenings for the sake of an easily remembered and forceful story, recent archaeological evidence supports the Bible's account of the general historical and cultural setting in which these happenings occurred. The description of the Fathers' way of life fits the period 2000–1700 B.C. too accurately to have been invented in a later age.

The wandering nature of the Fathers' lifestyle forced them to find their security in their God. Each of them accepted personal covenants (or treaties) with God as one important way of showing their own personal dependence on him. The people of Israel did not dress up or cover up the moral failures of the Fathers. This candidness recurs throughout the Bible.

Egypt, Exodus, and Sinai (1550–1250 B.C.)

Jacob's clan entered Egypt at about the same time foreign people called Hyksos ruled Egypt. After the Egyptians expelled the Hyksos in 1550 B.C., most foreigners left behind in Egypt were made slaves. The Hebrews of the Bible were such slaves for more than two hundred years. But they were not the only Hebrews in the world. "Hebrews" was used to describe a low class of society, perhaps workers who owned no land themselves or who wandered in search of work. They were scattered over the ancient Near East at this time. Some of Jacob's clan may have returned to Canaan before the Egyptians overthrew the Hyksos. Some groups of Hebrews who would later join the people of Israel may never have gone to Egypt at all.

After God called Moses in the wilderness of Sinai, he returned to Egypt and was a leader in the Exodus (departure) of a number of Hebrews. They became a new people called Israel, or the Israelites, after the new name God had earlier given Jacob, the name *Israel*. Once out of Egypt, the group had to struggle to keep its trust in its God. Indications are, for example, that they had not been fully convinced that there was only one God—even though they felt that only one God was taking care of them. They sometimes turned to other gods. Even the great treaty or covenant, concluded at Mount Sinai (or Horeb), which was a formal statement of appreciation and loyalty to God, did not stop them from murmuring and rebelling against God from time to time. Moses did, however, manage to hold them together during the forty years in the desert. They may even have added new members from among people they met in the desert during those years. Their religious rites centered on the Tent of Meeting (a portable shrine where Moses spoke with God) and on the Ark of the Covenant, or Covenant Box (a portable throne for God's invisible presence).

Conquest, Settlement, and Judges
(1250–1030 B.C.)

After Moses died, the Israelites were led by Joshua. They started to infiltrate Canaan. That land was split up into many small kingdoms, and Egypt could no longer control them. Therefore, the land could be slowly taken over by just such a small, but determined group. The Israelites came in from the West, across the Jordan River Valley, at the country's midpoint. Through a series of battles, Joshua managed to establish the people in the poorer, hillier sections of the land. In general, they did not take fertile, strongly defended areas like the Valley of Jezreel and the strip along the Mediterranean coast.

In those days, people often killed everyone in a town when they captured it and took it over. The Bible suggests the Israelites occasionally followed this custom. More often, though, they let the people live. In fact, some of the local inhabitants (perhaps "persuaded" by local Hebrews) joined the covenant with Israel's God. Others maintained their independence throughout the period of Judges.

Because the land that Israel won was mountainous and because there were Canaanite towns throughout the hills which had not been conquered, the various parts of the Israelite people were often isolated from each other. They were held together by their devotion to God. They met to worship, and probably to renew their covenant, at various holy places in the hills where the Tent of Meeting was set up. These holy places—Shechem, Gilgal, and Shiloh—were not, however, the only places where Israel's God was worshiped.

When a military threat arose, the people looked to God to raise up someone to lead one or more of the tribes against the invader. They called this person a "Judge." They felt a Judge possessed special abilities from God which enabled him or her to win battles against Israel's enemies and to govern the people in God's way. Israel's heroes, her God-sent saviors or champions, were anything but perfect. For example, Jephthah was a mountain bandit who offered his only child as a sacrifice to God. Samson loved too much the company of women. Gideon took a lot of divine persuading before he accepted God's call.

The situation became desperate when the Philistines began to push northward from their five cities on the Mediterranean coast into the Israelite interior. The Philistines were the survivors of a Greek invasion of Egypt that had failed. The survivors had sailed along the coast and captured some rich land. They established their five cities on the pattern of Greek city-states.

Samuel, the last of the Judges, a man also called a prophet, found himself and his people torn between two ways of responding to the

Philistine threat. The old system of trusting that God would provide a champion did not seem to work against the Philistines. However, to install a king who could lead the people with royal authority might deny any real trust in God. Samuel took the middle path: he annointed as king a man to whom God had given gifts of strength and prophecy. His name was Saul. The debate over how God leads his people— through specially gifted leaders or through human intelligence and regular institutions—was to continue for many years. The northern parts of Israel tended to choose the special leader; the southern parts the regular system of royal government.

The United Kingdom (1030–931 B.C.)

After King Saul and his son, Jonathan, were killed by the Philistines in battle, Saul's son, Ishbosheth, was installed as king in the North and a former lieutenant of Saul's, David, was chosen king in the South. Seven years later the elders of the North offered David kingship over them also. For many years David had been a fugitive from Saul, who was jealous of him. During these years in the barren wastes of the desert in the far south, David had built up a personal army. This army did not depend on the approval of the tribal elders. Its members did not have to return regularly to work their crops. David used his army in the south to make the Philistines subject to his power, in the northeast to extend Israel's control and influence all the way to Damascus, and in the southeast to annex or control Ammon, Moab, and Edom. David conquered those Canaanite areas within Israel's territory which had not yet been conquered. All this was possible because the surrounding great powers were temporarily weak and were unable to control Palestine themselves.

There remained, however, a deep division between the North and South in Israel. It reappeared when David's grandson, Rehoboam, went north to Shechem in order to be accepted as king by northern Israel. The northerners rejected him, and the northern and southern kingdoms went their separate ways from then on. One reason why David and Solomon were able to hold the two together was the fact that David chose Jerusalem to be his capital. Jerusalem had been an independent Canaanite city. David's personal army captured it and gave it to him as his private property. It was located on the boundary between North and South. It had belonged to neither and could be a center of unity. David enhanced Jerusalem's unifying role by transferring the Ark of the Covenant there. His son, Solomon, further linked his subjects to Jerusalem by surrounding the Ark with the (immovable) Temple.

Solomon was not the soldier his father had been—and Israel's empire shrank as a result. He was, however, an able political administrator; and his commercial arrangements brought increased prosperity. He reorganized the land into twelve parts (not exactly along old tribal lines) and this made possible the efficient gathering of the resources which were necessary for Solomon's great building program. He built an elaborate palace complex (fourteen years in building) in Jerusalem next to the Temple (seven years in building). He strengthened fortifications throughout the land. All this construction had its price. Heavy demands for labor and other taxes on free Israelite landowners began to anger these people whose traditions stressed the fact that God had delivered them from servitude to an earthly king. The Bible records at least one revolt against Solomon. Jeroboam led that revolt, and he eventually became king of the North. As Solomon had to go outside Israel for help and advice on organizing his government, or building, or setting up state-run businesses, foreign influences increased. Many foreigners worshiped their own gods and often influenced Israelites to worship these gods also. Ever since the Israelites had settled into a routine, stable life based on agricultural seasons, they were prone to worship the old Canaanite gods of the land. Now foreigners brought in their gods, who appealed to many Israelites. The growth of urban life and the fact that people who were newly rich could buy up small farms led to the spread of social stresses and injustices.

Two Kingdoms: Israel and Judah (931–735 B.C.)

The northern tribes called themselves "Israel." For much of its existence, the northern kingdom was the more important economically and militarily. It was *the* Israelite country. Despite its retention of Jerusalem, "Judah," the name of the southern kingdom, lived in the shadow of "Israel."

Furthermore, despite the dangers of religious compromise posed by the presence of the fertility cults in the more heavily agricultural north, the North could still consider itself more faithful than Judah to the religion of the old tribal confederacy. God intervened directly and vividly in national policies. His representatives were the prophets. These men of God, who judged the North by the standards of the Sinai covenant, did not hesitate to depose kings and to anoint successors.

The South, though it too had outspoken prophets, tended to adopt new ways. It worshiped Israel's God in a Temple which Solomon designed after a Phoenician model. It also emphasized a new covenant.

Unlike the Sinai covenant, which was between the whole people and God, this new covenant was a personal covenant between God and David in the style of the early covenants with the Fathers. David's descendants were promised the throne of the South forever with no clearly evident "if" clauses. The results of these two different covenants on political life were dramatically different. The North went through king after king, family after family. In the South the kings were all chosen on the basis of descent from King David and according to regular inheritance rules. Furthermore, in the minds of some, David's city, Jerusalem, and its Temple came to share in some of the promises made to David.

There were five outstanding northern kings, members of three different families. *Jeroboam I*, the first king of the North, ruled for twenty-two years. His sanctuaries at the ancient shrines of Dan and Bethel served as places where Israel's God, enthroned invisibly on the back of a bull, could be worshiped. *Omri* built the northern capital at Samaria. His son, *Ahab*, was the husband of Jezebel and the enemy of Elijah the prophet. *Jehu* persecuted and killed his political rivals and a large number of the worshipers of Baal, a Canaanite god who was still worshiped by many Israelites. The reign of Jehu's great-grandson, *Jeroboam II*, was marked by such great political, military, and economic power that the prophet Amos warned him that all was not well. After Jeroboam II things went down so quickly and so clearly that the next prophet, Hosea, did not have to tell people how bad things were. They already knew. So Hosea added words of comfort to his warnings. Though many Israelites did not connect their peril with the fact that injustice had been done against the powerless within Israel, and that the Israelites had failed to live according to the covenant, they could not ignore the looming presence of the ever-expanding Assyrian empire. In 722 B.C., almost exactly two hundred years after the union between North and South had broken down, Assyria captured the northern capital. They took part of the population of the North away and brought in foreigners as replacements.

Refugees who fled south to Judah brought with them their loyalty to the Sinai covenant. One result was an immediate reform under King Hezekiah and an even more ambitious reform fifty years later under King Josiah.

During the two hundred years of the northern kingdom's existence, not much of note occurred in the South. At the beginning Jerusalem had been saved for Judah by annexing and fortifying the territory just north of the city (the land of the tribe of Benjamin) as a buffer area. Judah generally maintained its independence during this period— although it saw the Temple looted twice (once by Egypt and once by

Israel). It had to pay tribute to Damascus at one period, and it was subject to Israel at times.

Judah's Last Days (735–587 B.C.)

Judah's story gained in importance as Israel's ended. In 735 B.C., Israel and Damascus (capital of Aramea) invaded Judah to try to force it to join them in trying to stop Assyria, a growing Mesopotamian power. The prophet Isaiah urged King Ahaz to trust in God, and not to rely on foreign nations to stop the Israelite-Aramean invasion. But Ahaz spurned Isaiah's advice and submitted his nation to Assyrian policies in return for Assyria's support against Israel and Damascus.

Submission to Assyria made an already bad religious situation worse. Judging from the sermons of the prophets Micah and Isaiah, the land was full of social injustice and religious practices that ran directly counter to the Sinai covenant and to all of Israel's traditions. In light of this situation, those who wanted the ancient ways restored (some of whom had witnessed firsthand in the North what happened when the covenant was no longer followed) were overjoyed when the next king, Hezekiah, began his program of reform. The king attempted to supervise all worship by allowing worship only in the Temple. But this was not acceptable to the Assyrians, who themselves worshiped many gods. Worship of the Assyrian gods was a symbol of loyalty to the Assyrian king. About twenty years after the Assyrians destroyed the northern kingdom, they also devastated almost all of Judah and besieged Hezekiah (and Isaiah) in Jerusalem. Though God preserved the city, Hezekiah had to submit once again to Assyria. His son, Manasseh, undid his father's reforms and returned to the old ways during his forty-five-year reign.

Two years after Manasseh's death, his grandson, Josiah, came to the throne at the age of eight. Josiah soon attempted to reinstitute Hezekiah's reforms. Since his program was contained in "The Book of the Law," the nucleus of the later book of *Deuteronomy*, his reform is referred to as "deuteronomic." As in the reform of Hezekiah, both the nation's covenant with God at Sinai and the Temple at Jerusalem were emphasized. The reformers formally renewed the nation's covenant with God and attempted to spread its spirit. Prophets like Jeremiah supported the movement at first, but then rejected it as the religious leaders began to overemphasize externals. Finally, the death of Josiah at the age of forty (in 609 B.C.) probably convinced many Judaites that they had better hedge their bets between the power of Israel's God and that of foreign gods. In the twenty years or so between Josiah's death and the destruction of Jerusalem, foreign religious practices and doctrines returned with a vengeance—even into the Temple grounds.

The external threat was still from Mesopotamia—but now the rising power was Babylon. Just after Josiah's death, Assyria had been finally and completely defeated. The burning question in Judah in the next few years was whether or not Egypt could stop Babylon. Twice Judah decided that Egypt could and sided with Egypt in the struggle. Twice (597 and 587 B.C.) Babylon captured Jerusalem and deported large numbers of the leading citizens to Babylon. At the second deportation Jerusalem's walls and Temple were pulled down. Some refugees fled to Egypt, beginning the large Jewish settlements there. Although some stayed on in Judah, to a large degree the land was depopulated over the next few years. Babylon did not import foreign colonists to take the place of those who had been deported.

Exile in Babylon (587–538 B.C.)

In the ancient world, events on earth were seen as the visible results of clashes on the divine level. When a nation was destroyed, people believed that the nation's god(s) had been defeated by more powerful gods. The fact that Judah-in-exile did not think this way was due to the influence of a number of religious thinkers who pointed out another way to understand what had happened.

Some of these thinkers collected the sacred traditions to show how Israel and Judah themselves had made their destruction inevitable— in spite of many warnings to return to the ways laid down in the covenant. Other religious thinkers looked to a future restoration. Two prophets in this second category stand out—Ezekiel and the man whose prophecies are collected in chapters 40–55 of the book of *Isaiah*, often called "Second Isaiah."

The exiles in Babylon were allowed to live as communities and to exercise a good deal of freedom. They did not want to be absorbed by the surrounding population and so lose their national and religious identity. With the Temple in ruins, the Promised Land far away, and the Davidic heir powerless, many of the old unifying elements were no longer effective. The Sinai covenant, however, was still effective; and its prestige had been increased by the events which had clearly shown that to ignore the covenant was to walk a path of death. Finding out what God's will was and doing it became the main concern. This meant that the Judean deportees began to emphasize certain practices that had not been so prominent a part of their religious practice in earlier times. Elements of God's will that served to set his people apart from their neighbors became especially important. Circumcision, dietary rules, opposition to marrying outside the community, and observance of the Sabbath became central concerns for the devout. These new emphases changed Israel's religion so much that it could now be described as "Jewish" (from "Judean") instead of "Israelitic," (as it was before 587 B.C.).

When Cyrus the Persian challenged the power of Babylon, he was hailed by Second Isaiah as a deliverer anointed by God (a "messiah") who would rescue God's people. The prophet stirred up the exiles with visions of a second exodus through the desert back to the Promised Land. And, a year after Cyrus took Babylon, just about fifty years after the Babylonians destroyed Jerusalem, he did allow Jewish exiles to return home. But for many, remaining in Babylon seemed better than returning. The Jewish community in Mesopotamia survived to make many great contributions to Judaism.

Persian and Greek Rule in Palestine (538–198 B.C.)

Cyrus agreed to give the sacred vessels of the Temple to those who went home. He also agreed to pay for the rebuilding of the Temple. There were a number of returns scattered over at least a hundred years. The first was led by a prince of the royal line of David named Sheshbazzar. His relative, Zerubbabel, and Joshua, the high priest, finished rebuilding the Temple with the help of two prophets, Haggai and Zechariah. The Second Temple was completed in 515 B.C., twenty-three years after Cyrus' decree offering to pay for the work.

The time taken in restoring the Temple shows the difficulties that the returned exiles faced. They had to rebuild a devastated, depopulated land. They also had to deal with hostile neighbors. It was during this time that hatred began between the Samaritans and the Jews. The Samaritans were the people who had been brought into the North by the Assyrians to replace the deported Israelites. They had intermarried with some of the Israelites who had remained there. The Jews thought they were inferior because of their mixed ancestry.

Two men played large roles in making the survival of Judah possible. Both came from Babylon around 450 B.C. (The precise relationship between the work of each is not clear because of chronological difficulties in the biblical texts.) Nehemiah was a Jewish eunuch at the Persian court who got himself appointed a governor of the Persian province of Judah. Ezra was a priest with an official Persian position who led a group back to Judah. Both adopted Ezekiel's vision of Israel as a priestly people set apart from other nations in order to worship God properly. Therefore, they concentrated their religious efforts on proper observance of the Sabbath, proper worship in the Temple, and proper marriages (i.e., only with Jews). Rules originally meant for priests were gradually extended to all pious Jews. Nehemiah provided for the physical safety of this new priest-like nation by rebuilding the walls of Jerusalem—a task made difficult by the opposition of the governors of the neighboring provinces of Samaria and Ammon.

Judah was now considered by her people to be ruled by God, and the high priest governed the province in his name. This Judah was in many ways different from the Judah of pre-exilic days. But Judah's thinkers were careful to show the connections between the new ways and the old days. It was in this period that the intense study of the Torah, or "Law," (a better translation would be "Teaching"), the first five books of the Hebrew Scriptures, became very popular among the devout.

The Greek conquest of Persia by Alexander the Great was completed by about 330 B.C. This meant new rulers for Judah and important new influences. Soon after Alexander's early death (323 B.C.), four of his generals divided his empire four ways. The Ptolemies of Egypt, descendants of one of these generals, controlled Judah for the next hundred years (c. 300–200 B.C.). Then the Seleucids of Syria, descendants of another one of Alexander's generals, took over control of Judah.

The new influences on Judah are called "Hellenization" (*Hellas* is the Greek name for "Greece"). The Greek rulers deliberately set out to share their civilization with the native populations. To do so, they established Greek cities throughout their domain to serve as examples. In Judah, reaction to Greek culture was divided. Some Jews openly and enthusiastically accepted the new ways. Others, called "pious ones," intensified their devotion to the Law and shut themselves completely off from Greek ways of living. It was harder to avoid the influence of Greek ways of thinking.

Maccabean Revolt and Hasmonean Independence (198–63 B.C.)

Judah's Seleucid (Syrian) rulers had to collect large sums of money to pay for the expansion of their power. They looted the Judean Temple treasury. The Seleucid rulers even auctioned off the high priesthood to the highest bidder. When one Seleucid ruler decided to force unity in his realm on the basis of the Hellenization of every one of his subjects, those Judeans who were loyal to the old ways began guerilla warfare in resistance. The rebels were first led by Mattathias, and then in turn by three of his sons: Judas (166–160 B.C.), Jonathan (160–143 B.C.), and Simon (143–134 B.C.). The struggle gradually turned from a resistance movement into a revolt aimed at creating a separate state. The last brother, Simon, became high priest and king.

The descendants of Simon, known as the Hasmoneans, ruled from 134 to 63 B.C. They gradually extended their control to the north, first taking Samaria and then northern Galilee. Northern Galilee was Judaized. Because of this, in New Testament times there were two Jewish areas, Galilee and Judah, separated by Samaritan territory. Eventually, the Hasmoneans ruled an area almost as large as David's empire. There was a good deal of civil war throughout Hasmonean times as rival factions struggled for control. It was in these years that the Pharisee party, the Essene group, and the Sadducean party each came into being.

Even though the Pharisees championed the old ways, they were able to adjust to new situations and ideas so well that they merit the label of "liberal." Descendants of the "pious ones" who had supported the Maccabean revolt until it lost its religious motivation, they earned the name "Pharisee" ("The Separated") by avoiding contact with Gentiles, sinners, and any Jew who did not try to be meticulous in his observance of the Law. They wanted to protect the holiness of the written Law. To do so they emphasized a complicated oral Law that kept people so involved in trying to keep it in all its detail that they could not penetrate the layers of rules to the point of breaking the written Law. One of the new ideas that made them different from the Sadducees was their belief in the resurrection of the body.

Another group that developed out of the "pious ones" was the Essenes. This group vigorously separated itself from most things political and religious in Jewish life. Whether they lived at their monastery at Qumran in the desert near the Dead Sea or as sympathizers scattered throughout the nation, they had given up on human efforts to achieve God's Kingdom. They were preparing themselves for "the day" when God would set things right himself. The Essenes are not mentioned by name in the Bible.

The Sadducees were the priestly and aristocratic party at Jerusalem. As priests, they resented the Pharisees' intrusions into the priestly duty of interpreting the Law. Perhaps because they were not all that interested in religious questions, they did not develop new theological positions to meet the changing situations and questions. They accepted only the first five books of the Scriptures (the Torah, or Law) as authoritative. However conservative they were theologically, their life-style was liberal; they embraced Hellenization wholeheartedly.

The Romans, the Herods, and Early Christianity
(63 B.C.–A.D. 66)

In 63 B.C., the Romans intervened in the growing civil turmoil in Palestine and made it part of the Roman province of Syria. The Hasmoneans were kept on for a time in various capacities, but they were gradually set aside due to the growing power of the family of an ambitious Idumean, Antipater. He and his sons reacted with great agility to each of the rapid shifts in power at Rome. Palestine found itself ruled in turn by Pompey, Julius Caesar, Cassius, Mark Antony, and Octavian (also known as "Augustus" when he became Emperor of Rome). Finally, under Augustus, one of Antipater's sons, Herod the Great took control of Palestine in 37 B.C. as a king subject to the Roman emperor. He spent the first twelve years of his reign making sure of his power by killing off all possible rivals. He spent the next twelve years engaged in a great building program all over Palestine, including a restoration of the Temple. Despite all this, the final years of his thirty-three-year reign were not peaceful for him. As a foreigner, he was hated by the Jews in spite of all that he had done for them. He was the Herod of the infancy stories about Jesus. Jesus was born before 4 B.C., the year in which Herod the Great died.

The New Testament mentions three other Herods. The first, *Herod Antipas,* is the Herod of the Passion accounts. After receiving Galilee and Perea as his portion of the kingdom of his father, Herod the Great, he ruled for forty-two years. The second was *Herod Agrippa I,* a grandson of Herod the Great. Beginning with a small territory in northern Transjordan in A.D. 37, Herod Agrippa I gradually received more and more territory to rule until his kingdom was almost as large as that ruled by Herod the Great. He persecuted the early Christian church and killed James the son of Zebedee shortly before his own death in A.D. 44. The third Herod was *Agrippa II,* the son of Herod Agrippa I. He ruled one, then another, small area beginning in A.D. 48. Paul appeared before this Herod just before sailing for Rome to have his case heard by the Emperor.

Direct Roman rule in some parts of Palestine was an off and on thing as various members of the family of Herod the Great lost and took over various territories. But after one of his sons, Archelaus, was removed from control of Judea, Samaria, and Idumea at the request of the populace in A.D. 6, Rome governed this particular area directly through Roman officials called "procurators," except for the brief period of A.D. 41–44, when Herod Agrippa I held it for a time. The procurators were unsuccessful in dealing with the Jews of Palestine. They did not respect Jewish religious feelings, acted in a high-handed fashion, and were often corrupt. Gradually, opposition to the Roman presence grew. A nationalistic group called Zealots began a program of terrorism that fed the fires of unrest.

It was in this atmosphere of resentment against foreign rule, disagreement about what God wanted his people to do, and widespread expectations that God was about to intervene dramatically in history to straighten things out for his people that Jesus and his earliest followers lived. The Gospel accounts and the Acts of the Apostles must be read with this turbulent background in mind.

The Great Revolt, the Destruction of the Temple, and the Second Revolt (A.D. 66–135)

Finally, one procurator pushed the Jews beyond their ability to endure. From A.D. 66 to 70, the land was devastated by bitter fighting between Romans and Jews, and also between various factions of Jews. The Roman army seized Jerusalem in A.D. 70, and utterly destroyed it. Jewish prisoners of war were sold all over the Mediterranean. By A.D. 73, Masada fell. It was the last remaining Jewish stronghold.

After the revolt was crushed, the Jewish community closed ranks around a group of rabbis at Jamnia, to the west of Jerusalem. A form of Phariseeism influenced by a rabbi named Hillel became the standard for Jews to follow. Essenic, Christian, and other kinds of Jews were excommunicated from the synagogue. It was at this time that Judaism and Jewish Christianity clearly split.

The disastrous outcome of the great revolt did not quiet hopes for a revival of Judean independence. As the people remembered the restoration after Babylon had once destroyed Jerusalem, they yearned for a new national restoration following the devastation of Jerusalem by Rome. They looked for a new anointed leader, or Messiah. In A.D. 132, Judea erupted once more in rebellion under Rabbi Aqiba, Eleazar the priest, and Simon ben Kosibah (Bar Cochba) the soldier and political leader. Even though Rome recalled her best general from Britain to deal with the revolt, it was only in A.D. 135 that the rebel army was completely defeated.

With this event, the period of biblical history came to an end.

LITERARY FORMS OF THE BIBLE

Eugene A. LaVerdiere, S.S.S.

Literature cannot be separated from the *form* in which it is written. A literary form is the exact type of writing which an author uses to express his ideas. The literary form of this article, for instance, is a prose essay. A poem is another kind of literary form, as is a novel, a short story, a sermon, or a listing of the members of a family. Each form has its own rules, special vocabulary, type of punctuation, and style of expression. Only in recent years have scholars tried to identify the various literary forms which the writers of the Bible used to convey their message.

They discovered that the biblical writers used literary forms that were in use by other writers of other books during the same period. This discovery helped scholars answer many questions about the historical accuracy of the biblical text.

Sometimes two different biblical passages by different authors described the same event, but there are obvious differences in what is said about the event. These differences no longer need to be explained on the basis of what actually happened. They can be explained by paying close attention to the nature of the particular literary form which the author used to discuss the event.

Biblical authors took full advantage of available literary resources in their efforts to share their message with others. They used appropriate language, drawing words and phrases from accepted usage, both religious and secular. However, they also drew on the broader forms of literary expression, writing in *prose* and *poetry* and expressing themselves through various types of *narrative* and with a wide range of other forms. In 1943, this expanded approach to understanding the Scriptures was formally endorsed by Pius XII as the right way to study the Bible (*Divino Afflante Spiritu*, Nos. 35–41).

This approach of studying the literary forms of the Bible has helped clarify questions of a historical nature. It has also opened the Bible to a much richer religious appreciation. The forms of biblical literature are literary "incarnations" of fundamental religious experience in the Israelite and Christian tradition. Because of this, they became the basic language of the heart and mind for all who continue to live in that tradition to express their own religious experience in ways that are true to that tradition. In this way, biblical *prayers* and *hymns* readily become our own prayers and hymns; biblical *narratives* become our story; its *discourses* address us; and its *dialogues* voice our own dialogue with God and the Lord Jesus. *Vocation narratives* continue to call us forth, and the *parables* of Jesus are ever-present challenges to all whose ears are truly open to hear.

Awareness of the literary forms of the Bible will help the reader to understand more accurately the ancient meaning of the text and will help release the power of this divine and human word in modern living. While special consideration is given in this article to the major forms found in the two Testaments, some of the minor forms which have been woven into their rich fabric will also be treated.

Prose and Poetry

As in all literature, the most general distinction in biblical literature is between prose and poetry. In the Old and New Testaments, both prose and poetry appear in a wide variety of forms. However, since biblical prose will be amply treated in later sections of this essay, the present section is devoted mainly to poetry.

Characteristics of biblical poetry include its concise and rhythmic expression, specialized diction, parallelism, balance of ideas, concrete imagery, and symbolic language. Poetry expresses its ideas at a high level of intensity. It is quite distinct from biblical prose, which is much closer to spoken language. However, since many elements of biblical poetry also appear in prose, it is sometimes difficult to distinguish the two. This is especially true for people who think mostly of rhyme and meter when they think of poetry. Neither rhyme nor meter are found very often in biblical poetry. A good approach to the question of what is prose or poetry in the Bible is to think of placing the passage someplace along a line from pure prose to the very poetic.

Among all the features that make biblical poetry, *parallelism* and *balance* are the most distinctive. Biblical poems are divided into stanzas of two or more lines, each of which is usually subdivided into two or three parallel segments.

Sometimes a parallel segment repeats an idea in the previous segment, but uses different words to do this (*synonymous parallelism*):

> I recognize my faults;
> I am always conscious of my
> sins. (Ps. 51:3)

At other times, the parallel segment sets forth a contrast to the idea in the first segment (*antithetic parallelism*):

> The righteous are guided and
> protected by the LORD,
> but the evil are on the way to
> their doom. (Ps. 1:6)

And sometimes the parallel segments add to the thought formed in the first segment (*cumulative* or *"staircase" parallelism*):

> Praise the LORD, you heavenly
> beings;
> praise his glory and power.
> Praise the LORD's glorious name;
> bow down before the Holy One
> when he appears. (Ps. 29:1–2)

By its very nature as poetry, biblical poetry communicates mainly by calling forth experiences and perceptions rather than by making direct statements about reality. This aspect of poetic communication is extremely important for grasping the purpose for which the biblical word was written. An image or symbolic statement which presents God as a rock or a shield, or which compares him to an eagle bearing its young across the sky, is true. However, to be seen as true, the statement must be understood to be an image. Only then will it call forth the picture of the firm ground of life and not just a rock, or the protective presence of God and not just a shield, or the soaring power of God's loving care and not just a bird. The author intended to convey these deeper truths by the use of imagery.

One of the most important aspects of biblical poetry is its relation to the poet's own understanding through faith of the nature of God. God exists at a level above his creation, and human life; but he nevertheless reveals himself through them. The biblical poet is thus challenged to tell about experiences of reality which human words can never adequately express. Straining at the limits of language, the writer turns to poetry and its power to call forth direct insight. Poetry is thus intimately related to the very nature of religious inspiration and the communication of that experience in the words of the Bible.

Fully one-third of the Old Testament is poetry. Although poetry can be found in the historical books, it is most often found in the prophetic and wisdom literature. And, of course, there are the many hymns, laments, and other poetic forms which were gathered into the book of *Psalms*. Not all the poetry in the Bible is of the same quality. It is generally agreed that Israel's highest poetic achievement is found in the books of *Isaiah* and *Job*. The widespread use of poetry in Israel's liturgy as well as in the parts of the Bible devoted to teaching accounts in part for the strong influence of poetry on Hebrew prose writing. The constant appearance of poetic prose in the Bible can also be explained by the intensity of the experience the author wants to present to his readers.

The poetic form appears far less frequently in the New Testament, where no single book can be described as primarily poetic. However, there are evidences in the New Testament of Christian hymns which were coming into being in the early Church. Many hymns are quoted in whole or part in several New Testament works. Along with Old Testament and Jewish hymns, these Christian hymns contributed to the poetic quality of New Testament prose passages.

Narrative and Direct Address

The Bible may tell its story by use of narrative and direct address, two important literary forms. In *narrative* the writer uses the third person ("he" or "she") to tell the story of Israel or the early Christian community. In *direct address* the writer uses the second person ("you," "your") to express his religious or ethical concern.

In the Old Testament, *narrative* is the form used by the writers of Israel's historical writings, as well as a number of short stories such as the books of *Ruth*, *Jonah*, and *Judith*. It is also present in a wide range of other works, however, including prophetic, wisdom, and apocalyptic literature. *Direct address* is not used as widely as narrative. It is found in some psalms, in prophetic books (especially *Jeremiah*), and in "didactic" or "instructive" wisdom literature.

In the New Testament, narrative is characteristic of the Gospels, *Acts*, and the book of *Revelation*; but narrative sections are also found in some of the letters. While direct address is the basic form of the letters, it also appears as a secondary form in the narrative literature (as in Luke 1:1–4; Acts 1:1–2; John 20:30–31).

Narrative and direct address are not rigidly separate from each other. They often interpenetrate and complement one another. That they do so is quite normal, since the biblical story (narrative) was told with its implications for the religious and ethical life of the readers (direct address) made very clear. In the Bible, ethical teaching is rooted in God's showing of himself in history. The very nature and purpose of biblical literature made it easy for authors to move freely from narrative to direct address and back, depending on whether they were focusing on the subjects of the stories or on the readers being addressed.

In order to understand whether narrative or direct address is being used, the reader should look to see whether the subject or the people for whom the book was written appears uppermost in the writer's mind at any given point in the writing. In John 20:24–29, for example, the writer's clear attention is on how Thomas the doubter became a believer. The writer does have an eye, however, on the readers who, unlike Thomas, must believe without having seen Jesus. In these verses, the story is in sharp focus with indirect reference to the readers. In John 20:30–31, on the other hand, the reader is brought into sharp focus when the author comments on the purpose of the entire Gospel. The readers are addressed in a comment arising from the story. These two successive units show both the difference and the close relationship between the two forms as the biblical author seeks to make his message clear.

Even though narrative and direct address in the Bible are closely associated, we must carefully distinguish between them. This is especially so when we approach a literary work from the standpoint of the readers.

Narrative makes its points with the reader primarily through a process of identification. The people in the story, their characteristics and attitudes as well as their relationships to one another, act as mirrors in which the readers can see all of themselves and their own life-situations. The story is told concretely, but with an openness to other times and contexts which is characteristic of all classical literature. Thus the story is read as the reader's story. Any change which takes place in the story makes possible a similar change in the reader.

In historical narrative, the entire process is made easier by the fact that the readers belong to a new moment in the same history which is being read or heard. The story of Abraham, Isaac, and Jacob, the story of Moses, the story of Jesus and of Peter and Paul is thus more than a historical account which is able to arouse feelings in us because we are caught up in the people and events in the story. It is also a part of our very own story. Even though the event happened a long time ago, we live in a stream of history which continues to be affected by that event. We are challenged to live daily in its light.

In all such narratives, it is the story and the people in the story which inspire us. It is not the writer. His literary presence remains hidden behind the voice of the narrator. Only when the author tends to use second-person address does he surface to speak to us directly. At such moments, the story and its people recede into the background only to emerge once more when the third-person narrative starts again.

Direct address communicates with the reader by insisting on some kind of response from him or her. It discusses issues directly. It analyzes current behavior; it argues; confronts; exhorts; condemns; and commends. By these means it calls the readers to initial or renewed conversion. It shapes their attitudes. It confirms them in their faith and demands action as the outworking of their faith.

In direct address, the writer's own person is usually at the fore. To the extent that this literary form involves identification, it is with the person and attitudes of the writer that readers are called to identify. Therefore, the writer uses the first person ("I," "me") along with the second ("you," "your"). There are moments, however, when the author steps aside and turns to narrative, using the third person ("he," "she"). A good example of this shift from direct address to narrative and back again can be found in 1 Corinthians 10:1–13. Paul begins by addressing his readers directly: "I want you to remember, my brothers" (v. 1a). Then, in a narrative setting, he tells about Moses and the Israelites in the Exodus. Paul does this to call forth the reader's memory of that great event (vv. 1b–5). He then returns to the use of the first and second person in verses 6–13. This is his application of the narrative to the readers.

The minor literary forms used in narrative and direct address are quite different. Biblical narratives include the many forms found in the *literary traditions* of antiquity. Direct address includes the various forms used in ancient oratory.

Dialogue and *discourse* are two of the most important forms found in biblical narrative.

Dialogues suggest the face-to-face nature of direct communication between people. They also give the author the opportunity to put into words the readers' own searching and response to challenges by the use of spoken language. This is done as the author interprets for his readership the meaning of each life of the people who appear in the story. The questions, answers and confessional statements of Abraham, Moses, and Christian disciples thus become those of every reader who joins in their story. When God himself or Jesus participates in the dialogue, they retain the initiative; the people addressed respond. In this context of divine address and human response in the Bible, many psalms and prayers can be understood as our human response in a dialogue for which a divine address is presupposed.

According to ancient literary custom, *discourses* and especially *farewell discourses* give writers an opportunity to speak directly to current situations. In *Deuteronomy*, for example, the writer through Moses' voice speaks to the Israelites of the seventh and sixth centuries B.C. He emphasizes that the covenant is not something only in the remote past. It is also a present and immediate reality. In John 13–17, Jesus' statements are used to shed light on the nature of the community which centered about the Apostle John toward the end of the first century A.D. in Ephesus. In Acts 20:17–35, the voice of Paul addresses the Lukan churches of the mid-eighties. Narrative writers could thus speak to their contemporary readers in a manner that seemed like direct address while still telling their story.

Some of the literary forms used by biblical writers are rooted more in the significance of the history and the importance of the people whose story is told than in the literary customs of the time. Thus Israel's ancient and evolving laws were included in the story of Moses the lawgiver. Thus the prophetic oracles and messages were incorporated in the story of the prophet who uttered them. Thus Jesus' proclamation of the good news of the kingdom, his pithy sayings, and his parabolic teachings were placed in the gospel accounts of what God accomplished in and through Jesus' person. Thus apostolic teaching was presented in Acts' story of the early growth and development of the Christian communities. Biblical narratives closely reflect the spoken word and the life context of the communities from which they sprang.

In the Old Testament, direct address includes (1) the traditional styles of *prophetic speech* in which the prophet often says his message is the word of God to Israel, and (2) Israel's *teaching* tradition in which tested sayings for practical living were recorded for the education of officials and the general public. *Isaiah* is an example of prophetic speech and *Proverbs* of teaching. The writers in both forms used vocabulary and figures of speech which were long established in many parts of the ancient world. The written word reflects the original spoken word. The prophet's function was to speak God's word to the king or the people. The wise teacher taught young Israelites by word of mouth. He had to phrase his teaching so that it could easily be remembered. He used parallelism and other devices to assist his learner's memory.

In the New Testament, the direct address form of the *letters* uses long-accepted patterns of letter writing. For instance, there is an address which starts with the name of the writer. This is followed by naming the person or group to whom the letter is sent. This is followed by greetings from the writer. Then the body of the letter comes, followed by final greetings from the writer. The New Testament letters combined some of the characteristics of Semitic letters with others from the Greek world. Profoundly Christian in spirit, this form was deeply influenced by the tradition of preaching of the apostles and other early church leaders. So much was this so that we must speak of a new, distinctively Christian letter form which is best described as a "Christian apostolic letter."

These letters were substitutes for a personal visit by one of the apostles and for the personally spoken word of the apostle. The letters therefore are close to the writer's spoken word. They proclaim and teach. The often contain long segments which are modeled on the oratorical methods of the day. Paul and others write in a sharp imaginary debate in their letters with people who oppose the truth of the Christian faith. Some supposed objector states his case; the writer answers the objection, and this raises another question which needs answering. The effect is similar to listening to a tight rhetorical argument. Good examples may be found in James 2:2–4, Romans 2:1–20, and 1 Corinthians 9 and 15:35–36. Sometimes Paul may use methods of argumentation used by the rabbis. Good examples are found in Romans 1:17 and Galatians 4:21–31.

The letters were intended to be read when the people to whom they were sent gathered for the Eucharist. It is therefore understandable that they used many traditional forms of expression current in the early liturgy. For instance, there is the influence of the *homily* with its discussion of faith issues and its exhortation to Christian living, as in Romans 1:16–11:36 and 12:1–15:13. The letters also include many of the Christian community's *prayers, creeds, hymns, liturgical greetings,* and *blessings.*

History, the Covenant Formulary, and Myth

Most of the Old Testament is very concerned with *history.* This is true of the historical books and of Israel's prophetic and wisdom literature. This concern with history is closely linked to the historical nature of Israel's religious experience of God. He is ever seen as the God of Israel's Fathers, the God of Abraham, Isaac, and Jacob.

This section focuses primarily on historical writing in the *Pentateuch, Joshua, Judges, 1* and *2 Samuel, 1* and *2 Kings, 1* and *2 Chronicles, Ezra,* and *Nehemiah.* Since the historical nature of these works varies considerably, they provide ample grounds for observing the forms of historical writing used in ancient Israel.

Similar to the writing of history in other ancient cultures of the Near East, Israel's history was written so that the past was always seen from the point of view of the time of writing and the need at that time to help shape the future. Historical writings summed up the meaning of Israelite life in order to express the meaning of the present at a time when events seemed to have broken the line with the past. This kind of writing is very different from modern historical writing. It is a different literary form. There is also a religious value system which underlies the account of events and gives meaning to those events.

The writers of biblical history intended to inspire their readers and to help them live purposefully within their own historical tradition. Accordingly, the focus of biblical history is on the meaning of events rather than on the "objective" description of those events. Modern historical writing is also interpretive, of course, but it emphasizes precise chronology, geography, and comprehensiveness.

The writers of Israel's history believed that God is both creator

71

and lord of history. For Israel, God showed himself in all of creation and in every facet of history, but especially in human life and in those historical events in which life is saved from death and provided with expansive development. Biblical writers frequently referred to these events as God's signs and wonders on humankind's behalf. Modern historical writing, however, is mainly secular in orientation. It does not view events with faith in the God of history as its basic understanding of the meaning of history. It presents history in purely humanistic terms. It finds historical order in the succession and linking together of human events without reference to God's creative and saving presence.

The literary form of Israel's historical writing was greatly influenced by the wording of ancient covenants. These were *treaties* between nations, people, and the gods, associated especially with the Hittite people of Anatolia about 1800–1500 B.C. These treaty forms outlined the past, present, and expected future relationship between a vassal kingdom and its Hittite sovereign. They provided Israel with a good model for understanding its own life and history in relation to its divine Lord.

The form of these treaties is fairly simple. Like the Hittite or other human sovereign, God introduces himself, recalls his prior history with Israel, and sets forth the law which must govern those who enter into a covenant relationship with him. He also outlines the curses which will befall the unfaithful as well as the blessings which those who are faithful will enjoy. These elements recur at many points in Israel's historical writing. In *Exodus'* presentation of the decalogue, for example, the text begins with God's self-introduction, "I am the LORD your God," and continues with a historical statement, "who brought you out of Egypt, where you were slaves" (Ex. 20:2). Then the commandments or laws of the covenant (Ex. 20:3–17) follow. Much of the book of *Deuteronomy* is modeled on the covenantal form. *Deuteronomy* provides a good example of covenantal blessings (28:1–14) and curses (28:15–68). The book of *Joshua* concludes with a covenantal renewal ceremony which sets forth the basic charter of Israelite life within the Promised Land (24:1–28).

Given the importance of the covenantal form, it is possible to view all of Israelite historical writing as an expansion of the recitation of God's relations with his people used in the covenantal form. The religious significance of historical writing in the Bible is thus very carefully defined.

The nature of biblical history, especially when seen as an expression of the covenantal relationship between God and his people, provided scope for varying degrees of historical accuracy in matters of chronology, geography, and comprehensiveness. When the events narrated were closer to the writer's own times, personal observation and court records rendered the account far more reliable in terms of modern methods in the writing of history. This accounts for the distinctive flavor of *1* and *2 Samuel*, *1* and *2 Kings*, *Ezra*, and *Nehemiah*. The story of earlier periods, however, is marked by the heroic or romantic nature of epic and saga traditions. The people written about and the fundamental significance of their lives and actions are indeed historical, but the presentation emphasizes God's initiatives and purposes in forming the Israelite nation with relatively less interest in details of historical precision. Such is the case in most of the Pentateuch as well as in parts of *Joshua* and *Judges*.

The first eleven chapters of *Genesis* are much closer to mythical forms of writing. *Myth,* in this case, must not be understood to mean that the events told were fictional or untrue. A myth is a profoundly true statement which speaks to universal aspects of life and reality. It is a statement whose meaning rises above time and space. Although biblical myths were influenced by other mythical statements of the ancient world, they are used by the biblical writers to express history's relationship to God. They point to history's origins at the moment of the world's creation. They speak of the beginnings where history touches eternity, and, therefore, to moments which cannot be historically described. Myth is thus essential to biblical faith. We do the Scriptures a serious injustice if we read myth as though it were history. Such a tendency must be resisted along with the opposite tendency to read biblical history as though it were mythical. By reading the early chapters of *Genesis* with sensitivity to poetic symbolism and imagery, we can easily avoid such temptations.

Gospel, Tradition, and Midrash

The narratives of Mark, Matthew, Luke, and John use the literary form called *gospel.* All four tell the story of Jesus Christ. They include the general outline of Jesus' life, but focus especially on the end of that life with Jesus' crucifixion and resurrection. Jesus' story, however, is not told for its own sake, but it is told to enable Christians to develop a self-understanding with which to face the challenges of the last third of the first century. Accordingly, the various conditions in which the early Christians lived and the situations they had to face influenced the gospel form. They affected the context, wording, and emphases of the narrative.

The gospels were written in the historical context of the first century. Besides the contemporary situations, the tradition of *preaching, teach-*

ing, and *liturgy* used in the growing Christian communities also influenced the gospel form. The most important source of the gospel form is thus the shape and nature of the early Christian assembly. What makes the gospels distinctive is their origin from the traditional patterns of expression in the assembly with its *gospel proclamation, teaching, eucharistic celebration, hymns,* and *prayers.*

While all four gospel narratives have a great deal in common, they also vary considerably. *Mark* is the oldest gospel and is an important literary source for *Matthew* and *Luke.* It focuses chiefly on the deeds of Jesus and his urgent call to suffering discipleship. *Matthew* relies more heavily on formal discourses of Jesus which are appropriate for a Jewish-Christian church which has been excluded from Judaism. Writing for Gentile Christians, Luke transforms Mark's minor journey theme into a major structure about which to organize his data. Viewing his work far more in the manner of a historian, Luke even wrote a second volume, *Acts,* which presents the missionary development of the early church. In *John,* Jesus speaks a long farewell discourse. More than any other, John's Gospel tends to poetic prose. This characteristic is seen clearly in the opening section. It is an adaptation of an early Christian hymn used by believers in the Johannine community.

One of the characteristics of all gospel writing is *reflection* on the meaning of events in the light of the Scriptures. From the beginning, this kind of reflection had been the most fundamental principle in New Testament methods of arriving at theological understanding. Standing in the Jewish and biblical tradition, Jesus himself had presented his work and message in relation to the Scriptures.

To best understand the gospels, however, one must go further and note the various ways such reflections were carried out. At times the Scriptures were cited directly and applied. A Scripture text thus illumined the meaning of later events in the life of Jesus and of the Christian community. Frequently, however, the same effect could be achieved by the simple use of well-recognized biblical language when referring to an event. The most extensive use of this procedure appears in the Jewish form called *midrash.* It is the retelling of a biblical story with a view to bringing out its meaning for a later generation. The Christian community developed from Jewish roots. Therefore, the early Christians and the gospel writers readily used this form of writing. However, the Christian intent was usually to bring out the meaning of a present event in the light of the Hebrew Scriptures rather than to provide a formal commentary on the ancient biblical story. The result was a kind of *midrash-in-reverse.*

Midrashic writing is especially prominent in Matthew's and Luke's accounts of Jesus' birth and infancy. In those accounts the meaning and implications of Jesus' life and work are set forth in highly biblical terms. Although there are frequent direct quotations from the Scriptures in these narratives, biblical language and phrases are present throughout. The infancy narratives can thus be compared to gospels in miniature in which multiple biblical references from many parts of the Old Testament form a marvelous theological tapestry. Elements in the infancy narratives which are more biblical and poetic than historical should not be considered untrue. Rather, they are meant to pierce beneath the surface of historical observation and to present the divine truth concerning the significance of Jesus for human history.

Through a better understanding of the literary forms of the Bible, today's reader can find more clearly that the Bible is truly good news for today.

BIBLICAL THEMES

Carolyn Osiek, R.S.C.J.
Donald Senior, C.P.
Carroll Stuhlmueller, C.P.

The richness and scope of the Bible is far greater than any series of categories can contain. The following themes, however, are central to the Bible's reflections on God and his relationship to us. Seven themes have been selected because they are basic concepts that span the entire Bible (Salvation, Spirit, Covenant, and Worship) or because they are of particular interest to the Christian reader of Scriptures (Kingdom, Church, and Christology). These themes are related to each other. That fact will be noted by referring the reader to other themes at various points in the article. Numerous references to Bible passages enable the reader to trace the themes throughout the Bible itself.

Salvation

The triumph of life over death is one of the Bible's most basic concerns. Death is seen in the biblical tradition to be the result of sin. It is part of the curse laid upon Adam as a consequence of his transgression of the command of God (Gen. 2:17; 3:19; Rom. 5:12–14). Other actors in the drama, however, are also sometimes blamed: the devil (Wisd. Sol. 2:24) or Eve (Sir. 25:24; 1 Tim. 2:14). Death is thus now decreed by God (Sir. 41:1), but it was not originally intended (Wisd. Sol. 1:13–14; 2:23).

Life was originally seen as long survival (Isa. 38). It quickly takes on a spiritual dimension. It is the result of keeping God's commandments (Deut. 30:15–19) and, above all, of loving him (Deut. 30:6). Life is, therefore, for all (Ezek. 18). In the later writings of the Old Testament, the sense of life as immortality beyond the grave begins to emerge (Wisd. Sol. 3:1–3).

The experience of the Exile in Babylon and the search to return to restore the nation is symbolized by Ezekiel's vision of the dry bones restored to life by the breath of God (Ezek. 37). This experience caused people to think of reward and retribution based on an individual's faith and actions instead of being only the result of the sins or merits of the community or of one's ancestors (Ezek. 18). This faith is most strikingly expressed in the account of the martyrdom of the mother and her seven sons under the persecution of Antiochus Epiphanes. Here the reward of the martyr clearly includes a hope of bodily resurrection from the dead (2 Macc. 7:9, 11, 23, 29).

The hope of salvation as bodily resurrection is based on a strong sense of looking forward to the final Day of the Lord. It is rooted in the belief and hope that God's power and ultimate triumph will be made clear to all on the last day. (*See* Kingdom.) This looking to the future for ultimate salvation is already strong in the prophetic tradition (Isa. 35:4; 56:1; 62:1). The prophets affirm that the faithful remnant of Israel will surely be saved (Isa. 10:20–21; 28:5; Amos 3:12; 5:15). Salvation is not limited to the people of Israel alone, however. Yahweh's saving power can extend to all the nations of the earth (Isa. 45:22). (*See* Covenant.)

Out of this yearning for God's future salvation comes a kind of writing that looks into the Last Days in highly symbolic language. These ideas appear in some of the later writers of the Old Testament, for example, in Ezekiel and in Daniel, and are well developed in the New Testament. In this dramatic kind of writing the account of how God will come at the Last Day to save is given to the writer in a revelation (Mark 13; Matt. 24; Luke 21; Rev. 1:19; 4:1). The future saving action of God will be accompanied by frightful cosmic signs (Mark 13:24–25; Matt. 24:29; Luke 21:11; 21:25; Rev. 6:8, 12–17), but this revelation of what will occur is meant to be the consolation and encouragement of the just while they still live (Matt. 10:22; Luke 21:28).

While *2 Maccabees* suggests that bodily resurrection is part of God's act of salvation only for martyrs, or at least only for the just (2 Macc. 7:14), the New Testament seems to assume that bodily resurrection will occur both for the reward of the just in eternal life and for retribution to the wicked in eternal punishment (Matt. 25:46; John 11:24). The principal focus in the New Testament, however, is still on the resurrection of the just (John 11:24; Rev. 20:4).

John and the *Letters of John* explain salvation as eternal life in yet another way. Jesus himself is the Life (John 1:4; 6:33, 35, 51; 11:25; 14:16). True life is hearing and believing in him (John 3:36; 5:24), and knowing the Father and Son (17:3), and loving one another (1 John 3:14).

In the Gospels, salvation is intimately connected with present bodily or mental well-being (Mark 15:30–31; Matt. 8:25; 9:21–22; 14:30; Luke 8:36,50), yet it also is something that will also come about in the future (Mark 8:35 and parallels; Luke 13:23; John 12:47). For Paul, salvation is closely connected with being put into a right standing with God. This new standing comes not through works of the Law (Rom. 3:28) but through the saving death of Christ which reconciles us to God

(Rom. 5:10, 18). We too must be dead to sin as Christ was in order to remain in that salvation (Rom. 6:3–11; Col. 3:3–5).

The prophets saw God as Savior of Israel (Isa. 12:2–3; 63:8; Jer. 4:14). The New Testament writers saw Jesus' mission in the world as that of saving his people (Matt. 1:21; Luke 2:11; 19:10; John 4:42; Phil. 3:20; 2 Tim. 1:10; 2 Peter 1:11). This is accomplished through his presence and deeds (Mark 5:34 and parallels; 10:52; Luke 7:50; 19: 9) and through the proclamation of salvation made in his name by his ministers (Acts 4:12; 16:17). (*See* Kingdom.)

Salvation is intended by God for all (1 Tim. 2:3–4; 4:10) but demands a response of repentance, faith, obedience, and good deeds (2 Cor. 7:10; Acts 2:21; Phil. 2:12; Mark 10:17 and parallels; Matt. 7:14).

Spirit

The biblical theme of Spirit also deals with the penetration of God's life in the world. In the Old Testament the Hebrew word for *spirit* means a mysterious and penetrating force. It is used for what was truly strong, durable, and beyond human control (Gen. 1:2; 2 Sam. 22:16; Isa. 11:4; Ezek. 13:13; 27:26). The word can be translated into English as "wind," "breath," or "spirit." In the earliest texts the Spirit of the Lord clothed or seized warrior-judges (Judg. 3:10; 6:34; 14:6, 19; 1 Sam. 11:6). The prophets who often spoke the word of God under the direct control of the Spirit of God were passive under this mighty force (Num. 24:2; 1 Sam. 10:5–13). At times the Spirit settled more quietly and permanently on a person. It still gave exceptional gifts to that person: Joseph (Gen. 41:38–40), Moses with the elders (Num. 11:17, 25), and Joshua (Num. 27:18).

The classical prophets, those with books to their names, avoided performing external wonders, and so turned attention away from emphasizing the Spirit. A few exceptions would be Hosea 9:7 or Isaiah 4:4 and 11:1–9. During the Exile, prophets like Ezekiel and Second Isaiah reintroduced the Spirit as the powerful agent for purifying and restoring the despondent people (Ezek. 36:23–28; 37:1–14; Isa. 42:1; 44:1–4). Still later in the postexilic age, the Spirit is viewed as the principle of creation (Gen. 1:1; 2:7; Job 26:13).

God's power and guidance also came through *angels.* At first they appear as messengers (Gen. 19:1; 28:12; Ps. 104:4) or as members of God's heavenly court (Isa. 6:2–3; 14:13–14; Deut. 32:8–9; 1 Kings 22:19–23; Jer. 23:18, 22). Called "Cherubim" or "Seraphim," statues were made of them to "protect" the Ark of the Covenant (Ex. 37:6–9; 1 Kings 6:22–28; Isa. 6:2–3). Angels symbolized God's majesty (Ezek. 1:1–28).

The term "angel of the LORD" was often used to refer to God himself (Gen. 18; Ex. 3:2; Judg. 6:11–24). Popular devotion to the angels increased at the time of the Exile and after (Zech. 1:6; 2:1; Dan. 7:10; Tobit 12:15; Job 4:18; 15:15). Guardian angels are mentioned for individuals (Tobit 5:27; Ps. 91:11–12) or for nations (Dan. 11:13–21; 12:1). They were sometimes healers (Tobit 3:17; 12:15) or mediators for prayer (Zech. 1:12; Job 5:1).

While the doctrine of *spirit* and *angel* appeared in a vague form throughout Old Testament times, that of *demons* was not as clear. Witchcraft was forbidden (Lev. 19:31). At first Satan was thought to be an opponent of people, but still in God's throne room (Job 1:6; Zech. 3:1–5; cf. 2 Sam. 24:1 with 1 Chron. 21:1). Very late, Satan is seen also as God's enemy (Wisd. Sol. 2:24). Books written in the years between the writing of the Old and New Testaments expanded the activity of spirit, angels, and demons.

In the New Testament, angels appear as messengers and agents of God to people (Luke 1:11, 26; Matt. 1:20; 2:13, 19; 28:2–7; Acts 5:19; 12:7, 11), and as representatives of individual people to God (Matt. 18:10; Acts 12:15). They are thought to be brilliant in appearance (Matt. 28:3; Acts 6:15), and will accompany the Son of Man when he returns in glory (Mark 8:38 and parallels; Matt. 25:31). In *Revelation*, seven spirits stand before the throne of God. They seem to represent the seven cities to whom the letters of Revelation 1–3 are addressed (Rev. 1:4; 3:1; 4:5), even though they are later sent out upon the whole earth (Rev. 5:6). The "angels" of the churches in the headings of the seven letters (Rev. 2:1, 8, 18; 3:1, 7, 14) are best understood, however, as the human leaders of those communities.

Evil spirits are often spoken of as "unclean spirits" (for example, Mark 1:23; 3:11; 6:7; Matt. 12:43–45; Luke 4:33). The devil, or Satan, is their leader, just as Michael is leader of God's angels (Rev. 12:7–9). Satan tempts both Jesus (Mark 1:13; Matt. 4:1; Luke 4:2) and his followers (Acts 5:3; 1 Cor. 7:5; 2 Cor. 2:11; 12:7). The devil and his angels are subject to God, even through Jesus' disciples (Luke 10:17–20), but not without the struggle of the cosmic battle in which they have been ultimately defeated and cast out of heaven (Judg. 6: 2; Peter 2:4; Matt. 25:41; Rev. 12:7–9). (*See* Kingdom.)

God himself is Spirit (John 4:24), yet the "Holy Spirit" is usually spoken of as one sent by the Father, as the principal agent in the conception of Jesus (Matt. 1:18; Luke 1:35) and in the casting out of demons (Matt. 12:28). The Spirit is a power received by believers after the resurrection of Jesus (John 7:39; Acts 1:8; 15:8). The Holy Spirit hovered over Jesus at his baptism (Mark 1:10 and parallels; John 1:32–33) and is the source of the divine power flowing from Jesus which was able to transform disciples into fearless apostles (John 1:33; Acts 1:5; 2:4).

The Holy Spirit is advocate (one who pleads on behalf of a needy person) and intercessor (John 14:16–17; 15:26; 16:7), teacher of truth (John 14:26; 16:13; 1 John 4:6), gift and pledge of future glory (2 Cor. 1:22; 5:5). The Spirit is the inspirer of prophecy (Luke 1:41, 67; 1 Cor. 14; Rev. 1:10; 17:3; 19:10; 21:10), and Christian prophecy is seen as carrying Old Testament prophecy forward in a new age (Acts 2:16–21, 33; 4:25; 28:25). Indeed, it is the presence of the Spirit in the Church that guarantees and gives it validity as the assembly of God's faithful. (*See* Church.)

Covenant

The Greek word for *"covenant"* can also be translated *"testament,"* the name often given to the entire Bible as the Old and New Testaments (Heb. 7–9). Covenant, therefore, brings us into the heart of the Scriptures, and also into the heartrending division between Judaism and Christianity (Rom. 9:1–3).

The idea of covenant originated with *treaties* between nations. As such, it was used to describe events in the secular world of the ancient patriarchs (Gen. 14:13; 21:32; 26:28). Among the various types of treaties between nations, the one between a strong overlord and a vassal nation gradually became the model for the covenant between God and Israel at Mount Sinai. According to this type, frequently called a *Suzerainty Treaty,* the overlord had shown exceptional kindness in protecting the vassal. The vassal, in turn, pledged loyalty and obedience toward the more powerful nation. For Israel, covenant was able to transform religion and law into an expression of gratitude for God's deliverance.

Six elements of the Suzerainty Treaty, especially as it evolved in *Deuteronomy,* occur in the biblical covenant: (1) the *preamble,* with the name of the Great King (Deut. 5:6); (2) *benefits* bestowed by the Great King upon the vassal (Deut. 5:6); (3) *laws* which demand exclusive loyalty (Deut. 17–21); (4) depositing the text in a sanctuary with *periodic rereading* (Deut. 31); (5) lists of *witnesses* (Deut. 32:1); and (6) *blessings and curses* (Deut. 27–28).

Covenantal laws were either *"apodictic"* (straightforward and self-evident), like the Ten Commandments (Ex. 20:1–17; Deut. 5:6–19) or *"casuistic"* (arrived at by a process of argumentation and reasoning), like the majority in Exodus 21 and 22. The apodictic laws were nonnegotiable. Still they did evolve, as a comparison between Exodus 20 and Deuteronomy 5 reveals. The casuistic laws were actually famous cases, remembered more as standards to direct future decisions than as absolute laws. Development and change can be seen as well in the liturgical celebration of the covenant. A careful reading of Exodus 19 and 24, as well as Deuteronomy 25 and 31, Joshua 24, or Psalm 68, shows that the renewal of covenant in a sanctuary setting became ever more evident; and the religious meaning became ever more at the heart of the covenant.

Covenant presumes a specially *chosen people,* a concept appreciated especially by Deuteronomy (Deut. 4:37; 7:6–7; 10:15; 14:2). This sense of being an elect people was symbolized liturgically by the holy city of Jerusalem or its sacred Temple (Deut. 12; 16–17). (*See* Worship.)

The prophets further developed the notion of covenant and election by making them refer to the inner religious and moral condition of a person. Amos stressed the idea of *"remnant,"* meaning not all Israelites by birth but only those endowed with a true spirit (Amos 3:1–2, 12). Hosea compared the covenant to the marriage bond (Hos. 2:19–20) while Jeremiah and Ezekiel began to foresee a *new covenant* written on the heart (Jer. 31:31–34; Ezek. 36:26–27), an idea inspired by Deuteronomy 6:4–9. During the Exile, Isaiah 42:6 and 49:6 foresaw a *universal covenant* with the Gentiles achieved through Israel as the suffering servant. This vision can be traced to such passages as Hosea 2:21–24 and Jeremiah 31:35–37. Although covenant seemed to separate one elect people from all the nonelect, still it evolved in such a way as to become more of an inner disposition which God breathed into the heart of all peoples, regardless of race or nationality.

Jesus continued this development. He did restrict his apostolate "only to those lost sheep, the people of Israel" (Matt. 15:24). Nonetheless, he saw himself as the suffering servant of Isaiah 42, 49–50, and 53 (Luke 9:21–27) and in still other ways endorsed a bond or covenant that expanded the Mosaic covenant beyond its customary interpretation (Matt. 12:1–7; 15:1–20; Luke 19:1–9). Jesus instructed his disciples to celebrate a new covenant in his body and blood. The Eucharist was not intended to replace the Passover sacrifice of Judaism, but to bring it to a new perfection (Mark 14:24; Matt. 26:28; Luke 22:20; 1 Cor. 11:25). (*See* Worship.)

At first, the followers of Jesus worshiped at the Temple as faithful Jews. They offered their Eucharistic service at home (Acts 2:42–47). Unfortunately, many factors contributed to a rift between Jesus' disciples and their Jewish kinsfolk. However, right to the end, Paul admitted that "my people (Israel), my own flesh and blood . . . (remain) God's (chosen) people" who continue to possess "his covenants . . . true worship (and) . . . God's promises" (Rom. 9:1–5). The Church considered itself the true Israel, the rightful offspring of Abraham (Gal. 4:24–31; 1 Cor. 3). (*See* Church.)

Later New Testament writings reflect the ever-growing split between Christianity and Judaism. *Hebrews* argues that Jesus' sacrifice on the cross and his heavenly priesthood replaced the many Jewish sacrifices and the hereditary priesthood of the Levites and Aaron. The longest quotation of the Hebrew Scriptures in the New Testament (Jer. 31:31–34) concludes that Jesus' "priestly work . . . is superior to theirs . . . his covenant . . . better . . . based on promises of better things" (Heb. 8:1–13). The special rights and privileges of Israel as a priestly people were now applied to all Christians (Ex. 19:5–6; 1 Peter 2:9; Rev. 5:9–10; 21:2–3,9).

Covenant, then, is a political idea, which was religiously applied to Israel as God's chosen people. It was then made personal and inward as it was extended to all peoples, while still maintaining its essential mystery of God's personal, redemptive love.

Worship

Biblical worship developed within *salvation history* (the history of the saving acts of God for his people). Different from all other ancient religions, Israel's story did not begin with the mighty act of first creation, but with God's compassionate response to the people's cries of oppression (Ex. 3:7). (*See* Kingdom; Salvation.) The earliest creeds of the Old or New Testament are frequently records of what God has done in the midst of human history, such as the Exodus out of Egypt or the occupation of the Promised Land, or the public ministry of Jesus, his death, resurrection, and the sending of the Spirit (Deut. 26; Josh. 24; Judg. 5; Pss. 68; 105; Rom. 1:1–5; Acts 2; 7; 13:16–41). These events of themselves would have made little or no impression upon human history. Only as salvation history recorded in the Scriptures and celebrated in the liturgy, in other words as worship, were these actions remembered and thus able to exercise an impact eventually upon world history.

At first, during the formative age of Moses and desert wandering, Israelite worship possessed no sacred place, only a sacred object called the "Ark of the Covenant," or *"Covenant Box,"* a chest some 3'3" long and 2'3" in width and height (Ex. 25:10–22). It contained at least the two tablets of the Decalogue (Ten Commandments) (Deut. 10:1–5), perhaps the rod of Aaron, and some manna (Ex. 16:32–34; Heb. 9:4). Above the Ark was a golden plate, called the "propitiatory" (or "place of meeting") (Ex. 25:10–22); and it was considered God's throne (Ps. 132:7; 1 Chron. 28:2). The Ark symbolized the Lord's continuous protection and guidance (Num. 10:33), especially in times of war (Num. 10:34–35; 1 Sam. 4:4–5).

David brought the Ark to Jerusalem (2 Sam. 6:12–19) as a way of linking his dynasty and capital with Mosaic origins. (*See* Kingdom; Covenant.) In building a *Temple* as a permanent abode for the Ark, Solomon was responsible for a radical shift in Israel's religion. The Ark no longer led the people in their journeys; rather they now journeyed in pilgrimage to the sacred *place* of the Temple. In 587 B.C., the Ark was destroyed along with the Temple, city, and dynasty (Jer. 3:16–17; 7; 26), but it was thought to reappear at least symbolically at the end of time (2 Macc. 2:4–8; Rev. 11:19).

Many qualities of the Ark and the Temple were said to apply to Jesus, the Church, and individual Christians (John 2:21; Rom. 3:25; 1 Cor. 3:10–17; 6:19). (*See* Christology; Church.)

Israel's *feastdays* combined great historical moments of salvation with the cycles of the agricultural life of a farmer: the lunar cycle appeared in the *Sabbath* (Ex. 20:8–11) and the *new moons* (2 Kings 4:23); the solar cycle with the spring festival of *Passover* (Pasch) (relating the celebration of the Exodus out of Egypt and the barley harvest) and *Pentecost* (relating the giving of the law on Sinai and the wheat harvest), or with the fall festival of *Tabernacles* (relating the Ark or Temple and the olive harvest). See Exodus 12, 23:14–17, Leviticus 23, and Deuteronomy 16. A *New Year's* festival (Num. 29:1–6) and a *Day of Atonement* (Lev. 16) probably existed very early. During the Exile, *fasting* took on an important religious meaning (Zech. 7:1–7). After the Exile, two new feasts became very popular: *Purim* (Est. 9:20–32) and *Hanukkah,* or Rededication of the Temple (1 Macc. 4:52–59).

The Church began to substitute Sunday for the Sabbath (Acts 20:7; 1 Cor. 16:2; Rev. 1:10), while Passover was associated with the death and resurrection of Jesus (Luke 22:1–20; 1 Cor. 5:7–8), Pentecost with the descent of the Holy Spirit (Acts 2), and Tabernacles with the exaltation of the Holy Cross in the Basilica of the Holy Sepulcher at Jerusalem.

Temple worship included: the reading of the Scripture (Deut. 31:9–13, 24–29; Neh. 8:8), the psalms as adapted to many communal and individual needs, and liturgical actions such as processions (Pss. 24; 68), holocausts with the gift entirely burnt in adoration (Lev. 1–7), peace offerings or sacred meals such as the Passover (Ex. 12; Deut. 26), and the sprinkling of blood to symbolize a renewed bond of life (Ex. 24:3–8; Lev. 16; 17). Another important ceremony was circumcision (Gen. 17:9–14; Lev. 12:3), which the prophets linked with purity of heart (Jer. 4:4; Deut. 10:12–22).

These ritual elements were absorbed within the Church in various ways. Baptism combined the purpose of circumcision and ceremonial washing with water with the mystery of Jesus' death and resurrection (Gal. 5:6; 1 Cor. 10; Acts 2:38–41; Rom. 6:3). The Eucharist united traditions about the manna and miracles in the desert with the Jewish Passover and the redemptive death and second coming of Jesus (John 6; Luke 22; 1 Cor. 10:23–24).

Kingdom of God

The "Kingdom of God," or Rule of God, is an important theme in the entire Scriptures, but takes on special significance in the New Testament because of the mission of Jesus.

The concept is ultimately rooted in Israel's experience of God as one upon whom the people depended for their very life and hope. (*See* Worship.) It was Yahweh who had rescued them from slavery in Egypt and had given them their nation and their land. The rule of Yahweh directly over his people was one reason why Israel was reluctant to accept human monarchy as its form of government (cf. Judg. 8:23). At first, the people had been content with a loose confederacy among the various clans, but the need for a more centralized government and the influence of the surrounding Canaanite cultures led Israel to establish a monarchy (cf. 1 Sam. 8–9). But Israel still stoutly maintained that Yahweh alone was ruler over them; the king was merely the instrument of God's power (1 Sam. 8:22; 1 Chron. 28:5).

Israelite monarchy reached its highest point quickly. After the Hamlet-like Saul came the promising David. Under his rule, the land was united and the central government established in Jerusalem. Political consolidation went hand in hand with religious centralization. Worship at local shrines was suppressed in favor of worship at the Jerusalem Temple. (*See* Worship.) David's ruthless misuse of his power to gain Bathsheba as his wife (2 Sam. 11–12) was a preview of the flawed history that would follow. Solomon, David's brilliant son, brought further glory to Israel, but he also significantly contributed to that strange pattern of infidelity which Israel's kings would practice down to the Hasmonean dynasty only a century before Jesus.

But even if the succession of kings in Israel died out, the dream of the "kingdom of God" did not. The people still longed for the day when their true ruler, Yahweh himself, would come to claim Israel for his own. On that day, as the prophets and poets had repeatedly affirmed, justice and peace and prosperity would abound. Thus the theme of the Kingdom of God was one of the ways Israel expressed its longing for God himself. To speak of David as the ideal king and to hope for the restoration of a renewed Davidic dynasty became a way of expressing hope in future salvation. (*See* Salvation.)

Although the theme of the coming of the Kingdom was only one way among many to express Israel's hope for salvation, it is the one Jesus used as the keynote of his own ministry (Mark 1:14). The synoptic Gospels, in particular, organize the entire ministry of Jesus around this theme. Jesus' message about the Kingdom can be summarized under the following points:

1. The Kingdom of God Is Near. In his preaching and parables, Jesus proclaims that the Kingdom is not merely an elusive future hope, but it is "near" (Mark 1:15), "has already come" (Matt. 12:28). Jesus speaks, too, of a future bringing of the Kingdom to perfection when all will be accomplished, but he also says that the effects of God's rule can be experienced now by those who are open to God's grace. The presence of the Kingdom is hidden, but the harvest is sure and the seed is already growing (Mark 4:26–29). (*See* Salvation.)

2. The God of the Kingdom Is Gracious and Merciful. Contrary to the emphases taken by some of the people of his time, Jesus does not speak of the coming of God's rule primarily in terms of judgment. The God of the Kingdom is a God of forgiveness and compassion. This is reflected in Jesus' own ministry of compassion to outcasts and sinners (Luke 15:1–32) and in his call for reconciliation and limitless forgiveness (Matt. 18:21–35). The mercy of God's rule is also transmitted through the miracles of Jesus. His healing touch, his victory over evil in all its forms, his restoration of sight and life demonstrate that the saving God of Israel "has already come to you" (Luke 11:20). The miracle activity of Jesus shows that the ultimate goal of his Kingdom ministry is the salvation of all creation. Paul reflects this view when he speaks of God's rule being complete when the "last enemy," death itself, has been defeated (1 Cor. 15:24–28). (*See* Salvation.)

3. The Presence of the Kingdom Demands Response. When Jesus announces the Kingdom, he calls for the hearer to "turn away from your sins and believe in the good news" (Mark 1:15). Much of Jesus' preaching is an urgent call to respond to the graciousness of his Father. The parables of the buried treasure and the pearl of great price (Matt. 13:44–46) are typical of Jesus' eloquent plea for commitment. Conversion is not just a turning away from obstacles to God's rule, but it is a pledge to follow Jesus (Matt. 19:21). The disciples are invited to take up the same ministry of proclaiming the Kingdom's presence and of healing and teaching that Jesus himself inaugurates (Matt. 10:7–8).

The Kingdom of God is one of the New Testament's most fundamental images for speaking of the nature of God as merciful, the person of Jesus as the fulfillment of Israel's hope, and the mission of the Church as continuing the work of establishing God's rule. (*See* Covenant; Christology; Church.)

Church

The early Christians' understanding of their identity and their role in history is expressed in the concept of "church." In the Hellenistic Greek world, the *ekklēsia* ("the assembly of those who are called") was a gathering of citizens to exercise their political rights. The Septuagint often adopted the same word as a translation for two Hebrew words, each of which meant the "assembly" of Israel, brought together for religious instruction or worship (Deut. 4:10; Judg. 20:2), though often, too, the word *synagōgē* is used in the Septuagint for those same Hebrew words (Ex. 35:1; Lev. 19:2; Num. 1:2; in Judg. 20:1–2, the two terms seem interchangeable). Regardless of the word used, the "assembly of Israel" is the gathering of its citizens with full awareness of their identity as the People of God. (*See* Covenant; Worship.)

Probably under the influence of both Greek and Jewish usage, *ekklēsia* became the usual term for the gathering of Christians to worship or to determine together their course of action (Acts 5:11; 9:31; 11:22; 12:5; Rom. 16:1, 5; 1 Cor. 1:2). By New Testament times, a *synagōgē* was a local Jewish assembly for the purpose of prayer, reading of the Scriptures, and instruction. Christian writers usually restricted its use to Jewish congregations (though in James 2:2, *synagōgē* may mean a Christian assembly, as it does in some later Christian writings). (*See* Worship.)

The first generations of Christians looked back to Jesus as founder of the Church (Matt. 16:18), which was established on the foundation stones of the apostles and prophets (Eph. 2:20; Rev. 21:14). Responsibility for leadership was entrusted to the twelve whom Jesus chose from among his disciples to send out as missionaries to announce the good news of the Kingdom (Mark 3:14–19; Matt. 10:1–5; Luke 6:13–16; John 6:67–71), first to Israel but ultimately to the whole world (Matt. 28:16–20). (*See* Kingdom.) The *Acts of the Apostles* dramatizes the missionary movement as it progresses from Jerusalem to Samaria and eventually ends with the arrival of Paul in the heart of the pagan world, Rome (Acts 1:8).

The original group of apostles, under the leadership of Peter (Matt. 16:18; Acts 1:15; 2:14, 37), bore witness boldly to the resurrection of Jesus and took the lead in establishing a community of believers who were of "one in mind and heart" (Acts 4:32–37), united in common worship and sharing of the Eucharist in their homes (Acts 2:44–47). Even in the first days of the Church, however, human failings were present, as the dishonesty of Ananias and Sapphira (Acts 5:1–11), the dispute between Greek-speaking and Hebrew-speaking Christians (Acts 6:1–2), and the dissension between Paul and Barnabas (Acts 15:36–41) show.

Leadership in the Church was never confined to the twelve. Already in the Jerusalem community "James, the Lord's brother," one of its "leaders" (Gal. 1:19; 2:9), was a prominent figure who participated in major decisions. The members of the Jerusalem Council of Acts 15 assembled to ponder the extent to which gentile converts to the Christian faith should be required to observe the Mosaic Law. The members of the Council are referred to consistently as "the apostles and elders" (Acts 15:2, 4, 6, 22–23). Moreover, Paul unflinchingly considers himself an apostle with the rest (1 Cor. 9:1; 15:9–10).

The first generation of apostles appointed elders or presbyters in the communities they established (Acts 14:23) for the work of guiding the Church in living the gospel. Paul usually refers to "churches" in the plural (Rom. 16:4, 16; 1 Cor. 11:6; Gal. 16:19). This expresses his way of seeing each local community of Christians as whole in itself. Yet, at the same time, he stresses communication and communion among the churches. He worked hard toward that goal. Elsewhere, the term *churches* is used collectively to include all local Christian communities (Acts 9:31).

The Church is the community of the saved (Acts 4:47; 1 Cor. 1:18), the assembly of the holy People of God (1 Cor. 1:2; cf. Num. 23:2–4) in which all discriminatory distinctions are to be dissolved in the waters of baptism (1 Cor. 12:13; Gal. 3:27–28; Col. 3:11; Eph. 2:14). It is the great mystery planned by God from all ages and revealed in Christ (Eph. 1:9–10). It is born with the outpouring of the Spirit at Pentecost.

The Church is compared to the branches that grow upon Christ the true Vine (John 15:1–8) and the flock tended by the Good Shepherd (John 10:1–18). The most familiar image is that of the body with many members, all of whom perform different roles but together make a smoothly functioning whole (1 Cor. 12:12–27; Rom. 12:5), whose head is Christ (Eph. 1:22–23; 5:23).

The Church is the bride of Christ (Eph. 5:25–27, 33; Rev. 21:2), a city (Eph. 2:19), the Jerusalem from on high (Gal. 4:24), in its final form the new Jerusalem descending from heaven (Rev. 21:2–4).

Though the expression "new Israel" is never used in the New Testament, Christians are given new commandments (Matt. 5:21–48; John 13:34); and already Paul seems to consider Christians "God's people" (Gal. 6:16). The Eucharist is seen as ratification of the new Covenant in the blood of Christ (Luke 22:20; 1 Cor. 11:25), and Paul sees himself and his co-workers as ministers of this new Covenant (2 Cor. 3:6). The letter to the *Hebrews* expands on this theme (Heb. 8:8–12 and 10:16, quoting Jer. 31:31–34; Heb. 9:12–15). Christians are called "the temple of the living God" (2 Cor. 6:16), "a sacred temple dedicated to the Lord" (Eph. 2:21–22), a "spiritual temple" and "holy priesthood" which offers acceptable spiritual sacrifices (1 Peter 2:5). Many writers in the New Testament, therefore, felt that the Church was for them not only what the Covenant had been for the Jewish people, but also the fulfillment and completion of that which the first Covenant had foreshadowed. (*See* Covenant.)

Christology

Christology is a technical term which means "an ordered process of reflection on the nature and meaning of Jesus." Although none of the New Testament writers are theologians in the technical sense of the word, they did reflect on the mystery of Jesus' person and mission. Therefore, they present us with a variety of christologies.

This reflection seems to have begun with the resurrection itself. (*See* Salvation, Spirit.) Faced with Jesus' victory over death and his risen presence in the community, the early Christians looked with new understanding upon the entire life, death, and mission of Jesus. They connected this history of Jesus with the message of the Hebrew Scriptures. They pondered the meaning of Jesus for their hopes in the future. All of the New Testament books are written from this resurrection perspective. The Gospels, for example, are not a detached collection of historical information about Jesus. They present that history through the lens of the Church's understanding of Jesus as one who had been raised from the dead and who was alive in his Church.

One of the most important ways the New Testament writers expressed their reflection upon the person of Jesus was to give him special titles drawn mainly from the Old Testament, but now filled with new meaning when applied to Jesus. Some of the most important titles include the following:

1. Christ. The word *Christos* means "anointed one" in Greek. It was used to translate the Hebrew word **Messiah.** The title was first used to speak of the king who was anointed, or consecrated, for Yahweh's service (cf. the so-called royal psalms which speak of this anointment: Pss. 2, 20, 21, 45, 89). David soon is thought to be the ideal example of the Lord's anointed: one who liberates, unites, and protects his people on behalf of Yahweh (2 Sam. 7:3–16). When the monarchy went into decline, the image of the ideal king was connected with Israel's hope for future salvation: a new David, a new Messiah, would be sent by God to deliver his people (Isa. 9:1–7; Mic. 5:2–4). (*See* Kingdom of God.) It seems that Jesus himself was hesitant to accept the title of "Christ" because of the nationalistic hopes it suggested (Mark 8:28–30). In the light of the resurrection, Jesus was clearly seen by the Christians as the expected Messiah, the leader sent by God to rescue his people. Thus Christians applied to Jesus the promises and prophecies which refer to the Messiah in the Old Testament. The frequency of this title in the New Testament gives the impression that in many passages "Christ" has become a surname rather than a title.

2. Son of God. This title, too, was first applied to the king in Israel, because he was chosen by God to rule his people (2 Sam. 7:14; Ps. 2:7). The title was also used of the faithful Israelite who obeyed God and trusted in his love (Wisd. Sol. 2:13, 16–18; 5:5). When this title is used of Jesus in the New Testament, it refers to his roles both as kingly Messiah and as obedient Israelite. It is also a way of stressing the intimate bond between Jesus and his Father (Matt. 4:1–11). In later Christian reflection, this dimension of the "Son of God" title will become even more important: Jesus is the Son of God because he shares in the Father's own divine life.

3. Lord. One of the most important New Testament titles for expressing the divine power and status of Jesus was "Lord." The title may have originated as a title of respect for a dignitary, not unlike the English word "sir." But it came to be used in the Old Testament as a reference to Yahweh himself. In the New Testament, the title affirms Christian faith in Jesus as one who has been exalted through his resurrection (Phil. 2:1; Acts 2:36) and who will come in triumph at the end of time (1 Cor. 16:22). This title seems to have been used often in the Church's prayer as an exclamation of worship and praise (Rev. 22:20; Matt. 7:21).

4. Son of Man. This is perhaps the most mysterious of the titles used of Jesus in the New Testament. In Aramaic, "Son of Man" is simply a way of referring to "man" or "human being." But "Son of Man" seems to be used in a more technical sense in *Daniel* (Dan. 7:13–14, translated in the GNB as "human being") where it refers to a mysterious figure (perhaps a symbol of the nation of Israel) who will be given majesty and power at the end of time. This title is used frequently of

Jesus in all four Gospels. It is, in fact, the title Jesus most often uses of himself. Some scholars believe that "Son of Man" is not a technical term, but it refers simply to Jesus' share in humanity: he is *the* human being. But it is more likely that the vagueness of the title allowed the early Church to give it a specific Christian meaning. Therefore, it is used to identify Jesus as the one who will come in triumph at the end of time (Mark 13:26), who had authority even on earth to heal and forgive (Matt. 9:6), but who also had to suffer and to give his life for others (Mark 10:45).

Many other titles are used of Jesus in the New Testament: for example, Lamb of God, High Priest, Emmanuel, Savior, Holy One, New Adam, King of Israel, Word, and Servant. The plurality of titles illustrates the depth and richness of the early Church's faith in Jesus. No single title or any combination of them was adequate to express the overwhelming mystery of Jesus' person. Later theology would reflect on this mystery in a more organized fashion, but the ingredients for the Church's confession of Jesus as fully human and yet fully divine are already present in the New Testament itself.

PART II

INTRODUCTION
TO
BIBLE
STUDY

✠ ✠ ✠

HOW TO STUDY THE BIBLE
Orlando R. Barone

The Believer and the Bible

The Bible is a book—no, a library of books of, by, and for believers. As a believer, one like you wrote it, first read it, and lived by it. In its words you will recognize your highest ideals and deepest realities. It is your book, so your desire to study it is sound. And yet you will often find the Bible strange and difficult, for it springs from a distant and ancient culture. With its numerous editors and authors spanning many centuries, the Bible is really the raw material of your faith, not its finished product. How you go about studying the Bible is crucial. We all need help—help to begin, to continue, and to deepen in our understanding of that very old book, that early witness of a tribe of people who dared to wrestle with their God.

Beginning

A sound introduction to the Bible requires the expert services of a knowledgeable tour guide and the lively company of fellow tourists. To visit the land and times of the Bible is to visit a foreign land and an ancient time. We need to be shown those special, sometimes out-of-the-way places that give us a feel for this vast and alien territory. We need a group to help spark excitement, to share ideas, and to provide an incentive to stick to the tour. In short, we ought to be a part of a Bible study group.

A group can have as few as two members or as many as ten. Intimacy and full participation begin to fade as the number grows. Each one in the group should be seeking, as St. Luke puts it, to "know the full truth about everything which you have been taught" (Luke 1:4). Deliberately quarrelsome or negative persons tend to use a group for personal display. They should gently (and privately) be asked to honor the purpose of the group or to stop coming. The group should meet about once every other week, either in a central place or alternating at members' homes. There should not be elaborate food preparation arrangements, lest the hosting of a group become a burden out of proportion to the reason the group is meeting. At the beginning there should be a set number of meetings in the series corresponding to an agreed reading and study program. Some homework is to be assigned and done before each meeting. Following this introductory sequence, the group can continue indefinitely.

To help make all this happen, a group needs a knowledgeable and believing Bible study leader. This leader should be one who is more prone to ask questions to stimulate the group's thinking than to give answers to cut off the searching process. An experienced leader has access to a healthy program, materials, and a sound grasp on the shades and highlights of Scripture. The leader may be a priest or religious, but there are a growing number of competent laypersons to whom the group might turn. In fact, people may feel freer to talk if the group is led by a layperson.

Finding the right person to lead the group could be a problem. Your pastor might know someone. Or it is quite possible that a well-credentialed teacher of things biblical can be located in a nearby church school. In any event, an able Bible study leader is a pearl of great price and well worth the search.

Important as a leader is as a resource to the group, it is possible that one cannot readily be found. Then one of the several series of Bible study guidebooks can be called into service. Here care is needed; different publications take decidedly differing points of view. One series may insist on a highly literalistic point of view and would thus severely limit a Catholic group in interpreting the word of God. Another series might take an argumentative viewpoint—its author may be trying to prove some personal religious point. By using his material, your group could be the victim of his limitations. This article makes no suggestions of a specific series, but it offers two guidelines. First, a Catholic group would do best to select a Catholic publication. In the field of biblical studies, Catholic publications on the whole are less constricting than are many of the other guides on the market, that is, *if* they are recent. And that is the second guideline. Volumes published before 1960 are apt to reflect the era prior to the current days of superb Catholic biblical scholarship.

Once we have formed our group, acquired a leader or good study guide, and set up a schedule of meetings, we are well on our way. The group now finds joy in welcoming that Other Leader who promised that where two or three gather in his name, he is there among them. Jesus is the source and center, our true point of departure, and he is the goal, the mark, our prize at journey's end. Our attitude and approach must be woven tightly with prayer. At the start of each meeting a member could offer a prayer relating to the evening's reading. To end a meeting the group can draw on the ideas just exchanged and developed and from them forge a gift of thanks. At times during a given meeting, an occasion for spontaneous prayer may arise. These songs from the heart are evidence of the Spirit's presence and should be welcomed, but never forced. If such a prayer is not part of one meeting, that fact in no way takes away from the value of the session. The urge to common prayer cannot be scheduled. It simply happens. The point is that a prayerful attitude is the hallmark of the group that has welcomed Jesus into its midst.

Continuing

Our next task is to determine the approach we will take in our Bible readings. Guidebooks have the approach all laid out for us, of course. Yet, we should be aware that there are good and poor ways of entering into Bible study. Catholics, when they begin Bible study, are often surprised by the breadth of interpretation allowed by their Church. Current scriptural scholarship and the relationship of modern disciplines such as science, history, and literary criticism to the study of the Bible have had an incredible impact on biblical interpretation. Adults who are just beginning to study the Bible are sometimes shocked to feel the impact of this openness to ideas. It can disturb set notions, notions nourished in the remembrance of bygone catechism lessons. These notions may have lain unchanged in the back of the mind for years. They are childish notions, for it was a child who learned them so long ago. And now they are going to be challenged by adult thought and serious reflection. Then those early notions give way to the far more fruitful and meaningful understanding appropriate to the mature Christian's approach to the Bible.

Nonetheless, a wrongheaded approach to the Bible study can hurt one's faith. It might constrict it into a needlessly literal and simplistic interpretation. Or it might spread that delicate faith out toward theological distortion or outright heresy. A well-designed, sensitive approach to Bible study enlivens faith and rouses the Spirit that tells us the full truth of the matters which we have been taught.

Two of the poorest approaches to Bible study are considered next, only because many people consider them to be the most logical approaches. They are the "Words-to-live-by" approach and the "So there!" approach.

The Words-to-live-by approach searches the Bible for a text to prove a moral point that one has already decided on. Usually it seeks to make its point at the expense of the other person. It tends to flaunt one's own knowledge of biblical references and to suggest that the

Bible-quoter is somehow more moral than the person whose knowledge of the Bible's words is less. This approach often quotes a text out of its proper context.

Now, no one is saying that the Bible contains no words to live by. However, proper use of Scriptures for moral guidance is deceptively simple and requires in fact a high degree of understanding of these books and the culture and causes that brought them forth. The very fact that Jesus himself forthrightly superseded certain Old Testament laws should give a person pause to consider which quotes one ought to hold to. Most notables, from politicians to movie stars, complain of being quoted out of context. The quote may be one sentence in a context of only one paragraph; still, the author deserves his framework. If one does decide to use a quote, that quote must be representative of the work as a whole, or it misrepresents the work. Now, the Bible is a diverse collection of writings by diverse authors. Incorrectly chosen quotes can present a false picture of a given author's intent.

There are other problems with the Words-to-live-by approach to Bible reading. These concern interpretation. Different Bible writers sometimes contradict one another. Or a proverb or an aphorism may be culture-bound and have no current application. Or an author might express a private thought on a matter, a thought that should not be interpreted as the final word on that matter. Or the proper conclusion to draw on a given passage may lie in a hard-to-translate quirk of the Hebrew or Greek language. A host of dangers await the habitual Bible-quoter. The words that the Bible has to live by are words of wisdom that we must search for and ponder. There are few shortcuts. The mystery of the divine is beyond simple explanation; and that mystery is pressed between the pages of those sacred songs and stories, proverbs and prayers. Before we can live by its words, its word must live with us and us with it. The Bible is a demanding book.

Like the Words-to-live-by approach, the So there! method misuses quotes. It views the Bible as a collection of religious proofs, the last word in any debate. It holds the Bible text to be the answer to all the theological, historical, and scientific problems that confront mankind. Need an answer to the problem of man's origins? Well, we have the first chapter of *Genesis,* says the So there! person and so the biologists and archaeologists in quest of truth can put away their microscopes and shovels. From the trifling to the transcendent, the answer hides in a verse or two. No problem is too large or too small; the Bible has the solution. So there!

The Scripture does indeed supply legitimate conclusions on religious matters. But those conclusions are not reached easily and are seldom found in one pointed quote. And as for answers to scientific questions, the Bible is not really the place to look for them. The science of the Bible writers was primitive, and it is doubtful God thought to accelerate human knowledge in this field by infusing scientific facts into the mind of the sacred authors. People cannot make of Scripture a weapon to use superficially against all those with whom they wish to disagree.

Another approach to Bible study is the Bible viewed as literature. This approach is not as dangerous as the two above, but it is not very helpful religiously. The Bible is literature, much of it elegant and lofty, some of it banal and boring, but that is not the point. Approaching the Bible only as literature skirts the all-important faith perspective. It looks at the Bible and sees a collection of Semitic sonnets and short stories, mideast myths, and masterpieces. We formed our Bible study group so that we can better appreciate our faith. For us, the Bible's importance lies in its real contact with the divine throughout all its pages.

There are other approaches which are excellent but too scholarly for a lay Bible study group. A group should avoid an approach that takes more understanding than it yet possesses. There is too much to be gained from that magnificent book.

Deepen

Of course, there is more than one sound approach to Bible study. This writer holds that the best approach begins with the context: in what setting did the book take shape? For what audience was it intended? What problem or situation motivated the sacred author to write? If you know, for example, that there are definite streams of tradition in Genesis and the broad characteristics of those streams (*see* How the Bible Came About), you know a great deal about Genesis. To understand the agonizing controversy that generated St. Paul's angry letter to the Galatians is to understand the essential meaning of that letter. The *contextual approach*, then, attempts to view the particular biblical work as a whole. It seeks to give the reader a feel for the forces that shaped the book, to enable today's reader to sense the earliest readers' situation and response to the book. The purpose for doing this is to enable today's reader to respond in faith and understanding along with those ancient believers.

A relatively simple example is Paul's First Letter to the Thessalonians. This letter is regarded as the earliest work in the New Testament as we have it. It was written by Paul some twenty years after Jesus' resurrection. Paul has two purposes in mind in writing the letter. The first is to bolster their faith. The young community of Christians was experiencing attacks from people without, and Paul wished to reconfirm their commitment to the faith he had preached a short time before. Paul was sure of their steadfastness from reports he had received, so the letter is upbeat, joyful in tone. The second purpose is to respond to the most serious problem that had yet confronted those new Christians. They believed that the risen Lord would soon return on the clouds of heaven and that they all would meet him. In fact, they lived in wait for him. What caused them extreme confusion was the natural deaths of some of their community. Would those who had died not return to greet the coming Lord? Paul's answer begins some two thousand years of theological reflection of the Second Coming of Christ.

By understanding this context, one can now read 1 Thessalonians in its entirety with much profit and understanding. And the letter should be read through at a sitting. A well-guided discussion would center on the meaning of the Second Coming for the first Christians and its meaning for our time. The discussion would bring out the point that biblical truth grew from the experience of the Church and from reflection on that experience. There is a fundamental article of faith underlying Thessalonians: the Bible grew from the Church, the community; the Church did not grow from the Bible. Thus, the inspiration that was with the Church in the days when the sacred authors wrote is with it still. And as it reads these Spirit-filled words, a Bible study group taps into the same vital breath of inspiration. The contextual approach is well suited to catch that breath, be it in the wail of a prophet's lamentation, the melody of a lover's song, or the steady cadence of a missionary's exhortation.

Complementing the contextual approach is the *thematic approach*. After the reader to some extent feels what key Bible writers felt, that reader is ready to pursue a theme. The thematic approach can be extremely fruitful for a Bible study group. A concept, such as "love," can be explored with great benefit through a varied and representative list of readings. Discussion of the theme is always lively, interesting, and enjoyable because, with proper guidance, the consistency and reinforcement of a theme as different authors deal with it sets the Scripture crackling with the flame of discovery and new appreciation. Of course, the group should be brought back often to the individual biblical works as whole pieces with a purposeful human writer or editor. Failure to return to the context can lead to a disjointed view of the Bible. The thematic approach can complement, but must never replace, the contextual approach.

Themes properly used provide a nearly endless array of fresh ways to understand the Bible. Themes can be theological: God, sin, death, hope, faith, joy, and peace. They may explore key words and their use in the Bible. Such words include "poor," "love," and "righteous-ness." Tracing the origins of words and the biblical use of these words requires expert guidance, but it is enjoyable and fruitful. Another use of the thematic approach centers on an author. A group might study "the mind of St. Paul," or "St. John's approach to gospel-writing," or "Jeremiah as a prophet." Finally, there are combinations: "St. Paul on sin," "the development of the word 'love' in St. John," or "Jeremiah's view of poverty."

One of the most beautiful biblical themes, and an excellent model, is *love*. Love can be broken down into "God's love for humans" and "humans' love for God." A good first reading is the entire First Letter of John in the New Testament. The entire message of this letter is love. Its essence is summed up in the following quote:

> We love because God first loved us. If someone says he loves God, but hates his brother, he is a liar. For he cannot love God, whom he has not seen, if he does not love his brother, whom he has seen. The command that Christ has given us is this: whoever loves God must love his brother also. (4:19–21)

God's love for us can be the first theme studied. In the first chapter of Genesis, one reads of God's pleasure in his entire creation and in the pinnacle of creation, man, who is like God and resembles God. In Exodus 23 and 24, one reads of the nature of covenant love, God's protective care, a love that requires fidelity in worship and in living. In 2 Samuel 12:1–25 and chapter 22, a bold portrait of God's wrath and mercy is etched against a background of infidelity, murder, tragedy, repentance, and boundless gratitude. Numerous Psalms, such as 11, 16, 23, and 27, provide an opportunity for prayer and reflection of God's covenant love. In the New Testament, we learn of God's favored ones, all who are "tired from carrying heavy loads" (Matt. 11:25–30). The parable of the lost son (Luke 15:11–32) illustrates God our Father's love and mercy, and the passion of Jesus (Luke 22:39–23:49) expresses the ultimate self-giving of the Son of God.

The second sub-theme for study is our love for God. In Exodus 20:1–17, the Ten Commandments make clear the Old Testament view that the heart of love for God is fidelity, and one can detect the beginnings of the notion that love of neighbor is implied in love of God. Further exposition of this point is given in Deuteronomy 1–11. Psalm 119 is a lengthy song of the love of God as seen throughout the Old Testament. In the New Testament, the joining of love of God and love of neighbor is brought to its clearest statement. This is seen first in the Sermon on the Mount (Matt. 5–7), then in the parable of the

Good Samaritan (Luke 10:25–37), and supremely in the last discourse of Jesus (John 13–17). St. Paul's famous passage on love (1 Cor. 13) makes that virtue the one that gives value to all other virtues, including faith and hope. And this all completes the cycle back to the First Letter of John and the ultimate revelation of all Scripture:

> God is love, and whoever lives in love lives in union with
> God and God lives in union with him. (4:16)

To sum up, an understanding of whole books of the Bible, the author's mind, and the environment that gave rise to a work can be coupled with a study of major biblical themes. The two approaches nourish one another, keep the reader on a level and exciting course, and provide a balanced and fruitful method of Bible study. First, *key* authors must be dealt with. Among these are the four sources of the Pentateuch (J, E, D, and P; see How the Bible Came About), the historian of David, David, Isaiah, Ezekiel, Mark, Luke, John, and Paul. Then, central themes are to be carefully looked at. Among these are faith, hope, love, poverty, peace, righteousness, the kingdom or reign of God, and God. A group can branch out from this basic scheme with further aid from its leader or by delving into the tremendous wealth of literature, popular and more scholarly, on Scripture. Our group has entered a world infinitely profound and vast, the seedbed of divine revelation, the inner space of God.

A Last Word

We have become aware of some salient reasons to pursue Bible study. We have seen the value of a group, a leader, and a careful, sensible approach to such study. There are misuses of this sacred book, and there are good uses that exceed the grasp of the beginner. We are gifted with two thousand years of reflection and scholarly study of Scripture. It is very wise to take advantage of that gift of history. This is a golden age of Bible study for Catholics, an age of excellent and accurate English translation. It is an age of vivid, readable authors in the biblical field and of exemplary periodicals promoting popular appreciation of the Word of God. True, it is also an unsettling era. Sincere and pious beliefs about the Bible are regularly called into question, and some are even discarded. The essential truths remain and always will, but some confusion and uncertainty are inevitable in this time of ferment and distillation of the fruits of the scriptural revival.

The risk that a person might question something that should not be questioned is really unwarranted if that person is a humble and faithful seeker after truth. Proper guidance, support, and prayer will ensure a bountiful quest. When we unite with Christ's Church, his people, we partake of the very inspiration that authored the Bible. We can be confident. We must search the Scriptures. The words of eternal life are there.

Of course, the Bible is not an easy book to read and comprehend. It is as diverse as the many authors and many centuries it took to compose it. It is as simple as a housekeeper searching for a lost penny, as profound as the holy man hearing God's voice in the lilting breeze. Its words reveal this God. They are the seed words spoken by a people who reached up to love this God, and, finally they are the words on the breath of that very God, who bent down to live with his people in flesh and blood, spirit and truth.

PART III

INTRODUCTIONS TO THE BOOKS OF THE BIBLE

✠ ✠ ✠

✠

GENESIS

The Book of Genesis

The first book of the Bible is appropriately named Genesis, or "beginning." The book reaches back past the beginnings of our most ancient history-writing to the beginning of the world. It also gives us an account of the beginnings of Israel and God's call to Abraham, and his relatives, the patriarchs, or "first fathers" of his people.

A description is given of the beginning of the universe in images and phrases which have become classical in Catholic thought and in all Western literature. God's action in bringing about this world of ours out of nothing is called Creation. Genesis presents the divine origin of the world in various ways, accompanied by deep insight into human nature. Mankind's "prehistory" is followed up in the first eleven chapters in a somewhat sketchy fashion, until we come to Abraham, the great father of all believers. The series of events in the lives of the heroic forefathers—Abraham, Isaac, Jacob, and Joseph— bring us, by the book's end, to the time when the people of Israel came to live in Egypt.

Subsequent books of the Bible will speak of how God saves his people, but the stage is set in Genesis for that salvation, since it is here we are told of Creation, sin, and God's first promises to save mankind which he had made "in his own image and likeness." The book thus provides, not only a logical introduction to the Book of Exodus, but also an inspired introduction to the whole of the biblical literature.

The Author of Genesis

The simplest and most honest thing we can say about who wrote Genesis is that we do not know. Although Genesis does not record the name of its author, by Jesus' time the rabbis had come to agree that Moses wrote Genesis and the four books which follow it, sometimes called in a group by the Greek name "Pentateuch," or "five scrolls." In the New Testament Jesus makes reference to "the Law of Moses" (Luke 2:22) and early Christians accepted the tradition of the Mosaic authorship of the "five scrolls."

Some modern critical scholars of the Pentateuch come to a quite different conclusion. Their theory is that Genesis, Exodus, Leviticus, and Numbers, in their present form, constitute one largely connected narrative. They were not written as separate books.

Behind the narrative, as we now have it, lie previously existing sources. In the Hebrew text of the narrative, there are different words for God, either Yahweh or Elohim, used fairly consistently in different sections of the text. This is a clue that leads some scholars to conclude that the present text was probably put together from previously existing sources. They point out that sources, namely, the Yahwistic, the Elohistic, and the Priestly, are found in Genesis, Exodus, Leviticus, and Numbers. (A fourth source found in the Pentateuch—the Deuteronomic—is thought to lie behind the Book of Deuteronomy.) It is not possible, according to this view, to speak of merely one author of these sources or traditions. They are seen as the result of the combined insights of many generations of teachings in ancient Israel. At some point these sources or traditions were skillfully united by a final editor into the narrative we find in the first four books of the Old Testament.

It was only when this narrative was combined with the Book of Deuteronomy that the whole literary work was divided into five scrolls, known as the Pentateuch. When the Hebrew Pentateuch was translated into Greek (c. third century B.C.), each scroll was given a Greek title which more or less defined its content. This is how we came to call the books by the names Genesis, Exodus, Leviticus, Numbers, and Deuteronomy.

In Catholic theology the matter of human authorship is not of central importance to the issue of the inspiration or inerrancy of a particular book of Scripture. The Council of Trent in 1546 declared the seventy-two books of the Bible "inspired" and belonging to a "canon" or list which had previously been accepted by the entire Christian church since the time of St. Augustine.

The Time of Genesis

Just as our knowledge is limited regarding the question of the authorship of the Pentateuch, so too, are we uncertain about a good deal of the time period which the book we call Genesis describes.

The time period of chapters 1 through 11 of Genesis takes us back to the very beginning of all things. It must never be forgotten, however, that chapters 1 through 11 are not a scientific account of the beginning of the universe or of life. They are Israel's faith statement of God's activity in the origins of the universe and of mankind. These chapters use simple language which has been adapted to the mentality of a particular people in a particular culture. The chapters state the principal truths which are fundamental for our salvation and give a popular description of how the human race and the chosen people began.

It is the teaching of the church that the first duty of scholars who investigate these chapters consists, above all, in the attentive study of the literary, scientific, historical, cultural, and religious problems connected with chapters 1 through 11. The church also encourages scholars to examine closely the literary processes of the early Oriental people, their psychology, their way of expressing themselves, and their very notion of historical truth. In a word, scholars should collate, without prejudice, all the subject matter of the paleontological and historical, epigraphic, and literary sciences. It is only in this way that scholarship can discover the true nature of certain narratives in chapters 1 through 11.

We can be more exact in estimating the period of the patriarchs— Abraham, Isaac, Jacob, and Joseph. Most historians would agree that Abraham would have lived in the middle of the eighteenth century B.C. Very recent archaeological discoveries, such as those at Ebla in modern Syria, may be able to throw even more light on the history behind the Genesis narratives.

A word of caution about dating will perhaps not be out of order here. History, as we know it, is a kind of writing which is very modern. In the ancient world when not many people were even literate, and when most of one's day was consumed in the arduous task of physical survival, not much attention was paid to things like exact dates and times. Depending on the country, very different systems of dating were used, and so the modern historian has a very difficult time making precise judgments about the dating of ancient events. Since the Bible, however, is God's ancient but ageless Word, it is addressed to all believers of every age. The precise dates of the particular events, then, have a relatively minor part to play in the message of Genesis, which is a religious message, not a scientific one.

Survey of Genesis

The work can be rather neatly divided between chapters 1 through 11 and 12 through 50. In the first section, the author has interwoven several basic theological traditions to introduce not only the Book of Genesis, but the whole Pentateuch—here begins the story of Israel's salvation. Obviously, the Creation stories (1:1 through 2:3; 2:4 through 2:25) do not have their roots in what we know as history, but the author has skillfully edited several traditions to form an organic whole of what had been separate stories.

There are several themes which likewise appear continually throughout the narrative. Genesis is rigorously faithful to Israel's belief in one God (monotheism). The origin of the entire universe is founded on that belief, for Israel's God is also Creator. And the Creator is also provident: he cares for his people and promises their salvation.

In the second half of Genesis, Israel's founding fathers, or patriarchs—Abraham, Isaac, Jacob, and Joseph—all personify her faith in the one God who is the source of all that is, and who is still personally involved in her history. The call of Abraham (ch. 12) is the beginning of the Judeo-Christian religion since he affirms his belief in the one God. God's promises to Abraham are given in a covenant, or pact, in which God will give Abraham land, descendants, and blessings, and Abraham will return to God faithful worship and obedience. Isaac (ch. 21), is the incarnation of God's promise of descendants. In Jacob (ch. 27), God enlarges Abraham's family and Jacob's twelve sons are the fathers of Israel's twelve tribes. The life of Joseph (ch. 37) brings Israel to Egypt and sets the stage for the great Exodus, the single most memorable of all God's saving acts on behalf of his chosen people.

OUTLINE OF GENESIS

Creation of the universe and of mankind	1:1–2:25	The Patriarchs:	
		a. Abraham	12:1–25:18
		b. Isaac	25:19–26:35
The beginning of sin and suffering	3:1–24	c. Jacob	27:1–35:29
From Adam to Noah	4:1–5:32	The descendants of Esau	36:1–43
Noah and the flood	6:1–9:29	Joseph and his brothers	37:1–45:28
From Noah to Jobab	10:1–32	The Israelites in Egypt	46:1–50:26
The tower of Babylon	11:1–9		
From Shem to Abram	11:10–32		

FOCUS	CREATION; ORIGIN AND CAUSE OF EVIL				PATRIARCHAL NARRATIVES			
REFERENCE	1.1———3.1———6.1———10.1———12.1———25.1———27.1———37.1—50.26							
DIVISION	CREATION	FALL	FLOOD	NATIONS	ABRAHAM	ISAAC	JACOB	JOSEPH
TOPIC	SIN, EVIL, AND THEIR CONSEQUENCES INTRODUCED INTO GOD'S GOOD CREATION				GOD'S PLAN OF SALVATION OPERATIVE IN PATRIARCHAL PROMISES; TENSION IN FULFILLMENT			
SETTING	FERTILE CRESCENT				CANAAN			EGYPT

GENESIS

EXODUS

The Book of Exodus

This second book of the Pentateuch tells the story of the departure, the "Exodus," of God's chosen people from the land of Egypt, with all the hardships it involved, as well as the story of the covenant God made with his people at Mount Sinai, when he gave Moses his Law, the Ten Commandments. This second part of the story, the giving of the Law, was so important that the rabbis called all five books the "Torah," or the Law. It would not be an exaggeration to say that the Book of Exodus is the most important book of the Pentateuch, and, perhaps, of the entire Hebrew Bible. This is because it contains the two most basic experiences which the Jewish people had which made them into a nation: God saved them from the hands of the Egyptians and made them "his own," by revealing to them his will, carved in the tablets of the Law given to Moses. So important are these events for the people of Israel that they will always celebrate them at Passover, the time when they remember that the angel of death "passed over" the homes of the Jews, and God allowed his people to "pass over" the Great Sea, saved from those who tried to harm them.

The Author of Exodus

Certainly, Moses is the "hero" and central figure of the Book of Exodus. The inspired author recorded the precious memories his people still cherished about Moses, the escape from Egypt, and the covenant by which they became God's special nation. Those memories nourished their faith and here take the form of the book called "Exodus."

In the discussion of the author of Genesis, it was pointed out that the memory of who actually wrote the Pentateuch is now long clouded over. For a fuller view of this very complex question, please turn to the section, "The Author of Genesis."

The Time of Exodus

The *general consensus of* scholarly *opinion* seems to be that the Exodus took place sometime in the thirteenth century B.C., perhaps during the reign of Pharaoh Ramses II, who was reigning in the year 1270 B.C. and who gave his name to a number of building sites (cf. Ex. 12:37). It should be noted, however, that the author was writing about events which had fundamental importance for the religious history of his people and so can hardly be expected to conform to our modern criteria for secular or civil historiography. He shows no interest, for example, in telling us the dates of the events he is describing. Students of the ancient history of Israel and Egypt try to incorporate the objective data of archaeology to throw some light on this period, but the certainty of time estimates is not assured.

Survey of Exodus

The story of the Book of Exodus can roughly be divided into two parts: the rescue from Egypt (chs. 1 through 18) and the giving of the Law of the covenant (chs. 19 through 40).

The Rescue from Egypt (chs. 1 through 18): The story of Genesis left the Jewish people in Egypt, where they had gone to escape famine while Joseph was a favorite of Pharaoh. Exodus quickly tells us (1:8) that there was a new king in Egypt "who knew nothing about Joseph." The reduction of the Jews to slavery, under their cruel Egyptian masters, is paralleled by the rise of Moses, born a son of Israel but raised in the Egyptian court. God reveals himself to Moses and calls him to leadership over his people. Moses, initially rejected by Pharaoh, finally succeeds in persuading Pharaoh to let God's people go. Pharaoh relents because of the devastating ten plagues which God sends on the land and the people of Egypt. Pharaoh changes his mind, however, and pursues the Jews as they try to leave. God intervenes once more and Pharaoh's army and chariots are cast into the sea (Ex. 15:4).

The Covenant (chs. 19 through 40): Having saved his people from the most imminent danger of Pharaoh and his armies, God now speaks his will to his people. In chapter 20, we find the first recording of the Ten Commandments, or the "Decalogue," in Greek, the "ten words" (cf. Deut. 5). The remaining chapters of Exodus are largely taken up with more explicit details of God's Law. The Law spells out how his people will live: in such a way that they will be his people. One of the concrete ways in which Israel will always be able to show her connection to God is that he gave to her, and to her alone, his Law.

OUTLINE OF EXODUS

The Israelites set free from Egypt	1:1–15:21	from Egypt	12:1–15:21
a. Slaves in Egypt	1:1–22	From the Red Sea to Mount Sinai	15:22–18:27
b. Moses' birth and early life	2:1–4:31	The Law and the covenant	19:1–24:18
c. Moses and Aaron confront the king of Egypt	5:1–11:10	The covenant Tent and instructions for worship	25:1–31:18
d. The Passover and the departure		The response of Israel to the covenant	32:1–40:38

FOCUS	LIBERATION FROM SLAVERY OF EGYPT				THE MAKING OF THE COVENANT			
REFERENCE	1.1———2.1———5.1———15.22———				19.1———25.1———32.1———35.1———40.38			
DIVISION	NEED FOR LIBERATION	PREPARATION FOR LIBERATION	LIBERATION OF ISRAEL	ISRAEL'S FIRST EXPERIENCE AS GOD'S PEOPLE	MAKING OF COVENANT	INSTRUCTIONS FOR BUILDING INSTRUMENTS OF WORSHIP	BREAKING AND RENEWAL OF COVENENT	EXECUTION OF INSTRUCTIONS REGARDING INSTRUMENTS OF WORSHIP
TOPIC	THE ACTUAL FORMATION OF ISRAEL				THE LEGAL FORMATION OF ISRAEL			
SETTING	EGYPT		WILDERNESS		MOUNT SINAI			

EXODUS

LEVITICUS

The Book of Leviticus

Leviticus is God's guidebook for his newly redeemed people, showing them how to worship, serve, and obey a holy God. Fellowship with God through sacrifice and obedience show the awesome holiness of the God of Israel. Indeed, "Be holy, because I, the LORD your God, am holy." (19:2).

Leviticus focuses on the worship and walk of the nation of God. In Exodus, Israel was redeemed and established as a kingdom of priests and a holy nation. Leviticus shows how God's people are to fulfill their priestly calling.

The Hebrew title is *Wayyiqra*, "And He Called." The rabbis, in their later commentaries on the Law called "Talmud," refer to Leviticus as the "Law of the Priests" and the "Law of the Offerings." The Greek title appearing in the Septuagint is *Leuitikon*, "That Which Pertains to the Levites." From this word, the Latin Vulgate derived its name *Leviticus* which was adopted as the English title. This title is slightly misleading because the book does not deal with the Levites as a whole but more with the priests, a segment of the Levites.

The Author of Leviticus

As in the cases of Genesis and Exodus, the traditional ascription of Leviticus to Moses is more honorary than strictly factual. Moses, who received the Law from God, is the source of Israel's knowledge of the Law. His intimate relationship with the God of Israel is without precedent or subsequent parallel, even in the case of the great prophets. In a way, Moses is the first and the greatest of the prophets. In that sense, the Torah can be called the Law of Moses (cf. Luke 2:22). Still, the actual writing of the text reveals a codifying tendency more reminiscent of the later monarchy than of the actual time of Moses himself.

The reader should turn to the discussion of this complex issue of Pentateuchal authorship which is found under "The Author of Genesis."

The Time of Leviticus

No geographical movement takes place in Leviticus: the children of Israel remain camped at the foot of Mount Sinai (25:1–2; 26:46; 27:34). The new calendar of Israel begins with the first Passover (Ex. 12:2); and, according to Exodus 40:17, the Tent of the Lord's presence is completed exactly one year later.

Leviticus picks up the story at this point and takes place in the first month of the second year. Numbers 1:1 opens at the beginning of the second month.

Survey of Leviticus

It has been said that it took God only one night to get Israel out of Egypt, but it took forty years to get Egypt out of Israel. In Exodus, Israel is redeemed and established as a kingdom of priests and a holy nation; and in Leviticus, Israel is taught how to fulfill their priestly call. They have been led out from the land of bondage in Exodus and into the sanctuary of God in Leviticus. They move from redemption to service, from deliverance to dedication. This book serves as a handbook for the Levitical priesthood, giving instructions and regulations for worship. Used to guide a newly redeemed people into worship, service, and obedience to God, Leviticus falls into two major sections: (1) sacrifice (chs. 1 through 17) and (2) sanctification (chs. 18 through 27).

Sacrifice (chs. 1 through 17): This section teaches that God must be approached by the sacrificial offerings (chs. 1 through 7), by the mediation of the priesthood (chs. 8 through 10), by the purification of the nation from uncleanness (chs. 11 through 15), and by the provision for national cleansing and fellowship (chs. 16 and 17). The blood sacrifices remind the worshipers that because of sin the holy God requires the costly gift of life (17:11). The blood of the innocent sacrificial animal becomes the substitute for the life of the guilty offerer: "sins are forgiven only if blood is poured out" (Heb. 9:22).

Sanctification (chs. 18 through 27): The Israelites serve a holy God who requires them to be holy as well. To be holy means to be "set apart" or "separated." They are to be separated from other nations unto God. In Leviticus the idea of holiness appears eighty-seven times, sometimes indicating ceremonial holiness (ritual requirements), and at other times moral holiness (purity of life). This sanctification extends to the people of Israel (chs. 18 through 20), the priesthood (chs. 21 and 22), their worship (chs. 23 and 24), their life in Canaan (chs. 25 and 26), and their special vows (ch. 27). It is necessary to remove the defilement that separates the people from God so that they can have a walk of fellowship with their Redeemer.

FOCUS	SACRIFICE				SANCTIFICATION				
REFERENCE	1.1————8.1————11.1————16.1—				—18.1——21.1——23.1——25.1————27.1–27.34				
DIVISION	THE LAWS OF				THE LAWS OF SANCTIFICATION				
	THE OFFERINGS	CONSECRATION OF THE PRIESTS	CONSECRATION OF THE PEOPLE	NATIONAL ATONEMENT	FOR THE PEOPLE	FOR THE PRIESTS	IN WORSHIP	IN THE LAND OF CANAAN	THROUGH VOWS
TOPIC	THE WAY TO GOD				THE WALK WITH GOD				
	THE LAWS OF ACCEPTABLE APPROACH TO GOD				THE LAWS OF CONTINUED FELLOWSHIP WITH GOD				
SETTING	MOUNT SINAI								

LEVITICUS

OUTLINE OF LEVITICUS

Laws about offerings and sacrifices 1:1–7:38
The ordination of Aaron and his sons as priests 8:1–10:20

Laws about ritual cleanness and uncleanness 11:1–15:33
The Day of Atonement 16:1–34

Laws about holiness in life and worship	17:1–27:34	c. Holiness in worship	23:1–24:23
a. Holiness of the people	17:1–20:27	d. Holiness with the land	25:1–26:46
b. Holiness of the priesthood	21:1–22:33	e. Holiness through vows	27:1–27:34

NUMBERS

The Book of Numbers

Numbers is the book of wanderings. It takes its name from the two numberings of the Israelites—the first at Mount Sinai and the second on the plains of Moab. Most of the book, however, describes Israel's experiences as they wander in the wilderness. The lesson of Numbers is clear. While it may be necessary to pass through wilderness experiences, one does not have to live there. For Israel, an eleven-day journey became a forty-year agony.

The title of Numbers comes from the first word in the Hebrew text, *Wayyedabber*, "And He Said." Jewish writings, however, usually refer to it by the fifth Hebrew word in 1:1, *Bermidbar*, "In the Wilderness," which more nearly indicates the content of the book. The Greek title in the Septuagint is *Arithmoi*, "Numbers." The Latin Vulgate followed this title and translated it *Liber Numeri*, "Book of Numbers." These titles are based on the two numberings: the generation of Exodus (ch. 1) and the generation that grew up in the wilderness and conquered Canaan (ch. 26). Numbers has also been called the "Book of the Journeyings," the "Book of the Murmurings," and the "Fourth Book of Moses."

The Author of Numbers

This fourth book of the Pentateuch, likewise, has Moses as its hero and inspiration. The book carries no explicit mention of its author's identity.

The reader should turn to "The Author of Genesis" for a more nearly complete treatment of this very complex issue of authorship.

The Time of Numbers

Leviticus covers only one month, but Numbers stretches over almost thirty-nine years. It records Israel's movement from the last twenty days at Mount Sinai (1:1; 10:11), the wandering around Kadesh Barnea, and finally the arrival in the plains of Moab in the fortieth year (22:1; 26:3; 33:50; Deut. 1:3). Their tents occupy several square miles whenever they camp since there are probably over two-and-a-half million people (based on the census figures in chapters 1 and 26). God miraculously feeds and sustains them in the desert—he preserves their clothing and gives them manna, meat, water, leaders, and a promise (14:34).

FOCUS	THE OLD GENERATION		THE TRAGIC TRANSITION				THE NEW GENERATION		
REFERENCE	1.1————5.1————		10.11—13.1—15.1————20.1—26.1—				28.1————31.1—36.13		
DIVISION	ORGANIZATION OF ISRAEL	SANCTIFICATION OF ISRAEL	TO KADESH	AT KADESH	IN WILDERNESS	TO MOAB	REORGANI-ZATION OF ISRAEL	REGULATIONS OF OFFERINGS AND VOWS	CONQUEST AND DIVISION OF ISRAEL
TOPIC	ORDER		DISORDER				REORDER		
	PREPARATION		POSTPONEMENT				PREPARATION		
SETTING	MOUNT SINAI		WILDERNESS				PLAINS OF MOAB		

NUMBERS

Survey of Numbers

Israel as a nation is in its infancy at the outset of this book, only thirteen months after the Exodus from Egypt. In Numbers, the book of divine discipline, it becomes necessary for the nation to go through the painful process of testing and maturation. God must teach his people the consequences of irresponsible decisions. The forty years of wilderness experience transforms them from a rabble of ex-slaves into a nation ready to take the Promised Land. Numbers begins with the old generation (1:1 through 10:10), moves through a tragic transitional period (10:11 through 25:18), and ends with the new generation (chs. 26 through 36) at the doorway to the land of Canaan.

The Old Generation (1:1 through 10:10): The generation that witnessed God's miraculous acts of deliverance and preservation receives further direction from God while they are still at the foot of Mount Sinai (1:1 through 10:10). God's instructions are very explicit, reaching every aspect of their lives. He is the Author of order, not confusion; and this is seen in the way he organizes the people around the sacred Tent. Turning from the outward conditions of the camp (chs. 1 through

4) to the inward conditions (chs. 5 through 10), Numbers describes the spiritual preparation of the people.

The Tragic Transition (10:11 through 25:18): Israel follows God step by step until Canaan is in sight. Then in the crucial moment at Kadesh they draw back in unbelief. Their murmurings had already become incessant, "The people began to complain to the LORD about their troubles . . . he became angry . . ." (11:1). But their unbelief after sending out the twelve spies at Kadesh Barnea is something God will not tolerate (cf. Deut. 1:19–46: a second, revised version of the reconnoitering [spying] of the land). Their rebellion at Kadesh marks the pivotal point of the book. The generation of the Exodus will not be the generation of the conquest.

Unbelief brings discipline and hinders God's blessing. The old generation is doomed literally to kill time for forty years of wilderness wanderings—one year for every day spent by the twelve spies in inspecting the land. They are judged by disinheritance and death as their journey changes from one of anticipation to one of aimlessness. Only Joshua and Caleb, the two spies who believed God, enter Canaan. Almost nothing is recorded about these transitional years.

The New Generation (chs. 26 through 36): When the transition to the new generation is complete, the people move to the plains of Moab, directly east of the Promised Land (22:1). Before they can enter the land they must wait until all is ready. Here they receive new instructions, a new census is taken, Joshua is appointed as Moses' successor, and some of the people settle in the Transjordan.

Numbers records two generations (chs. 1 through 14 and 21 through 36), two numberings (chs. 1 and 26), two journeyings (chs. 10 through 14 and 21 through 27), and two sets of instructions (chs. 5 through 9 and 28 through 36). It illustrates both the kindness and severity of God (Rom. 11:22) and teaches that God's people can move forward only as they trust and depend on him.

OUTLINE OF NUMBERS

The Israelites prepare to leave Mount Sinai	1:1–9:23	rael	26:1–27:23
a. The first census	1:1–4:49	Regulations of offerings and vows	28:1–30:16
b. Various laws and rules	5:1–8:26	Victory over Moab	31:1–54
c. The second Passover	9:1–23	Division of land east of the Jordan	32:1–42
From Mount Sinai to Moab	10:1–21:35	Summary of the journey from Egypt to Moab	33:1–49
Failure with the Moabites	22:1–25:18	Instructions before crossing the Jordan	33:50–36:13
A reorganization of Is-			

DEUTERONOMY

The Book of Deuteronomy

Deuteronomy, Moses' "Upper Desert Discourse," consists of a series of farewell messages by Israel's leader. It is addressed to the new generation destined to possess the land of promise—those who survived the forty years of wilderness wandering.

Like Leviticus, Deuteronomy contains a vast amount of legal detail, but its emphasis is on the laymen rather than the priests. Moses reminds the new generation of the importance of obedience if they are to learn from the sad example of their parents.

The Hebrew title of Deuteronomy is *Haddebharim*, "The Words," taken from the opening phrase in 1:1, "In this book are the words." The parting words of Moses to the new generation are given in oral and written form so that they will endure to all generations. Deuteronomy has been called "five-fifths of the Law" since it completes the five books of Moses. The Jewish people have also called it *Mishneh Hattorah*, "repetition of the Law," which is translated in the Septuagint as *To Deuteronomion Touto*, "This Second Law." Deuteronomy, however, is not a second law but an adaptation and expansion of much of the original law given on Mount Sinai.

The Author of Deuteronomy

The structure of Deuteronomy argues against its having been written at one time by one hand. The narratives, relative to the end of Moses' life, reveal a style that is different from that found in the main section of the book. Even in the main section of Deuteronomy there are additions, doublets, and a number of conclusions that force scholars to conclude to several stages of writing.

As the book now stands, it portrays Moses delivering a series of discourses to God's people on the plains of Moab. While most critical scholars contend that the author is anonymous, the prominence given to Moses throughout the book forbids us to deny him any part in the work. Moses left his people a basic teaching to regulate their convenant relationship with God. In later generations, new problems demanded new regulations in keeping with the spirit of Moses. Deuteronomy is a reinterpretation of Moses' teachings as they were understood in the seventh century B.C.

Those responsible for writing Deuteronomy were probably the Levites, the guardians of Moses' spirit and law. Following the fall of the northern kingdom in 722–721 B.C., some Levites fled to Jerusalem and brought with them their collections of reinterpretations. It was probably under Hezekiah (715–687 B.C.) that all the collections were gathered together and the first edition of Deuteronomy appeared. It was most likely during Josiah's reign (640–609 B.C.) that this was made known as part of a national reform in Judah.

The Time of Deuteronomy

Like Leviticus, Deuteronomy does not progress historically. It takes place entirely on the plains of Moab due east of Jericho and the Jordan River (1:1; 29:1; Josh. 1:2). It covers about one month: combine Deuteronomy 1:3 and 34:8 with Joshua 5:6–12.

Survey of Deuteronomy

Deuteronomy, in its broadest outline, is the record of the renewal of the covenant given at Mount Sinai. This covenant is reviewed, expanded, enlarged, and finally ratified in the plains of Moab. Moses accomplishes this primarily through three sermons that move from a retrospective, to an introspective, and finally to a prospective look at God's dealings with Israel.

Moses' First Sermon (1:1 through 4:43): Moses reaches into the past to remind the people of two undeniable facts in their history: (1) the moral judgment of God upon Israel's unbelief, and (2) the deliverance and provision of God during times of obedience. The simple lesson is that obedience brings blessing and disobedience brings punishment.

Moses' Second Sermon (4:44 through 26:19): This moral and legal section is the longest in the book because Israel's future as a nation in Canaan will depend upon a right relationship with God. These chapters review the three categories of the Law: (1) *The testimonies* (chs. 5 through 11). These are the moral duties—a restatement and expansion of the Ten Commandments plus an exhortation not to forget God's gracious deliverance. (2) *The statutes* (12:1 through 16:17). These are the ceremonial duties—sacrifices, tithes, and feasts. (3) *The ordinances* (16:18 through 26:19). These are the civil (16:18 through 20:20) and social (chs. 21 through 26) duties—the system of justice, criminal laws, laws of warfare, rules of property, personal and family morality, and social justice.

Moses' Third Sermon (chs. 27 through 34): In these chapters Moses writes history in advance. He predicts what will befall Israel in the near future (blessings and curses) and in the distant future (dispersion among the nations and eventual return). Moses lists the terms of the covenant soon to be ratified by the people. Because Moses will not be allowed to enter the land, he appoints Joshua as his successor and delivers a farewell address to the multitude. God himself buries Moses in an unknown place.

OUTLINE OF DEUTERONOMY

Moses' first discourse	1:1–4:49	a. Instructions for entering Canaan	27:1–28:68
Moses' second discourse	5:1–26:19	b. The covenant renewed	29:1–30:20
a. The Ten Commandments	5:1–10:22	c. Moses' last words	31:1–33:29
b. Laws, rules, and warnings	11:1–26:19	The death of Moses	34:1–12
Moses' third discourse	27:1–33:2		

FOCUS	FIRST SERMON	SECOND SERMON				THIRD SERMON		
REFERENCE	1.1———4.44———	12.1———	16.18—21.1—27.1—			——29.1———	—31.1—34.12	
DIVISION	REVIEW OF GOD'S ACTS FOR ISRAEL	EXPOSITION OF THE DECALOGUE	CEREMONIAL LAWS	CIVIL LAWS	SOCIAL LAWS	RATIFICATION OF COVENANT	PALESTINIAN COVENENT	TRANSITION OF COVENANT MEDIATOR
TOPIC	WHAT GOD HAS DONE	WHAT GOD EXPECTED OF ISRAEL				WHAT GOD WILL DO		
	HISTORICAL	LEGAL				PROPHETICAL		
SETTING	PLAINS OF MOAB							

DEUTERONOMY

THE BOOK OF

JOSHUA

The Book of Joshua

The Book of Joshua, traditionally listed as the first of the historical books of the Old Testament, forges a link between the Pentateuch (the first five books of the Old Testament) and the remainder of Israel's history. Under the leadership of Joshua, the successor to Moses, the people of Israel complete the conquest of the land of Canaan, thereby bringing to fulfillment God's promise to Abraham (Gen. 15:7). Their military campaigns and settlement of Canaan lead the people to a newer realization of God in their midst: victory comes through faith in God and obedience to his Word, rather than through military might or numerical superiority.

The book is appropriately titled after its central figure, Joshua, whose name means "salvation" or "Yahweh is salvation." The purpose of the book is to demonstrate the faithfulness of God in fulfilling his promise to give the people the land of Canaan as a special inheritance and to explain the distribution of the lands to the various tribes of Israel. In the course of the story, the people are called to continued faithfulness to their covenant with God.

The Author of Joshua

The traditional view is that Joshua was the author of this book. Some modern scholars have proposed that the Book of Joshua is too complex to have been written by a single author. The book is considered to be a compilation of oral and written records which were later edited in several stages to produce its present form. Among scholars today, there is recognition of a long tradition of battle narratives and important place-name listings, all woven into a continuous story of the period surrounding the initial settlement of the Israelites in Canaan. While the work of several editors is perceived by modern scholarship, there remains no reason to deny outright the historical leadership of Joshua, nor the military character of the Israelite conquest of Canaan. Archaeological evidence of destruction in the period at sites like Lachish, Debir, and Hazor, and the lack of such evidence at sites like Jericho and Ai, present an inconsistent witness to the historicity of the Book of Joshua at this time.

The Time of Joshua

The setting of the Book of Joshua is clearly given as that period of Joshua's leadership of Israel after the death of Moses, and the subsequent time of settlement in Canaan. Yet, because the dating of the Exodus and the wilderness experiences of the Israelites is much debated by scholars today, no fixed date may be determined absolutely for the Joshua period. Also, scholars debate the duration of events narrated in the book, some allowing for a slow, drawn-out period of gradual settlement in Canaan, while others support a more traditional picture of compact invasion and victory within a short period of years. At least three geographical settings are included in the book: (1) the Jordan River (chs. 1 through 5); (2) Canaan (chs. 6 through 12); and (3) the twelve tribes in their proper areas of inheritance (chs. 13 through 24). The final distribution of lands to the tribes, as described in the second half of the book, may represent a summary of a lengthier process of settlement, rather than a single event as may appear. Rather than a precise dating of events, the chief concern of the inspired authors and editors is Israel's possession of the land in fulfillment of God's promises to Abraham, Moses, and Joshua, and in response to the people's faithfulness to the covenant made at Mount Sinai.

Survey of Joshua

Joshua resumes the narrative where Deuteronomy leaves off, and takes Israel from the wilderness to the Promised Land. Israel has now reached its climactic point of fulfilling the centuries-old promise in Genesis of a homeland. The first half of Joshua (1:1 through 12:24) describes the seven-year conquest of the land, and the second half (13:1 through 24:33) gives the details of the division and settlement of the land.

Conquest (1:1 through 12:24): The first five chapters record the spiritual, moral, physical, and military preparation of Joshua and the people for the impending conquest of Canaan. Joshua is given a charge by God to complete the task begun by Moses (1:2). After being encouraged by God, Joshua sends out two spies who come back with a favorable report (in contrast to the spies of the previous generation). Obedience and faith are united in the miraculous crossing of the Jordan River (3:1 through 4:24).

Joshua's campaign in central Canaan (6:1 through 8:35) places a strategic wedge between the northern and southern cities preventing a massive Canaanite alliance against Israel. This divide-and-conquer strategy proves effective, but God's directions for taking the first city (Jericho) sound like foolishness from a military point of view. The Lord uses this to test the people and to teach them that Israel's success in battle will always be by his power and not their own might or cleverness. Sin must be dealt with at once because it brings severe consequences and defeat at Ai (7:1–26).

The southern and northern campaigns (9:1 through 12:24) are also successful, but an unwise oath made to the deceptive Gibeonites forces

Israel to protect them and to disobey God's command to eliminate the Canaanites.

Settlement (13:1 through 24:33): Joshua is growing old, and God tells him to divide the land among the twelve tribes. Much remains to be won, and the tribes are to continue the conquest by faith after Joshua's death. Chapters 13:1 through 21:45 describe the allocation of the land to the various tribes as well as the inheritances of Caleb (chs. 14 and 15) and the Levites (ch. 21).

The last chapters (22:1 through 24:33) record the conditions for continued successful settlement in Canaan. Access to God, as well as his forgiveness, comes only through the divinely established sacrificial system; and civil war almost breaks out when the eastern tribes build an altar that is misinterpreted by the western tribes.

Realizing that blessing comes from God only as Israel obeys his covenant, Joshua preaches a moving sermon, climaxed by Israel's renewal of her allegiance to the covenant.

OUTLINE OF JOSHUA

The conquest of Canaan — 1:1–12:24
The division of the land — 13:1–21:45
a. The land east of the Jordan — 13:1–33
b. The land west of the Jordan — 14:1–19:51
c. The cities of the refuge — 20:1–9
d. The cities of the Levites — 21:1–45
The eastern tribes return to their territory — 22:1–34
Joshua's farewell address — 23:1–16
The covenant renewed at Shechem — 24:1–33

FOCUS	CONQUEST OF CANAAN		SETTLEMENT IN CANAAN			
REFERENCE	1.1———————6.1———————		13.8———————14.1———————		20.1———————22.1———————24.33		
DIVISION	PREPARATION OF ISRAEL	CONQUEST OF CANAAN	SETTLEMENT OF EAST JORDAN	SETTLEMENT OF WEST JORDAN	SETTLEMENT OF RELIGIOUS COMMUNITY	CONDITIONS FOR CONTINUED SETTLEMENT
TOPIC	ENTERING CANAAN	CONQUERING CANAAN	DIVIDING CANAAN			
	PREPARATION	SUBJECTION	POSSESSION			
SETTING	JORDAN RIVER	CANAAN	TWO AND A HALF TRIBES—EAST JORDAN NINE AND A HALF TRIBES—WEST JORDAN			

JOSHUA

THE BOOK OF
JUDGES

The Book of Judges

The Book of Judges is titled after twelve heroes of Israel, whose deeds it records. The book continues the history of Israel in Canaan from the conquest of the land until the period of the kings. "There was no king in Israel at that time. Everyone did whatever he pleased" (21:25). Over several hundred years, Israel's tribes were rather independent, usually linking together in response to a particular crisis under the leadership of a charismatic military leader called "a judge," whom the ancient theologians of Israel understood to have been sent by God to rescue his people. Thus the book is called in Hebrew *Shophetim*, meaning "Judges" or "Deliverers."

The story as a whole develops a series of repeated cycles of events in four stages: (1) Israel forgets God and sins; (2) God responds in anger and allows a foreign power to oppress Israel; (3) Israel repents of its sin and pleads for God's help; and (4) God raises up a judge to deliver his people and restore faithfulness in Israel. The book reaffirms that the future of Israel depends upon the people's obedience or disobedience to God's law and their fidelity to the worship of God alone.

The Author of Judges

The Book of Judges represents an extensive period of oral and written tradition passed down and assembled over a number of stages. While the Hebrew Talmud (Jewish commentary) scholars attributed authorship to Samuel, and some of the materials evidently date from that period, most modern scholars support a multiple authorship, and suggest that Judges includes a series of independent accounts from the northern and southern kingdoms, finally compiled in its present form, sometime after the collapse of the north in 721 B.C.

The Time of Judges

The book clearly speaks of the period of Israel's history between the initial conquest of the land and the beginning of the monarchy under Saul. Its earliest stories reflect a time of changing relationships among the tribes, although there may have been a more centralized tribal structure in this period. During this time, a number of Canaanite strongholds remained to be brought under Israelite rule. The events of Judges cover a period of 335 or 400 years. To explain some inconsistencies in recording between the data of Judges and that of First Kings 6, some scholars have suggested that the stories of the individual judges need not be successive, but at times simultaneous tales from different regions of Canaan. It should be clear that the death of Joshua begins a new stage in Israel's life and history until the coming of Saul at about 1040 B.C. This interval is the time of the judges.

Survey of Judges

After Joshua and the generation of the conquest pass on, "the next generation forgot the LORD and what he had done for Israel" (2:10; see also 2:7–10; Josh. 24:31). Judges opens with a description of Israel's deterioration, continues with seven cycles of oppression and deliverance, and concludes with two illustrations of Israel's depravity.

Deterioration (1:1 through 3:4): Judges begins with short-lived military successes after Joshua's death, but quickly turns to the repeated failure of all the tribes to drive out their enemies. The people feel the lack of a unified central leader, but the primary reasons for their failure are a lack of faith in God and a lack of obedience to him (2:1–3). Compromise leads to conflict and chaos. Israel does not drive out the inhabitants (1:21, 27, 29 and 30); instead of removing the moral cancer spread by the inhabitants of Canaan, they contract the disease. The Canaanite gods literally become a trap to them (2:3). Judges 2:11–23 is a microcosm of the pattern found in chapters 3 through 16 of Judges.

Deliverances (3:5 through 16:31): This section describes seven apostasies (fallings away from God), seven servitudes, and seven deliverances. Each of the seven cycles have five steps: sin, servitude, supplication, salvation, and silence. These also can be described by the words rebellion, retribution, repentance, restoration, and rest. The seven cycles connect together as a descending spiral of sin (2:19). Israel vacillates between obedience and apostasy as the people continually fail to learn from their mistakes. Apostasy grows, but the rebellion is not continual. The times of rest and peace are longer than the times of bondage. The monotony of Israel's sins can be contrasted with the creativity of God's methods of deliverance.

Depravity (17:1 through 21:25): These chapters illustrate (1) religious apostasy (chs. 17 and 18) and (2) social and moral depravity (chs. 19 through 21) during the period of the judges. Chapters 19 through 21 contain one of the worst tales of degradation in the Bible. Judges closes with a key to understanding the period: "Everyone did whatever he pleased" (21:25). The people are not doing what is wrong in their own eyes, but "sinned against the Lord again."

OUTLINE OF JUDGES

Description of Israel's deterioration 1:1–3:4

Oppression and deliv-erance 3:5–16:31

Israel's depravity 17:1–21:25

FOCUS	DETERIORATION		DELIVERANCE						DEPRAVITY		
REFERENCE	1.1——— 2.1—	3.5—	4.1—	6.1——	10.6—	12.8—	13.1—	17.1—	19.1—	20.1—21.25
DIVISION	ISRAEL FAILS TO COMPLETE THE CONQUEST	GOD JUDGES ISRAEL	SOUTHERN CAMPAIGN	NORTHERN CAMPAIGN (1st)	CENTRAL CAMPAIGN	EASTERN CAMPAIGN	NORTHERN CAMPAIGN (2nd)	WESTERN CAMPAIGN	SIN OF IDOLATRY	SIN OF IM-MORALITY	SIN OF CIVIL WAR
TOPIC	CAUSES OF THE CYCLES		CURSE OF THE CYCLES						CONDITIONS DURING THE CYCLES		
	LIVING WITH THE CANAANITES		WAR WITH THE CANAANITES						LIVING LIKE THE CANAANITES		
SETTING	CANAAN										

JUDGES

THE BOOK OF

RUTH

The Book of Ruth

The Book of Ruth is named after the woman of Moab who married Boaz of Bethlehem, and so is joined to the people of Israel. It tells a beautiful story of love and devotion, set in the days of the judges. Because of Ruth's faithfulness to God and her mother-in-law, Naomi,

God rewards her by giving her a new husband (Boaz) and a privileged position in the family line of David and Christ. She became the great-grandmother of David.

The aim of the book is to demonstrate God's care for those who are faithful to family and to the Lord, regardless of nationality, and to accent the special favor of the house of David in the plan of God for the people of Israel.

The Author of Ruth

The author of the Book of Ruth is not indicated anywhere in its text, nor from any other biblical passages. While the book tells of events in the period of the judges, it is clearly written at a later period. Some descriptions of Israelite social customs and the great stress upon family and clan solidarity reflect an early period of history, yet the obvious concern with the Davidic ancestry and the survival of the line of Elimelech indicate that it was written after the firm establishment of the Davidic house on the throne. While Greek and Latin canons (approved list of inspired books) list Ruth after the Book of Judges (because of its time associations), the Hebrew tradition has included it among the Writings (a grouping of Old Testament books) of the later age of scriptural composition. One need not consider the book merely a good tale, without any roots in historical fact. The events show God's faithfulness to his saving design for all nations. Ruth is a Moabite. All are urged to imitate Ruth's faith.

The Time of Ruth

The events of the book are set in the time of the judges, and cover a rather short period of years between the life of Ruth in Moab, her trip to Bethlehem to work in the fields, and her marriage to Boaz in that town. The book draws a contrast between the unfaithfulness of Israel during this period and the faith of Ruth—a foreign girl. The assignment of a precise time is difficult. It takes place "Long ago, in the days before Israel had a king" (1:1).

Survey of Ruth

Ruth is the story of a virtuous woman who lives above the norm of her day. She is "a fine woman" (3:11) who shows loyal love to her mother-in-law, Naomi, and her near-kinsman, Boaz. In both relationships, goodness and love are clearly manifested. Her love is demonstrated in chapters 1 and 2 and rewarded in chapters 3 and 4.

Ruth's Love Is Demonstrated (chs. 1 and 2): The story begins with a famine in Israel, a sign of disobedience and apostasy (Deut. 28 through 30). An Israelite named Elimelech ("My God Is King") in a desperate act moves from Bethlehem ("House of Bread"—note the irony) to Moab. Although he seeks life in that land, he and his two sons Mahlon ("Sick") and Chilion ("Pining") find only death. The deceased sons leave two Moabite widows, Orpah ("Stubbornness") and Ruth ("Friendship"). Elimelech's widow, Naomi, hears that the famine in Israel is over and decides to return, no longer as Naomi ("Pleasant") but as Marah ("Bitter"). She tells her daughters-in-law to remain in Moab and remarry since there was no security for an unmarried woman in those days. Orpah chooses to leave Naomi and is never mentioned again. Ruth, on the other hand, resolves to cling to Naomi and follow God, the God of Israel. She therefore gives up her culture, people, and language because of her love. God's providential care brings her to the field of Boaz, Naomi's kinsman. Boaz ("In Him Is Strength") begins to love, protect, and provide for her.

Ruth's Love Is Rewarded (chs. 3 and 4): Boaz takes no further steps toward marriage, so Naomi follows the accepted customs of the day and requests that Boaz exercise his right as kinsman-redeemer. In 3:10–13, Boaz reveals why he has taken no action: he is older than Ruth (perhaps twenty years her senior), and he is not the nearest kinsman. Nevertheless, God rewards Ruth's devotion by giving her Boaz as a husband and by providing her with a son, Obed, the grandfather of David.

FOCUS	RUTH'S LOVE DEMONSTRATED		RUTH'S LOVE REWARDED	
REFERENCE	1.1————————1.19————		—3.1——————4.1————————4.22	
DIVISION	RUTH'S DECISION TO STAY WITH NAOMI	RUTH'S DEVOTION TO CARE FOR NAOMI	RUTH'S REQUEST FOR REDEMPTION BY BOAZ	RUTH'S REWARD OF REDEMPTION BY BOAZ
TOPIC	RUTH AND NAOMI		RUTH AND BOAZ	
	DEATH OF FAMILY	RUTH CARES FOR NAOMI	BOAZ CARES FOR RUTH	BIRTH OF FAMILY
SETTING	MOAB	FIELDS OF BETHLEHEM	THRESHING FLOOR OF BETHLEHEM	BETHLEHEM

RUTH

OUTLINE OF RUTH

Ruth's love demonstrated	1:1–2:23	c. Ruth gleans for food	2:1–23
a. Ruth stays with Naomi	1:1–18	Ruth's love rewarded	3:1–4:22
b. Naomi and Ruth return to Bethlehem	1:19–22	a. Naomi seeks security for Ruth	3:1–18
		b. Boaz marries Ruth	4:1–22

THE FIRST BOOK OF

SAMUEL

The Book of First Samuel

The books of First and Second Samuel were originally one book in the Hebrew Bible. Through its transmission, the materials have been realigned, notably in the Septuagint (the third century B.C. Greek translation of the Hebrew Old Testament) wherein the earlier, united, presentation is divided into First and Second Kings, resulting in the listing of First and Second Kings of the Hebrew Bible as Third and Fourth Kings—much to our confusion. Today, scholars are agreed in listing these twin works as First and Second Samuel.

The First Book of Samuel continues the historical record from the days of the judges into the early monarchy in Israel, largely by recounting events in the lives of three men: Samuel, Saul, and David. Throughout the story, which is continued in Second Samuel, a consistent theme is maintained. Israel's success and prosperity depend upon their faithfulness to the Lord. The lives of Israel's kings reflect the pattern of the people themselves, swinging from faith to sin and then repentance. Israel's political fortunes go hand-in-hand with their life of faith.

These books do not present a complete and continuous history, but rather a series of events centered around the dominant persons of the time. Throughout the narration an ambiguous position regarding the monarchy is reflected: on the one hand, the Lord alone is King of Israel; on the other, the people want a king like the nations around them. As a result, the king is viewed both as the delegate of the Lord, and as a concession by God to the people. By the ending of the Samuel cycle, however, the place of the Davidic kingship in God's chosen plan is secured.

The Author of First Samuel

The author of First and Second Samuel is not known. The Talmud (Jewish commentary) attributes authorship to Samuel himself, and to the prophets Nathan and Gad. Most scholars today feel that the works are the product of a long period of transmission, combining some very early material from the period with several editorial revisions. At least three main sources of material are considered: written Samuel stories; two sets of stories about Saul and David; and the family lists of David. Without any certain dating, it has been suggested that the early material, the added sections, and final editing might not have been completed before the time of the Babylonian exile (586 B.C.), though some contend for a late seventh-century B.C. date.

The Time of First Samuel

First Samuel covers nearly one hundred years from the birth of Samuel to the death of Saul. During this time the people of Israel are oppressed again and again by the powerful Philistines, who reside along the Mediterranean coast and press inward to Israel's territories. It is in the midst of these wars that Saul and David assert their respective leadership and influence among the people of Israel. In the course of the story of First and Second Samuel, the transition from tribal association to a political empire is shown.

Survey of First Samuel

First Samuel records the crucial transition from the theocracy under the judges to the monarchy under the kings. The book is built around three key men: Samuel (chs. 1 through 7), Saul (chs. 8 through 31), and David (chs. 16 through 31).

Samuel (chs. 1 through 7): Samuel's story begins late in the turbulent time of the judges when Eli is the judge-priest of Israel. The birth of Samuel and his early call by God are found in chapters 1 through 3. Because of his responsiveness to God (3:19), he is confirmed as a prophet (3:20–21) at a time when "there were very few messages from the LORD, and visions from him were quite rare" (3:1).

Corruption at Shiloh by Eli's notoriously wicked sons leads to Israel's

129

defeat in the crucial battle with the Philistines (4:1–11). The Covenant Box (ark of the covenant), God's "throne" among the people, is lost to the Philistines; the priesthood is disrupted by the deaths of Eli and his sons; and the glory of God departs from the tabernacle (Ichabod, "God's glory has left Israel," 4:21). Samuel begins to function as the last of the judges and the first in the order of the prophets (Acts 3:24). His prophetic ministry (7:3–17) leads to a revival in Israel, the return of the Covenant Box, and the defeat of the Philistines. When Samuel is old and his sons prove to be unjust judges, the people wrongly cry out for a king. They want a visible military and judicial ruler so they can be "as other countries" (8:5–20).

Saul (chs. 8 through 15): In their impatient demand for a king, Israel chooses less than God's best. Their motive (8:5) and criteria (9:2) are wrong. Saul begins well (chs. 9 through 11), but his good characteristics soon degenerate. In spite of Samuel's solemn prophetic warning (ch. 12), Saul and the people begin to act wickedly. Saul presumptuously assumes the role of a priest (cf. 2 Chron. 26:18) and offers up sacrifices (ch. 13). He makes a foolish vow (ch. 14) and disobeys God's command to destroy the Amalekites (ch. 15). Samuel's powerful words in 15:22–23 evoke a pathetic response in 15:24–31.

Saul and David (chs. 16 through 31): When God rejects Saul, he commissions Samuel to anoint David as Israel's next king. God's king-elect serves in Saul's court (16:14 through 23:29) and defeats the Philistine Goliath (ch. 17). Jonathan's devotion to David leads him to sacrifice the throne (20:30–31) in acknowledgment of David's divine right to it (ch. 18). David becomes a growing threat to the insanely jealous Saul; but he is protected from Saul's wrath by Jonathan, Michal, and Samuel (ch. 19).

Saul's open rebellion against God is manifested in his refusal to give up what God has said cannot be his. David is protected again by Jonathan from Saul's murderous intent (ch. 20), but Saul becomes more active in his pursuit of David. The future king flees to a Philistine city where he feigns insanity (ch. 21), and flees again to Adullam where a band of men forms around him (ch. 22).

David continues to escape from the hand of Saul, and on two occasions spares Saul's life when he has the opportunity to take it (chs. 24 through 26). David again seeks refuge among the Philistines, but is not allowed to fight on their side against Israel. Saul, afraid of impending battle against the Philistines, foolishly consults a medium at Endor to hear the deceased Samuel's advice (ch. 28). The Lord rebukes Saul and pronounces his doom; he and his sons are killed by the Philistines on Mount Gilboa (ch. 31).

OUTLINE OF FIRST SAMUEL

Samuel as judge of Israel	1:1–7:17	reign	11:1–15:35
Saul becomes king	8:1–10:27	David and Saul	16:1–30:31
The first years of Saul's		The death of Saul and his sons	31:1–13

FOCUS	SAMUEL		SAUL		
REFERENCE	1.1——————4.1————		—8.1——————13.1————15.10————31.13		
DIVISION	FIRST TRANSITION OF LEADERSHIP: ELI—SAMUEL	JUDGESHIP OF SAMUEL	SECOND TRANSITION OF LEADERSHIP: SAMUEL—SAUL	REIGN OF SAUL	THIRD TRANSITION OF LEADERSHIP SAUL—DAVID
TOPIC	DECLINE OF JUDGES		RISE OF KINGS		
	ELI	SAMUEL	SAUL		DAVID
SETTING	CANAAN				

I SAMUEL

THE SECOND BOOK OF

SAMUEL

The Book of Second Samuel

This segment of the originally united Samuel story treats the highlights of David's reign, first over Judah and then over Israel as a whole. It traces David's ascension to the throne, the days of his prosperity and faithfulness, and the period of David's sins and repentance. All the people share in the consequences of David's blessings and curses. The book offers a vivid picture of both internal and external conflict in the young monarchy, and David himself models both devotion to the Lord and the limits and failures of the king before God. A central concern of the book is the affirmation of the dynasty of David as

God's chosen family, as revealed in the prophecy of Nathan (ch. 7), which becomes the foundation of a theme that the future Messiah would come from the royal family of David, which continues through later books in the Bible and on into the New Testament period as well. For more information on the original form of Samuel, see First Samuel.

The Author of Second Samuel

Please refer to comments under First Samuel. Some authors propose that the core of material found in the so-called Narrative of Succession (chs. 9 through 20) represents the hinge around which later data was written, and the historical focal point around which newer materials were expanded. The four-chapter appendix (chs. 21 through 24) offers a reflective interpretation of the impact of the Davidic reign on the history of God's people. The date of final composition remains uncertain.

The Time of Second Samuel

The story of David begins with First Samuel 16 and ends in First Kings 2. Second Samuel records the major events of David's forty-year rule. His reign in Hebron begins in 1011 B.C. and ends in 1004 B.C. (5:5). His thirty-three-year reign over the united Judah and Israel lasts from 1004 B.C. to 971 B.C.

Survey of Second Samuel

Second Samuel continues the account of the life of David at the point where First Samuel concludes. Soon after the death of Saul, the king-elect becomes the king enthroned, first over Judah when he reigns in Hebron for seven-and-a-half years and finally over all Israel when he reigns in Jerusalem for thirty-three years. This book reviews the key events in the forty-year reign of the man who is the halfway point between Abraham and Christ. It can be surveyed in the three divisions: the triumphs of David (chs. 1 through 10), the transgressions of David (ch. 11), and the troubles of David (chs. 12 through 24).

The Triumphs of David (chs. 1 through 10): Chapters 1 through 4 record the seven-year reign of David over the territory of Judah. Even though Saul is David's murderous pursuer, David does not rejoice in his death because he recognizes that Saul has been divinely anointed as king.

Saul's son Ishbosheth is installed by Abner as a puppet king over the northern tribes of Israel. David's allies led by Joab defeat Abner and Israel (2:17; 3:1). Abner defects and arranges to unite Israel and Judah under David, but Joab kills Abner in revenge. The powerless Ishbosheth is murdered by his own men, and David is made king of Israel (5:3). David soon captures and fortifies Jerusalem and makes it the civil and religious center of the now united kingdom. Under David's rule the nation prospers politically, spiritually, and militarily. David brings the Covenant Box (ark of the covenant) to Jerusalem and seeks to build a house for God (ch. 7). His obedience in placing the Lord at the center of his rule leads to great national blessing (chs. 8 through 10). "The LORD made David victorious everywhere" (8:14).

The Transgressions of David (ch. 11): David's crimes of adultery and murder mark the pivotal point of the book. Because of these transgressions, David's victories and successes are changed to the personal, family, and national troubles which are recorded throughout the rest of Second Samuel.

The Troubles of David (chs. 12 through 24): The disobedience of the king produces chastisement and confusion at every level. David's glory and fame fade, never to be the same again. Nevertheless, David confesses his guilt when confronted by Nathan the prophet and is restored by God. A sword remains in David's house as a consequence of the sin: the baby born to David and Bathsheba dies, his son Amnon commits incest, and his son Absalom murders Amnon.

The consequences continue with Absalom's rebellion against his father. He shrewdly steals the hearts of the men of Israel (15:6). David is forced to flee from Jerusalem, and Absalom sets himself up as king. David would have been ruined, but God keeps Absalom from pursuing him until David has time to regroup his forces. Absalom's army is defeated by David's, and Joab kills Absalom in disobedience of David's orders to have him spared.

David seeks to amalgamate the kingdom, but conflict breaks out between the ten northern tribes of Israel and the two southern tribes of Judah and Benjamin. Israel decides to follow a man named Sheba in a revolt against David, but Judah remains faithful to him. This leads to war, and Joab defeats the rebels.

The closing chapters are actually an appendix to the book because they summarize David's words and deeds. They show how intimately the affairs of the people as a whole are tied to the spiritual and moral condition of the king. The nation enjoys God's blessing when David is obedient to the Lord, and suffers hardship when David disobeys God.

OUTLINE OF SECOND SAMUEL

David's triumphs	1:1–10:19	umphs of David	8:1–10:19
a. David's reign		David's transgression	11:1–27
over Judah	1:1–4:12	David's troubles	12:1–24:25
b. David's reign in		a. Troubles in Da-	
Jerusalem	5:1–25	vid's house	12:1–13:36
c. The spiritual tri-		b. Troubles in Da-	
umphs of David	6:1–7:29	vid's kingdom	13:37–20:26
d. The military tri-		c. The later years	21:1–24:25

FOCUS	DAVID'S TRIUMPHS			DAVID'S TRANSGRESSIONS	DAVID'S TROUBLES	
REFERENCE	1.1————6.1————8.1————			11.1————————	12.1————13.37————24.25	
DIVISION	POLITICAL TRIUMPHS	SPIRITUAL TRIUMPHS	MILITARY TRIUMPHS	SINS OF ADULTERY AND MURDER	TROUBLES IN DAVID'S HOUSE	TROUBLES IN THE KINGDOM
TOPIC	SUCCESS			SIN	FAILURE	
	OBEDIENCE			DISOBEDIENCE	JUDGMENT	
SETTING	DAVID IN HEBRON	DAVID IN JERUSALEM				

II SAMUEL

THE FIRST BOOK OF

KINGS

The Book of First Kings

Like the two books of Samuel, the two books of Kings were originally one in the Hebrew Bible, and only later divided into units in the Septuagint (ancient Greek translation of the Hebrew Bible). Nevertheless, the unity of material remains not only for First and Second Kings, but also through the whole historical corpus of Joshua through Kings. The Book of First Kings traces the life of Solomon from his ascent to the throne, during his powerful reign and the building of the Temple, and until the division of the kingdom among his successors. In general, the two books of Kings portray the kings of the north (Israel) as unfaithful, while the southern kings (in Judah) are somewhat more faithful to the Lord. In the end, both kingdoms are doomed to defeat and collapse because of their sins.

First and Second Kings are not a modern-styled history book, but rather a religious history; theological purpose determined the selection of material and the interpretation of events. Kings are measured upon faithfulness to the covenant, and the nation's success depends upon the people's loyalty to the Lord. The books also include cycles of early prophetic literature in the persons of Elijah (First Kings) and Elisha (Second Kings).

The Author of First Kings

The author of First and Second Kings is unknown, and although the Talmud (Jewish commentary) attributes these works to Jeremiah, most modern scholars would not be content with a single author theory. Scholars debate what sources have been drawn upon for the two-volume story of Kings. Various materials, including some from the sources explicitly cited in the Kings (The History of Solomon, 11:41; The History of the Kings of Israel, 14:19; and The History of the Kings of Judah, 14:29), evidently have been assembled into the kingly narratives in an early edition to be dated either shortly before the Exile (621–597 B.C.) or during the first stages of the Exile, and a second revised edition completed during the Exile, either at Babylon or in Palestine itself (562–539 B.C.).

More important for our understanding is the point of view of history reflected in the narrative, and the principal purpose for which it was written: First and Second Kings were written to explain to a devastated people why their nation had collapsed (because of their disobedience to the Lord and the covenant worship of the Lord alone) and to offer encouragement that God's promise of Davidic rule would once again be realized in the future. The books of Kings do share with the other books in the historical section of the Old Testament a common theme of interpreting events in light of the covenant and the people's response in faith.

The Time of First Kings

The Book of First Kings deals with the reign of Solomon primarily, and covers a period of about 120 years from the beginning of his reign in 971 B.C. through Ahaziah's reign ending in 851 B.C. The key date is 931 B.C., the year in which the kingdom was divided into the northern nation of Israel and the southern nation of Judah. It is somewhat arbitrarily separated from the continued narrative of Second Kings at the point of Ahaziah's rule.

Survey of First Kings

The first half of First Kings concerns the life of one of the most amazing men who ever lived. He brings Israel to the peak of its size and glory, and yet, the kingdom is disrupted soon after his death, torn in two by civil strife. This book divides clearly into two sections: the united kingdom (chs. 1 through 11) and the divided kingdom (chs. 12 through 22).

United Kingdom (chs. 1 through 11): These chapters given an account of Solomon's attainment of the throne, wisdom, architectural achievements, fame, wealth, and tragic unfaithfulness. Solomon's half-brother Adonijah attempts to take the throne as David's death is nearing, but Nathan the prophet alerts David who quickly directs the coronation of Solomon as coregent (ch. 1). Solomon still has to consolidate his power and deal with those who oppose his rule. Only when this is done is the kingdom in his complete control (2:46). Solomon's ungodly marriages (cf. 3:1) eventually turn his heart from the Lord, but he begins well with a genuine love for God and a desire for wisdom. This wisdom leads to the expansion of Israel to the zenith of her power. Solomon's empire stretches from the border of Egypt to the border of Babylonia, and peace prevails.

From a divine perspective, Solomon's greatest achievement is the building of the Temple. The Covenant Box (ark of the covenant) is placed in this exquisite building, which is filled with the Lord's presence. Solomon offers a magnificent prayer of dedication and binds the people with an oath to remain faithful to God.

Because the Lord is with him Solomon continues to grow in fame, power, and wealth. However, his wealth later becomes a source of trouble when he begins to purchase forbidden items. He acquires many foreign wives who lead him into idolatry. It is an irony of history that this wisest of men acts as a fool in his old age. God pronounces judgment and foretells that Solomon's son will rule only a fraction of the kingdom (Judah).

Divided Kingdom (chs. 12 through 22): Upon Solomon's death, God's words come to pass. Solomon's son Rehoboam chooses the foolish course of promising more severe taxation. Jeroboam, an officer in Solomon's army, leads the ten northern tribes in revolt. They make him their king, leaving only Judah and Benjamin in the south under Rehoboam. This is the beginning of a chaotic period with two nations and two sets of kings. Continual enmity and strife exists between the northern and southern kingdoms. The north is plagued by apostasy (Jeroboam sets up a false system of worship) and the south by idolatry. Of all the northern and southern kings listed in this book, only Asa (15:9–24) and Jehoshaphat (22:41–50) do what is pleasing and right in the eyes of the Lord (15:11; 22:43). All of the others are idolaters, usurpers, and murderers.

Ahab brings a measure of cooperation between the northern and southern kingdoms, but he reaches new depths of wickedness as a king. He is the man who introduces Jezebel's Baal worship to Israel. The prophet Elijah ministers during this low period in Israel's history, providing a ray of light and witness of the word and power of God. But Ahab's encounter with Elijah never brings him to turn from his false gods to God. Ahab's treachery in the matter of Naboth's vineyard causes a prophetic rebuke from Elijah (ch. 21). Ahab repents (21:27–29) but later dies in battle because of his refusal to heed the words of Micaiah, another prophet of God.

OUTLINE OF FIRST KINGS

The end of David's reign	1:1–2:12	northern tribes	12:1–14:20
Solomon becomes king	2:13–46	b. The kings of Judah and of Israel	14:21–16:34
Solomon's reign	3:1–11:43	c. The prophet Elijah	17:1–19:21
a. The early years	3:1–4:34		
b. The Temple is built	5:1–8:66	d. King Ahab of Israel	20:1–22:40
c. The later years	9:1–11:43	e. Jehoshaphat of Judah and Ahaziah of Israel	22:41–53
The divided kingdom	12:1–22:53		
a. The revolt of the			

FOCUS	UNITED KINGDOM			DIVIDED KINGDOM		
REFERENCE	1.1———3.1———		9.1———12.1———	14.21———17.1———22.53		
DIVISION	ESTABLISHMENT OF SOLOMON	RISE OF SOLOMON	DECLINE OF SOLOMON	DIVISION OF THE KINGDOM	REIGNS OF VARIOUS KINGS	REIGN OF AHAB WITH ELIJAH
TOPIC	SOLOMON			MANY KINGS		
	KINGDOM IN TRANQUILLITY			KINGDOMS IN TURMOIL		
SETTING	JERUSALEM: CAPITAL OF UNITED KINGDOM			SAMARIA: CAPITAL OF ISRAEL JERUSALEM: CAPITAL OF JUDAH		

I KINGS

137

THE SECOND BOOK OF

KINGS

The Book of Second Kings

The Book of Second Kings continues the drama begun in First Kings—the tragic history of two nations on a collision course with captivity. The author systematically traces the reigning kings of Israel and Judah, first by carrying one nation's history forward, then retracing the same period for the other nation.

Nineteen consecutive ungodly kings rule in Israel, leading to the captivity by Assyria. The picture is somewhat brighter in Judah, where godly kings occasionally emerge to reform the evils of their predecessors. In the end, however, sin outweighs righteousness and Judah is marched off to Babylon. See "The Book of First Kings" for more detail concerning the title.

The Author of Second Kings

For a discussion of the question of authorship and sources of composition, please see parallel section under First Kings. While the case for a single author-editor of the Joshua through Second Kings cycle remains seriously challenged today, few scholars contest the unity of authorship of First and Second Kings themselves. Some have seen a literary relationship in style and, at times, content between Kings and the Book of Jeremiah, but few would identify a common author for both of them.

The Time of Second Kings

This work may be divided into two main sections: (1) a record of the two kingdoms and their rulers, from Ahaziah to the collapse of the north in 721 B.C., with the fall of Samaria; and (2) the story of Judah from 721 B.C., until its collapse in 586 B.C., with the Exile of the Jews to Babylon. The last recorded event in Second Kings is the release of Jehoiachin (25:27–30) which takes place in 560 B.C. Chapters 1 through 17 describe events from about 853–721 B.C., where chapters 18 through 25 continue the story until the release of Jehoiachin. In sum, the united kingdom lasted roughly 1043–931 B.C., the northern kingdom of Israel for another 210 years, and the southern kingdom of Judah a total of 336 years. During this long period of history, great shifts in world power among Egypt, Assyria, and Babylon dominate the Palestinian world. At its close, Israel's glory age of political independence and religious autonomy has ended. It is also during this period of Israel's history that the prophetic movement develops in both north and south, as time and again the kings are warned and invited to repentance by God's messengers. The books of Kings make known to their readers the consequences of the people's unfaithfulness: ruin, exile, and the end of the Temple. Yet, even the very fulfillment of the prophets' dreadful warnings provides confidence in God's mastery of human history, and allows the people in exile to trust anew in God's promise of restoration.

Survey of Second Kings

Without interruption Second Kings continues the narrative of First Kings. The twin kingdoms of Israel and Judah pursue a collision course with captivity as the glory of the once united kingdom becomes increasingly diminished. Division has led to decline and now ends in double deportation with Israel captured by Assyria and Judah by Babylon. This book traces the history of the divided kingdom in chapters 1 through 17 and the history of the surviving kingdom in chapters 18 through 25.

Divided Kingdom (chs. 1 through 17): These chapters record the story of Israel's corruption in a relentless succession of bad kings from Ahaziah to Hoshea. The situation in Judah during this time (Jehoram to Ahaz) is somewhat better, but far from ideal. This dark period in the northern kingdom of Israel is interrupted only by the ministries of such godly prophets as Elijah and Elisha. At the end of Elijah's miraculous ministry, Elisha is installed and authenticated as his successor. He is a force for righteousness in a nation that never served the true God or worshiped at the Temple in Jerusalem. Elisha's ministry is characterized by miraculous provisions of sustenance and life. Through him God demonstrates his gracious care for the nation and his concern for any person who desires to come to him. However, like his forerunner Elijah, Elisha is basically rejected by Israel's leadership.

Elisha instructs one of his prophetic assistants to anoint Jehu king over Israel. Jehu fulfills the prophecies concerning Ahab's descendants by putting them to death. He kills Ahab's wife Jezebel, his sons, and also the priests of Baal. But he does not depart from the calf worship originally set up by Jeroboam. The loss of the house of Ahab means the alienation of Israel and Judah and the weakening of both. Israel's enemies begin to get the upper hand. Meanwhile, in Judah, Jezebel's daughter Athaliah kills all the descendants of David, except for Joash, and usurps the throne. However, Jehoiada the priest eventually removes her from the throne and places Joash in power. Joash restores the Temple and serves God.

Syria gains virtual control over Israel, but there is no response to God's chastisement: the kings and people refuse to repent. Nevertheless, there is a period of restoration under Jeroboam II, but the continuing series of ungodly kings in Israel leads to its overthrow by Assyria.

Surviving Kingdom (chs. 18 through 25): Of Israel's nineteen kings, not one is righteous in God's sight. All but one of its nine dynasties are created by murdering the previous king. In Judah, where there is only one dynasty, eight of its twenty rulers do what is right before God. Nevertheless, Judah's collapse finally comes, resulting in the Babylonian Exile. Chapters 18 through 25 read more easily than chapters 1 through 17 because alternating the histories of the northern and southern kingdoms is no longer necessary. Only Judah remains.

Six years before the overthrow of Israel's capital of Samaria, Hezekiah becomes king of Judah. Because of his exemplary faith and reforms, God spares Jerusalem from Assyria and brings a measure of prosperity to Judah. However, Hezekiah's son Manasseh is so idolatrous that his long reign leads to the downfall of Judah. Even Josiah's later reforms cannot stem the tide of evil, and the four kings who succeed him are exceedingly wicked. Judgment comes with three deportations to Babylon. The third occurs in 586 B.C. when Nebuchadnezzar destroys Jerusalem and the Temple. Still, the book ends on a note of hope with God preserving a remnant for himself.

FOCUS	DIVIDED KINGDOM			SURVIVING KINGDOM		
REFERENCE	1.1————8.15———————17.1—			18.1————22.1—————25.1—25.30		
DIVISION	MINISTRY OF ELISHA UNDER AHAZIAH AND JEHORAM	REIGNS OF TEN KINGS OF ISRAEL AND EIGHT KINGS OF JUDAH	FALL OF ISRAEL	REIGNS OF HEZEKIAH AND TWO EVIL KINGS	REIGNS OF JOSIAH AND FOUR EVIL KINGS	FALL OF JUDAH
TOPIC	ISRAEL AND JUDAH			JUDAH		
	AHAZIAH TO HOSHEA			HEZEKIAH TO ZEDEKIAH		
SETTING	ISRAEL DEPORTED TO ASSYRIA			JUDAH DEPORTED TO BABYLONIA		

II KINGS

OUTLINE OF SECOND KINGS

The divided kingdom	1:1–17:41	dom	18:1–25:30
a. The prophet Elisha	1:1–8:15	a. From Hezekiah to Josiah	18:1–21:26
b. The kings of Judah and of Israel	8:16–17:4	b. Josiah's reign	22:1–23:30
c. The fall of Samaria	17:5–41	c. The last kings of Judah	23:31–24:20
The surviving king-		d. The fall of Jerusalem	25:1–30

THE FIRST BOOK OF

CHRONICLES

The Book of First Chronicles

The books of First and Second Chronicles form part of a four-fold unity with the books of Ezra and Nehemiah, and are listed as the final canonical works of the Hebrew Bible. While the Chronicles cover the same period of Jewish history described in Second Samuel through Second Kings, they are presented in a different perspective. The books are not simply a repetition of the same material, but rather a theological reinterpretation of that material in connection with the people's lives after the Exile. Their theological aim is to affirm the priority of the Davidic dynasty in God's plan for Israel and to reassert the centrality of Temple worship in the postexile period. Thus a priestly and spiritual perspective dominates the books. As was true of Samuel and Kings, First and Second Chronicles, in their original form, were likely a single work by a common author. While many nineteenth-century scholars presented a harsh judgment on the historical record of the books, modern scholars treat with keener appreciation the specifically theological history so well developed by the four-volume work of the so-called Chronicler.

The Author of First Chronicles

Although the text does not identify the author, the Talmud (Jewish commentary) has attributed the work to Ezra, the priest who was responsible for the religious aspects of Israel's restoration after the Exile. Modern scholars argue in favor of a single author, called the Chronicler, as responsible for all four books in the series (including Ezra and Nehemiah), and suggest he may have been a Levite cantor at the Temple. The date of the composition has been debated, with some agreement on a postexilic date of 400 B.C., although others offer dates ranging from 550 B.C. to as late as 200 B.C. The author of the series drew from many varied sources and incorporated his own theological perspective in his narratives of the Davidic family and the Temple ceremonies in particular. Additional comments on the use of sources may be found under "The Author of Second Chronicles."

The Time of First Chronicles

The genealogies in chapters 1 through 9 cover the time from Adam to David, and chapters 10 through 29 focus on the thirty-three years of David's rule over the united kingdoms of Israel and Judah (1004–971 B.C.). However, the genealogies extend to about 500 B.C., as seen in the mention of Zerubbabel, grandson of King Jeconiah, who leads the first return of the Jews from exile in 538 B.C., and also Zerubbabel's two grandsons Pelatiah and Jeshaiah (3:21).

Chronicles spends considerable time on the reigns of David and Solomon because they bring the nation to its pinnacle. The book is written to the people of Israel's "Second Commonwealth" to encourage them and to remind them that they must remain the covenant people of God. This reminds the Jews of their spiritual heritage and identity during the difficult times they are facing.

Survey of First Chronicles

Chronicles retraces the whole story of Israel's history up to the return from captivity in order to give the returned remnant a divine perspective on the developments of their past. The whole Book of First Chronicles, like Second Samuel, is dedicated to the life of David. It begins with the royal line of David (chs. 1 through 9) before surveying key events of the reign of David (chs. 10 through 29).

Royal Line of David (chs. 1 through 9): These nine chapters are the most comprehensive genealogical tables in the Bible. They trace the family tree of David and Israel as a whole, but in a highly selective manner. The genealogies place considerable emphasis on the tribes of Judah and Benjamin because Chronicles is not concerned with the northern kingdom but with the southern kingdom and the Davidic dynasty. They show God at work in selecting and preserving a people for himself from the beginning of human history to the period after the Babylonian Exile. The genealogies move from the patriarchal period (Adam to Jacob; 1:1 through 2:2) to the national period (Judah, Levi, and the other tribes of Israel; 2:3 through 9:44). They demonstrate God's keeping of his covenant promises in maintaining the Davidic line through the centuries. The priestly perspective of Chronicles is evident in the special attention given to the tribe of Levi.

Reign of David (chs. 10 through 29): Compared with Second Samuel, David's life in First Chronicles is seen in an entirely different light. This is clear from both the omissions and the additions. Chronicles completely omits David's struggles with Saul, his seven-year reign in Hebron, his various wives, and Absalom's rebellion. It also omits the event in Second Samuel that hurt the rest of his life—his sin with Bathsheba. Chronicles is written from a more positive perspective, emphasizing God's grace and forgiveness, in order to encourage the Jews who have just returned from captivity. Chronicles adds events not found in Second Samuel, such as David's preparations for the Temple and its worship services.

Only one chapter is given to Saul's reign (ch. 10), because his heart was not right with God. David's story begins with his coronation over all Israel after he has already reigned for seven years as king over Judah. Chronicles stresses his deep spiritual commitment, courage, and integrity. It emphasizes his concern for the things of the Lord, including his return of the Covenant Box (ark of the covenant) and his desire to build a Temple for God. God establishes his crucial covenant with David (ch. 17), and the kingdom is strengthened and expanded under his reign (chs. 18 through 20). His sin in numbering the people is recorded to teach the consequences of disobeying God's law. The rest of the book (chs. 22 through 29) is primarily concerned with David's preparations for the building of the Temple and the worship associated with it. The priestly perspective of Chronicles can be seen in the considerable space given to the Temple and the priests. David is not allowed to build the Temple (28:3), but he designs the plans, gathers the materials, prepares the site, and arranges for the Levites, priests, choirs, porters, soldiers, and stewards. The book closes with his beautiful public prayer of praise and the accession of Solomon.

OUTLINE OF FIRST CHRONICLES

Genealogies and lists	1:1–9:44	b. Troubles and	
The death of Saul	10:1–14	achievements	13:1–22:1
The reign of David	11:1–29:30	c. Preparations for	
a. David becomes		building the	
king	11:1–12:40	Temple	22:2–29:30

FOCUS	ROYAL LINE OF DAVID	REIGN OF DAVID				
REFERENCE	1.1————————10.1—————	13.1—————	18.1—————	22.1—————	28.1———	29.30
DIVISION	GENEALOGIES OF DAVID AND ISRAEL	ACCESSION OF DAVID AS KING	ACQUISITION OF THE ARK	VICTORIES OF DAVID	PREPARATION FOR THE TEMPLE	LAST DAYS OF DAVID
TOPIC	GENEALOGY	HISTORY				
	ANCESTRY	ACTIVITY				
SETTING	ISRAEL					

I CHRONICLES

THE SECOND BOOK OF

CHRONICLES

The Book of Second Chronicles

The book parallels the history of First and Second Kings, but virtually ignores the northern kingdom of Israel, apparently because of its abandonment of worship at the Jerusalem Temple. The Chronicler focuses on the kings of Judah who pattern their lives and rules after the model of David, thus offering extensive treatment of reformers like Asa, Joash, Hezekiah, and Josiah.

The Temple and Temple worship are central throughout the book. The author is concerned to demonstrate that the fortunes of the people depend upon their faithful worship of God alone. The book begins with Solomon's Temple and concludes with Cyrus' decree to rebuild the Temple more than four hundred years later. As mentioned in the consideration of First Chronicles, this work should be viewed as a segment of a continuous religious history, running through Ezra and Nehemiah.

The Author of Second Chronicles

For comments about the Chronicler himself, please refer to "The Author of First Chronicles." One major concern of modern scholarship focuses upon the question of sources for this writer's work. The influences of First and Second Samuel, First and Second Kings, and dependence upon the Pentateuch (first five books of the Old Testament) are acknowledged by most scholars today. Chronicles also reflects the influence of prophetic teachings, suggesting that the prophetic books were completed in some form by the time of the Chronicler's work. This author, however, has composed a history which reaches beyond a mere reediting of materials, and represents a genuine literary work in itself. This work includes a reworking of themes and theological meaning, the addition of elements not found in the earlier books, and still a fidelity to the authority of those books as part of Scripture, even before a fixed collection (canon) of sacred writings had been established.

The Time of Second Chronicles

Please refer to "The Time of First Chronicles" for the background of both these works. Chapters 1 through 9 of the second book cover the forty years from 971 through 931 B.C., and chapters 10 through 36 cover the period from 931 through 538 B.C. The closing verses of Second Chronicles (36:22–23) are repeated with minor changes as the opening verses of Ezra (1:1–3), to suggest the continuation of the story of return from exile and the restoration of Israel under the leadership of Ezra and Nehemiah.

Survey of Second Chronicles

This book repeatedly teaches that whenever God's people forsake him, he withdraws his blessings, but trust in and obedience to the Lord bring victory. Since everything in Chronicles is related to the Temple, it is not surprising that this concludes with Cyrus' edict to rebuild it. Solomon's glory is seen in chapters 1 through 9, and Judah's decline and deportation in chapters 10 through 36.

Solomon's Reign (chs. 1 through 9): The reign of Solomon brings in Israel's golden age of peace, prosperity, and Temple worship. The kingdom is united and its boundaries extend to their greatest point. Solomon's wealth, wisdom, palace, and Temple become legendary.

His mighty spiritual, political, and architectural feats raise Israel to her zenith. However, it is in keeping with the purpose of Chronicles that six of these nine chapters concern the construction and dedication of the Temple.

The Reign of Judah's Kings (chs. 10 through 36): Unfortunately, Israel's glory is short-lived. Soon after Solomon's death the nation is divided, and both kingdoms begin a downward spiral that can only be delayed by the religious reforms. The nation generally forsakes the Temple and the worship of God, and is soon torn by warfare and unrest. The reformation efforts on the part of some of Judah's kings are valiant, but never last beyond one generation. Nevertheless, about seventy percent of chapters 10 through 36 deals with the eight good kings, leaving only thirty percent to cover the twelve ungodly rulers. Each king is seen with respect to his relationship to the Temple as the center of worship and spiritual strength. When the king serves God, Judah is blessed with political and economic prosperity. Second Chronicles nevertheless ends on a note of hope at the end of the captivity, when Cyrus issues the decree for the restoration of Judah: "Now, all of you who are God's people, go there, and may the LORD your God be with you" (36:23).

OUTLINE OF SECOND CHRONICLES

The reign of Solomon	1:1–9:31	The revolt of the northern tribes	10:1–19
a. The early years	1:1–17	The kings of Judah	11:1–36:12
b. The Temple is built	2:1–7:10	The fall of Jerusalem	36:13–23
c. The later years	7:11–9:31		

FOCUS	REIGN OF SOLOMON			REIGNS OF THE KINGS OF JUDAH		
REFERENCE	1.1————2.1————8.1————			10.1————14.1————		36.1———36.23
DIVISION	INAUGURATION OF SOLOMON	COMPLETION OF THE TEMPLE	THE GLORY OF SOLOMON'S REIGN	THE DIVISION OF THE KINGDOM	THE REFORMS UNDER ASA, JEHOSHAPHAT, JOASH, HEZEKIAH, AND JOSIAH	THE FALL OF JUDAH
TOPIC	THE TEMPLE IS CONSTRUCTED			THE TEMPLE IS DESTROYED		
	SPLENDOR			DISASTER		
SETTING	JUDAH					

2 CHRONICLES

THE BOOK OF
EZRA

The Book of Ezra

Ezra continues the Old Testament narrative of First and Second Chronicles by showing how God fulfills his promise to return his people to the land after their exile in Babylon. The book relates the story of the first return to Jerusalem under Zerubbabel (chs. 1 and 2), the rebuilding of the Temple (chs. 3 through 6), and the second group's return under the leadership of Ezra to renew the spiritual life and worship of the people there.

Ezra is an expert in the Law and is known in the Talmud (Jewish commentary) as a second Moses, so devoted is he to the Torah (first five books of the Old Testament) given to Moses in the traditional history. He is responsible for the religious renewal of the people in Jerusalem.

The books of Ezra and Nehemiah were originally bound together as part of the larger historical record, compiled by the Chronicler, and are included in the Septuagint (Greek translation of the Hebrew Old Testament 250 B.C.) with the title Second Esdras. In the Hebrew Bible, Ezra and Nehemiah are listed prior to First and Second Chronicles.

The Author of Ezra

Although Ezra is not specifically mentioned as the author, the Talmud (Jewish commentary) attributes the book to Ezra himself. Modern scholars acknowledge the possibility that portions of the work written in the first person may in fact be the Chronicler's use of a work called the Memoirs of Ezra (note a similar case for the Memoirs of Nehemiah). Some scholars argue that Ezra is responsible for the final editing of the Pentateuch (first five books of the Old Testament), while the Chronicler wrote his own record of Israel's history to balance the point of view given in the Pentateuch, with a greater stress upon the Davidic covenant and Temple worship. It is clear, however, that Ezra's and Nehemiah's religious perspective and devotion to the Law exerted a profound influence on the people of Israel in the postexilic age.

The Time of Ezra

The books of Ezra and Nehemiah address a new period of Israel's history, the time of restoration after the Babylonian exile. Under the authority of Cyrus, the Persian king who defeated the Babylonians in 539 B.C., the Jews are granted permission to return to Jerusalem and to rebuild the Temple. The first wave of returning exiles, under the leadership of Zerubbabel, begin the Temple in 536 B.C., but progress is slow. The prophets, Haggai and Zechariah, encourage the Temple's completion, which is accomplished by around 515 B.C. The people, however, are still in need of spiritual reformation. A second wave of returnees, under the leadership of Ezra, about 457 B.C., during the rule of Persian Emperor Artaxerxes I (464–423 B.C.), fosters the reform of Temple worship and a rededication of the people to the Lord. Further remarks on the dating of the returns to Jerusalem by Ezra and Nehemiah may be found in the sections "The Author of Nehemiah" and "The Time of Nehemiah."

Survey of Ezra

Ezra continues the story exactly where Second Chronicles ends and shows how God's promise to bring his people back to their land is fulfilled (Jer. 29:10–14). God is with these people, and although their days of glory seem over, their spiritual heritage still remains and God's rich promises will be fulfilled. Ezra relates the story of the first two returns from Babylon, the first led by Zerubbabel and the second led decades later by Ezra. Its two divisions are the restoration of the Temple (chs. 1 through 6) and the reformation of the people (chs. 7 through 10), and they are separated by a fifty-eight-year gap during which the story of Esther takes place.

The Restoration of the Temple (chs. 1 through 6): King Cyrus of Persia overthrows Babylon in 539 B.C. and issues a decree in 538 B.C. that allows the exiled Jews to return to their homeland. Isaiah prophesied two centuries before that the Temple would be rebuilt and actually named Cyrus as the one who would bring it about (Isa. 44:28 through 45:4). Cyrus may have read and responded to this passage.

Zerubbabel, a "prince" of Judah (a direct descendant of King David), leads the faithful remnant back to Jerusalem. Those who return are from the tribes of Judah, Benjamin, and Levi; but it is evident that representatives from the other tribes eventually return as well. The ten "lost tribes" are not entirely lost.

Zerubbabel's priorities are in the right place; he first restores the altar and the religious feasts before beginning work on the Temple itself. The foundation of the Temple is laid in 536 B.C., but opposition arises and the work ceases from 534 to 520 B.C. While Ezra 4:1–5 and 24 concerns Zerubbabel, 4:6–23 concerns opposition to the building of the wall of Jerusalem some time between 464 and 444 B.C. These verses may have been placed here to illustrate the antagonism to the work of rebuilding. The prophets Haggai and Zechariah exhort the people to get back to building the Temple (5:1–2), and the work begins again under Zerubbabel and Joshua the High Priest. Tattenai, a Persian governor, protests to Emperor Darius about the Temple building and challenges their authority to continue. Darius finds the decree of Cyrus and confirms it, even forcing Tattenai to provide whatever is needed to complete the work. It is finished in 515 B.C.

The Reformation of the People (chs. 7 through 10): A smaller return under Ezra takes place in 457 B.C., eighty-one years after the first return under Zerubbabel. Ezra the priest is given authority by Emperor Artaxerxes I to bring people and contributions for the Temple in Jerusalem. God protects this band of less than two thousand men and they safely reach Jerusalem with their valuable gifts from Persia. Many priests but few Levites return with Zerubbabel and Ezra (2:36–42; 8:15–19). God uses Ezra to rebuild the people spiritually and morally. When Ezra discovers that the people and the priests have intermarried with foreign women, he identifies with the sin of his people and offers a great intercessory prayer on their behalf. During the gap of fifty-eight years between Ezra 6 and 7, the people fall into a confused spiritual state and Ezra is alarmed. They quickly respond to Ezra's confession and weeping by making a solemn promise to put away their foreign wives and to live in accordance with God's law. This confession and response to the Word of God brings about a great revival and changes lives.

FOCUS	STORY OF JUDAH FROM JOSIAH TO READING OF LAW BY EZRA					
REFERENCE	1.1———2.1———3.1———5.7———6.1———8.1———9.55					
DIVISION	LAST KINGS OF JUDAH	RESPONSES TO CYRUS' DECREE	STORY ABOUT ZERUBBABEL	RETURN FROM CAPTIVITY	RECONSTRUCTION OF TEMPLE	STORY OF EZRA
TOPIC	RETURN FROM EXILE			RECONSTRUCTION		
SETTING	BABYLON AND PALESTINE					

1 ESDRAS

149

OUTLINE OF EZRA

The first return from exile	1:1–2:70	and dedicated Ezra returns with other	3:1–6:22
The Temple is rebuilt		exiles	7:1–10:44

THE BOOK OF
NEHEMIAH

The Book of Nehemiah

This book offers the second part of the story of Israel after the Exile. Although Ezra and Nehemiah were considered one continuous book in the Hebrew Bible, they now stand as independent books in the canon of Scripture. The book is named after its chief character, Nehemiah, whose name is cited in the opening lines of the work. The main topic of the book is the story of Nehemiah's efforts to rebuild the walls of Jerusalem, and the subsequent events of his administration of the people's welfare. The task of reviving and reforming the people within the new city walls demands years of Nehemiah's devotion and leadership. The book includes four main sections: Nehemiah's return to Jerusalem, the rebuilding of the wall of the city, the reading of the Law by Ezra, and the rule of Nehemiah as governor of Judah.

Please refer to "The Book of Ezra" for details about the place of this work along with "The Book of Nehemiah" in the Greek and Hebrew Bibles.

The Author of Nehemiah

Much of this book can reasonably be traced to the personal memoirs of Nehemiah, which may have served as a primary source for the Chronicler as he compiled his four-part history. Some have argued that Ezra was the one who combined his own work in chapters 7 through 13 of the Book of Nehemiah, with some diary of the man Nehemiah. A fairer assessment of the data leads to the conclusion that a number of sources including the memoirs of both Ezra and Nehemiah may have provided the materials for the Chronicler for these twin books.

Nehemiah himself served as wine steward to the king, and later as the governor of Judah (444–432 B.C.). Nehemiah 13:6 recounts Nehemiah's return to Persia and a second trip to Jerusalem between 432 and 425 B.C. It is clear that Nehemiah accomplishes for the political community what Ezra achieves for the religious spirit of Israel: a restored order and a sense of unity among the people under their Lord.

The Time of Nehemiah

See "The Time of Ezra," because both Ezra and Nehemiah share the same historical background. The Book of Nehemiah fits within the reign of Artaxerxes I of Persia (464–423 B.C.). Esther is Artaxerxes' stepmother, and it is possible that she is instrumental in Nehemiah's appointment as the emperor's wine steward. Nehemiah leaves Persia in the twentieth year of Artaxerxes (2:1), returns to Persia in the thirty-second year of Artaxerxes (13:6), and leaves again for Jerusalem "after some time" (13:6), perhaps about 425 B.C. This book could not have been completed until after his second visit to Jerusalem.

The historical reliability of this book is supported by the Elephantine papyri. These ancient documents mention Sanballat (2:19) and Jehohanan (6:18) and indicate that Bigvai replaces Nehemiah as governor of Judah by 410 B.C.

Survey of Nehemiah

Nehemiah is closely associated with the ministry of his contemporary, Ezra. Ezra is a priest who brings spiritual revival; Nehemiah is a governor who brings physical and political reconstruction and leads the people in moral reform. They combine to make an effective team in rebuilding the postexilic remnant. Malachi, the last Old Testament prophet, also ministers during this time to provide additional moral and spiritual direction. Its two divisions are: the reconstruction of the wall (chs. 1 through 7), and the restoration of the people (chs. 8 through 13).

The Reconstruction of the Wall (chs. 1 through 7): Nehemiah's great concern for his people and the welfare of Jerusalem leads him to take bold action. The walls of Jerusalem, destroyed by Nebuchadnezzar in 586 B.C., were nearly complete when Artaxerxes I took the throne of Persia (see Ezra 4:6–23). When he hears that opposition led to their second destruction, Nehemiah prays on behalf of his people and then secures Artaxerxes' permission, provision, and protection for the massive project of rebuilding the walls.

Nehemiah inspects the walls and challenges the people to "rebuild the city walls" (2:17). Work begins immediately on the wall and its gates, with people building portions corresponding to where they are living.

However, opposition quickly arises, first in the form of mockery, then in the form of conspiracy when the work is progressing at an alarming rate. Nehemiah overcomes threats of force by setting half of the people on military watch and half on construction. While the external opposition continues to mount, internal opposition also surfaces. The wealthier Jews are abusing and oppressing the people, forcing them to mortgage their property and sell their children into slavery. Nehemiah again deals with the problem with prayer and action. He also leads by example when he sacrifices his governor's allowance. In spite of deceit, slander, and treachery, Nehemiah continues to trust in God and to press on with singleness of mind until the work is completed. The task is accomplished in an incredible fifty-two days, and even the enemies recognize that it can only have been accomplished with God's help (6:16).

The Restoration of the People (chs. 8 through 13): The construction of the walls is followed by consecration and consolidation of the people. Ezra the priest is the leader of the spiritual revival (chs. 8 through 10), reminiscent of the reforms he led thirteen years earlier (Ezra 9 and 10). Ezra stands on a special wooden platform after the completion of the walls and gives the people a marathon reading of the Law. They respond with weeping, confession, obedience, and rejoicing. The Levites and priests lead them in a great prayer that surveys God's past work of deliverance and loyalty on behalf of his people, and magnifies God's attributes of holiness, justice, mercy, and love. The "solemn written agreement" is then renewed with God as the people commit themselves to separate from the Gentiles in marriage and to obey God's commandments.

Lots are drawn to determine who will remain in Jerusalem and who will return to the cities of their inheritance. One-tenth are required to stay in Jerusalem, and the rest of the land is resettled by the people and priests. The walls of Jerusalem are dedicated to the Lord in a joyful ceremony accompanied by instrumental and vocal music.

Unfortunately, Ezra's revival is short-lived; and Nehemiah, who returned to Persia in 432 B.C. (13:6), makes a second trip to Jerusalem about 425 B.C. to reform the people. He purifies the Temple, enforces the Sabbath, and requires the people to put away all foreign wives.

OUTLINE OF NEHEMIAH

Nehemiah returns to Jerusalem	1:1–2:20	the covenant is renewed	8:1–10:39
The walls of Jerusalem are rebuilt	3:1–7:73	Further activities of Nehemiah	11:1–13:31
The Law is read, and			

FOCUS	RECONSTRUCTION OF THE WALL		RESTORATION OF THE PEOPLE	
REFERENCE	1.1 ——————— 3.1 ———		——— 8.1 ——————— 11.1 ——————— 13.31	
DIVISION	PREPARATION TO RECONSTRUCT THE WALL	RECONSTRUCTION OF THE WALL	RENEWAL OF THE COVENANT	OBEDIENCE TO THE COVENANT
TOPIC	POLITICAL		SPIRITUAL	
	CONSTRUCTION		INSTRUCTION	
SETTING	JERUSALEM			

NEHEMIAH

THE BOOK OF
ESTHER

The Book of Esther

The Book of Esther comes to us in two forms. There is a short Hebrew version and a longer Greek one. Here we are dealing with the Hebrew version of Esther. In the Hebrew Bible, Esther is one of the Kethubim or "writings" that constitute the third part of the Old Testament (Law and Prophets being the other two). Also, in the Hebrew Bible, Esther is the last of the megilloth, or scrolls, which are read on special feasts of the Jewish liturgical year. The institution of the festival of Purim is described in Esther 9:20–32.

The Author of Esther

Augustine suggested that Ezra wrote the book. Clement of Alexandria, on the basis of 9:20–32, put forward the opinion that Mordecai wrote Esther. The best that can be said is that the book was written by an unknown Jew of the tribe of Benjamin (2:5).

The author probably wrote the book by drawing from various sources. Some modern scholars think there once existed three separate but unrelated stories: the Vashti story, the Mordecai story, and the Esther story. These the author combined in the book we know as Esther. Other modern scholars see the author as a very gifted writer who wove together different traditions into his narrative: e.g., the festival of Purim, the sage at the foreign court, wisdom, and persecution of the Jews in the Persian Empire.

What the author has produced is a historical novel. He set his novel against a historical figure, Xerxes, and some accurate references to Persian customs. The author is more interested in communicating a certain moral attitude than in writing a history.

The Time of Esther

The story is set in Susa, the capital city of Elam, a winter residence of Persian kings. Ahasuerus is the Hebrew name and Zerxes the Greek name of Khshayarsh, who was king of Persia from 486–464 B.C. Not everyone agrees, however, that this was the time Esther was written. Esther is the only Old Testament book not represented among the Dead Sea Scrolls. Although the emperor of Persia is mentioned almost two hundred times, God is not mentioned once. The law and the covenant are not alluded to or acknowledged. Sirach does not mention Esther. These factors have caused many scholars to give up in attempting to date this book. There are some who see a way out of the confusion by distinguishing between the first edition of Esther and the final edition. More and more, opinion favors the fourth century or Persian period for the first edition, and the second century or Hellenistic period for the final edition.

Esther is addressed to Jews who are living in a predominantly secular society. In such a situation, Jews should not flee the society. Rather, they should accept the challenge of changing the society for the better. Each person's contribution can make a difference. No one can say he or she is insignificant. Surely Mordecai and Esther did not think that way.

Survey of Esther

The author certainly explains the origin, meaning, and date of the festival of Purim (the fourteenth and fifteenth of Adar which is our February-March). More importantly, however, the author teaches that God delivers his people from oppression in any age. The wicked may prosper for a time while the virtuous suffer, but there will be a reversal of fortunes in God's good time. To accomplish this reversal, God often uses ordinary men and women like Mordecai and Esther. Chapters 1 through 4 describe the threat to the Jews, and chapters 5 through 10 describe the triumph of the Jews.

The Threat to the Jews (chs. 1 through 4): The story begins in King Xerxes' winter palace at Susa. The king provides a lavish banquet and display of royal glory for the people of Susa, and proudly seeks to make Queen Vashti's beauty a part of the program. When she refuses to appear, the king is counseled to depose her and seek another queen, because it is feared that the other women will become insolent if Vashti goes unpunished. Esther later finds favor in the eyes of King Xerxes and wins the royal "beauty pageant." At her cousin Mordecai's instruction, she does not reveal that she is Jewish. With her help, Mordecai is able to warn the king of an assassination plot, and his deed is recorded in the palace records. Meanwhile, Haman becomes prime minister, but Mordecai refuses to bow to him. When he learns that Mordecai is Jewish, Haman plots for a year to eliminate all Jews, as his rage and hatred grow. He casts lots (purim) daily during this period until he determines the best day to have them massacred. Through bribery and lies he convinces King Xerxes to issue an edict that all Jews in the empire will be slain eleven months hence in a single day. Haman conceives his plot in envy and a vengeful spirit, and he executes it with malicious craft. The decree creates a state of confusion, and Mordecai asks Esther to appeal to the king to spare the Jews. At the peril of her life, Esther decides to see the king and reveal her nationality in a desperate attempt to dissuade King Xerxes. Mordecai convinces her that she has been called to her high position for this purpose.

The Triumph of the Jews (chs. 5 through 10): After fasting, Esther appears before the king and wisely invites him to a banquet along with Haman. At the banquet she requests that they attend a second banquet, as she seeks the right moment to divulge her request. Haman is flattered but later enraged when he sees Mordecai. He takes his wife's suggestion to build a large gallows for Mordecai (he cannot wait the eleven months for Mordecai to be slain). That night King Xerxes decides to treat his insomnia by having the palace records read to him. Reading about Mordecai's deed, he wants him to be honored. Haman, mistakenly thinking the king wants to honor him, tells the king how the honor should be bestowed, only to find out that the reward is for Mordecai. He is humbled and infuriated by being forced to honor the man he loathes. At Esther's second banquet King Xerxes offers her as much as half of his empire for the third time. She then makes her plea for her people and accuses Haman of his treachery. The infuriated king has Haman hanged on the gallows that Haman intended for Mordecai. The gallows, seventy-five feet high, was designed to make Mordecai's downfall a city-wide spectacle, but it ironically provides Haman with unexpected public attention—posthumously.

Persian law sealed with the king's ring (3:10) cannot be revoked, but at Esther's request the king issues a new proclamation to all the provinces that the Jews may assemble and defend themselves on the day when they are attacked by their enemies. This decree changes the outcome intended by the first order and produces great joy. Mordecai is also elevated and set over the house of Haman. When the fateful day of the two proclamations arrives, the Jews defeat their enemies in their cities throughout the Persian provinces, but do not take the plunder. The next day becomes a day of celebration and an annual Jewish holiday called the festival of Purim. The word is derived from the Assyrian *puru*, meaning "lot," referring to the lots cast by Haman to determine the day decreed for destroying the Jews. The narrative closes with the advancement of Mordecai to a position second only to the king.

FOCUS	THREAT TO JEWS						TRIUMPH OF JEWS		
REFERENCE	A.1———1.1—3.1—B.1———3.14—C.1———D.1———5.3—6.1———————8.4———E.1———8.13—F.1———F.10								
DIVISION	ESTHER CROWNED		HAMAN'S PLOT AGAINST JEWS				MORDECAI'S TRIUMPH OVER HAMAN	ISRAEL'S TRIUMPH	
	MORDECAI'S DREAM		XERXES' DECREE		PRAYERS	ESTHER FAINTS		XERXES' DECREE	MORDECAI'S DREAM
TOPIC	GRAVE DANGER						GREAT DELIVERANCE		
SETTING	PERSIA								

ESTHER

OUTLINE OF ESTHER

Esther becomes queen	1:1–2:23	The Jews defeat their	
Haman's plot	3:1–5:14	enemies	8:1–10:3
Haman is put todeath	6:1–7:10		

THE BOOK OF

JOB

The Book of Job

Job tells the story of a man who loses everything—his wealth, his family, his health—and wrestles with the question, Why? The book is a poetic dialogue in a prose-narrative setting, dealing with the problem of evil and suffering in the life of a just man. The theme of Job is also found in the writings of ancient Mesopotamia and Egypt.

The book begins with a heavenly debate between God and Satan, moves through three cycles of earthly debates between Job and his friends, and concludes with a dramatic "divine diagnosis" of Job's problem. In the end, Job acknowledges the sovereignty of God in his life and receives back more than he had before his trials.

Iyyob is the Hebrew title for this book, and the name has two possible meanings. If derived from the Hebrew word for persecution, it means "Persecuted One." It is more likely that it comes from the Arabic word meaning "To Come Back" or "Repent." If so, it may be defined "Repentant One." Both meanings apply to the book.

The Author of Job

The author of Job is unknown, and there are no textual hints as to his identity. Whoever he was, he has produced one of the literary masterpieces of all time. He may have been familiar with similar stories in the Mesopotamian and Egyptian literature. His theology and literary genius far surpasses them, however. The author-poet is probably draw-

157

ing from his own experience of suffering and tragedy, and offers his inspired insights into very difficult theological issues.

The Time of Job

Lamentations 4:21 locates Uz in the area of Edom, southeast of the Dead Sea. This is also in the region of northern Arabia, and Job's friends come from nearby countries.

It is important to distinguish the date of the events in Job from the date of its writing. Accurate dating of the events is difficult because there are no references to contemporary historical occurrences. However, a number of facts indicate a patriarchal date for Job: (1) Job's wealth is measured in terms of livestock (1:3; 42:12) rather than gold or silver; (2) like Abraham, Isaac, and Jacob, Job is the priest of his family and offers sacrifices; (3) there are no references to Israel, the Exodus, the Mosaic Law, or the sacred Tent; (4) fitting Abraham's time, the social unit in Job is the patriarchal family-clan; (5) the Chaldeans who murder Job's servants (1:17) are nomads and have not yet become city dwellers; (6) Job uses the characteristic patriarchal name for God, *Shaddai* ("the Almighty").

Several theories have been advanced for the date of writing: (1) it was written shortly after the events occurred, perhaps by Job or Elihu; (2) it was written by Moses in Midian (1485–1445 B.C.); (3) it was written in the time of Solomon (c. 950 B.C.); (4) it was written during or after the Babylonian captivity.

The date of the writing of Job is not easy to determine. Rabbinic opinions as to the date of writing range from 2100 B.C. to 400 B.C.. Early church writers such as Eusebius and Gregory of Nazianzus, also assign the writing of Job to an early period (pre-Mosaic or Solomonic). Most modern scholars reject such an early date. They tend to think that the author lived in the cosmopolitan atmosphere of the sixth to the fourth century B.C.

The Survey of Job

The book is permeated by the idea of a unique God who is Creator and Lord of all, and who is beyond all human reckoning. Job's trust in God (chs. 1 and 2) changes to complaining and growing self-righteousness (chs. 3 through 31; see 32:1 and 40:8), but his repentance (42:1–6) leads to his restoration (42:7–17). The trials bring about an important transformation: The man after the process is different from the man before the process. The Book of Job divides into three parts:

the dilemma of Job (chs. 1 and 2), the debates of Job (chs. 3 through 37), and the deliverance of Job (chs. 38 through 42).

The Dilemma of Job (chs. 1 and 2): Job is not a logical candidate for disaster (see 1:1 and 8). His moral integrity and his selfless service to God heighten the dilemma. Behind the scenes, Satan ("Accuser") charges that no one loves God from pure motives, but only for material blessings (1:9–11). To refute Satan's accusations, God allows him to strike Job with two series of assaults. In his sorrow Job laments the day of his birth but does not deny God (1:21; 2:10).

The Debates of Job (chs. 3 through 37): Although Job's "comforters" reach wrong conclusions, they are his friends; of all who know Job, they are the only ones who come; they mourn with him in seven days of silent sympathy; they confront Job without talking behind his back. However, after Job breaks the silence, a three-round debate follows in which his friends say Job must be suffering because of his sin. Job's responses to their simplistic assumptions make the debate cycles increase in emotional fervor. He first accuses his friends of judging him, and later appeals to the Lord as his judge and refuge.

Job makes three basic complaints: (1) God does not hear me (13:3 and 24; 19:7; 23:3–5; 30:20); (2) God is punishing me (6:4; 7:20; 9:17); and (3) God allows the wicked to prosper (21:7). His defenses are much longer than his friends' accusations; in the process of defending his innocence, he becomes guilty of self-righteousness.

After Job's five-chapter closing monologue (chs. 27 through 31), Elihu freshens the air with a more perceptive and accurate view than those offered by Eliphaz, Bildad, or Zophar (chs. 32 through 37). He tells Job that he needs to humble himself before God and submit to God's process of purifying his life through trials.

The Deliverance of Job (chs. 38 through 42): After Elihu's preparatory discourse, God himself ends the debate by speaking to Job from the storm. In his first speech God reveals his power and wisdom as Creator and Preserver of the physical and animal world. Job responds by acknowledging his own ignorance and insignificance; he can offer no rebuttal (40:3–5). In his second speech God reveals his sovereign authority and challenges Job with two illustrations of his power to control the uncontrollable. This time Job responds by acknowledging his error with a repentant heart (42:1–6). If Job cannot understand God's ways in the realm of nature, how then can he understand God's ways in the spiritual realm? God makes no reference to Job's personal sufferings and hardly touches on the real issue of the debate. However, Job catches a glimpse of the divine perspective when he acknowledges God's sovereignty over his life; his worldly goods are restored twofold. Job prays for his three friends who have cut him so deeply, but Elihu's speech is never rebuked. Thus, Satan's challenge becomes God's opportunity to build up Job's life. "We call them happy because they endured. You have heard of Job's patience, and you know how the Lord provided for him in the end. For the Lord is full of mercy and compassion" (James 5:11; see James 1:12).

OUTLINE OF JOB

Prologue	1:1–2:13	e. In praise of wisdom	28:1–28
Job and his friends	3:1–31:40	f. Job's final statement	29:1–31:40
a. Job's complaint	3:1–26	The speeches of Elihu	32:1–37:24
b. The first dialogue	4:1–14:22	The Lord answers Job	38:1–42:6
c. The second dialogue	15:1–21:34	Epilogue	42:7–17
d. The third dialogue	22:1–27:23		

FOCUS	DILEMMA OF JOB	DEBATES OF JOB					DELIVERANCE OF JOB
REFERENCE	1.1————3.1——————15.1————22.1————28.1————32.1————38.1————42.17						
DIVISION	CONTROVERSY OF GOD AND SATAN	FIRST CYCLE OF DEBATE	SECOND CYCLE OF DEBATE	THIRD CYCLE OF DEBATE	FINAL DEFENSE OF JOB	SOLUTION OF ELIHU	CONTROVERSY OF GOD WITH JOB
TOPIC	CONFLICT	DEBATE					REPENTANCE
	PROSE	POETRY					PROSE
SETTING	LAND OF UZ (NORTH ARABIA)						

JOB

PSALMS

The Book of Psalms

The Book of Psalms is the largest and perhaps most widely used book in the Bible. It explores the full range of human experience in a very personal and practical way. Its 150 "songs" run from the Creation through the patriarchal, theocratic, monarchical, exilic, and postexilic periods. The tremendous breadth of subject matter in the Psalms includes diverse topics, such as jubilation, war, peace, worship, judgment, messianic prophecy, praise, and lament. The Psalms were set to the accompaniment of stringed instruments and served as the Temple hymnbook and devotional guide for the Jewish people.

The Book of Psalms was gradually collected and originally unnamed, perhaps due to the great variety of material. It came to be known as *Sepher Tehillim*—"Book of Praises"—because almost every psalm contains some note of praise to God. The Septuagint uses the Greek word *Psalmoi* as its title for this book, meaning poems sung to the accompaniment of musical instruments. It also calls it the *Psalterium* ("a collection of songs"), and this word is the basis for the term *Psalter*. The Latin title is *Liber Psalmorum*, "Book of Psalms."

The Authors of Psalms

Critics have challenged the historical accuracy of the superscriptions regarding authorship. Almost half (seventy-three) of the psalms are designated as Davidic: Psalms 3–9; 11–32; 34–41; 51–65; 68–70; 86; 101; 103; 108–110; 122; 124; 131; 133; and 138–145. The New Testament attributes the anonymous Psalms 2 and 95 to this king whose name means "Beloved of Yahweh" (Acts 4:25; Heb. 4:7). In addition to these seventy-five, twelve are attributed to Asaph, "Collector," a priest who headed the service of music (50; 73–83; Ezra 2:41); ten are attributed to the sons of Korah, "Bald," a guild of singers and composers (42; 44–49; 84; 85; 87; Num. 26:9–11); two to Solomon, "Peaceful," Israel's most powerful king (72 and 127); one to Moses, "Son of the Water," a prince, herdsman, and deliverer (90); one to Heman, "Faithful," a wise man (88; 1 Kings 4:31; 1 Chron. 15:19); and one is attributed to Ethan, "Enduring," a wise man (89; 1 Kings 4:31; 1 Chron. 15:19). The remaining fifty psalms are anonymous: 1; 2; 10; 33; 43; 66; 71; 91–100; 102; 104–107; 111–121; 123; 125; 126; 128–130; 132; 134–137; and 146–150. Some of the anonymous psalms are traditionally attributed to Ezra.

The Time of Psalms

Psalms cover a wide time span from Moses (c. 1250 B.C.) to the postexilic community under Ezra and Nehemiah (c. 430 B.C.). Because of their broad chronological and subject range, the Psalms were written to different audiences under many conditions. Therefore, they reflect a wide variety of devotional attitudes and thus of value for a great variety of readers.

The five divisions of the Book of Psalms were compiled over several centuries. As individual psalms were written, some were used in Israel's worship. A number of small collections were made independently, like the pilgrimage songs and groups of Davidic psalms (1–41; 51–70; 138–145). These smaller anthologies were gradually collected into the "five books," perhaps in imitation of the Pentateuch. How and when the five books were put together is still debated. The first major collection was probably under the patronage of David. The Levitical collections of Korah and Asaph were added soon after this. Then came Book Four. Finally, the Hallel collection formed Book Five. The five books were then united and edited. Literary type and subject matter were at least two criteria used in placing an individual psalm within one of the five books.

Survey of Psalms

The Psalter is really five books in one, and each book ends with a doxology. The last psalm is the closing doxology for Book Five and for the Psalter as a whole. After the Psalms were written, editorial superscriptions or instructions were added to 116 of them.

The following classification divides the Psalms into ten types: (1) *Individual Lament Psalms:* Directly addressed to God, these psalms petition him to rescue and defend an individual. They have these elements: (a) an introduction (usually a cry to God), (b) the lament, (c) a confession of trust in God, (d) the petition, (e) a declaration or vow of praise. Most psalms are of this type (e.g., 3–7; 12; 13; 22; 25–28; 35; 38–40; 42; 43; 51; 54–57; 59; 61; 63; 64; 69–71; 86; 88; 102; 109; 120; 130; 140–143). (2) *Communal Lament Psalms:* The only difference is that the nation rather than an individual makes the lament (e.g., 44; 60; 74; 79; 80; 83; 85; 90; and 123). (3) *Individual Thanksgiving Psalms:* The psalmist publicly acknowledges God's activity on his behalf. These psalms thank God for something he has already done or express confidence in what he will yet do. They have these elements: (a) a proclamation to praise God, (b) a summary statement, (c) a report of deliverance, and (d) a renewed vow of praise (e.g., 18; 30; 32; 34; 40; 41; 66; 106; 116; and 138). (4) *Communal Thanksgiving Psalms:* In these psalms the acknowledgment is made by the nation rather than by an individual (see 124 and 129). (5) *General Praise Psalms:* These psalms are more general than the thanksgiving psalms. The psalmist attempts to magnify the name of God and boast about his greatness (see 8; 19; 29; 103; 104;

139; 148; 150). The joyous exclamation "praise the LORD!" is found in several of these psalms. (6) *Descriptive Praise Psalms:* These psalms priase God for his attributes and acts (e.g., 33; 36; 105; 111; 113; 117; 135; 136; 146; 147). (7) *Enthronement Psalms:* These psalms describe God's sovereign reign over all (see 47; 93; 96–99). Some anticipate the kingdom rule of Christ. (8) *Pilgrimage Songs:* Also known as Songs of Zion, these psalms were sung by pilgrims traveling up to Jerusalem for the three annual religious feasts of Passover, Pentecost, and Tabernacles (see 43; 46; 48; 76; 84; 87; 120–134). (9) *Royal Psalms:* The reigns of the earthly king and the heavenly king are portrayed in most of these psalms (e.g., 2; 18; 20; 21; 45; 72; 89; 101; 132; and 144). (10) *Wisdom and Didactic Psalms:* The reader is exhorted and instructed in the way of righteousness (see 1; 37; 119).

There is a problem with the so-called imprecatory ("to call down a curse") psalms. These psalms invoke divine judgment on one's enemies (see 7; 35; 40; 55; 58; 59; 69; 79; 109; 137; 139; 144). These are difficult for us to understand because they seem unreasonably harsh. A few things should be kept in mind: (1) they call for divine justice, rather than human vengeance, on those who are unjust and insolent; (2) there is no plan to make war against enemies; (3) these psalms arise from the psychological states of those who are experiencing dehumanizing suffering; (4) they are a way of letting off steam, a way of controlling anger by releasing it in a torrent of violent words; (5) there is no sharp distinction in the Hebrew mind between a sinner and his sin.

OUTLINE OF PSALMS

The 150 psalms are grouped into five collections, or books, as follows:

Psalms 1–41
Psalms 42–72
Psalms 73–89
Psalms 90–106
Psalms 107–150

BOOK	BOOK I (1—41)	BOOK II (42—72)	BOOK III (73—89)	BOOK IV (90—106)	BOOK V (107—150)
NUMBER OF PSALMS	41	31	17	17	44
BASIC CONTENT	SONGS OF WORSHIP	HYMNS OF NATIONAL INTEREST		ANTHEMS OF PRAISE	
TOPICAL LIKENESS TO PENTATEUCH	GENESIS: MAN AND CREATION	EXODUS: DELIVERANCE AND REDEMPTION	LEVITICUS: WORSHIP AND SANCTUARY	NUMBERS: WILDERNESS AND WANDERING	DEUTERONOMY: SCRIPTURE AND PRAISE
CLOSING DOXOLOGY	41.13	72.18-19	89.52	106.48	150.1-6
POSSIBLE COMPILER	DAVID	HEZEKIAH OR JOSIAH		EZRA OR NEHEMIAH	

PSALMS

PROVERBS

The Book of Proverbs

The age of the patriarchs was but a distant memory at the time Proverbs was written. So, too, were the periods of the Exodus and the monarchy. The kingdoms of Israel and Judah had both suffered humiliating and devastating defeats. The Babylonian Exile of the Jews was cruel and harsh. God's people were now an oppressed people. Some foreign power was always present exerting its secular influence. This was no time for theological idealism or for dreams of deliverance. A person had to deal with the practical realities of life in the world.

The key word in Proverbs is *wisdom*, "the ability to live life skillfully." A godly life in an ungodly world, however, is no simple assignment. Proverbs provides God's detailed instructions for his people to deal successfully with the practical affairs of everyday life: how to relate to God, parents, children, neighbors, and government. The authors of this book use a combination of poetry, parables, pithy questions, short stories, and wise maxims to give in strikingly memorable form the common sense and divine perspective necessary to handle life's issues.

The Authors of Proverbs

The Book of Proverbs is titled *Mishle Shelomoh*. The word *mashal* can mean many things. Here it is generally taken to mean "rule." A "mashal" or proverb then is a moral injunction which should rule a person's conduct in day-to-day living.

That Solomon would be considered the leading author of Proverbs comes as no surprise. His role in the development of Wisdom Literature in Israel was so emphasized in Jewish and Christian traditions that almost all the books that comprise the wisdom collection were attributed to him.

Despite this long-standing tradition, scholars today feel certain that only chapters 10 through 22 and 25 through 29 of Proverbs can be dated to the preexilic period when Solomon lived. No one can be sure whether Solomon is indeed the author of any of the material found in these chapters. It is important to recall here that it was a custom of the time to attribute writings to a famous prophet, priest, or king. By doing so, the author was teaching that this particular writing enjoys the authority and inspiration of God's spirit that was usually associated with the famous name of the past.

In the case of Solomon, God is said to have given him wisdom that surpassed that of all the people of the East and all the wisdom of Egypt. He was one of those specially chosen ones through whom God acted for the benefit of all the people.

Solomon organized his court along Egyptian lines. In doing so, he introduced a group of men known as "advisors to the king." These were principally learned Egyptian men who brought with them the wisdom tradition of Egypt. In this way Solomon was known as the patron and founder of wisdom tradition in Israel.

The Time of Proverbs

Proverbs is a collection of topical maxims and is not a historical book. It is a product of the wisdom school in Israel. One of the most difficult tasks in biblical studies is the dating of Israel's Wisdom Literature, including Proverbs. The wisdom movement was international. Wise men and their literature were to be found in Egypt, Phoenicia, Babylon, and Canaan. In Egypt, written examples of Wisdom Literature can be found as early as 2700 B.C. The biblical wisdom tradition must be viewed against this wide background.

There surely would have been some borrowing on the part of Israel from the rich wisdom tradition of her neighbors. There is a close similarity, some would even say dependence, of Proverbs 22:17 through 24:22 to the Egyptian "Instruction of Amenemope." While this borrowing took place, it must be pointed out that Israel injected her own theism and morality into any material she took from the surrounding cultures. Israel, of course, developed her own wisdom tradition. Some of the material found in Proverbs is preexilic, even before the kings of Israel. Much of it is postexilic. The collection of proverbs was edited over many years. The form of the book, as we now have it, most likely comes from the end of the fifth century B.C.

Survey of Proverbs

Proverbs is the most intensely practical book in the Old Testament because it teaches skillful living in the multiple aspects of everyday life. Its specific precepts include instruction on wisdom and folly, the righteous and the ungodly, the tongue, pride and humility, justice and vengeance, the family, laziness and work, poverty and wealth, friends and neighbors, love and lust, anger and strife, masters and servants, life and death. Proverbs touches upon every facet of human relationships, and its principles transcend the bounds of time and culture.

The Hebrew word for "proverb" (*mashal*), means "comparison, similar, parallel." A proverb uses a comparison or figure of speech to make a pithy but poignant observation. Proverbs have been defined as simple illustrations that expose fundamental realities of life. These maxims are not theoretical but practical; they are easily memorized, based on real-life experience, and designed for use in the mainstream of life. The proverbs are general statements and illustrations of timeless truth, which allow for, but do not condone, exceptions to the rule. The key word is *hokhmah*, "wisdom": it literally means "skill" (in living). Wisdom is more than shrewdness or intelligence. Instead, it relates to practical righteousness and moral acumen. The Book of Proverbs may be divided into six segments: the purpose of Proverbs (1:1–7), the proverbs to the youth (1:8 through 9:18), the proverbs of Solomon (10:1 through 24:34), the proverbs of Solomon copied by Hezekiah's men (25:1 through 29:27), the words of Agur (30:1–33), and the words of King Lemuel (31:1–31).

The Purpose of Proverbs (1:1-7): The brief prologue states the author, theme, and purpose of the book.

The Proverbs to the Youth (1:8 through 9:18): Following the introduction, there is a series of ten exhortations, each beginning with "son or sons" (1:8 through 9:18). These messages introduce the concept of wisdom in the format of a father's efforts to persuade his son to pursue the path of wisdom in order to achieve godly success in life. Wisdom rejects the invitation of crime and foolishness, rewards seekers of wisdom on every level, and wisdom's discipline provides freedom and safety (chs. 1 through 4). Wisdom protects one from illicit sensuality and its consequences, from foolish practices and laziness, and from adultery and the lure of the harlot (chs. 5 through 7). Wisdom is to be preferred to folly because of its divine origin and rich benefits (chs. 8 and 9). There are four kinds of fools, ranging from those who are naive and uncommitted to scoffers who arrogantly despise the way of God. The fool is not mentally deficient; he is self-sufficient, ordering his life as if there were no God.

The Proverbs of Solomon (10:1 through 24:34): There is a minimal amount of topical arrangement in these chapters. There are some thematic clusters (e.g., 26:1–12, 13–16, 20–22), but the usual units are one-verse maxims. It is helpful to assemble and organize these proverbs according to such specific themes as money and speech. This Solomonic collection consists of 375 proverbs of Solomon. Chapters 10 through 15 contrast right and wrong in practice, and all but nineteen proverbs use parallels of paired opposite principles. Chapters 16:1 through 22:16 offer a series of self-evident moral truths and all but eighteen proverbs use parallels of paired identical or similar principles. The words of wise men (22:17 through 24:34) are given in two groups. The first group includes thirty distinct sayings (22:17 through 24:22), and six more are found in the second group (24:23–34).

The Proverbs of Solomon Copied by Hezekiah's Men (25:1 through 29:27): This second Solomonic collection was copied and arranged by the men of King Hezekiah (25:1). These proverbs in chapters 25 through 29 further develop the themes in the first Solomonic collection.

The Words of Agur (30:1–33): The last two chapters of Proverbs form an appendix of sayings by two otherwise unknown sages, Agur and Lemuel. Most of Agur's material is given in clusters of numerical proverbs.

The Words of King Lemuel (31:1–31): The last chapter includes an acrostic of twenty-two verses (the first letter of each verse consecutively follows the complete Hebrew alphabet) portraying a capable wife (31:10–31).

OUTLINE OF PROVERBS

| In praise of wisdom | 1:1–9:18 | The words of Agur | 30:1–33 |
| The proverbs of Solomon | 10:1–29:27 | The words of Lemuel | 31:1–31 |

FOCUS	PURPOSE OF PROVERBS	PROVERBS TO YOUTH	FIRST COLLECTION OF THE PROVERBS OF SOLOMON	SECOND COLLECTION OF THE PROVERBS OF SOLOMON (HEZEKIAH)	WORDS OF AGUR	WORDS OF LEMUEL
REFERENCE	1.1—————	—1.8—————	—10.1—————	—25.1—————	—30.1—————	—31.1——31.31
DIVISION	PURPOSE AND THEME	FATHER'S EXHORTATIONS	FIRST COLLECTION OF SOLOMON	SECOND COLLECTION OF SOLOMON	NUMERICAL PROVERBS	VIRTUOUS WIFE
TOPIC	PROLOGUE	PRINCIPLES OF WISDOM			EPILOGUE	
	COMMENDATION OF WISDOM	COUNSEL OF WISDOM			COMPARISONS OF WISDOM	
SETTING	JUDAH					

PROVERBS

ECCLESIASTES

The Book of Ecclesiastes

The word "vanity," or "useless" in this translation, (*hebel* in Hebrew), opens and closes Ecclesiastes. The author uses this word thirty-six times in the course of his writing. He had lived a long life and obviously had sufficient time to reflect on life. His conclusions were not all positive ones. He was very critical of what he saw happening in his day. So-called wise men had categories for everything and everyone, including God. In doing so they were making undue claims of divine privileges. This is vanity of vanities.

The Hebrew title is *Qoheleth*. It comes from the word *qahal*, "to convoke an assembly." It designates one who has some relationship to the assembly, one who performs a function or has an office, possibly teaching. Qoheleth has lost faith in the triump of human justice. He thinks it is futile for anyone to try independently to figure out the meaning of life. He imagines at first that God does not wish to reveal true wisdom to man. One initial theme of his reflections is pursuit of the mere enjoyment of life. He also observes that sadness always seems to be around the corner. However, the teacher at last discovers that obedience of God's law is the key to life's fulfillment (12:13).

The Author of Ecclesiastes

The opening verse states that the words are those of David's son, Qoheleth, king in Jerusalem. This has led to the traditional view that Solomon is the author. Some scholars today doubt this. Language considerations alone argue against Solomon's authorship. The language of Qoheleth appears to be a late form of Hebrew, possibly from the third century B.C. The author may have been an anonymous Jew who sought to restore God to his rightful transcendent place.

The Time of Ecclesiastes

In determining the time of Qoheleth, several factors should be kept in mind: (1) Qoheleth has been influenced by Greek ideas. Alexander the Great died in 323 B.C., but Greek influence became significant several decades later; (2) Qoheleth's Hebrew theology represents a period later than the sixth century B.C.; (3) Ben Sira is familiar with Qoheleth. With these and other considerations, a common date given today for the book of Qoheleth is 250 B.C.

Survey of Ecclesiastes

Ecclesiastes is a profound and problematic book. It is the record of an intense earth, especially in view of all the iniquities and apparent absurdities that surround us. It takes the perspective of the greatest answers that wisdom under the sun can produce. Ecclesiastes is extremely difficult to synthesize, and several alternate approaches have been used. The one used here is: the thesis that "life *is* useless" (1:1–11), the proof that "life is useless" (1:12 through 6:12), the counsel for living with uselessness (7:1 through 12:14).

The Thesis That "Life Is Useless" (1:1–11): After a one-verse introduction, Qoheleth states his theme: "Life is useless, all useless" (1:2). Life under the sun appears to be futile and perplexing. Verses 3–11 illustrate this theme in the endless and apparently meaningless cycles found in nature and history.

The Proof That "Life Is Useless" (1:12 through 6:12): Qoheleth describes his multiple quest for meaning and satisfaction as he explores his vast personal resources. He begins with wisdom (1:12–18) but finds that "the more you know, the more it hurts." Due to his intense perception of reality he experiences just the reverse of "ignorance is bliss." Qoheleth moves from wisdom to laughter, pleasure, and wine (2:1–3) and then turns to works, women, and wealth (2:4–11); but all lead to emptiness. He realizes that wisdom is far greater than foolishness, but both seem to lead to futility in view of the brevity of life and universality of death (2:12–17). He concludes by acknowledging that contentment and joy are found only in God.

At this point, Ecclesiastes turns from his situation in life to a philosophical quest; but the conclusion remains the same. Qoheleth considers the unchanging order of events and the fixed laws of God. Time is short, and there is no eternity on earth (3:1–15). The futility of death seems to cancel the difference between righteousness and evil (3:16–22). Chapters 4 and 5 explore the uselessness in social relationships (oppression, rivalry, covetousness, power) and in religious relationships (formalism, foolish prayer, promises). In addition, the world's offerings produce disappointment, not satisfaction. Ultimate meaning can be found only in God.

The Counsel for Living with Uselessness (7:1 through 12:14): A series of lessons on practical wisdom are given in 7:1 through 9:12. Levity and pleasure-seeking are seen as superficial and foolish; it is better to have sober depth of thought. Wisdom and self-control provide perspective and strength in coping with life. One should enjoy prosperity and consider in adversity that God made both. Avoid the twin extremes of self-righteousness and immorality. Sin invades all men, and wisdom is cut short by evil and death. The human mind cannot grasp ultimate meaning. Submission to authority helps one avoid unnecessary hardship, but real justice is often lacking on earth. The uncertainties of life and certainty of the grave show that God's purposes and ways often cannot be grasped. One should, therefore, magnify opportunities while they last, because fortune can change suddenly.

Observations on wisdom and folly are found in 9:13 through 11:6. Wisdom, the most powerful human resource, is contrasted with the meaningless talk and effort of fools. In view of the unpredictability of circumstances, wisdom is the best course to follow in order to minimize grief and misfortune. Wisdom involves discipline and diligence. In 11:7 through 12:7 Qoheleth offers exhortations on using life well. Youth is too brief and precious to be squandered in foolishness or evil. A person should live well in the fullness of each day before God and acknowledge him early in life. This section closes with an exquisite allegory of old age (12:1–7).

Qoheleth concludes that the "good life" is only attained by revering God. Those who fail to take God and his will seriously into account are doomed to lives of foolishness and futility. Life will not wait upon the solution of all its problems; nevertheless, real meaning can be found by looking not "under the sun" but beyond the sun to the "one Shepherd" (12:11).

FOCUS	THESIS: "ALL IS VANITY"		PROOF: "LIFE IS VAIN"		COUNSEL: "FEAR GOD"		
REFERENCE	1.1————1.4————1.12————3.1————7.1————10.1————12.9————12.14						
DIVISION	INTRODUCTION OF VANITY	ILLUSTRATIONS OF VANITY	PROOF FROM SCRIPTURE	PROOF FROM OBSERVATIONS	COPING IN A WICKED WORLD	COUNSEL FOR UNCERTAINTY	CONCLUSION: FEAR AND OBEY GOD
TOPIC	DECLARATION OF VANITY		DEMONSTRATION OF VANITY		FROM VANITY		
	SUBJECT		SERMONS		SUMMARY		
SETTING	UNIVERSE: "UNDER THE SUN"						

ECCLESIASTES

OUTLINE OF ECCLESIASTES

Life is useless	1:1–11	Counsel for living with	
Proof that life is useless	1:12–6:12	uselessness	7:1–12:14

SONG OF SONGS

The Book of Song of Songs

The Hebrew title *Shir Hashirim* comes from 1:1. This was the way the Hebrews expressed the superlative. The meaning is "The Greatest Song." Throughout the history of interpretation, theories abound as to how to interpret this book. The traditional approach of both Jews and Christians is to interpret the book allegorically. The text is speaking about human love, but the real meaning was either the mystical love of God for his people, Israel; or, for Christians, the love between Christ and his church. Other scholars see it as a type of drama.

Many contend that the book is a collection of secular love songs. These would have been written, developed, and edited over a long period of time. These songs celebrated the pain and joy of human love.

It is important to remember, however, that the Song of Songs belongs to the collection of "wisdom writings" in the canon of Scripture. Therefore, it must be read and interpreted as "wisdom literature." The Song is a reflection of the joyful and mysterious nature of love. The love between a man and a woman is a strong and divinely ordained force in human experience. The author seeks to understand it as one of those many mysteries within the created order.

The Author of Song of Songs

The superscription tells us that Solomon is the author of this most excellent book. His name appears in six other verses (1:5; 3:7, 9, 11; 8:11–12). This has led many to believe that Solomon is indeed the author.

Most critical scholars today, however, reject Solomon's authorship. While the poem in 3:6–11 was probably composed on the occasion of one of Solomon's many marriages, there is nothing to indicate that

Solomon is its author. Authorship was conceived of differently in the Near East from the way it is in the Western world. Solomon could be conceived as the author in the sense that he was the patron and perhaps founder of the wisdom tradition in Israel. Literary authorship is another question entirely. The traditional attribution of authorship of the Song of Songs comes from the presence of his name in 3:6–11.

Some unknown person probably collected a series of love songs that had been written over a period of years. These were brought into the wisdom collection, making sure they agreed with the theology of Israel's religion. This unknown editor has produced a masterful reflection on human love.

The Time of Song of Songs

The poems that make up the anthology that is called Song of Songs cannot be dated with any certainty. Some of them could have originated at the time of Solomon since they resemble lyrics composed in Egypt before 1000 B.C.

Many scholars today agree that the poems span five centuries, beginning with the period of Solomon and reaching to the Persian period. The many geographical references found in Song of Songs point to a different provenance for the various songs, but offer no clue as to the time of their composition. Scholars are divided on whether most of the poems are preexilic or postexilic, but are agreed that the final editing took place in the Persian period, no later than the fifth century.

Survey of Song of Songs

The great literary value of the Song of Songs can be seen in its rich use of metaphor and oriental imagery, as it extols the purity, beauty, and satisfaction of love. It is never crass, but often intimate, as it explores the dimensions of the relationship between two lovers: attraction, desire, companionship, pleasure, union, separation, faithfulness, and praise.

The book is a collection of lyrics, some of which have little to do with wedding ceremonies or with married love. Scholars do not agree on how many songs make up the anthology. Some find as many as fifty-four; others find as few as six.

Like Ecclesiastes, this book is not easily outlined, and various schemes can be used. Song of Songs abounds with sudden changes of speakers, and they are not identified. Also, the songs do not seem to be arranged in any kind of thematic way.

Chapters 1 through 3 give a series of recollections of courtship. These include the beloved's longing for affection at the palace before the wedding. There are expressions of mutual love in the banquet hall and a springtime visit of the lover to his beloved's home in the country. The beloved's dream of separation from her lover is related. There is also a wedding ceremony and procession, probably the marriage of Solomon to one of his many foreign brides.

In chapters 4:1 through 5:1 the lover praises his beloved from head to foot with a superb chain of similes. Her delectable qualities are like a walled garden which is entered only when the marriage is consummated. The lover accepts his beloved's invitation to marriage and announces the joy of love's consummation.

The section 5:2 through 6:3 contains the longest and most elaborate song in the anthology. The beloved has a troubled dream. Her lover is knocking at her door. She delays answering, and when she finally opens the door he is gone. She panics and searches for him at night in Jerusalem.

In 6:4–12 the lover praises the beauty of his beloved and assures her of his love. She is compared to the beauty of Jerusalem and Tirzah. She is unique among all the women in the king's court and can be compared to the beauties of nature.

Chapter 7:1–14 begins with another song by a company of singers in praise of the young woman's beauty. Another song follows, this time by the lover, in which the beloved's beauty is compared to the stately form of the palm tree. The concluding song of chapter 7 is the beloved's invitation to her lover to go forth into the field where she will give him her love.

Chapter 8:1–14 contains yet again a diversified collection of songs. The love between the beloved and her lover cannot be overthrown by jealousy, but only deepens. Their ardent love burns like a flame which not even death can destroy (8:6).

OUTLINE OF SONG OF SONGS

First Song	1:1–2:7	Fourth Song	5:2–6:3
Second Song	2:8–3:5	Fifth Song	6:4–8:4
Third Song	3:6–5:1	Sixth Song	8:5–14

FOCUS	BEGINNING OF LOVE			BROADENING OF LOVE		
REFERENCE	1.1————4.1————5.2————			6.4————7.1————8.1————8.14		
DIVISION	COURTSHIP	FIRST PRAISE OF BELOVED	BELOVED'S DREAM	SECOND PRAISE OF BELOVED	THIRD PRAISE OF BELOVED	CONTINUING QUALITY OF LOVE
TOPIC	FOSTERING OF LOVE	JOY OF LOVE'S CONSUMMATION	LOVE'S FRUSTRATIONS	UNIQUE QUALITIES OF BELOVED	SINGER'S PRAISE OF BELOVED / BELOVED'S INVITATION	GROWTH AND FAITHFULNESS OF LOVE
SETTING	ISRAEL					

SONG OF SONGS

THE BOOK OF

ISAIAH

The Book of Isaiah

The central insight and message of "Isaiah," in its present form, focuses around God's evaluation of the efficacy of his own word: "It [my word] will do everything I send it to do" (55:11). Through the mouth of Isaiah, God proclaims his redemptive plan for all history. Israel, the community of God's people yesterday and today, is described as the recipient of both divine judgment and forgiveness. Guilty Israel will always be the object of God's terror; repentant Israel will receive his forgiveness. This is God's word to Israel, and this word will be fulfilled in history.

The destruction of Jerusalem and the subsequent exile in Babylon will confirm the prophecies of Isaiah of Jerusalem. Defeat and bondage, however, will not be the final word. Just as assuredly, the message of God's final and decisive redemption of Israel holds out hope for the future. The parable of the farmer (28:23–29) announces God's hidden and strange plan which becomes manifest to the world in the creation of "a new earth and new heavens" (65:17), an idyllic age in which earlier promises (11:6, 9) will be fulfilled (65:25). The Book of Isaiah then testifies to the strands of continuity in God's plan for Israel first announced in chapters 1 through 39 and confirmed in chapters 40 through 66, "This plan, which God will complete when the time is right" (Eph 1:10) will be executed through the guaranteed agency of God's Word: "Yes, grass withers and flowers fade, but the word of our God endures forever" (40:8). An excellent summary to the book's sixty-six chapters appears in its title, "Isaiah," which means "God will give salvation."

The Author of Isaiah

The Book of Isaiah is an eminent example of the amazing vitality of the prophetic Word in the Old Testament. The pronouncements of an eighth century B.C. prophet, Isaiah of Jerusalem had a literary ripple effect in the Israelite and early Jewish communities as late as the third century B.C.

Isaiah of Jerusalem was the son of a certain Amoz (1:1). The prophet fathered at least two children to whom he gave symbolic names that reflected the urgency of his message (7:3; 8:1ff.). The vitality of Isaiah's prophetic vision produced a series of anonymous disciples over the subsequent five hundred years. These disciples kept Isaiah's word and theological intent alive by their preaching. Their inspired interpretations of his words gradually found a place in this book, alongside the work of Isaiah himself. On the one hand their interpretations appear as strategic expansions (called interpolations), interspersed among the prophet's original oracles (e.g., 2:2–4). On the other hand, massive appendices (e.g., chs. 40 through 55 and 56 through 66) became attached to the material already assembled in chapters 1 through 39. Both types of reinterpretation had the effect of bestowing on the entire work its characteristic future orientation, and of making Isaiah's original preaching a continuing message of God's plan of salvation for his people of every age.

The Time of Isaiah

Isaiah of Jerusalem exercised his ministry from 740–701 B.C. He preached to Judah and Jerusalem during the reigns of Jotham, Ahaz, and Hezekiah. This was a politically turbulent era during which four Assyrian kings, Tiglath Pilesar III (745–727 B.C.), Shalmaneser V (726–722 B.C.), Sargon II (721–705 B.C.), and Sennacherib (704–681 B.C.), attempted to overrun the western sector of the Fertile Crescent.

Almost two hundred years later, on the eve of the fall of Babylon to Cyrus of Persia (44:28; 45:1; 42:1, 25), the anonymous prophet responsible for the oracles found in chapters 40 through 55 preached divine forgiveness and deliverance to his fellow Jewish exiles held in captivity (40:2). He and his prophecies have commonly been given the designation "Deutero" (or Second) Isaiah, because of the agreement between his basic message and the content of the interpolations found alongside the oracles of Isaiah of Jerusalem.

Chapters 56 through 66 are often attributed to yet another anonymous prophet, or group of prophets, who ministered to the Jewish community in the Persian province of Judea in the generations following the return of the exiles to the land of their forefathers. These oracles from the so-called Trito (or Third) Isaiah at once speak to the sobering realities of life in the restored community (59:1–21) and share in Deutero-Isaiah's vision of the universal establishment of God's justice and the conversion of all people to faith in him (66:18).

Survey of Isaiah

A clear theology of the Word of God guided the formulation of the Book of Isaiah in the shape in which we now read it. Five convenient divisions suggest themselves for a brief survey of the book: (1) judgment and redemption for Judah (chs. 1 through 12); (2) universal judgment and Israel's redemption (chs. 13 through 27); (3) judgment and redemption for Jerusalem (chs. 28 through 35); (4) Babylonian Exile foretold (chs. 36 through 39); (5) comfort and consolation for Israel (chs. 40 through 66).

Judgment and Redemption for Judah (chs. 1 through 12): Chapter 1 provides a commentary on the entire book. The oracles contained therein describe Israel's rebellion against God and the consequent divine judgment on the nation now in ruins. God rejects the false worship of Israel through which it tries to barter its way back into his good graces. Instead, God invites Israel to repentance and promises that salvation will come and Jerusalem will one day be called a "faithful city" (1:26). Sinful Israel of every age is not doomed to eternal judgment. Rather, through repentance, it has a real future with God.

Chapters 2 through 11 reiterate in alternating sequences the proclamation of judgment and redemption. Judgment, however, dominates the prophet's words. The call of Isaiah (ch. 6), set strategically in the midst of these oracles, highlights the decision of God which pronounces the destruction of Israel, a word already rendered in the heavenly council and now relayed to the prophet. All is not lost, though. Redemption from doom is as much a part of the divine plan as judgment (6:13b). The litany in chapter 12 anticipates the promise of the coming salvation.

Universal Judgment and Israel's Redemption (chs. 13 through 27): Chapters 13 through 27 raise the themes of judgment and redemption onto a worldwide plane. The judgment spoken against the nations (chs. 13 through 23) merges into the final and universal judgment against all the world (ch. 24) from which Israel emerges redeemed (chs. 25 through 27).

Judgment and Redemption for Jerusalem (chs. 28 through 35): Again, chapters 28 through 35 lay a pathway from initial judgment against the drunkards of the land (28:1f.) and the rebellious leaders of Judah (30:1f.) to the rescue of Jerusalem from judgment (chs. 34 and 35).

Babylonian Exile Foretold (chs. 36 through 39): Chapters 36 through 39 sound the death knell for Judah and Jerusalem by announcing the Babylonian captivity. Thus God's word of judgment is effective in history (6:11f.). Yet the stage is also set for the rebirth of the nation through the power of that same word (40:8).

Comfort and Consolation for Israel (chs. 40 through 66): God's will for Israel (40:10f.) headlines the script of chapters 40 through 66. As certainly as the word of judgment is rendered, just as surely God's word concerning Israel's final and decisive redemption will be fulfilled. The prophecy now comforts Israel with God's promises of hope and restoration. The basis for this hope is the sovereignty and majesty of God (chs. 40 through 48). God the Creator is contrasted with idols, which are the creations of humans. His people may indeed be enslaved, but redemption is his final word to his people (44:26). Their present sufferings will receive meaning from their future salvation (53:11), and at the same time usher in a kingdom of peace and righteousness throughout the earth. In that day Jerusalem will be rebuilt, Israel's borders enlarged, and the people's enemies judged. Peace, prosperity, and justice will prevail. God will "make all things new."

OUTLINE OF ISAIAH

Warnings and promises	1:1–12:6
Oracles against the nations	13:1–23:18
God's judgment of the world	24:1–27:13
Further warnings and promises	28:1–35:10
King Hezekiah of Judah and the Assyrians	36:1–39:8
Messages of promise and hope	40:1–55:13
Warnings and promises	56:1–66:24

FOCUS	PROPHECIES OF CONDEMNATION				HISTORICAL PARENTHESIS	PROPHECIES OF COMFORT			
REFERENCE	1.1———————13.1———————24.1———————28.1—				—36.1————————	40.1———————49.1———————58.1—66.24			
DIVISION	PROPHECIES AGAINST		PROPHECIES OF		HEZEKIAH'S DELIVERANCE, SICKNESS, AND RECOVERY	ISRAEL'S DELIVERANCE	ISRAEL'S DELIVERER	ISRAEL'S GLORIOUS FUTURE	
	JUDAH	THE NATIONS	DAY OF LORD	JUDGMENT & BLESSING					
TOPIC	PROPHETIC				HISTORIC	REDEMPTIVE			
	JUDGMENT				TRANSITION	HOPE			
SETTING	JUDAH					BABYLON		JUDEA	

ISAIAH

THE BOOK OF
JEREMIAH

The Book of Jeremiah

Like other preexilic prophets, Jeremiah was called to proclaim God's judgment on his people for their idolatry and wanton disregard for the Sinai covenant. He not only announced the coming catastrophe, which would be inflicted by the Babylonians, but he also endured it. He saw Jerusalem captured, destroyed, and burned. He witnessed two deportations: one in 597 B.C. and the other in 587 B.C. Jeremiah's task, however, was twofold: to announce judgment, but also to proclaim salvation. Jerusalem would one day be rebuilt (31:38f.). God would make a "new covenant" with his people, writing it upon their hearts. "I will forgive their sins and I will no longer remember their wrongs . . ." (31:31–34).

The Author of Jeremiah

The superscription (1:1) informs us that "this book is the account of what was said by Jeremiah." Jeremiah was from Anathoth, a little village about three miles northeast of Jerusalem. He was the son of Hilkiah, a priest, and probably a descendant of the priestly family of Abiathar (1 Kings 2:26f.). His prophetic ministry extended over forty years. Called to proclaim God's judgment upon Judah, his task was extremely difficult and painful. His fellow townsmen threatened his life if he continued preaching in God's name (11:21). Following his proclamation of the destruction of the Temple, priests and prophets charged him with blasphemy, a crime which carried the death penalty (7:1f.; 26:1f.). For having declared Jerusalem's destruction, he was beaten and chained (19:40 through 20:6). He was scorned, denounced, considered a traitor, and thrown into a cistern and left to die. Throughout his ordeal the prophet was deeply conscious that his message was God's (1:7–9), and that he was under compulsion to deliver it (20:9). His hope and trust were in God.

In 605 B.C., Jeremiah dictated all his prophecies from the beginning of his ministry to his secretary Baruch. After King Jehoiakim destroyed this work, Jeremiah dictated another scroll which contained even more material (ch. 36).

Modern scholarship holds that the Book of Jeremiah is a compilation of collections consisting of: poetic oracles delivered by Jeremiah; biographical narratives written by Baruch or other disciples; and prose sermons resembling Deuteronomy, which were edited, expanded, and interpreted by priests and others belonging to the Deuteronomic school.

The Time of Jeremiah

When Jeremiah received his prophetic call (627 B.C.), Josiah (640–609 B.C.) was king of Judah. He was a good king. He initiated a religious reform and commanded that the book of the Law which was found in the Temple (c. 622–621 B.C.) be proclaimed to the people (2 Kings 22:3; 23:1f.). In 609 B.C., Josiah was killed in a battle against the Egyptians. By this time Babylon had already overthrown Nineveh, the capital of Assyria (612 B.C.). Jehoahaz, the new king of Judah (609 B.C.), reigned for three months, until he was deposed and taken to Egypt. Jehoiakim (609–598 B.C.) succeeded him. For the first four years of his reign Jehoiakim was an Egyptian vassal. However, following the Babylonian defeat of the Egyptians at Carchemish in 605 B.C., Judah became a vassal state of Babylon. Meanwhile, the reform of Josiah had collapsed, and idolatry was once again rampant. In 601 B.C., Jehoiakim rebelled against Babylon, and the Babylonian army marched against Judah. Jehoiakim died before Jerusalem was taken, and his son, Jehoiakin (598–597 B.C.) succeeded him. Shortly thereafter, in March 597 B.C., the city fell. The king, along with other prominent citizens, was taken into exile (2 Kings 24:14). Zedekiah (597–587 B.C.), the uncle of Jehoiakin became the new king of Judah. In time, he also rebelled. In July of 587 B.C., the Babylonians captured Jerusalem. To ensure no further uprisings, the Temple was destroyed, the walls of the capital were torn down, and Zedekiah and the leading citizens were deported to Babylon. Judah became a Babylonian province, ruled by a governor, Gedaliah. Within two months Gedaliah was slain. Fearful of Babylonian retaliation, a number of Judeans fled to Egypt, and the prophet Jeremiah was forced to go along.

Thus there were three stages in Jeremiah's ministry: (1) from 627 to 605 B.C. he prophesied while Judah was threatened by Assyria and Egypt; (2) from 605 to 587 B.C. he proclaimed God's judgment while Judah was threatened and besieged by Babylon; (3) from 587 to c. 580 B.C. he ministered in Jerusalem and Egypt after Judah's downfall.

Survey of Jeremiah

The Book of Jeremiah may be divided as follows: the call of Jeremiah (ch. 1); the prophecies to Judah (chs. 2 through 45); the prophecies to the Gentiles (chs. 46 through 51); and the fall of Jerusalem (ch. 52).

The Call of Jeremiah (ch. 1): Jeremiah is called and sanctified before birth to be God's prophet. This introductory chapter surveys the identification, inauguration, and commission of the prophet.

The Prophecies to Judah (chs. 2 through 45): Jeremiah's message is communicated through a variety of parables, sermons, and object lessons. The prophet's life becomes a daily illustration to Judah, and most of the book's object lessons are found in this section (13:1–14; 14:1–9; 16:1–9; 18:1–12; 19:1–13; 24:1–10; 27:1–11; 32:6–15; 43:8–13). In a series of graphic messages, Jeremiah lists the causes of Judah's coming judgment. The Gentile nations are more faithful to their false gods than Judah is to God. The people are condemned for their empty profession, their disobedience to God's covenant, and their spiritual harlotry. God has bound Judah to himself; but like a rotten waistband, Judah has become corrupt and useless. Their sin is very great. Jeremiah can only lament for them. As a sign of imminent judgment Jeremiah is forbidden to marry and to participate in the feasts. Because the nation does not trust God or keep the Sabbath, the land will receive a Sabbath rest when they are in captivity. Jerusalem will be invaded, and the rulers and people will be deported to Babylon. Restoration will only come under the new Shepherd, the Messiah, the nation's future King. Jeremiah announces the duration of the captivity as seventy years, in contrast to the messages of the false prophets who insist it will not happen.

Because of his message (2:25) Jeremiah suffers misery and opposition (chs. 26 through 45). He is rejected by the prophets and priests who call for his death, but he is spared by the elders and officials. In his sign of the yoke he proclaims the unpopular message that Judah must submit to divine discipline. But he assures the nation of restoration and hope under a new covenant (chs. 30 through 33). A remnant will be delivered and there will be a coming time of blessing. Jeremiah's personal experiences and sufferings are the focal point of chapters 34 through 45, as opposition against the prophet mounts. Since he is no longer allowed in the Temple, he sends his assistant Baruch to read his prophetic warnings. His scroll is burned by Jehoiakim, and Jeremiah is imprisoned. After the destruction of the city, Jeremiah is taken to Egypt by fleeing Jews, but he prophesies that Nebuchadnezzar will invade Egypt as well.

FOCUS	CALL OF JEREMIAH	PROPHECIES TO JUDAH				PROPHECIES TO THE GENTILES	FALL OF JERUSALEM
REFERENCE	1.1—————	2.1—————	26.1—————	30.1—————	34.1—————	46.1—————	52.1————52.34
DIVISION	PROPHETIC COMMISSION	CONDEMNATION OF JUDAH	CONFLICTS OF JEREMIAH	FUTURE RESTORATION OF JERUSALEM	PRESENT FALL OF JERUSALEM	CONDEMNATION OF NINE NATIONS	HISTORIC CONCLUSION
TOPIC		BEFORE THE FALL			THE FALL	AFTER THE FALL	
	CALL	MINISTRY					RETROSPECT
SETTING		JUDAH					

JEREMIAH

The Prophecies to the Gentiles (chs. 46 through 51): These chapters are a series of prophetic oracles against nine nations: Egypt, Philistia, Moab, Ammon, Edom, Damascus (Syria), Arabia, Elam, and Babylon. Only Egypt, Moab, Ammon, and Elam are given a promise of restoration.

The Fall of Jerusalem (ch. 52): Jeremiah's forty-year declaration of doom was finally vindicated in an event so significant that it is recorded in detail four times in the Scriptures (2 Kings 25; 2 Chron. 36; Jer. 39 and 52). In this historical supplement Jerusalem is captured, destroyed, and plundered. The leaders are killed and the captives taken to Babylon.

OUTLINE OF JEREMIAH

The call of Jeremiah	1:1–19	Events in Jeremiah's life	26:1–45:5
Prophecies during the reigns of Josiah, Jehoiakim, Jehoiakin, and Zedekiah	2:1–25:38	Prophecies against the nations	46:1–51:64
		The fall of Jerusalem	52:1–34

LAMENTATIONS

The Book of Lamentations

The Book of Lamentations consists of five poems lamenting the destruction, desolation, and ruin of Jerusalem in 587 B.C. The cessation of worship in the Temple, the exile of the king and leaders, the ravages of famine, and the broken spirit of the survivors are vividly described with much feeling. The laments not only express profound grief, but manifest a deep faith and hope in the Lord. The poet sees that God brought about the fall of Jerusalem in order to chastise his elect for their unrighteousness and unfaithfulness. The people were guilty, and the punishment was deserved. But the poet looks beyond the present to the future. The Lord's love is steadfast. He is merciful and forgiving. He has the power to restore.

The Hebrew Bible places the Book of Lamentations among the Writings (the third section of its threefold division of the Bible). The ancient Greek translation of the Old Testament (Septuagint) and the Latin translation of the Bible (Vulgate) place the book among the Prophets, after the Book of Jeremiah.

The Author of Lamentations

The author of Lamentations is unnamed in the book. However, early Jewish and Christian tradition ascribes the book to Jeremiah. This conclusion is probably based on Second Chronicles 35:25, where the author states that Jeremiah composed a lament for King Josiah (640–609 B.C.), and is supported by the fact that Lamentations fits the final days of Jeremiah. However, modern scholarship, based on literary considerations within the book itself, is almost unanimous in agreeing that Jeremiah is not the author. The author is unknown. Some scholars perceive a single author; others see more than one author. It is generally held that the poems are not much later than 587 B.C., the year Jerusalem fell.

The Time of Lamentations

Following a stalemate between Egyptian and Babylonian military forces in 601 B.C., King Jehoiakim (609–598 B.C.) of Judah rebelled against Babylon. The result was tragic. The Babylonian army marched against Judah. Jehoiakim died before Jerusalem was taken, and his son Jehoiakin (598–597 B.C.) succeeded him. When Jerusalem fell in March of 597 B.C., Jehoiakin was taken into exile along with the prominent citizens (2 Kings 24:14). Zedekiah (597–587 B.C.), the uncle of Jehoiakin, was placed on the throne by the Babylonians. Later he also rebelled, and the Babylonians captured Jerusalem in July 587 B.C. To ensure no further uprisings they destroyed the Temple, tore down the city walls, and burned Jerusalem. Zedekiah and leading citizens were taken into exile. Lamentations was composed shortly thereafter.

Survey of Lamentations

The five laments can be entitled: the destruction of Jerusalem (ch. 1); the wrath of God (ch. 2); the prayer for mercy (ch. 3); the siege of Jerusalem (ch. 4); and the prayer for restoration (ch. 5).

The Destruction of Jerusalem (ch. 1): This poem consists of a description of Jerusalem's wretched state (1:1–11), and a lamentation by Jerusalem, as if the city were a person (1:12–22). The city has been left desolate because of grievous sins, and her enemies "laughed at her downfall" (1:7). Jerusalem pleads with the Lord to regard her misery and repay her adversaries.

The Wrath of God (ch. 2): In this poem the author moves from Jerusalem's desolation to a description of her destruction. Babylon has destroyed the city, but only as God's instrument of judgment. This lament presents an eyewitness account of the thoroughness and severity of Jerusalem's devastation. Through the action of the Babylonians, the Lord has terminated all religious observances, removed the priests, prophets, and kings, and leveled the Temple and palaces. The poet grieves over the suffering the people brought on themselves through rebellion against God (2:1–17). He urges them to cry out in prayer to the Lord (2:18–19), and he, himself, prays for the whole nation (2:20–22).

The Prayer for Mercy (ch. 3): The poet enters into the misery and despair of his people and makes their suffering his own (3:1–18). There is an abrupt turn in verses 19 through 39, as the poet reflects on the faithfulness and loyal love of the compassionate God of Israel. These truths enable him to find comfort and hope in spite of his dismal circumstances. He expresses his deep sorrow as he prays to the Lord for deliverance and for the punishment of Israel's traditional enemy, Edom.

The Siege of Jerusalem (ch. 4): The prophet rehearses the siege of Jerusalem and remembers the suffering and starvation of rich and poor. He also reviews the causes of the siege, especially the sins of the prophets and priests and their foolish trust in human aid. This poem closes with a warning to Edom of future punishment and with a glimmer of hope for Jerusalem.

The Prayer for Restoration (ch. 5): Lamentations' last sorrowful poem is a description of the people's sad state. Their punishment is complete, and the prophet prayerfully desires the restoration of his nation.

OUTLINE OF LAMENTATIONS

The destruction of Jerusalem	1:1–22	The siege of Jerusalem	4:1–22
The wrath of God	2:1–22	The prayer for restoration	5:1–22
The prayer for mercy	3:1–66		

FOCUS	DESTRUCTION OF JERUSALEM	WRATH OF GOD	PRAYER FOR MERCY	SIEGE OF JERUSALEM	PRAYER FOR RESTORATION
REFERENCE	1.1	2.1	3.1	4.1	5.1———5.22
DIVISION	MOURNING CITY	BROKEN PEOPLE	SUFFERING	RUINED KINGDOM	PENITENT NATION
TOPIC	GRIEF	CAUSE	HOPE	MISERIES	PRAYER
SETTING	JERUSALEM				

LAMENTATIONS

THE BOOK OF

EZEKIEL

The Book of Ezekiel

The Book of Ezekiel gives evidence of the early Jewish community's deepening appreciation of the calling and office of a prophet. Perhaps no greater identification between the word of a prophet and God's own Word is achieved in any other book of the Bible than in the Book of Ezekiel. Told to eat a scroll that is inscribed on both sides with "cries of grief . . . and wails and groans" (2:10), the prophet Ezekiel is commanded to proclaim God's judgment to the house of Israel (2:8 through 3:4). Even the unique manner in which Ezekiel behaves and speaks throughout the book forges an unmistakable link between his word and God's will. In expressing God's will for sinful Israel, Ezekiel realizes that the initiative, whether for judgment or redemption, lies solely in the hands of God and nowhere else (37:1ff.) In this book the prophet acts only when God, through the Spirit, causes him to act. Missing from the Book of Ezekiel are the debates with God so characteristic of Jeremiah and other prophets. Instead, the oracles Ezekiel delivers are none other than the word of God that is put into his mouth (3:27).

At the same time, no other prophet's message disengages itself so totally from the particulars of its historical situation to find an application for readers of any era than Ezekiel's. In this book, the concrete features of time and place fade into abstraction. While, in other prophetic books, the reader can easily imagine the circumstances leading up to a prophet's strongly worded accusation or threat against the people, the Book of Ezekiel possesses a more universal and less time-bound character. Absent from this book are the cues that aid the reader in forming a concrete picture of the prophet's audience. Instead, we hear law-court terminology and priestly judgments concerning righteousness and unrighteousness. In addition, we have presented here an abundance of symbolic actions, visions, and allegories. These literary forms engage readers from diverse backgrounds, and various cultures and eras, and conspire to produce the effect of the immediacy of God's word to every generation. This message is summed up in a formula which is used some seventy-two times throughout the book, and issues in a challenge to the Israel of every age: to acknowledge "that I am the LORD," the God who shows himself to be who he is in his power, a providential God who longs to be acknowledged by his unfaithful people.

The Author of Ezekiel

In the biblical world, parents customarily gave their children names which expressed a wish for the newborn. Considering Ezekiel's depressing message of Jerusalem's destruction and the bitter opposition he would receive from those who steadfastly denied that city's demise, no more appropriate name could have been bestowed on him than Ezekiel: "May God make strong." The son of a certain Buzi (1:1), Ezekiel was a priest enlisted as a prophet of the Lord. His prophetic ministry showed a priestly emphasis in his concern with the Temple, priesthood, sacrifices, and the "glory of God," a particular mode of the divine presence which the Jerusalem clergy called the Shekinah. Ezekiel was privileged to receive a number of visions of the power and plan of God. He was quite imaginative and artistic in the lengthy oracles he delivered, especially in those dealing with the history of the Israelites and their apostasy (chs. 16 and 23). Indeed, the prophet endured the charge that he was merely a maker of metaphors (20:49). Not spared the grief of the people who suffered the downfall of Judah, Ezekiel saw his own wife die as a sign of the destruction of his country when Nebuchadnezzar began his final siege on Jerusalem.

The Time of Ezekiel

Ezekiel ministered during the darkest days of Judah's history: the period of Babylonian captivity. This was an era of intense political and religious crises for many of Ezekiel's countrymen. In 597 B.C. King Nebuchadnezzar of Babylonia retaliated against the rebellion of his vassal king, Jehoiakim of Judah, by marching against Jerusalem and forcing the city to surrender. The assassinated Jehoiakim's successor, Jehoiakin, was carried off into exile in Babylon together with royal officials and the upper class of the city, among whom was Ezekiel, the prophet-to-be. With Jehoiakin in exile, and his uncle Zedekiah placed on the Jerusalem throne by the Babylonians, political confusion reigned. Certain factions backed one or the other of the two kings, while various parties advocated either compliance with or opposition to Nebuchadnezzar. Holding sway, the latter groups renewed rebellion against Babylon. Finally, in 587 B.C., Nebuchadnezzar destroyed Jerusalem after a long siege. Many more exiles from Palestine joined those previously settled in Babylonia.

From 592 to 587 B.C., Ezekiel found it necessary to convince the disbelieving Jewish exiles that there was no hope of immediate deliverance. It was not, however, until those exiles heard that Jerusalem was destroyed that their false hopes of returning were finally abandoned. During the first stage of his ministry, Ezekiel communicated the message that the rebellious people of Israel deserved the punishment of exile because their behavior had been an abomination to God (6:13; 14:23).

Yet the Exile was not the end but only a turning point in Judah's fortunes. No more affliction, suffering, or punishment from God would follow in the immediate future. In this, the second stage of his ministry, Ezekiel prepared his fellow exiles for the coming new age. This appears best in his discourses in chapters 33 through 39. Both Israel and Judah will return from Exile. Israel will be given a new heart and a new spirit. God will pour out his Spirit upon his people and make a new covenant with them, a covenant of peace.

Survey of Ezekiel

The Book of Ezekiel may be divided as follows: the commission of Ezekiel (chs. 1 through 3); the judgment on Judah (chs. 4 through 24); the judgment on the Gentiles (chs. 25 through 32); and the restoration of Israel (chs. 33 through 48).

The Commission of Ezekiel (chs. 1 through 3): God gives Ezekiel an overwhelming vision of his divine glory, and commissions him to be his prophet. Ezekiel is given instruction, enablement, and responsibility.

The Judgment on Judah (chs. 4 through 24): Ezekiel directs his prophecies against the nation God chose for himself. The prophet's signs and sermons (chs. 4 through 7) point to the certainty of Judah's judgment. In chapters 8 through 11, Judah's past sins and coming doom are seen in a series of visions of the abominations in the Temple, the slaying of the wicked, and the departing glory of God. The priests and princes are condemned as the glory leaves the Temple, moves to the Mount of Olives, and disappears in the east. Chapters 12 through 24 speak of the causes and extent of Judah's coming judgment, through dramatic signs, powerful sermons, and parables. Judah's prophets are counterfeits and her elders are idolatrous. They have become a fruitless vine and an adulterous wife. Babylon will swoop down like an eagle and pluck them up. The people are responsible for their own sins, and they are not being unjustly judged for the sins of their ancestors. Judah has been unfaithful, but God promises that her judgment will be followed by restoration.

The Judgment on the Gentiles (chs. 25 through 32): Judah's nearest neighbors may gloat over her destruction, but they will be next in line. They, too, will suffer the fate of siege and destruction by Babylon. Ezekiel shows the full circle of judgment on the nations that surround Judah by following them in a clockwise circuit: Ammon, Moab, Edom, Philistia, Tyre, and Sidon (chs. 25 through 28). Chapters 29 through 32 contain a series of oracles against Egypt. Unlike the nations in chapters 25 through 28 that were destroyed by Nebuchadnezzar, Egypt will continue to exist, but as "the weakest kingdom of all" (29:15).

The Restoration of Israel (chs. 33 through 48): The prophecies in these chapters were given after the overthrow of Jerusalem. Now that the promised judgment has come, Ezekiel's message no longer centers on coming judgment but on the positive theme of comfort and consolation. Just as surely as judgment has come, blessing will also come; God's people will be regathered and restored. The mouth of Ezekiel, God's watchman, is opened when he is told that Jerusalem has been taken. Judah has had false shepherds (rulers), but the true Shepherd will lead them in the future. The vision of the valley of dry bones pictures the reanimation of the nation by the Spirit of God. Israel and Judah will be purified and reunited. There will be a future invasion by the northern armies of Gog, but Israel will be saved because the Lord will destroy the invading forces.

In 573 B.C., fourteen years after the destruction of Jerusalem, Ezekiel returns in a vision to the fallen city and is given detailed specifications for the reconstruction of the Temple, the city, and the land (chs. 40 through 48). After an intricate description of the new outer court, inner court, and Temple (chs. 40 through 42), Ezekiel views the return of the glory of the Lord to the Temple from the east. Regulations concerning worship in the coming Temple (chs. 43 through 46) are followed by revelations concerning the new land and city (chs. 47 and 48). "The LORD Is Here!" (48:35).

OUTLINE OF EZEKIEL

Ezekiel's call	1:1–3:27	God's promise to his people	33:1–37:28
Messages of doom on Jerusalem	4:1–24:27	Prophecy against Gog	38:1–39:29
God's judgment of the nations	25:1–32:32	A vision of the future Temple and land	40:1–48:35

FOCUS	COMMISSION OF EZEKIEL		JUDGMENT ON JUDAH	JUDGMENT ON GENTILES	RESTORATION OF ISRAEL	
REFERENCE	1.1————2.1———————————4.1———————————			25.1—————————33.1———————40.1———48.35		
DIVISION	EZEKIEL SEES THE GLORY	EZEKIEL IS COMMISSIONED TO THE WORK	SIGNS, MESSAGES, VISIONS, AND PARABLES OF JUDGMENT	JUDGMENT ON SURROUNDING NATIONS	SALVATION FOR ISRAEL	RESTORATION OF THE NEW ISRAEL
TOPIC	JUDAH'S FALL			JUDAH'S FOES	JUDAH'S FUTURE	
SETTING	BABYLON					

EZEKIEL

THE BOOK OF

DANIEL

The Book of Daniel

The figure of Daniel is depicted as the best representation of the way to balance adherence to God's ways with the rule and domination of gentile kings. Daniel interprets dreams and has visions. In this way he helps his countrymen and the Gentiles to see that the God of Daniel is superior to all foreign gods. Daniel's God is the Lord of history. He uses the rise and fall of kings and nations to accomplish his plan. Daniel's people are suffering terrible indignation. Their country has been destroyed; their exile is shameful. Daniel encourages them to be faithful to their values. They should be willing to lay down their lives for their faith.

The Author of Daniel

The traditional view among both Jews and Christians is that Daniel the prophet is a historical person who wrote this entire book. The name *Daniye'l* or *Dani'el* means "God Is My Judge" and the book is, of course, named after the principal character. Ezra 8:2 and Nehemiah 10:7 mention a Daniel as one of those who returned from the Babylonian Exile. The prophet Ezekiel speaks of a Daniel (Dan'el) who was renowned for his piety and wisdom, but who lived at the time of Noah.

The neo-Platonic philosopher, Porphyry (A.D. 304), was the first to question the traditional view. He attributed the book to an anonymous person living around 170–160 B.C. For centuries Porphyry's view was ignored. Recent critical scholarship has revived it, however. They point out that the language is late Hebrew or a form of Aramaic that is surely later than the end of the fifth century B.C. They also point out that the historical perspective of the book reflects the Hellenistic age.

The author wrote principally in two languages, Hebrew and Aramaic. (The Greek parts of the book will be treated under the Deuterocanonical section.) The author probably took previously existing Aramaic stories about Daniel (chs. 1 through 6) and combined them with his own visions (chs. 7 through 12). The book in its final form could well be the work of an unknown editor who added his own material to the original composition.

The Time of Daniel

To discuss the time of Daniel from the narrative of the book is easy enough. The book tells about a Jew, Daniel, who lived in exile in Babylon. To discuss the time of Daniel from an analysis of its language, content, and structure is a very complex undertaking.

The events recorded in chapters 1 through 6 take place during the Babylonian Exile. The material of chapters 7 through 12 seems to be set in Palestine, or at least concerns events that took place there. Critical studies of this book suggest: (1) Daniel is not a historical person; (2) a long period of development lies behind the book as we now have it; (3) the stories in chapters 1 through 6 were written in the Exile but probably in the Hellenistic age; (4) chapters 7 through 14 were written during the persecution of Antiochus IV (Epiphanes), about 170–160 B.C.; (5) the book's theology, language, and historical perspective point to a time long after the Babylonian Exile.

Survey of Daniel

The first six chapters refer to and presuppose some definite historical time frame, but should not be read as though they were actual historical accounts. They should be taken seriously, however, since they aim to edify, to teach, and to shape people's lives.

The visions of chapters 7 through 12 are revelations received in visions or through the mediation of angels. The revelations are about past and present history and about God's establishment of his kingdom in the final age. The overlapping of Hebrew and Aramaic in the text does not fit neatly with the division of the book into two sections: stories about Daniel, 1:1 through 6:29, and visions of Daniel, 7:1 through 12:13. After an introductory chapter in Hebrew, Daniel switches to Aramaic in chapters 2 through 6. The first vision (7:1–28) is in Hebrew, while the final visions (8:1 through 12:13) are in Aramaic.

The Book of Daniel can be divided into the following sections: Daniel and his companions at the court of Babylon (1:1 through 6:29); Daniel's visions (7:1 through 12:13).

Daniel and His Companions at the Court of Babylon (1:1 through 6:29): Chapter 1 introduces the book by giving the background and preparation of the prophet. Daniel is deported along with other promising youths and placed in an intensive training program in Nebuchadnezzar's court. Their names and diets are changed so that they will lose their Jewish identification, but Daniel's resolve to remain faithful to the Lord is rewarded. He and his friends are granted skill and knowledge.

Only Daniel can relate and explain Nebuchadnezzar's disturbing dream of the great statue (ch. 2). God empowers Daniel to foretell the way in which he will sovereignly raise and depose four gentile empires. The Messiah's kingdom will end the time of the Gentiles. Because of his position revealed in the dream, Nebuchadnezzar erects a gold statue and demands that all bow to it (ch. 3). The persecution and preservation of Daniel's friends in the blazing furnace again illustrate the power of God. After Nebuchadnezzar refuses to respond to the warning of his vision of the tree (ch. 4), he is humbled until he acknowledges the supremacy of God and the foolishness of his pride.

The banquet of Belshazzar marks the end of the Babylonian kingdom (ch. 5). Belshazzar is judged because of his arrogant defiance of God. In the reign of Darius, a plot against Daniel backfires when he is divinely delivered in the den of lions (ch. 6). Daniel's courageous faith is rewarded, and Darius learns a lesson about the might of the God of Israel.

Daniel's Visions (7:1 through 12:13): The vision of the four beasts (ch. 7) supplements the four-part statue vision of chapter 2 in its portrayal of the Babylonian, Persian, Greek, and Roman empires. But once again "the people of the Supreme God will receive royal power and keep it forever and ever" (7:18). The focus in chapter 8 narrows to a vision of the ram and goat that shows Israel under the Medo-Persian and Grecian empires. Alexander the Great is the large horn of 8:21, and Antiochus Epiphanes is the little horn of 8:9. After Daniel's prayer of confession for his people, he is privileged to receive the revelation of the seventy weeks, including the Messiah's atoning death (ch. 9). This gives the chronology of God's perfect plan for the redemption and deliverance of his people. Following is a great vision that gives amazing details of Israel's future history (chs. 10 and 11). Chapter 11 chronicles the coming of kings of Persia and Greece, the wars between the Ptolemies of Egypt and the Seleucids of Syria, and the persecution led by Antiochus. God's people will be saved out of tribulation and resurrected (ch. 12).

OUTLINE OF DANIEL

Daniel and his friends	1:1–6:28	weeks	9:1–27
Daniel's visions	7:1–11:45	d. The heavenly	
a. The four beasts	7:1–28	messenger	10:1–11:45
b. The ram and the		e. The time of the	
goat	8:1–27	end	12:1–13
c. The seventy			

FOCUS	HISTORY OF DANIEL	PLAN FOR GENTILES			PLAN OF ISRAEL	WISDOM TRIUMPHS	FALSENESS OF IDOL WORSHIP
REFERENCE	1.1———2.1———	3.23———	———3.24———	7.1———	———13.1———	———14.1——14.42	
DIVISION	PERSONAL VISION OF DANIEL AND OTHERS	PRAYER OF AZARIAH AND THREE YOUNG MEN (GREEK)	VISIONS CONTINUED	DANIEL'S VISIONS	SUSANNA (GREEK)	BEL AND THE DRAGON (GREEK)	
TOPIC	DANIEL'S BACKGROUND	KING'S DREAM	PRAYER	DREAMS BANQUET LION'S DEN	ANGEL INTERPRETS DANIEL'S DREAMS	JUDGMENT	WISDOM AND COURAGE
SETTING	BABYLON OR PERSIA						

DANIEL

191

THE BOOK OF

HOSEA

The Book of Hosea

The message of Hosea, an eighth-century B.C. prophet, was profoundly influenced by his personal marital experience. Gomer, his wife, who may have been a cultic prostitute, was unfaithful. She symbolized faithless Israel. Just as Hosea's love was so profound that he could not abandon Gomer or cease loving her, so likewise God's love for faithless Israel was so unfathomable that he would seek to bring her back. To recapture the love of their early days, God longed for a return to their desert experience.

Israel's infidelity was evidenced in her participation in the fertility rites of foreign gods, to whom she attributed her prosperity. Her rejection of God was further seen in her disregard for the Law, her ruthless oppression of the poor, and her reliance upon military might. God, a jealous lover, would chastise her to bring her back. He would remove the ornaments bestowed by her false lovers, so that she might recognize the true Giver of Gifts and return to him. When humbled, she would seek her husband, God.

In all probability the marriage with Gomer is a real experience in the prophet's life rather than an allegory or vision.

The Author of Hosea

The superscription (1:1) attributes authorship to Hosea, the son of Beeri. Other than the name of his father, we have no knowledge of Hosea's family background or of his birthplace. Unfortunately, he experienced marital difficulties. Gomer, his wife, was unfaithful. He was the father of three children, having two sons and one daughter. Some scholars believe that he was a priest, others that he was a cultic prophet. A contemporary of Amos, Hosea prophesied in the northern kingdom of Israel, more than likely in the capital city of Samaria, or in the areas of Bethel and Gilgal. As those of other prophets, his message was received with hostility (9:7–8). He was well educated. This is apparent in his effective imagery, his elevated language, and his grasp of the historical and political situation. The word Hosea means "Yahweh Saves."

Modern scholarship attributes the book to Hosea and his immediate disciples; subsequently, additions were made to the book.

The Time of Hosea

According to the superscription (1:1) Hosea prophesied during the reigns of Uzziah (783–742 B.C.), Jotham (742–735 B.C.), Ahaz (735–715 B.C.), and Hezekiah (715–687/668 B.C.), kings of Judah, and during the reign of Jeroboam II (786–746 B.C.), king of Israel. Hosea's long career continued after the time of Jeroboam II and spanned the reigns of the last six kings of Israel from Zechariah (746–745 B.C.) to Hoshea (732–724 B.C.). Many modern scholars would date Hosea's prophecies from about the mid-eighth century B.C. to c. 725 B.C..

When Hosea began his ministry, Israel was enjoying a temporary period of political and economic prosperity under Jeroboam II. However, the nation soon began to crumble after Tiglath Pileser III (745–727 B.C.) strengthened Assyria. The reigns of Israel's last six kings were relatively brief: four were murdered and a fifth was taken captive to Assyria. Confusion and decline characterized the last years of the northern kingdom, and her people refused to heed Hosea's warning of imminent judgment. The people were in a spiritual stupor, riddled with sin and idolatry.

Survey of Hosea

The Book of Hosea may be divided as follows: (1) the adulterous wife and faithful husband (chs. 1 through 3); (2) adulterous Israel and her faithful Lord (chs. 4 through 14).

The Adulterous Wife and Faithful Husband (chs. 1 through 3): Hosea marries a woman named Gomer who bears him three children appropriately named by God as signs to Israel. The names Jezreel ("God Scatters"), Unloved, and Not-My-People indicate the fate of the nation. Israel will be scattered, will no longer experience God's love, and will no longer be his special people.

Gomer seeks other lovers and deserts Hosea. In spite of the depth to which her sin carries her, Hosea's love is so profound that he redeems Gomer from the slave market and restores her as his wife.

Adulterous Israel and Her Faithful Lord (chs. 4 through 14): Because of his own painful experience, Hosea has a better perception of God's sorrow over the sinfulness of his people. His loyal love for Gomer is a reflection of God's concern for Israel. Israel has fallen into the dregs of sin and is hardened against God's gracious last appeal to return. The people have flagrantly violated the stipulations of the Sinai covenant. Priests, false prophets, and elders sin and lead others astray. God now arraigns them for their crimes. Although God wants to heal and redeem them (7:1, 13), in their arrogance and idolatry they continue to rebel against him.

Chapters 9 and 10 give the verdict of the case God has just presented. Israel's disobedience will lead to her dispersion. She has spurned repentance; the judgment of God can no longer be delayed.

God is just, but he is also loving and merciful. God must discipline; but because of his endless love he will ultimately save and restore his wayward people (chs. 11 through 14). "How can I give you up, Israel? How can I abandon you?" (11:8). "I will bring my people back to me. I will love them with all my heart" (14:4).

OUTLINE OF HOSEA

Hosea's marriage and family	1:1–3:5	Messages of love, warning, and promise	11:1–14:9
Messages against Israel	4:1–10:15		

FOCUS	ADULTEROUS WIFE AND FAITHFUL HUSBAND			ADULTEROUS ISRAEL AND FAITHFUL LORD			
REFERENCE	1.1————2.2————3.1—			—4.1————6.4————9.1————11.1———14.9			
DIVISION	PROPHETIC MARRIAGE	APPLICATION OF GOMER TO ISRAEL	RESTORATION OF GOMER	SPIRITUAL ADULTERY OF ISRAEL	REFUSAL OF ISRAEL TO REPENT	JUDGMENT OF ISRAEL BY GOD	RESTORATION OF ISRAEL TO GOD
TOPIC	MARRIAGE OF HOSEA			MESSAGE OF HOSEA			
	PERSONAL			NATIONAL			
SETTING	ISRAEL						

HOSEA

THE BOOK OF

JOEL

The Book of Joel

The Book of Joel is characterized by prophetic overtones regarding the end of history. Joel perceives a locust plague as a type and a portent of the day of the Lord (the Day of Judgment). Just as repentance and prayer enable Israel to escape the plague, so the same means will save Israel on the day of the Lord when he comes to judge all nations.

Further revelation will take us beyond the nationalism of Joel to reveal that God's salvation will be extended to all the nations, not just to Israel. Likewise, the Spirit of the Lord will be poured forth, not only upon the Israelites, but also upon the Gentiles. In his Pentecost sermon (Acts 2:16–21), Peter sees the promise of the pouring forth of the Lord's Spirit (2:28–29) as being fulfilled by the gift of the Holy Spirit.

The Author of Joel

Nothing is known of Joel's family background, other than the fact that his father's name was Pethuel (1:1). Some believe that Joel may have been a cultic prophet, while others conclude that he was a priest. He was a preacher of repentance. He sought to get the people to turn toward the Lord and to turn away from sin. The Hebrew name *Yo'el* means "Yahweh Is God."

The Time of Joel

The Book of Joel contains no explicit time references. However, the majority of modern-day scholars, based on internal evidence, assign the work to the postexilic era, believing it to be composed during the time of the Persian Empire. A date around 400–350 B.C. is often given. Some scholars would date the book in the preexilic period, either in the ninth or seventh century.

Survey of Joel

The Book of Joel may be divided as follows: the plague of locusts (1:1 through 2:27), and the new age (2:28 through 3:21).

The Plague of Locusts (1:1 through 2:27): Joel describes a recent plague that has devastated the land. Locusts have stripped the vines and fruit trees and ruined the grain harvest. The situation is desperate (1:2–12). He exhorts the people to repent, to do penance, to fast, and to pray (1:13–14). For Joel, the plague has a deeper significance. It is a sign of what will happen to the nation unless it repents. Unless the people turn away from sin and turn toward the Lord, they will be destroyed on the coming day of the Lord. On that day the land will be invaded by a swarming army. Like locusts the army will be speedy and voracious. The destruction caused by the army will be dreadful: "How terrible is the day of the LORD! Who will survive it?" (2:11). Once again Joel exhorts the community to repent, to do penance, and to pray for deliverance (2:12–17). The Lord hears their prayer and has "mercy on his people" (2:18). He promises to deliver them from the plague, to bless the land with agricultural plenty, and to restore the land to its former condition (2:18–25). Their deliverance from the locust plague is a sign and assurance of their future deliverance, if they remain faithful to the Lord.

The New Age (2:28 through 3:21): Israel will receive many blessings on the coming day of the Lord. The Spirit of the Lord will be poured forth upon all (2:28–29). On that day the Lord will gather the nations for judgment. They will be judged for all the wicked atrocities they inflicted upon his elect people (3:1–8). The Lord will make war on the nations; they will be destroyed (3:9–15). On that day Israel will be restored and forever secure from her oppressors. The Lord dwells in their midst in Zion (3:16–21).

OUTLINE OF JOEL

The plague of locusts   1:1–2:27   The new age   2:28–3:21

FOCUS	THE PLAGUE OF LOCUSTS		THE NEW AGE	
REFERENCE	1.1————————1.13————————	2.17————————	2.28————————	3.21
DIVISION	LOCUST PLAGUE	MOURNING AND REPENTANCE	RESTORATION OF FERTILITY	DAY OF THE LORD
TOPIC	JUDGMENT ON JUDAH		FUTURE JUDGMENT AND RESTORATION OF JUDAH	
SETTING	JUDEA			

THE BOOK OF

AMOS

The Book of Amos

Amos, a mid-eighth-century B.C. prophet, delivered his oracles in the northern kingdom of Israel. Called and sent by God, he denounced the widespread social injustices, which were violations of the Mosaic covenant. Some oracles may have been delivered in the capital city of Samaria. In Bethel, the royal sanctuary, Amos prophesied the fall of Israel and the Exile of the people (7:11). Amaziah, the priest of Bethel, banished him from the shrine and ordered Amos to return to Judah (7:12–13). In 721 B.C. Israel fell to the Assyrians.

The book is an anthology of Amos's oracles and visions. It was probably written by Amos and by some of his disciples. Later, additions were made to the book. The final arrangement of the oracles is the work of an editor.

The Author of Amos

Amos was from the rural area of Tekoa in Judah. This small village was about ten miles south of Jerusalem. Amos was self-employed. He was a shepherd and tended fig trees (7:14). This latter task involved the puncturing of the fruit of the tree, hastening the maturing and ripening process. Amos was intelligent. He knew the wisdom taught by the elders, and he borrowed and adapted their techniques to proclaim his message. His vision was broad, and he was well acquainted with international events. His use of agricultural and pastoral images reveals his keen sense of observation. His prophetic activity lasted for only a brief period of time.

The Time of Amos

The first verse of the book informs us that Amos prophesied when Uzziah (783–742 B.C.) was king of Judah, and when Jeroboam II (786–742 B.C.) was king of Israel. In Judah, Uzziah's reign was a time of prosperity and successful military ventures. He fortified Jerusalem and subdued the Philistines and the Edomites. In Israel, under Jeroboam II, the Israelites attained the zenith of their power. This was a period of great material prosperity. However, only the merchants and the nobility shared the wealth. The rich got richer and the poor got poorer. Peasants, small landholders, and farmers were dispossessed of their holdings by the powerful, land-hungry upper classes. The oppressed had nowhere to turn. Priests, prophets, and judges were intimately associated with the corruption. Then, around 760 B.C., the Lord sent Amos to Israel to announce his judgment on the nation.

Survey of Amos

The Book of Amos may be divided as follows: the eight oracles against the nations (1:1 through 2:16), the three sets of oracles for Israel (3:1 through 6:14), five symbolic visions (7:1 through 9:8b), and a messianic perspective (9:8c–15).

The Eight Oracles Against the Nations (1:1 through 2:16): In this section Amos denounces the nations surrounding Israel. Each nation, in turn, is indicted for atrocities committed during war, for crimes against humanity. The final denunciation is reserved for Israel. Israel is castigated for its transgressions against fellow Israelites—the poor and the oppressed. Amos proclaims God's universal sovereignty. The Lord can make moral demands, not only upon Israel, but upon all the nations.

The Three Sets of Oracles for Israel (3:1 through 6:14): In these chapters, Amos delivers three sets of oracles, each beginning with the phrase, "Listen . . . to this . . ." (3:1; 4:1; 5:1). The first set (ch. 3) proclaims that because of Israel's iniquities, a foreign nation will plunder the land and bring about total destruction. The second set (ch. 4) castigates the women of Samaria, the social elite, who also bear responsibility for the sins of the nation. Repeatedly, the Lord chastises the Israelites so that they might repent and turn away from sin and back to him. But each time God proclaims, "You did not come back to me" (4:6, 8, 9, 10, 11). The third set (chs. 5 and 6) announces the Lord's judgment on the nation for its sins and for its failure to repent. The day of the Lord will be a day of wrath. The nation will be led into exile.

Five Symbolic Visions (7:1 through 9:8b): Amos' three sets of oracles are followed by five visions of coming judgment upon Israel. The first two visions of locusts and fire, which symbolize the coming judgment, do not come to pass because of Amos' intercession. The third vision of a plumb line reveals God's word as one of judgment—"I will not change my mind again about punishing them" (7:8). Amos' encounter with Amaziah, the priest of Bethel, follows (7:10–17). The fifth vision of the destruction of a building, probably the temple at Bethel, reveals that no one will escape God's punishment.

A Messianic Perspective (9:8c–15): The Book of Amos ends on a note of hope, not despair; a note of consolation, not condemnation. God himself will bring about a marvelous transformation. He will restore the Davidic kingdom, and the land will be filled with great prosperity.

OUTLINE OF AMOS

The eight oracles against the nations	1:1–2:16	Five symbolic visions	7:1–9:8b
The three sets of oracles for Israel	3:1–6:14	A messianic perspective	9:8c–15

FOCUS	EIGHT PROPHECIES	THREE SERMONS	FIVE VISIONS	FIVE PROMISES
REFERENCE	1.1————————3.1————————7.1————————9.11————————9.15			
DIVISION	JUDGMENT OF ISRAEL AND SURROUNDING NATIONS	SIN OF ISRAEL: PRESENT AND PAST	THE JUDGMENT OF ISRAEL	RESTORATION OF ISRAEL
TOPIC	PRONOUNCEMENTS OF JUDGMENT	PROVOCATIONS FOR JUDGMENT	FUTURE JUDGMENT	PROMISES AFTER JUDGMENT
	JUDGMENT			HOPE
SETTING	ISRAEL			

AMOS

THE BOOK OF

OBADIAH

The Book of Obadiah

Obadiah, the shortest book in the Old Testament, contains one of the strongest messages of judgment found in the Old Testament. Obadiah sternly proclaims the destruction of a hated enemy, the Edomites. Because they aided the Babylonian army when Jerusalem fell in 587 B.C., and later annexed Judean territory, the Edomites would be completely destroyed. On "the day of the Lord" Israel and Judah would again form one kingdom and triumph over their enemies.

The Book of Obadiah is difficult to date. There are vague references to hostilities that occurred over a long period of time. At one time a number of scholars thought that Obadiah was the earliest of the prophetic books. Hardly anyone holds this opinion today. It is generally agreed that verses 11 and 12 refer to the fall of Jerusalem. Therefore, the book was written sometime after 587 B.C. It could even be as late as the fifth century B.C.

The Author of Obadiah

Obadiah was an obscure prophet who probably lived in Judah. Nothing is known of his hometown or family. He offered hope to the Israelites living in the exilic or postexilic period. He assured them that their enemies would be defeated, that God would ultimately restore his people, and that the Lord would be King (1:21).

The Time of Obadiah

The Edomites and the Israelites were considered to be the descendants of Esau and Jacob, respectively, and tradition traced their ancestry and animosity back to the womb (Gen. 25:23). The Edomites, a nomadic people, settled in the land southeast of the Dead Sea, about 1300 B.C. When the Israelites were on their way to the land of Canaan, the Edomites denied them passage through their land (Num. 20:14–21). The Edomites fought against Saul (1 Sam. 14:47), and were later conquered by David (2 Sam. 8:14). Solomon exploited the Edomite copper mines, and greatly expanded his trade by using the Edomite port of Eziongeber on the Gulf of Aqaba (1 Kings 9:26–28). After the monarchy split, Edom struggled to free itself from the yoke of Judah. Edom successfully revolted during the reign of Jehoram (849–842 B.C., 2 Kings 8:20–22), and remained independent for about fifty or sixty years. However, Amaziah (800–783 B.C.) conquered the land as far south as Sela (2 Kings 14:7). His successor Azariah (783–742 B.C.) completed the conquest and, once again, extended the boundary of Judah to Eziongeber. During the reign of Ahaz (735–715 B.C.), Edom regained its independence. However, it was short-lived. In 732 B.C., Edom became a vassal state of the Assyrians, and paid them tribute for over a hundred years. Edom next fell under the Babylonian yoke. When Nebuchadnezzar conquered Jerusalem in 587 B.C., the Edomites rejoiced (Lam. 4:21–22; Ps. 137:7). Around the beginning of the fifth century B.C., Nabatean tribes from Arabia invaded Edom from the south and east. Toward the end of the fifth century B.C., the Nabateans ruled the region, with Petra as the capital city. During this time many Edomites moved into south Judea, a territory later designated as Idumaea. John Hyrcanus (134–104 B.C.) forcibly converted the Edomites to Judaism. Herod the Great (37–34 B.C.), the Roman puppet-king who was despised by the Jews, was an Idumaean. Ironically, in A.D. 70, when Jerusalem fell to the Romans, the Edomites were staunch defenders of the city. After that time they were never heard of again. As Obadiah predicted, they would be "destroyed and dishonored forever" (1:10), and "No descendant of Esau will survive" (1:18).

Survey of Obadiah

The Book of Obadiah may be divided as follows: the oracle against Edom (1:1–14), and the oracle against the nations in connection with "the day of the Lord" (1:15–21).

The Oracle Against Edom (1:1–14): This oracle declares that God will overthrow Edom. Edom is arrogant because of its secure position in Mount Seir, a mountainous region south of the Dead Sea. Its capital city of Sela (Petra), protected by a narrow mile-long gorge whose walls rise 320 feet, seemed inviolable. The Lord, however, will destroy and completely devastate Edom. Thieves and vintagers may leave something after them, but God will strip Edom of everything. Verses 11 and 12 describe Edom's stance during the Babylonian siege of Jerusalem in 587 B.C. Edom rejoiced when Jerusalem fell (Lam. 4:21–22; Ps. 137:7). The Edomites not only assisted the Babylonians; they also annexed Judean territory.

The Oracle Against the Nations in Connection With the Day of the Lord (1:15–21): This oracle proclaims the imminence of the day of the Lord. On that day, God will triumph over the nations; Judah and Israel will be united, and all the territories once ruled by David will be reclaimed.

OUTLINE OF OBADIAH

The oracle against Edom	1–14	nations in connection with "the day of the Lord"	15–21
The oracle against the			

FOCUS	ORACLE AGAINST EDOM		RESTORATION OF GOD'S PEOPLE	
REFERENCE	1————————10—	———————14—	——————17—	———————21
DIVISION	FUTURE PUNISHMENT OF EDOM	REASONS FOR EDOM'S PUNISHMENT	JUDGMENT UPON THE NATIONS	RESTORATION OF JUDAH AND ISRAEL
TOPIC	DEFEAT OF EDOM		RESTORATION OF GOD'S PEOPLE	
SETTING	JUDEA			

OBADIAH

THE BOOK OF

JONAH

The Book of Jonah

The Book of Jonah describes the adventures of a defiant prophet. When told to go and preach to the Ninevites, Israel's traditional enemy, Jonah sought escape. He boarded a ship, was tossed overboard, swallowed and rescued by a large fish, and sent to Nineveh. There he preached God's message. It was marvelously received. The people repented, and God spared them of his threatened punishment. Jonah was bitter because he wanted Nineveh destroyed.

The Book of Jonah is an instructive lesson. An unknown author composed it to convey a theological message. Jonah represents the typical Israelite of his day. He wanted to limit God's mercy and salvation exclusively to the chosen people. To his way of thinking, God's mercy should not extend to other nations, especially to the hated Ninevites. The Book of Jonah reveals the universality of God's offer of mercy and salvation.

The Author of Jonah

The author of Jonah is unknown. He lived in the postexilic era, probably in the fifth or fourth century B.C. He borrowed the protagonist, "Jonah the son of Amittai" (1:1), from the eighth century B.C. Under Jeroboam's reign (786–746 B.C.) the boundaries of Israel were restored, as the Lord had promised through his servant Jonah, the son of Amittai, from Gath Hepher (2 Kings 14:25). The town of Gath Hepher, near Nazareth, was in Galilee. The unknown author wanted his audience to think of this eighth-century prophet. During the eighth and seventh centuries, Assyria conquered, terrorized, and brutalized the people of the ancient Near East. Hence, they had no difficulty in understanding why the prophet Jonah balked at God's commission to preach to a people they hated.

The word *Jonah* means "dove."

The Time of Jonah

Most contemporary scholars place the writing of the Book of Jonah in the postexilic era. This period, especially following the reforms of Ezra and Nehemiah, was characterized by Jewish isolationism and nationalism. The Jews were the people of God. Many of them believed that Gentiles were to be hated and shunned. Rather than share God's salvation and mercy with foreign nations, they sought to limit God's mercy to themselves.

Survey of Jonah

The Book of Jonah may be divided as follows: the first mission (1:1 through 2:10) and the second mission (3:1 through 4:11).

The First Mission (1:1 through 2:10): A prophet is to go where he is sent and to preach what he is told. Told to go to Nineveh and preach repentance, Jonah refuses lest the Ninevites repent and the Lord should spare them. Seeking to escape from the Lord, Jonah sets sail for Spain, the farthest western point possible. But Jonah cannot escape from the Lord, who causes a storm to arise at sea. Believing a storm arose because someone angered a god, the terrified pagan sailors turn to their individual gods in prayer. Meanwhile, Jonah is sleeping, unaware of the storm sent as punishment. Later awakened and confronted by the evidence that he is the guilty party, Jonah confesses that his God is the Lord of the sea and land. Ironically, Jonah sought to use the sea to escape from the Lord of the sea. Realizing that the only way to save the ship and the sailors is to be thrown overboard, Jonah makes this request. The sailors grant his request, and the storm subsides. The pagan sailors then offer a sacrifice to the Lord.

A large fish, sent by the Lord, swallows Jonah. From within, in thanksgiving for his deliverance from the sea, he recites a psalm of praise. After three days and three nights of confinement, the Lord orders the fish to spew Jonah onto the shore.

The Second Mission (3:1 through 4:11): Jonah, receiving a second commission from the Lord, sets out for Nineveh where he proclaims, "In forty days Nineveh will be destroyed!" (3:4). The results were unbelievable. Accepting Jonah as a prophet, the Ninevites took his words to heart. Sackcloth, ashes, and fasting became the order of the day. Everyone was involved, especially the king of Nineveh. So sincere was the conversion that the Lord had compassion on the Ninevites and relented from inflicting the threatened punishment.

Jonah, the stubborn prophet who was the recipient of God's mercy, now begrudges that mercy to the Ninevites. Unable to deal with his own narrow-mindedness, and filled with rage, he asks to die. But the Lord confronts him and asks, "What right do you have to be angry?" (4:4). Unyielding, Jonah goes outside the city to await its destruction. To protect himself from the searing sun, be builds a hut. The Lord provides further protection by causing a plant to grow. Pleased with his newly found comfort, the next day the prophet sought relief from the heat. To his dismay, the plant had died; the Lord had caused a worm to attack it. The hut provided no solace, as there was no escaping a hot wind sent by the Lord. Once more the prophet wanted to die. Again God confronted him: "What right do you have to be angry about the plant?" (4:9). Why should he be so angry about something so fleeting, and with which he was never involved? If the demise of one plant so upset Jonah, that was all the more reason for the Lord to spare Nineveh. Jonah could not limit the Lord's mercy. The Lord extends his salvation where he wills, even to the hated Ninevites.

OUTLINE OF JONAH

Jonah's call and disobedi-ence	1:1–17	Jonah's message to Nineveh	3:1–10
Jonah's deliverance and thanksgiving	2:1–10	God's mercy on Nineveh	4:1–11

FOCUS	FIRST COMMISSION OF JONAH				SECOND COMMISSION OF JONAH			
REFERENCE	1.1————	1.4————	2.1————	2.10————	3.1————	3.5————	4.1————	4.4—4.11
DIVISION	DISOBEDIENCE TO THE FIRST CALL	JUDGMENT ON JONAH EXACTED	PRAYER OF JONAH IN THE FISH	DELIVERANCE OF JONAH FROM THE FISH	OBEDIENCE TO THE SECOND CALL	JUDGMENT ON NINEVEH AVERTED	PRAYER OF JONAH	REBUKE OF JONAH
TOPIC	GOD'S MERCY UPON JONAH				GOD'S MERCY UPON NINEVEH			
	"I WON'T GO"		"THANKS, LORD"		"REPENT"		"WHY, LORD?"	
SETTING	JUDEA							

JONAH

THE BOOK OF

MICAH

The Book of Micah

Micah, a prophet of social justice, saw the socioeconomic abuses of his day as violations of the Mosaic covenant. Although he also addressed the northern kingdom, his prophetic activity is centered in Judah. There he proclaimed that Jerusalem was as wicked as Samaria, and equally under the Lord's judgment. He boldly denounced corrupt rulers, false prophets, wordly priests, fraudulent merchants, and venal judges. He condemned the mere performance of religious rituals, devoid of a true spirit of religion. God's judgment, he proclaimed, would come upon Judah. Even Jerusalem and the Temple would be destroyed. However, Micah's prophecy goes beyond judgment; he also announces salvation. He provides hope, and proclaims that one day Judah will be restored.

Micah's most memorable passage presents his message as a synthesis of the teaching of the great eighth-century prophets: "The LORD has told us what is good. What he requires of us is this: to do what is just [Amos], to show constant love [Hosea], and to live in humble fellowship with our God [Isaiah]" (6:8).

The structure of the Book of Micah is such that oracles of judgment (1:2 through 2:11; 3:1–12; 6:1 through 7:7) alternate with oracles of salvation (2:12–13; 4:1 through 5:14; 7:8–20).

The book itself is a collection of oracles compiled over several centuries, from Micah's time down to the early postexilic period.

The Author of Micah

Micah, whose name means "Who Is Like Yahweh?" was a late eighth-century prophet and a contemporary of Isaiah. His father's name isn't recorded and we know nothing of his family background. He came from Moresheth, a small village of the Shephelah (lowlands) of Judah, about twenty-five miles southwest of Jerusalem. Micah was deeply aware that he had to speak out against the socioeconomic and religious abuses of his day, and that his message, authority, and strength came from the Lord (3:8). Hezekiah's religious reform was influenced by the preaching of Micah (Jer. 26:17–19).

The Time of Micah

The superscription (1:1) indicates that Micah prophesied during the reigns of Jotham (742–735 B.C.), Ahaz (735–715 B.C.), and Hezekiah (715–687 B.C.), kings of Judah. Thus the outside dates of his prophetic ministry are 742–687 B.C. Prosperity characterized Jotham's reign as king of Judah. During the reign of his son, Ahaz, Assyria was a power to be feared. In 732 B.C. the Assyrians conquered Syria. Then Samaria, the capital city of Israel, was taken in 721 B.C. At the same time, Judah became a vassal state of Assyria. Hezekiah, the next king, fortified and armed Judah and instituted a religious reform. In 705 B.C., Hezekiah rebelled against Assyria and refused tribute. Sennacherib marched against Judah in 701 B.C. He took forty-six of Judah's cities, and records that he confined Hezekiah in Jerusalem "like a bird in a cage." Hezekiah surrendered the city. In 688 B.C., Hezekiah once more rebelled against Assyria. This time Jerusalem was not taken by the Assyrians, and the belief in the inviolability of the city became firmly entrenched in the minds of the people.

Survey of Micah

The Book of Micah may be divided as follows: the Lord's judgment against his people (1:1 through 3:12), the restoration of the New Israel (4:1 through 5:14), and a message of warning and hope (6:1 through 7:20).

The Lord's Judgment Against His People (1:1 through 3:12): God leaves his heavenly temple and comes as an accuser and judge against his people. They are guilty. Their wanton treachery condemns both Israel and Judah, especially the respective capitals, Samaria and Jerusalem. Israel will be destroyed; Judah will be devastated (1:2–7). In a lament over the coming destruction of Judah, Micah conveys the distressing news by employing a series of puns on the names of the towns near Moresheth (1:8–16). Some specific causes of the judgment are then mentioned: the unethical schemes of land monopolists, the refusal to listen to God's Word spoken through his prophets, and the crippling demands creditors placed on borrowers (2:1–11). A message of hope is also given—the Lord will deliver a remnant (2:12–13). Secular leaders who prey on their people (3:1–4), prophets who prophesy favorable oracles to enrich themselves (3:5–7), and venal judges and priests are all harshly condemned. God's presence in the Temple will not save them, for the Temple and Jerusalem will be destroyed (3:11–12).

The Restoration of the New Israel (4:1 through 5:15): Micah's next two chapters contain oracles of messianic hope. Jerusalem will become a great religious center with nations flocking to the city, and there will be peace among the nations (4:1–5). The Lord, the Good Shepherd, will lead a remnant from exile, and will restore his people (4:6–8). Though exile is painful, God will redeem them (4:9–10). Zion's enemies will be crushed (4:11–13). The Messiah will come from the royal line of David. Then he will shepherd his people and inaugurate peace throughout the world (5:1–4). The remnant will become strong and prevail against their captors (5:6–8). Israel will be purified and delivered from instruments of military and political power, and from religious means of guaranteeing her self-security. Israel will put its trust in God (5:9–14).

A Message of Warning and Hope (6:1 through 7:20): In a court trial scene, God, the prosecutor and judge, presents his case against Israel, the defendant. The Lord inquires how he has mistreated his people that they behave as they do. He then enumerates his saving acts from the Exodus to the conquest of Canaan (6:1–5). In response to what they should offer God, Micah responds, "to do what is just, to show constant love, and to live in humble fellowship with our God" (6:8). Those who unjustly and violently acquire material goods will lose everything and be ruined (6:9–16). The faithful have disappeared; plunderers and murderers are everywhere. No one can be trusted; family members are alienated from one another (7:1–6). In the midst of wickedness the prophet places his trust in God, who will save him (7:7).

The nation will be reestablished when the Lord takes up its cause and establishes its right. Its enemies will be crushed (7:8–10). The walls will be rebuilt, boundaries reestablished, and Babylon laid waste (7:11–12). God is called upon to shepherd his flock and to rework the wonderful deeds of the Exodus (7:14–15). The nations will fall before the Lord's power and might (7:16–17). Who is like God? His love remains steadfast. He will forgive the sins of his people and wipe away their guilt (7:18–20).

OUTLINE OF MICAH

The Lord's judgment against his people	1:1–3:12	A message of warning and hope	6:1–7:20
The restoration of the New Israel	4:1–5:15		

FOCUS	JUDGMENT		SALVATION	JUDGMENT	SALVATION	JUDGMENT	SALVATION
REFERENCE	1.1————	—2.1————	—2.12————	—3.1————	—4.1————	—6.1————	—7.8——7.20
DIVISION	THE LORD'S JUDGMENT	SOCIAL EVILS	REMNANT	FAILURE AND DOWNFALL OF LEADERS	RESTORATION	ACCUSATION AND RESPONSE	PROMISE OF SALVATION
TOPIC	PUNISHMENT				RESTORATION	WARNING AND HOPE	
SETTING	JUDAH						

MICAH

THE BOOK OF

NAHUM

The Book of Nahum

The Book of Nahum celebrates the impending fall of Nineveh, the capital of Israel's ancient and fearful enemy, the Assyrians. The fall of Nineveh is seen as the Lord's judgment upon the nation for its wickedness. Nahum's prophecy is a powerful vindication of the Lord's kingship over all nations, however powerful they may appear. It also illustrates the ultimate triumph of God over human evil and national arrogance. The date of the book must be placed sometime after the year 663 B.C. since Thebes, the ancient capital of upper Egypt, fell to the Assyrians in that year, and Nahum mentions its destruction (3:8). Most scholars believe the book was composed before 612 B.C., the year Nineveh fell.

The Author of Nahum

Nahum is a late seventh-century prophet. We know nothing of his family and background. In the superscription, he is called an Elkoshite (1:1). The exact location of the town of Elkosh remains uncertain. Some scholars believe that Nahum was a prophet in the service of the Temple. Nahum is probably a shortened form of Nahumiah meaning "Yahweh Comforts."

The Time of Nahum

The hatred which the people of Nahum's day expressed toward Assyria was deeply ingrained. The Assyrians were brutal and savage in warfare, and Assyria's history was one of constant warfare. In 721 B.C., Sargon II (722–705 B.C.) destroyed Samaria, the capital city of Israel. Under Sennacherib (705–681 B.C.) the Assyrians devastated Judah in 701 B.C. Assyria reached the zenith of its power and prosperity under Ashurbanipal (669–633 B.C.). It extended its sway as far south as Thebes, the capital of upper Egypt, which fell in 663 B.C. Following the death of Ashurbanipal, the Assyrian empire began to disintegrate. New powers, the Medes and the Babylonians, were on the horizon. They attacked and conquered Assyrian outposts and cities until only the heartland remained. In 614 B.C. the ancient capital city, Asshur, was captured. In 612 B.C., the Medes and Babylonians assaulted Nineveh and utterly destroyed it.

Survey of Nahum

The Book of Nahum may be divided as follows: God's judgment on Nineveh (1:1–15), and the fall of Nineveh (2:1 through 3:19).

God's Judgment on Nineveh (1:1–15): Nahum portrays God's coming in a storm to rescue his people. He begins with a clear description of the character of God. Because of his righteousness, he is a God of vengeance (1:2). The Lord is also characterized by patience (1:3) and power (1:3–6). He is gracious to all who respond to him, but those who rebel against him will be overthrown (1:7–8). Because of its wickedness Nineveh will be utterly destroyed (1:9–10, 14), and Judah will be free of its yoke (1:13). Nothing can stand in the way of judgment, and this is a message of comfort to the people of Judah (1:15). The threat of an Assyrian invasion will soon be over.

The Fall of Nineveh (2:1 through 3:19): Assyria will be conquered, but Judah will be restored (2:1–2). Nahum's description of the siege (2:3–7) and plundering of Nineveh (2:8–13) is one of the most vivid portraits of battle in Scripture. The storming warriors and chariots can almost be seen as they enter the city through a breach in the wall. As the Ninevites flee in terror, the invading army plunders the treasures of the city. Nineveh is burned and cut off forever. Nineveh's destruction is the Lord's work.

Nahum closes his oracle of judgment with God's reasons for overthrowing Nineveh. The city is characterized by cruelty and corruption (3:1–7). Just as Assyria had crushed the Egyptian capital of Thebes, Assyria's capital city will also be destroyed (3:8–10). Nineveh is fortified so well that defeat seems impossible, but God proclaims that its destruction is inevitable (3:11–19). None of its resources can deter divine judgment.

OUTLINE OF NAHUM

Judgment on Nineveh 1:1–15   The fall of Nineveh 2:1–3:19

FOCUS	DESTRUCTION OF NINEVEH DECREED		DESTRUCTION OF NINEVEH DESCRIBED		DESTRUCTION OF NINEVEH DESERVED	
REFERENCE	1.1————————1.9		2.1————————2.3		3.1————————3.12————3.19	
DIVISION	GENERAL PRINCIPLES OF DIVINE JUDGMENT	DESTRUCTION OF NINEVEH AND DELIVERANCE OF JUDAH	THE CALL TO BATTLE	DESCRIPTION OF THE DESTRUCTION OF NINEVEH	REASONS FOR THE DESTRUCTION OF NINEVEH	INEVITABLE DESTRUCTION OF NINEVEH
TOPIC	VERDICT OF VENGEANCE		VISION OF VENGEANCE		VINDICATION OF VENGEANCE	
	WHAT GOD WILL DO		HOW GOD WILL DO IT		WHY GOD WILL DO IT	
SETTING	JUDAH					

NAHUM

THE BOOK OF

HABAKKUK

The Book of Habakkuk

The Book of Habakkuk deals with the problem of evil on an international scale. Habakkuk looks at Judean society in his day. Wickedness is widespread. The prophet cries to God and questions his ways. Why doesn't the Lord correct the situation? When God informs Habakkuk that he will send the Chaldeans (Babylonians) as his instrument to bring judgment upon the wicked Judeans, the prophet is deeply distressed. How can the Lord send the ruthless Chaldeans to punish his own people, who though guilty, are more just than their oppressors? (1:13). God assures Habakkuk that the wicked will be destroyed. He controls the outcome of history. He exercises his universal rule over all nations. He is preparing the final victory. Those who are just, if they put their trust in God, and if they are patient for his plan to unfold, will survive (2:4). Habakkuk sings God's praises (ch. 3), even though he doesn't fully understand his ways.

A commentary on the first two chapters of Habakkuk was found among the Dead Sea Scrolls in Qumran. The commentary was interpreted by the Essenes, a Jewish sect living in Qumran, in the light of their own history.

The Author of Habakkuk

In the introduction to the book (1:1) and in the introduction to the closing canticle (3:1) Habakkuk is identified as "the prophet." This special designation may indicate that Habakkuk was a professional prophet. Some believe that he may have been a prophet of the Temple. We know nothing of his family background, nor his place of origin. He was a contemporary of the prophet Jeremiah.

A late story in the deuterocanonical book of Daniel (Dan. 14:32–38 [Bel 33–39]) relates that Habakkuk was transported from Judah to Babylon and then back again in order to feed the imprisoned Daniel. This deuterocanonical story has no historical basis. The meaning and etymology of the name are uncertain.

The Time of Habakkuk

The introduction to the Book of Habakkuk (1:1), unlike earlier prophetical books, does not give us any information concerning the date of the prophet's prophecy. Some scholars maintain that Judah's oppressors are the Assyrians. These scholars would date the book somewhere between 626 B.C., when the Chaldeans appeared as a threat to the Assyrian empire, and 612 B.C., when the capital of Assyria, Nineveh, fell. However, the more widely held opinion is that the Chaldeans (Babylonians) (1:6) are in view throughout the book, and that they are God's instrument charged with executing his judgment on the wicked of Judah. This latter opinion would place the prophecy somewhere between 612 B.C. and 587 B.C.

In 626 B.C., a Chaldean by the name of Nabopolassar (626–605 B.C.) revolted against the Assyrians and seized the throne of Babylon. The mighty Assyrian empire was about to crumble. The ancient Assyrian capital, Asshur, fell to the Medes in 614 B.C. Two years later the Medes and Babylonians joined forces to capture and destroy Nineveh, the later Assyrian capital. In 609 B.C., Judah became a vassal state of Egypt, and Neco II (609–593 B.C.) placed Jehoiakim (609–598 B.C.) on the throne of Judah. During Jehoiakim's reign pagan practices set in, and the reform of his father Josiah completely collapsed. The Babylonians, under Nebuchadnezzar, defeated the Egyptians at Carchemish in 605 B.C. Shortly afterward, Nebuchadnezzar (605/4–562 B.C.) became the ruler of Babylon. Judah became a vassal state of Babylon. When the Egyptian and Babylonian forces were engaged in a stalemate in 601 B.C., Jehoiakim thought it was timely to revolt against Babylon. The Babylonian army marched against Judah. Jehoiakim died during the invasion and was succeeded by Jehoiakin (598–597 B.C.) his son. Within three months Jerusalem surrendered. In 597 B.C., the king, the high officials, and the prominent citizens were taken into exile in Babylon. The Babylonians enthroned Zedekiah, Jehoiakin's uncle (597–587 B.C.). Zedekiah also rebelled against the Babylonians. In July of 587 B.C. the Babylonian army broke through the walls of Jerusalem. The king, along with other citizens, was taken to Babylon. Jerusalem's walls were leveled and the city was burned.

Survey of Habakkuk

The Book of Habakkuk may be divided as follows: a dialogue between Habakkuk and God (1:1 through 2:4); doom on the unrighteous (2:5–20); and the canticle of Habakkuk (3:1–19).

A Dialogue Between Habakkuk and God (1:1 through 2:4): Habakkuk sees oppression and violence everywhere. He asks the Lord, "How long will you tolerate wicked deeds?" The wicked sin with impunity, and justice is perverted (1:2–4). God answers (1:5–11) that he is raising up the Chaldeans (Babylonians) as his instrument to punish sinful Judah. The Chaldeans will come against Judah swiftly, violently, and completely. The coming storm from the east will be the Lord's answer to Judah's wickedness.

God's answer prompts a second complaint from Habakkuk (1:12–17). The prophet, more perplexed than ever, asks how the Lord can punish Judah with a nation that is even more wicked. Babylonian captives are treated like animals. The Babylonians even worship their weapons of war. Will the Lord, whose eyes are too pure to gaze upon evil, reward the Babylonians for their cruelty and idolatry? Habakkuk will await his reply. God's reply comes in a vision, and it is to be written down. The vision will be fulfilled in the appointed time set by God. The righteous person, who patiently awaits the fulfillment of the divine plan and who firmly believes in the Lord's justice, will survive the coming doom (2:1–4).

Doom on the Unrighteous (2:5–20): Oppressed nations will taunt the oppressor. They will utter five oracles of doom against the oppressor: for greed (2:6b–8), for exploitation and extortion (2:9–11), for violence (2:12–14), for extreme cruelty (2:15–17), and for idolatry (2:18–20). The seed of wickedness sown by the oppressor will reap self-destruction. The Lord is aware of the wickedness of Babylon. Babylon will not escape his judgment. After the oracles are proclaimed, there is a call to worship God in awe-filled silence (2:20).

The Canticle of Habakkuk (3:1–19): Habakkuk concludes with a canticle of praise for the person (3:1–3), power (3:4–12), and plan (3:13–19) of God. He now acknowledges the Lord's wisdom in the coming invasion of Judah. He will await the day of distress that will come for the oppressors of his nation. God's creative and redemptive work in the past gives the prophet confidence in the divine purposes at a time when he would otherwise despair. "I will still be joyful and glad, because the LORD God is my savior" (3:18).

OUTLINE OF HABAKKUK

Habakkuk's complaints and the Lord's replies	1:1–2:4	
Doom on the unrigh- teous		2:5–20
Habakkuk's prayer		3:1–19

FOCUS	HABAKKUK'S COMPLAINTS AND THE LORD'S ANSWERS				HABAKKUK'S PRAYER OF PRAISE
REFERENCE	1.1————————1.5————————1.12————————2.2————————3.1————————3.19				
DIVISION	FIRST PROBLEM OF HABAKKUK	FIRST REPLY OF GOD	SECOND PROBLEM OF HABAKKUK	SECOND REPLY OF GOD	PRAYER OF PRAISE OF HABAKKUK
TOPIC	FAITH TROUBLED				FAITH TRIUMPHANT
	WHAT GOD IS DOING				WHO GOD IS
SETTING	JUDAH				

HABAKKUK

THE BOOK OF

ZEPHANIAH

The Book of Zephaniah

One of the central concepts of Zephaniah, if not *the* central concept, is the day of the Lord, which this prophet borrowed from Amos and Isaiah. There is also a strong emphasis on the covenant. Zephaniah hammers home his message repeatedly that the day of the Lord (Judgment Day) is coming when the malignancy of sin will be dealt with. Israel and her gentile neighbors will soon experience the crushing hand of God's wrath. But after the chastening process is over, blessing will come in the person of the Messiah, who will be the cause for praise and singing. The dispersed and conquered people of God will be restored. There will be a remnant who should be a humble, lowly people, completely dependent on God and fully trusting in him. Zephaniah strongly denounces idolatry. He has harsh words for those who try to mix faith in God with the religious teachings and practices of paganism.

The Author of Zephaniah

We know very little of this prophet, other than what we find in his writing. He is called the son of Cushi (which means "the Ethiopian"). Zephaniah traces his lineage back four generations to Hezekiah. This is probably Hezekiah the king of Judah. If he was the great-great-grandson of this king he would be the only prophet of royal descent. This could have given him freer access to the court of Josiah in whose reign he prophesied. His name means "The Lord Treasured" or "The Lord Protected."

The Time of Zephaniah

The superscription to the book tells us that Zephaniah prophesied during the days of Josiah who reigned in Judah from 640–609 B.C. The sins catalogued in 1:3–13 and 3:1–7 are taken as a clue by many scholars to indicate a date prior to Josiah's reforms, when the sins from the reigns of Manasseh and Amon still predominated. It is therefore likely that Zephaniah's ministry played a significant role in preparing Judah for the reforms that took place under Josiah. The first reform took place in the twelfth year of Josiah's reign (628 B.C.; 2 Chron. 34:3–7) when he tore down all the altars of Baal, destroyed the foreign incense altars, burned the bones of pagan priests, and broke all molten images in pieces. Six years later (622 B.C.) Josiah's second reform took place.

Some scholars date Zephaniah's ministry to the time of Josiah's death in 609 B.C. Babylon was a growing power and was a threat to Judah. The consensus today, however, is that Zephaniah was at work in Judah during Josiah's reign but prior to the reform of 621 B.C.

Survey of Zephaniah

On the whole, Zephaniah is a fierce and grim book of warning about the coming day of the Lord. Desolation, darkness, and ruin will strike Judah and the nations because of the wrath of God upon sin. Zephaniah looks beyond judgment, however, to a time of joy when God will cleanse the nations and restore the fortunes of his people Israel. The book begins with God's declaration, "I am going to destroy everything on earth" (1:2); but it ends with this promise, "The time is coming! I will bring your scattered people home" (3:20). Zephaniah moves three times from the general to the specific: (1)

215

from universal judgment (1:1–3) to judgment upon Judah (1:4 through 2:3); (2) from judgment upon surrounding nations (2:4–15) to judgment upon Jerusalem (3:1–7); (3) from judgment and cleansing of all nations (3:8–10) to restoration of Israel (3:11–20). The two broad divisions of the book are: the judgment in the day of the Lord (1:1 through 3:8), and the salvation in the day of the Lord (3:9–20).

The Judgment in the Day of the Lord (1:1 through 3:8): The prophetic oracle begins with an awesome statement of God's coming judgment upon the entire earth because of the sins of men (1:2–3). Zephaniah then concentrates on the judgment of Judah (1:4–18), listing some of the offenses that will cause it to come. Judah is polluted with idolatrous priests who promote the worship of Baal and nature, and her officials and princes are completely corrupt. Therefore, the day of the Lord is imminent; and it will be characterized by terror, desolation, and distress. However, by his grace, God appeals to his people to repent and humble themselves to avert the coming disaster before it is too late (2:1–3).

Zephaniah pronounces God's coming judgment upon the nations that surround Judah (2:4–15). He looks in all four directions: Philistia (west), Moab and Ammon (east), Sudan (south), and Assyria (north). Then he focuses on Jerusalem, the center of God's dealings (3:1–7). Jerusalem is characterized by spiritual rebellion and moral treachery.

The Salvation in the Day of the Lord (3:9–20): After a broad statement of the judgment of all nations (3:8), Zephaniah changes the tone of the remainder of his book to blessing; for this, too, is an aspect of the day of the Lord. The nation will be cleansed and will call on the name of the Lord (3:9–10). The remnant of Israel will be regathered, redeemed, and restored (3:11–20). They will rejoice in their Redeemer, and he will be in their midst. Zephaniah opens with idolatry, wrath, and judgment, but closes with true worship, rejoicing, and blessing.

OUTLINE OF ZEPHANIAH

The day of the Lord's judgment	1:1–2:3	bors	2:4–15
The doom of Israel's neighbors		Jerusalem's doom and redemption	3:1–20

FOCUS	JUDGMENT IN THE DAY OF THE LORD					SALVATION IN THE DAY OF THE LORD	
REFERENCE	1.1————1.4———————2.4————————3.1————————3.8———					——3.9————————3.14———3.20	
DIVISION	JUDGMENT ON THE WHOLE EARTH	JUDGMENT ON THE NATION OF JUDAH	JUDGMENT ON THE NATIONS SURROUNDING JUDAH	JUDGMENT ON THE CITY OF JERUSALEM	JUDGMENT ON THE WHOLE EARTH	PROMISE OF CONVERSION	PROMISE OF RESTORATION
TOPIC	DAY OF WRATH					DAY OF JOY	
	JUDGMENT ON JUDAH					RESTORATION FOR JUDAH	
SETTING	JUDAH AND THE NATIONS						

ZEPHANIAH

THE BOOK OF

HAGGAI

The Book of Haggai

With the Babylonian Exile in the past, and a newly returned group of Jews back in the land, the work of rebuilding the Temple can begin. However, sixteen years after the process is begun, the people have yet to finish the project, for their personal affairs have interfered with God's business. Haggai preaches a fiery series of sermonettes designed to stir up the nation to finish the Temple. He calls the builders to renewed courage in the Lord, renewed holiness of life, and renewed faith in God who controls the future.

The etymology and meaning of *haggay* is uncertain, but it is probably derived from the Hebrew word *hag*, "festival." It may also be an abbreviated form of *haggiah*, "festival of Yahweh." Thus, Haggai's name means "Festal" or "Festive," possibly because he was born on the day of a major feast, such as Tabernacles (Haggai's second message takes place during that feast, 2:1). The title in the Septuagint is *Aggaios* and in the Vulgate it is *Aggaeus*.

The Author of Haggai

We know very little about this postexilic prophet. His name is mentioned ten times (1:1, 3, 12–13; 2:1–2, 10, 13–14, 20). Haggai is known only from this book and from two references to him in Ezra 5:1 and 6:14. There he is seen working with the younger prophet, Zechariah, in the ministry of encouraging the rebuilding of the Temple.

The only other information we have about Haggai is what can be deduced from his oracles. A careful analysis of the text has led some scholars to say that Haggai practiced and preached Jewish exclusivism in the postexilic period. He might have been a member or a leader of a priestly party. These scholars view Haggai as a political activist. His program of rebuilding the Temple was more political than religious. Nevertheless he fulfilled an important teaching office at the time. He explained the conditions, both moral and ritual, under which a person could join the community. This was secondary, however, to his main message: "Build the Temple."

The Time of Haggai

In 538 B.C. Cyrus of Persia issued a decree allowing the Jews to return to their land and rebuild their Temple. The first return was led by Zerubbabel, and in 536 B.C. work on the Temple began. Ezra 4 through 6 gives the background to the Book of Haggai and describes how the Samaritans hindered the building of the Temple and wrote a letter to the Persian king. This opposition only added to the growing discouragement of the Jewish remnant. Their initial optimism upon returning to their homeland was dampened by the desolation of the land, crop failure, hard work, hostility, and other hardships. They gave up the relative comfort of Babylonian culture to pioneer in a land that seemed unproductive and full of enemies. Finding it easier to stop building than to fight their neighbors, the work on the Temple ceased in 534 B.C. The pessimism of the people led to spiritual lethargy, and they became preoccupied with their own building projects. They used political opposition and a theory that the Temple was not to be rebuilt until some later time (perhaps after Jerusalem was rebuilt) as excuses for neglecting the house of the Lord.

It was in this context that God called his prophets Haggai and Zechariah to the same task of urging the people to complete the Temple. Both books are precisely dated: Haggai 1:1, September 1, 520 B.C.; Haggai 1:15, September 24, 520 B.C.; Haggai 2:1, October 21, 520 B.C.; Zechariah 1:1, November, 520 B.C.; Haggai 2:10, 20, December 24,

520 B.C.; Zechariah 1:7, February 24, 519 B.C.; Zechariah 7:1, December 4, 518 B.C. Zechariah's prophecy commenced between Haggai's second and third messages. Thus, after fourteen years of neglect, work on the Temple was resumed in 520 B.C. and was completed in 516 B.C. (Ezra 6:15). The Talmud indicates that the Covenant Box, the Shekinah glory, and the Urim and Thummim were not in the rebuilt Temple.

Darius I (521–486 B.C.) was king of Persia during the ministries of Haggai and Zechariah. He was a strong ruler who consolidated his kingdom by defeating a number of revolting nations.

Survey of Haggai

Haggai is second only to Obadiah in brevity among Old Testament books, but this strong and frank series of four terse sermons accomplishes its intended effect. The work on the Temple has ceased, and the people have become more concerned with the beautification of their own houses than with the building of the central sanctuary of God. Because of their misplaced priorities, their labor is no longer blessed by God. Only when the people put the Lord first by completing the task he has set before them will his hand of blessing once again be upon them. Haggai acts as God's man in God's hour, and his four messages are: the completion of the latter Temple (1:1–15), the glory of the latter Temple (2:1–9), the present blessings of obedience (2:10–19), and the future blessings of promise (2:20–23).

The Completion of the Latter Temple (1:1–15): When the remnant returns from Babylon under Zerubbabel, they begin to rebuild the Temple of the Lord. However, the work soon stops and the people find excuses to ignore it as the years pass. They have no problem in building rich dwellings for themselves ("well-built houses," 1:4) while they claim that the time for building the Temple has not yet come (1:2). God withdraws his blessing and they sink into an economic depression. However, they do not recognize what is happening because of their indifference to God and indulgence of self; so God communicates directly to the remnant through his prophet Haggai. Zerubbabel the governor, Joshua the High Priest, and all the people respond; and twenty-three days later they again begin to work on the Temple.

The Glory of the Latter Temple (2:1–9): In a few short weeks, the enthusiasm of the people sours into discouragement; the elders remember the glory of Solomon's Temple and bemoan the puniness of the present Temple (see Ezra 3:8–13). Haggai's prophetic word of encouragement reminds the people of God's covenant promises in the past

(2:4–5), and of his confident plans for the future (2:6–9): "The new Temple will be more splendid than the old one" (2:9).

The Present Blessings of Obedience (2:10–19): Haggai's message to the priests illustrates the concept of contamination (2:11–13) and applies it to the nation (2:14–19). The Lord requires holiness and obedience, and the contamination of sin blocks the blessings of God. Because the people have obeyed God in building the Temple, they will be blessed from that day forward.

The Future Blessings of Promise (2:20–23): On the same day that Haggai addresses the priests, he gives a second message to Zerubbabel. God will move in judgment, and in his power he will overthrow the nations of the earth (2:21–22). At that time, Zerubbabel, a symbol of the Messiah to come, will be honored.

OUTLINE OF HAGGAI

| The command to rebuild the Temple | 1:1–15 | Messages of comfort and hope | 2:1–23 |

FOCUS	COMPLETION OF THE LATTER TEMPLE	GLORY OF THE LATTER TEMPLE	PRESENT BLESSING OF OBEDIENCE	FUTURE BLESSING THROUGH PROMISE
REFERENCE	1.1—————	———2.1—————	———2.10—————	———2.20————2.23
DIVISION	"CONSIDER YOUR WAYS ... MY HOUSE THAT IS IN RUINS."	"THE GLORY OF THIS LATTER TEMPLE SHALL BE GREATER."	"FROM THIS DAY FORWARD I WILL BLESS YOU."	"I WILL SHAKE HEAVEN AND EARTH."
TOPIC	THE TEMPLE OF GOD		THE BLESSINGS OF GOD	
	FIRST REBUKE (PRESENT)	FIRST ENCOURAGEMENT (FUTURE)	SECOND REBUKE (PRESENT)	SECOND ENCOURAGEMENT (FUTURE)
SETTING	JERUSALEM			

HAGGAI

THE BOOK OF

ZECHARIAH

The Book of Zechariah

For a dozen years or more, the task of rebuilding the Temple has been half completed. Zechariah is commissioned by God to encourage the people in their unfinished responsibility. Rather than exhorting them to action with strong words of rebuke, Zechariah seeks to encourage them to action by reminding them of the future importance of the Temple. The Temple must be built, for one day the Messiah's glory will inhabit it. But future blessing is contingent upon present obedience. The people are not merely building a building; they are building the future. With that as their motivation, they can enter into the building project with wholehearted zeal, for their Messiah is coming.

Zekar-yah means "God Remembers" or "God Has Remembered." This theme dominates the whole book: Israel will be blessed because God remembers the covenant he made with the fathers. The Greek and Latin version of his name is *Zacharias*.

The Author of Zechariah

Zechariah ("God Remembers") was a popular name shared by no fewer than twenty-nine Old Testament characters. It may have been given out of gratitude for God's gift of a baby boy. Like his predecessors, Jeremiah and Ezekiel, Zechariah was of priestly lineage as the son of Berechiah and grandson of Iddo (1:1; Ezra 5:1; 6:14; Neh. 12:4, 16). He was born in Babylon and was brought by his grandfather to Palestine when the Jewish exiles returned under Zerubbabel and Joshua the High Priest. If he was the "young man" of 2:4, he was called to prophesy at an early age in 520 B.C. According to Jewish tradition, Zechariah was a member of the Great Synagogue that collected and preserved the canon of revealed Scripture. Matthew 23:35 indicates he was "murdered between the Temple and the altar" in the same way that an earlier Zechariah was martyred (see 2 Chron. 24:20–21).

Some scholars attribute chapters 9 through 14 to another author. They place the composition of this section of the book later than the sixth century, possibly as late as the fourth century B.C.

The Time of Zechariah

Most scholars are of the opinion that chapters 1 through 8 are from the same time as Haggai. Both prophets dealt with the important issue of rebuilding the Temple. Zechariah's oracles in chapters 1 through 8 span a two-year period beginning in October-November, 520 B.C., to November-December, 518 B.C.

Chapters 9 through 14 are quite different. They are more visionary in tone than prophetic. They are dated two hundred years later than chapters 1 through 8 of Zechariah. These chapters show dependence on Joel (c. 400 B.C.). Sirach (c. 200 B.C.) speaks of the Twelve Prophets (cf. Sir. 49:10). The date for chapters 9 through 14 of Zechariah then is most likely sometime between 400–200 B.C., probably around 325 B.C.

Survey of Zechariah

Zechariah uses a series of eight visions, four messages, and two burdens to portray God's future plans for his covenant people. The first eight chapters were written to encourage the remnant while they were rebuilding the Temple; the last six chapters were written after the completion of the Temple to anticipate Israel's coming Messiah. Zechariah moves from gentile domination to messianic rule, from persecution to peace, and from uncleanness to holiness. The book divides into: the eight visions (chs. 1 through 6), the four messages (chs. 7 and 8), and the two burdens (chs. 9 through 14).

The Eight Visions (chs. 1 through 6): The book opens with an introductory appeal to the people to repent and return to God, unlike their fathers who rejected the warnings of the prophets (1:1–6). A few months later, Zechariah has a series of eight night visions, evidently in one troubled night (February 15, 519 B.C.; 1:7). The angel who speaks with him interprets the visions, but some of the symbols are not explained. The visions mix the work of the Messiah in both advents, and like the other prophets, Zechariah sees only the peaks of God's program without the intervening valleys. The first five are visions of comfort, and the last three are visions of judgment: (1) The horseman among the myrtle trees—God will rebuild Zion and his people (1:7–17). (2) The four horns and craftsmen—Israel's oppressors will be judged (1:18–21). (3) The man with a measuring line—God will protect and glorify Jerusalem (2:1–13). (4) The cleansing of Joshua the High Priest—Israel will be cleansed and restored by the coming Branch (3:1–10). (5) The golden lampstand—God's Spirit is empowering Zerubbabel and Joshua (4:1–14). (6) The flying scroll—individual sin will be judged (5:1–4). (7) The woman in the basket—national sin will be removed (5:5–11). (8) The four chariots—God's judgment will descend on the nations (6:1–8). The crowning of Joshua (6:9–15) anticipates the coming of the Branch who will be King and Priest (the composite crown).

The Four Messages (chs. 7 and 8): In response to a question about the continuation of the fasts (7:1–3), God gives Zechariah a series of four messages: (1) a rebuke of empty ritualism (7:4–7); (2) a reminder of past disobedience (7:8–14); (3) the restoration and consolation of Israel (8:1–17); and (4) the recovery of joy in the kingdom (8:18–23).

The Two Burdens (chs. 9 through 14): The first burden (chs. 9 through 11) concerns the first advent and rejection of Israel's coming King. Alexander the Great will conquer Israel's neighbors, but will spare Jerusalem (9:1–8) which will be preserved for her King (the Messiah; 9:9–10). Israel will succeed against Greece (the Maccabean revolt; 9:11–17), and although they will later be scattered, the Messiah will bless them and bring them back (10:1 through 11:3). Israel will reject her Shepherd-King and be led astray by false shepherds (11:4–17). The second burden (chs. 12 through 14) concerns the Second Advent of Christ and the acceptance of Israel's King. The nations will attack Jerusalem, but the Messiah will come and deliver his people (ch. 12). They will be cleansed of impurity and of falsehood (ch. 13), and the Messiah will come in power to judge the nations and reign in Jerusalem over the whole earth (ch. 14).

OUTLINE OF ZECHARIAH

Messages of warning and hope	1:1–8:23	bors	9:1–8
Judgment on Israel's neigh-		Future prosperity and peace	9:9–14:21

FOCUS	EIGHT VISIONS			FOUR MESSAGES	TWO BURDENS	
REFERENCE	1.1————1.7————6.9————			7.1————9.1————	————12.1————14.21	
DIVISION	CALL TO REPENTANCE	EIGHT VISIONS	CROWNING OF JOSHUA	QUESTION OF THE FASTS	FIRST BURDEN: REJECTION OF THE MESSIAH	SECOND BURDEN: REIGN OF THE MESSIAH
TOPIC	PICTURES			PROBLEM	PREDICTION	
	ISRAEL'S FORTUNE			ISRAEL'S FASTINGS	ISRAEL'S FORTUNE	
SETTING	JERUSALEM					

ZECHARIAH

THE BOOK OF

MALACHI

The Book of Malachi

Malachi, a prophet in the days of Nehemiah, directs his message of judgment to a people plagued with corrupt priests, wicked practices, and a false sense of security in their privileged relationship with God. Using the question-and-answer method, Malachi probes deeply into their problems of hypocrisy, infidelity, mixed marriages, divorce, false worship, and arrogance. So sinful has the nation become that God's words to the people no longer have any impact.

The meaning of the name *Mal'aki*, "My Messenger," is probably a shortened form of *Mal'akya*, "Messenger of Yahweh," and it is appropriate to the book which speaks of the coming of the "messenger of the covenant" ("messenger" is mentioned three times in 2:7; 3:1). The Septuagint used the title *Malachias* even though it also translated it "by the hand of his messenger." The Latin title in *Maleachi*.

The Author of Malachi

Most scholars think the author must remain anonymous. The traditional name, Malachi, is really an abbreviation of the term in 3:1, *Mal'akiya*, "Messenger of Yahweh." The Septuagint renders Malachi (1:1) an *Angelou Autou*, "His Messenger." It seems that the noun in 3:1 has become a proper name in 1:1. There is no historical information concerning a person by the name of Malachi. There are some who hold the theory that at one time there were eleven minor prophets. Then someone found three collections of prophecies, each having the same introductory words "Oracle of the Word of Yahweh." No name was attached to these three prophecies. The first two became chapters 9 through 11 and 12 through 14 of Zechariah. The third was called the Book of Malachi by making the noun of 3:1 into a proper name in 1:1. Thus the collection of minor prophets added up to twelve. Despite this theory, many today contend that the style and theological content point to a genuine prophetic figure as the source of the tradition found in this book.

The Time of Malachi

The fact that the prophet is recalling the people to proper religious observances indicates that he is preaching before the reforms of Ezra and Nehemiah have become effective. The middle of the fifth century, about 460–450 B.C., is the most likely date of this book.

Survey of Malachi

The great prophecies of Haggai and Zechariah are not yet fulfilled, and the people of Israel become disillusioned and doubtful. They begin to question God's providence as their faith imperceptibly degenerates into cynicism. Internally, they wonder whether it is worth serving God after all. Externally, these attitudes surface in mechanical observances, empty ritual, cheating on tithes and offerings, and crass indifference to God's moral and ceremonial law. Their priests are corrupt and their practices wicked, but they are so spiritually insensitive that they wonder why they are not being blessed by God.

Using a probing series of questions and answers, God seeks to pierce their hearts of stone. In each case the divine accusations are denied: How has God loved us? (1:2–5); How have we (priests) despised God's name? (1:6 through 2:9); How have we (people) profaned the covenant? (2:10–16); How have we tired God? (2:17 through 3:6); How have we robbed God? (3:7–12); How have we spoken against God? (3:13–15). In effect, the people sneer, "Oh, come on now; it's not that bad!" However, their rebellion is quiet, not open. As their perception of God grows dim, the resulting materialism and externalism become settled characteristics that later grip the religious parties of the Pharisees and Sadducees. In spite of all this, God still loves his people and once again extends his grace to any who will humbly turn to him. Malachi explores: the privilege of the nation (1:1–5), the pollution of the nation (1:6 through 3:15), and the promise to the nation (3:16 through 4:6).

The Privilege of the Nation (1:1–5): The Israelites blind themselves to God's love for them. Wallowing in the problems of the present, they are forgetful of God's works for them in the past. God gives them a reminder of his special love by contrasting the fates of Esau (Edom) and Jacob (Israel).

The Pollution of the Nation (1:6 through 3:15): The priests have lost all respect for God's name and in their greed offer only diseased and imperfect animals on the altar. They have more respect for the Persian governor than they do for the living God. Moreover, God is withholding his blessings from them because of their disobedience to God's covenant and because of their insincere teaching.

The people are indicted for their treachery in divorcing the wives of their youth in order to marry foreign women (2:10–16). In response to their questioning the justice of God, they receive a promise of the Messiah's coming but also a warning of the judgment that he will bring (2:17 through 3:6). The people have robbed God of the tithes and offerings due him, but God is ready to bless them with abundance if they will put him first (3:7–12). The final problem is the arrogant challenge to the character of God (3:13–15), and this challenge is answered in the remainder of the book.

The Promise to the Nation (3:16 through 4:6): The Lord assures his people that a time is coming when the wicked will be judged and those who fear him will be blessed. The day of the Lord will reveal that it is not "useless to serve God" (3:14).

Malachi ends on the bitter thought "destroy your country." Although the people are finally cured of idolatry, there is little spiritual progress in Israel's history. Sin abounds, and the need for the coming Messiah is greater than ever.

OUTLINE OF MALACHI

Israel's sins   1:1–2:16   mercy   2:17–4:6
God's judgment and his

FOCUS	PRIVILEGE OF THE NATION	POLLUTION OF THE NATION		PROMISE TO THE NATION		
REFERENCE	1.1———————1.6————————2.10—————		3.16———————4.1———————4.4———————4.6			
DIVISION	LOVE OF GOD FOR THE NATION	SIN OF THE PRIESTS	SIN OF THE PEOPLE	BOOK OF REMEMBRANCE	COMING OF CHRIST	COMING OF ELIJAH
TOPIC	PAST	PRESENT		FUTURE		
	CARE OF GOD	COMPLAINT OF GOD		COMING OF GOD		
SETTING	JERUSALEM					

MALACHI

DEUTEROCANONICALS/ APOCRYPHA

Introduction

The following books: Tobit, Judith, Esther (the Greek text), Wisdom of Solomon, Sirach, Baruch, Letter of Jeremiah, Song of the Three Young Men, Susanna, Bel and the Dragon, 1 Maccabees, and 2 Maccabees, formed part of the Septuagint Greek text and were interspersed among other books of the Old Testament.

This Greek text was not only widely used by Jews but was known as well by numerous "God-fearing" Gentiles who were attracted to the high moral teachings of the Old Testament, even though they had not themselves become converts to Judaism. One can thus readily understand how and why early Christianity, as it spread among Greek-speaking Jews and Gentiles, employed this Greek text. In fact, the majority of Old Testament quotations in the New Testament are based on this translation.

Precisely when Jewish leadership officially adopted the traditional 39 books of the so-called Hebrew Canon is not known; nor is there agreement as to exactly what criteria were used in determining the canon. According to tradition the determination of the books of the Hebrew canon was made about A.D. 90, but there is evidence to believe that official and widespread agreement on this issue came somewhat later.

Among Christians it was apparently only in the fourth century that the issue of the canonicity of these books arose, a situation which is reflected in Jerome's placing these books in a separated section in his Vulgate translation of the Old Testament.

In 1546 at the Council of Trent the Roman Catholic Church officially declared these books to be sacred and canonical and to be accepted "with equal devotion and reverence."

At the time of the Reformation Martin Luther did not regard these books as Scripture but as "useful and good for reading." In his German translation of the Bible he followed the practice of Jerome in placing them at the end of the Old Testament with the superscription "Apocrypha." Protestants generally continued this practice in their translations of the Bible into such languages as Swedish, Norwegian, Danish, Slovenian, French, Spanish, and English (King James Version).

Among Christians who do not accept these books as Scripture there is, however, widespread agreement as to their importance in providing much valuable information on Jewish history, life, thought, worship, and religious practice during the centuries immediately prior to the time of Christ. Accordingly, they make possible a clearer understanding of the historical and cultural situation in which Jesus lived and taught.

Catholics speak of these books as "deuterocanonical" to indicate that their canonical status as Scripture was settled later than that of the protocanonical books. Protestants usually refer to these books as Apocrypha.

THE BOOK OF

TOBIT

The Book of Tobit

The Book of Tobit is one of the Deuterocanonical books of the Old Testament. In the oldest Greek manuscripts it is placed with Judith and the Greek version of Esther, sometimes after the historical books and sometimes after the sapiential books. The Councils of Trent (A.D. 1546), Florence (A.D. 1441), Carthage (A.D. 419), and Hippo (A.D. 393) listed it among the canonical books of the Old Testament.

The purpose of the author is to give, not history, but an "edifying story." The book illustrates, in an effective way, many truths concerning the blessings derived from the practice of virtue, particularly from doing acts of charity.

To achieve this purpose the author made use of several sources, for example, the "Wisdom of Ahikar." One of his main sources, however, was Genesis and its stories of the patriarchs. The journey of Eliezer and the marriage of Issac and Rebecca served as a model for his account of Tobit's journey and marriage to Sarah. Raphael is the angel who was sent by God to guide Eliezer in finding a wife for Isaac. The story of Eliezer's quest is given in Genesis 24. Persian folklore lies behind the story of the demon, Asmodeus. With this and other older material the author of Tobit skillfully developed his double-plot story.

The clear artificiality of the plot shows that it is pure fiction, told for the sake of teaching so many excellent moral lessons.

The Author of Tobit

Tradition tells us practically nothing about the author of the book. In the text itself two pieces of data have led several scholars to argue that the book was written by Tobit and his son, Tobias. In most of the ancient versions, 1:1 through 3:6 is written in the first person. In 12:20, as he is leaving, Raphael admonishes Tobias: "Now I must go back to him who sent me. Write down everything that has happened to you." These two passages lead some to conclude that the book is the record of the memoirs of Tobit and Tobias.

It should be noted that in some versions, for example, the Latin Vulgate and the ancient Aramaic, 1:1 through 3:6 is written in the third person. If it is true that the narrative of 1:1 through 3:6, written in the first person, is older than the version which puts it in the third person, one cannot conclude that the book is written by Tobit, for it considers only the beginning of the history and it is possible that this is only a literary device. Some would say that if the Vulgate has substituted the third person for the first, this would indicate that Jerome did not believe it to be the work of Tobit. If it is not the work of Tobit, it does not appear possible to indicate any other author.

All that one can say from the general character of the work is that the author was a Jew. "Tobit" is the name of the book because Tobit is the principal character.

The place of composition is also unclear. The author, except for the locale of Tobit and Jerusalem, knows nothing of Palestinian or neighboring locales. The territory in which the narrative unfolds is Assyria (Nineveh) and Media—not Babylon (except 14:4), Persia, or other countries. The plot opens and closes in a period of exile and precisely that of exile in Nineveh. Therefore, the book would appear to be destined for exiled Hebrews. It is hard to defend Palestine as the place of writing, because there is no allusion to postexilic conditions there. The book was probably written in the Diaspora by Jews scattered throughout the ancient world.

The Time of Tobit

As far as the date of composition, the absence of all clear data on this subject obliges us to consider some hints furnished by the text.

It can be said that a very early date is not consistent with the data. According to 14:6 and 16 the destruction of Nineveh (612 B.C.) appears in the eyes of the author to belong to the distant past. Chapters 13 and 14, alluding to the devastation and destruction in the country of Judah, bring us at least to the time of the Babylonian captivity, including the destruction of Jerusalem and the Temple (13:11f.). Further indications of a late date are the insistence on paying tithes and firstfruits to the priests and Levites, and insistence on precise observance of the Mosaic Law.

On the other hand, the book lacks any indication of the troubled Maccabean period and the sharp division between the Pharisees and Sadducees. It is therefore suggested that the book was written about 200 B.C.

Survey of Tobit

As the story opens, Tobit as an old man speaks of all the sufferings of his life until the time in which the events of the book occur. An Israelite of the tribe of Naphtali, while living in the land of his ancestors, he was the only one among his contemporaries to practice the law faithfully. Deported to Nineveh, with his wife Anna and his son Tobias, he remained faithful there despite many sufferings, until the day when his scrupulous integrity drew almost blasphemous insults from his wife. Ruined, blind, and abandoned by all, he turned to God in humble and penitent prayer, asking to be taken from this evil world in which he had no hope (1:1 through 3:6).

At that same moment, in the city of Ecbatana in Media, Sarah, the daughter of Raguel, was also insulted by a servant who ridiculed her misfortune. Her seven husbands who had attempted to espouse her were dead; a jealous demon, Asmo deus, had killed them before they could approach her. Like Tobit, she too cried out to God in her distress, asking him to put an end to her days or to end her humiliation (3:7–15).

The prayers of Tobit and Sarah are heard, and God sends his angel, Raphael, who heals both of them (3:16).

The principal character in the story is the young Tobias. His father, Tobit, gives him a long admonition in chapter 4, a collection of proverbs dealing with good works. Then, he sends Tobias to recover a significant sum of money which he had deposited with a certain Gabael in Lower Media (5:1–3).

The angel Raphael, under the name of Azarias, then offers to lead the young man (5:4–22). The angel is not only a guide; he teaches the young Tobias how to face danger. He also teaches him the remedy for the blindness of his father and for the evil deeds of demons. He praises the charms of Tobias' cousin, Sarah, and invites him to ask for her in marriage (ch. 6).

Arriving in Ecbatana, Tobias demands the hand of his cousin, and to the great joy of her parents, the first night passes without incident. Forty days of rejoicing honor the happy spouses. In the interval, Azarias goes to recover the money and bring Gabael back to the wedding celebration (chs. 7 through 9).

During this time, Anna and Tobit are disturbed because their son has not returned to Nineveh. Tobias then leaves Ecbatana and takes the road back home with his wife, always led by the angel. At home he restores sight to his father with the aid of the remedy shown by Raphael. There is prolonged rejoicing in honor of the young spouses.

Raphael reveals his identity before his departure and reveals a new teaching on good works in his proverbs. Finally, he invites his hearers to give thanks to Providence (ch. 12). Tobit responds with a hymn which grows into prophetic utterances on the future glory of Jerusalem (ch. 13).

As Tobit lies dying, he reveals to his son the future. He again recommends to him filial piety, the practice of good works, and the fear of God (14:1–11). After the death of his mother and father, Tobias returns to Ecbatana to take care of the needs of his in-laws in their last days. He dies after seeing fulfillment of the prophecies of his deceased father (14:12–15).

OUTLINE OF TOBIT

Tobit in Nineveh and Sarah in Media suffer and pray 1:1–3:15
Their prayers are answered 3:16–11:18
a. In answer to their prayers God sends the angel Raphael 3:16–17
b. Tobit gives advice to his son, Tobias 4:1–21
c. Raphael travels with Tobias to Media 5:1–7:12
d. Tobias marries Sarah 7:13–9:6
e. Raphael returns with Tobias and Sarah, and cures Tobit's blindness 10:1–11:18
The angel Raphael reveals who he is 12:1–22
Tobit praises God and gives advice to Tobias 13:1–14:15

FOCUS	TOBIT'S FAITHFULNESS		FAITHFULNESS REWARDED	
REFERENCE	1.1————3.16		————12.1————13.1————14.15	
DIVISION	SUFFERING	EFFICACY OF PRAYER	RAPHAEL'S REVELATION	TOBIT PRAISES GOD
TOPIC	PRACTICE OF VIRTUE		TEACHING AND THANKSGIVING	
SETTING	NINEVEH			

TOBIT

THE BOOK OF

JUDITH

The Book of Judith

The book has been called a historical romance, written to inspire the Jewish people to continued trust in God, their historic Savior. As such, it falls within the Hebrew *haggadah* literature, largely fictional material in the Jewish Talmud, whose purpose was to make a moral point. The very name *Judith* is Hebrew for "Jewish woman," and thus represents Israel in her faith and courage in times of great crisis. Having saved them from the Egyptians (5:12) and from other dire circumstances (8:11–20), God will not fail to save his people. But the people themselves must be as faithful and trusting as Judith.

The Author of Judith

The work is anonymous and the author's identity is not known. Extant only in Greek, the book is probably a Greek translation of an earlier Hebrew form. Its wide-ranging review of Israel's troubled past suggests that it may have been written after a similar time of crisis. Some allusions to Greek customs of wearing olive wreaths (3:7; 5:13) might indicate the period of the Maccabees, after the overthrow of the Seleucid Greek kings, about 150 B.C. In his romantic view of Israel's history, the author is saying they defeated the Greeks in the same way they defeated the ancient Assyrians and all their other enemies.

The Time of Judith

The setting of the book is historically so confused that almost all scholars recognize it as a moral tale told in a way that only sounds historical.

Nebuchadnezzar was king of Babylon from 605–561 B.C. The Assyrian empire fell in 612 B.C. Holofernes, while a historical general, really belonged to the Persian army, which defeated Babylon. The author is equally free regarding his geographical details which represent places as being close when they are quite distant, or which are altogether unknown to us. It is sufficient to say that the author goes back to Israel's distant past, distant from the point of view of 150 B.C. He does not seem to be concerned that his history is inaccurate, because his purpose is not to write history but *haggadah*, Jewish teaching presented in a homiletic form. If the Jewish people of 150 B.C. will only be as faithful as Judith was, God will remain the Savior of Israel—his historical people.

Survey of Judith

The setting of the story is in the time of King Nebuchadnezzar, who is described as quite fierce and successful in all his campaigns, plundering every new country his armies enter. His principal general, Holofernes, is likewise formidable. As they prepare to attack Israel, the leader of the Ammonites, Achior, suggests in a speech before Holofernes' war council that defeating Israel will only be possible if the people have been unfaithful to their God. Otherwise, Holofernes himself will be defeated (ch. 5). The general is infuriated at this and binds Achior, sending him to be captured by the Israelites.

Meanwhile, Israel is terror stricken at the news that Holofernes is marching against Jerusalem, and prays fervently to God. The people begin to lose courage (7:19) and fear that all is lost as they see the size of the Assyrian army. Just at that time, Judith hears that the people are perplexed and she speaks publicly to them about the need for trust in God. She has a secret plan.

After prayer to God, she leaves Jerusalem and is arrested by an Assyrian patrol. She pretends to be fleeing the inevitable destruction of the city. She is so beautiful that when she is brought to the tent of Holofernes he is much attracted to her. He holds a large banquet, after which he is so drunk that he falls asleep. Judith takes advantage of this and kills him, beheading him. She brings the head back to the Israelites who rejoice, while the Assyrians panic at the loss of their great general. The Assyrians retreat and Israel is saved. Judith sings a hymn to the saving God of her people.

OUTLINE OF JUDITH

The Jews are threatened with destruction	1:1–7:32	Judith saves the nation	8:1–14:19
		The Jews are victorious	15:1–16:25

FOCUS	THREAT	SALVATION	VICTORY
REFERENCE	1.1——————————8.1—————————15.1————————16.25		
DIVISION	HOLOFERNES MARCHES AGAINST JERUSALEM	JUDITH KILLS HOLOFERNES	JUDITH'S SONG OF PRAISE
TOPIC	PREPARATION FOR WAR	PREPARATION FOR BLESSING	CELEBRATION OF BLESSING
SETTING	ASSYRIAN EMPIRE		

JUDITH

THE BOOK OF

ESTHER
(THE GREEK VERSION)

The Book of Esther (Greek)

The Book of Esther, as it comes down to us, is a combination of original Hebrew elements with embellishments originally written in Greek. These Greek sections are not accepted by non-Catholics, though they were defined as part of the Roman Catholic Canon of Scripture at the Council of Trent in A.D. 1546. The story line, however, is essentially identical with that of the Esther accepted by non-Catholics. It describes the providence of God for his people living in Persia in the reign of King Xerxes. The principal purpose of the book is to describe the victory of the Jews and their consequent salvation during attacks against them in Persia. The Jewish people continue to commemorate this victory at the annual Festival of Purim. The book, which mentions God or prayer only rarely, was considered very secular by some and is the single book of the Hebrew Bible not found in the excavations at Qumran among the famous Dead Sea Scrolls.

235

The Author of Esther (Greek)

The author is unknown to us since the work is essentially anonymous. At the end of the final Greek section, in the postscript, mention is made of a certian Lysimachus who may have been responsible for the actual Greek translation as well as the addition of the Greek sections. In any case he is otherwise unknown to us.

The Time of Esther (Greek)

The setting of the book is the court of King Xerxes of Persia, 486–464 B.C. Scholars are not in full agreement about the amount of history contained in the work, though its author is undoubtedly familiar with a number of authentic Persian customs of the period. There is no other known record that Xerxes had a Jewish consort, Esther, or a Jewish counselor, Mordecai, as the book relates.

The book's Greek translation and final additions were made in the Greek period sometime before 114 B.C.

Survey of Esther (Greek)

In order to show the parts of the original Greek and Hebrew sections, the Greek additions are conventionally lettered A-F and placed in the appropriate parts of the Hebrew text which retains its ancient chapter and verse divisions.

In A, the Prologue gives the strange dream of Mordecai, with the apocalyptic imagery added to show the cosmic significance of the Jewish victory over their enemies. Mordecai's loyalty to the king is noted, which will figure in the later story, chapter 6.

In B, the second section, 1:1 through 2:23, the story relates how Queen Vashti embarrasses the king and is deposed, giving Esther the opportunity to become queen. Esther, a beautiful Jewish girl, is being raised by her uncle, Mordecai. Apparently, Esther's renowned beauty caused her to be included in the king's harem. Then Haman, alluded to in A, hatches a plot to exterminate the Jews (3:1–15). The Greek author introduces a pompous letter of the king's, authorizing the slaughter.

In 4:1–16 and section C, Esther and her uncle are alarmed at the impending doom of their people, and Mordecai prays to God.

In an important addition to section D, the Greek author makes a vivid portrayal of God's power to intervene and change even hardened hearts for his purposes. Xerxes is enchanted by his beautiful wife and gives her the opportunity to reverse the tide of disaster which threatens the Jews.

In 5:1–14, Esther invites the king and Haman to a banquet. Haman is flattered and deceived into thinking all is well. He feels confident enough to prepare for the execution of Mordecai. The tables are turned, however, when Esther reveals that it is Haman who is responsible for her misery. Mordecai, instead of being hanged, is given the honored place of the now-executed Haman.

The Jews are warned by Esther that there is a plan to kill them. Confident of Esther's influence at court, the Jews are victorious over their enemies. Haman, who had thrown "lots" (*purim*) to determine the date of the massacre, gives the modern Jewish victory celebration its name, the Festival of Purim.

OUTLINE OF ESTHER (GREEK)

Esther becomes queen	A:1–2:23	The Jews defeat their ene-	
Haman's plot against the		mies	8:1–F:10
Jews	3:1–5:14	Postscript	
Haman is put to death	6:1–7:10		

FOCUS	THREAT TO JEWS					TRIUMPH OF JEWS		
REFERENCE	A.1——1.1—3.1—B.1——3.14—C.1——D.1——5.3—6.1————8.4——E.1——8.13—F.1—F.10							
DIVISION	ESTHER CROWNED	HAMAN'S PLOT AGAINST JEWS			MORDECAI'S TRIUMPH OVER HAMAN	ISRAEL'S TRIUMPH		
	MORDECAI'S DREAM	XERXES' DECREE	PRAYERS	ESTHER FAINTS		XERXES' DECREE	MORDECAI'S DREAM	
TOPIC	GRAVE DANGER					GREAT DELIVERANCE		
SETTING	PERSIA							

ESTHER

237

THE WISDOM OF SOLOMON

The Book of the Wisdom of Solomon

The Book of Wisdom, or as it is known in the Septuagint, the Wisdom of Solomon, is not a part of the Hebrew canon of Scripture, yet has long-standing support as one of the deuterocanonical works of the Christian Old Testament. The book was written to offer edification to a Jewish community during times of oppression and political suffering, and to reassure faithful members of that community that God indeed rewards those who remain steadfast in the faith. The work combines traditional Jewish material with ideas borrowed from Greek philosophy of the age, and has within its text some passages (notably 3:1–8) frequently used in Christian liturgy. Among its chief themes are divine wisdom, the Exodus event in Jewish history, the mercy of God, and individual retribution. The book is more in the form of an address that the classic teacher-to-pupil style of other wisdom literature.

The Author of the Wisdom of Solomon

Scholars generally acknowledge today that this book's claim to the person of Solomon as its author is a literary device to lend authority to its message. It is evidently the work of an unknown Jewish believer in the Alexandrian community, one devoted to religious learning and eager to affirm the power of Jewish wisdom in the face of the local philosophy of the larger Greek community at Alexandria. The author's work reflects a profound knowledge of the Old Testament writings and also of ideas which were popular in Egypt at the time. The book is written in Greek and is usually dated in the area of 100 B.C. Some scholars argue for more than a single author, and attempt to divide the book into several sections based on stylistic differences and textual study. There is more support at present for a unity of authorship for the whole book. Earlier debates among scholars regarding a possible Hebrew original to the Greek text have largely been settled in favor of Greek as the original language of the work. Its late date makes the Wisdom of Solomon the last book of the Christian canon of the Old Testament.

The Time of the Wisdom of Solomon

The first century before Christ, which is the setting for the book, was an age of intellectual and scientific development, especially at Alexandria among the Jews of the Diaspora (that is, those outside the Holy Land of Palestine). It was also a time of struggle and political unrest in Palestine under Greco-Roman rule. During most of the postexilic period (after 500 B.C.), the Jews in foreign lands especially felt the pressure of maintaining traditional religious beliefs in the face of the popular Greek philosophies of the time. Their faith was often put to the test in pagan surroundings, not only through direct religious persecution, but more subtly in the cultural norms of Greek society at large. The writer sought to affirm the value of Jewish belief in such a context and to support his fellow believers in a time of struggle. The period also produces a movement of clearer acceptability of an afterlife and eternal reward of the just, a movement carried forward in the Christian period soon to follow the time of the author.

Survey of the Wisdom of Solomon

The book may be divided into three major sections: (1) immortality is the reward of wisdom (1:1 through 6:21); (2) praise of wisdom by Solomon (6:22 through 10:21); (3) God's faithfulness and providence in the Exodus, with some side topics including God's mercy and the folly of idolatry (11:1 through 19:22).

Immortality is the Reward of Wisdom (1:1 through 6:21): The author contrasts the destinies of the wicked and the just. The wicked are rewarded with death, but the just receive eternal life. The sufferings of the just in this world can only be understood in light of the final judgment and the vindication of the just in eternal life.

Praise of Wisdom by Solomon (6:22 through 10:21): This is set forth as Solomon's speech on the power and glory of wisdom, his prayer for wisdom, and the place of wisdom, as the Spirit of God reflects the combination of Jewish and Greek themes. He demonstrates that Jewish belief is in no way inferior to Greek thought. It is here that the author uses the powerful model of King Solomon as the wisest of all the kings of Israel's history to affirm the high quality and value of Jewish wisdom traditions.

God's Faithfulness and Providence in the Exodus (11:1 through 19:22): After an introductory narrative, the author asserts his theme

239

that Israel is benefited by the very same things which God uses to punish and afflict Egypt. He offers a series of five contrasts between the plagues against Egypt and the corresponding blessings on Israel to illustrate this theme. Included in this section are also disgressions on such topics as God's power and mercy (11:17 through 12:22), false worship (13:1 through 15:17), God in creation (19:6–21), and a conclusion in 19:22. The author stresses that God's wisdom has guided the history of Israel in a providential way, even when the people felt most oppressed. God alone is master of all, and he alone will vindicate the just on the Day of Judgment.

OUTLINE OF THE WIDSOM OF SOLOMON

Immortality is the reward of wisdom	1:1–6:21	The foolishness of idolatry	13:1–15:13
Praise of wisdom	6:22–10:21	Blessing and punishment at the Exodus	15:14–19:22
Wisdom during the Exodus	11:1–12:27		

FOCUS	REWARD OF WISDOM	PRAISE OF WISDOM	WISDOM AS GUIDE
REFERENCE	1.1——————————6.22———————————11.2—————————19.22		
DIVISION	DESTINY OF RIGHTEOUS AND WICKED	WISDOM AND EARLY ISRAELITE HISTORY	WISDOM AND EXODUS
TOPIC	REWARD AND PUNISHMENT	SOLOMON, ADAM, ABRAHAM, JACOB, JOSEPH	REWARD AND PUNISHMENT
SETTING	PROBABLY ALEXANDRIA		

WISDOM OF SOLOMON

SIRACH
THE WISDOM OF JESUS, SON OF SIRACH

(ECCLESIASTICUS)

The Book of Sirach

The Book of Sirach, so-called because of the surname of its author, is also known by the designation *"Liber Ecclesiasticus,"* meaning "Church Book." This latter title may have arisen from its wide usage in the church. The book is not found in the Hebrew Bible nor in the Protestant canon.

The book, a compilation of maxims grouped by affinity, gives the appearance of being a collection of small essays. Among the various topics dealt with are the following: the rearing of children, pride and humility, patience, respect and obedience of parents, friendship, wealth, relationships with women, table etiquette, control of the tongue, retribution, care of the needy, and above all the quest for wisdom. Of special importance are the covenant and the law of Moses. The author, seeking to counter the Hellenistic influences of his day, stressed the religious and cultural heritage of Judaism in order to show where true wisdom could be found.

Although composed in Hebrew, there is no extant Hebrew text, since the Hebrew text disappeared in the early Christian era. Manuscript discoveries at the end of the last century and this century have accounted for about two-thirds of the Hebrew text.

The Author of Sirach

Scholars agree that the author of the book is "Jesus (*Joshua* in Hebrew), son of Sirach Eleazar" (50:27). Born and reared in the city, he was probably a scribe, as well as a sage. Possessing a profound knowledge and love of the Scriptures, he was especially well versed in the Book of Proverbs and the Pentateuch. He probably conducted an academy in Jerusalem, where he lectured young men on ethical and religious topics (51:23). He was a man of culture and traveled extensively (34:11).

The Time of Sirach

Scholars generally agree that the book was written sometime between 195 and 168 B.C., probably about 180 B.C. This is based on internal evidence. In his eulogy of Simon, the High Priest (50:1f.) who was probably Simon II (c. 220–195 B.C.), the author creates the impression that his death was rather recent. Secondly, there is no indication in the book that the Maccabean revolt had begun. The book was composed in Hebrew. From the foreword we discover that the author's grandson, while in Egypt, translated his grandfather's work into Greek sometime after 132 B.C.

Survey of Sirach

The Book of Sirach may be divided as follows: the foreword, part 1: in praise of wisdom (1:1 through 23:27); part 2: in praise of wisdom (24:1 through 50:21); and the epilogue and appendices (50:22 through 51:30).

The Foreword: This section was added by the author's grandson, who translated the book into Greek. He begs the reader to be indulgent for any weakness in the translation.

Part 1: In Praise of Wisdom (1:1 through 23:27): This section commences with a poem in praise of wisdom: all wisdom comes from the Lord and has its beginning in the fear of the Lord (1:1–20). The Lord will bestow wisdom on those who keep the commandments (1:26). Hypocrisy and pride have no place in true worship (1:27–30). Those who serve the Lord will be tested with trials; they should trust God, hope in him, and await his mercy (2:1–18). Respect and reverence for parents bring blessing and atone for sins (3:1–16). Almsgiving also atones for sins (3:30). Assist the hungry, the poor, the oppressed, widows, and orphans (4:1–10). Despite her discipline, wisdom brings blessings and happiness to those who seek her. Avoid sinful shame, reliance upon wealth, detraction, and calumny. Treasure a faithful friend; such a friend is rare and priceless (4:11 through 6:17). The search for wisdom is a lifetime quest. Wisdom is the Lord's gift. Beware of political ambition and lying. Fulfill family and religious responsibilities; be stern when necessary (6:18 through 7:36). Heed the advice of the sages and the aged. Be wise in choosing companions; beware of enemies. Be especially prudent and reserved in dealing with women. Treasure old friends. God rules the earth; therefore, rulers should be wise (8:8 through 10:5). Do not be proud; God brings down the arrogant.

Be humble and fear God. Do not anxiously seek short-lived goods; rather, cultivate wisdom and virtue. Avoid associating with those who are more powerful or wealthier. Use riches wisely and share them with others, for riches are left behind at death (10:6 through 14:19). The happy man is the one who meditates on wisdom. Wisdom will not disappoint him, but bring him joy. God gave man a free will; the sinner is responsible for his own conduct. It is better to die childless than to have wicked children. Weakness reaps destruction. God created the universe and made man in his image with dominion over all things. God gave man wisdom and knowledge that he might praise his creator. The Lord forgives those who return to him; his mercy is boundless. In times of prosperity, think of poverty and want (14:20 through 18:26). Control lustful desires; wine and immoral women can lead to ruin. Avoid malicious gossip. Give fraternal correction when necessary. The wise man, unlike the fool, knows the proper time to speak. A liar is dishonored and disgraced (18:30 through 20:26). The wise man, through prudent speech, will earn the esteem of the great. The path that sinners walk is smoothly paved, but leads to the world of the dead. A fool is a burden to others, heavier than salt, sand, or iron. Do not revile a friend; help a friend in need. The sage turns to the Lord, his Father and Master, and asks for help in avoiding sin. Do not make a habit of taking oaths, uttering the Holy Name, or using vulgarity. Nothing is hidden from the Lord. Those who commit sexual sins will be punished. Fear of the Lord and obedience to his law surpass everything (20:27 through 23:27).

Part 2: In Praise of Wisdom (24:1 through 50:21): This section, like part one, begins with a poem in praise of wisdom. Wisdom is personified and speaks in the first person. She is the word spoken by the Most High; her abode is in Zion; she is identified with the law of Moses. The author, filled with wisdom, puts forth his instruction for future generations (24:1–34). He praises brotherly love, love of neighbor, and conjugal love; he abhors their opposites. Among the ten kinds of people the author deems himself fortunate to know is the man with an understanding wife. A good wife, who is a gift from the Lord, delights her husband (25:1 through 26:18). The desire for profit leads many astray. Shun fools; linger with the serious-minded. Do not betray the confidence of a friend, nor be misled by those pretending friendship. Forgive; then your sins will be forgiven in prayer. Avoid strife and slander. The tongue can be more deadly than the sword. Lend to a neighbor in need, and repay debts as soon as possible. A simple life in one's humble abode is better than lavish banquets in another's house (26:29 through 29:28). Discipline children; provide for their education. Undisciplined children will lead to misery. A healthy body and a cheerful attitude are more precious than gold. Concern for wealth causes anxiety and sleeplessness, and leads to sin. Remember table etiquette. Drink wine moderately, and leave a banquet at a proper time (30:1 through 32:13). The Lord reveals himself through the discipline of his law. One should seek counsel in following the law. The author, the last of a series of great teachers, has been blessed by the Lord, and now labors to share his wisdom with the leaders of his people (32:14 through 33:18). The head of a household should retain his possessions until the hour of death. Make a slave work, but treat him fairly and charitably. Trust in the Lord, not in dreams. Travel makes one more learned. Ritual acts must be accompanied by the proper internal dispositions. God hears the cry of the oppressed. The author prays to God for deliverance from foreign nations, for return to the Promised Land, and for restoration of Zion and the Temple (33:19 through 36:17). Women, like food, differ in quality. The husband of a beautiful and gentle woman is blessed. A true friend stands near in troubling times. Seek advice from a religious person; but trust your own judgment, and pray for guidance. Pray and consult a physician when ill; medical knowledge is from God. Grieve for the departed, but not excessively. His fate will one day be yours (36:18 through 38:23). Artisans, though necessary for a community, hold no leadership positions. The scribe studies and meditates on the Law; he gives advice to rulers. He turns to the Lord in prayer and gives thanks for the wisdom he has been granted. The sage invites his disciples to praise God whose works are good (38:24 through 39:35). Physical and mental suffering, endured by all, is greater for the sinner. Wealth, acquired dishonestly, will vanish. Death embraces all, but a good name endures forever. Man should be ashamed for certain deeds; others need bring no shame. A daughter is a constant source of anxiety to her father (40:1 through 42:14).

Three relatively long poems complete this section: a poem praising God for his works in nature (42:15 through 43:33); a poem praising the great men of Israel's past (chs. 44 through 49); and a poem praising the High Priest, Simon (50:1–21).

Epilogue and Appendices (50:22 through 51:30): Praise is given to God for his wonderful works. May God continue to bestow happiness and peace (50:22–24). The author praises God with a psalm of thanksgiving for deliverance from every kind of evil (51:1–12). This is followed by an acrostic hymn in which the author recalls how he sought wisdom from his youth. He invites those in need of instruction to attend his school (51:13–30).

OUTLINE OF SIRACH

Foreword

In praise of wisdom (Part 1)   1:1–23:27

  a. Duty, reward, and practical advice   1:1–14:19

  b. Wisdom brings happiness   14:20–19:26

  c. God's wisdom and human response   19:27–23:27

In praise of wisdom (Part 2)   24:1–50:21

  a. Wisdom and virtue   24:1–32:13

  b. God's wisdom and man's worship and work   32:14–42:14

  c. God's glory in nature   42:15–43:33

  d. In praise of ancestors   44:1–50:21

Epilogue and Appendices   50:22–51:30

FOCUS	PRAISE OF WISDOM I		PRAISE OF WISDOM II				BLESSING OF WISDOM
REFERENCE	1.1————16.24————		24.1————32.14————	42.15————44.1————			50.22——51.30
DIVISION	DUTY REWARD ADVICE	GOD'S WISDOM AND HUMAN RESPONSE	WISDOM AND VIRTUE	WISDOM WORSHIP WORK	GOD'S GLORY	PRAISE OF ANCESTORS	PRAISE OF WISDOM
TOPIC	INSTRUCTION		EXHORTATION				THANKS-GIVING
SETTING	JERUSALEM AND EGYPT						

SIRACH

THE BOOK OF

BARUCH

The Book of Baruch

The Book of Baruch, supposedly, was written by the secretary of Jeremiah during the Babylonian captivity. His name was Baruch. Drawing from various religious traditions, the book is addressed to exilic Jews in Babylon. After a public proclamation, it was sent to Jerusalem where it was to be incorporated into the liturgy on certain feasts.

Actually, the book was composed many centuries after the time of Baruch. A compiler gathered the compositions of various authors and addressed the Jews of his day, with the exilic era as the setting for his work. These later Jews also lived in a stressful situation. Like their exilic ancestors, they should admit their sinfulness, turn to the Lord, and expectantly await his deliverance. The restoration of Jerusalem following the Babylonian Exile would be their guarantee of the future restoration of Jerusalem in the final messianic age.

The book, consisting of prose (1:1 through 3:8) and poetry (3:9 through 5:9), is extant today only in Greek, although a Hebrew original was probable for the entire book. The book is not found in the Hebrew Bible or in the Protestant canon.

The Author of Baruch

The traditional author of the book was Baruch, the secretary and confidant of the prophet Jeremiah (1:1). Modern scholarship, based on external and internal evidence, would deny that Baruch is the author. It is generally held that the book is a composite by unknown authors (usually three are mentioned), united by a redactor, and ascribed to Baruch. Attributing a work to a famous personage of old was a fairly common literary device in order to re-create for the readers the historical period during which that person lived. The Hebrew name *Baruch* means "Blessed."

The Time of Baruch

Many scholars are of the opinion that the various parts of the book were written sometime during the early second century B.C. and the middle of the first century B.C., and that the book was edited to appear in its present format about 50 B.C.

Survey of Baruch

The Book of Baruch may be divided as follows: The introduction (1:1–14); a prayer of confession and deliverance (1:15 through 3:8); a poem in praise of wisdom (3:9 through 4:4); and a poem of comfort and help for Jerusalem (4:5 through 5:9).

The Introduction (1:1–14): The opening verses provide the circumstances for the composition of the book. On the fifth anniversary (probably in 582 B.C.) of the fall of Jerusalem, Baruch composed this work.

He proclaimed it in the presence of the deposed king, Jeconiah (also called Jehoiakin) and all his fellow exiles (1:1–4). Profoundly affected by the proclamation, the people wept, fasted, and prayed. A collection was then taken up. Baruch brought it to Jerusalem, along with the sacred utensils which had been taken from the Temple (1:5–9). They asked the people of Jerusalem to use the money to purchase offerings for the altar of the Lord (1:10); to pray for their Babylonian captors (1:11–12; cf. Jer. 29:7); to pray for those in exile for they have sinned against the Lord (1:13); and to read this book publicly as a confession of sin in the Temple "on the first day of the Festival of Shelters and on other holy days of assembly" (1:14).

A Prayer of Confession and Deliverance (1:15 through 3:8): In the first part of the prayer (1:15 through 2:10) the exiles, addressing their fellow Jews in Jerusalem, humbly admit that they have been justly punished for their sins. The prayer opens with words similarly found in Daniel 9:7f. (cf. Ezra 9:6–15; Neh. 1:5–11; 9:6–37). "The Lord our God is righteous, but we are still covered with shame . . . because we have sinned against the Lord our God and have disobeyed him. We did not listen to him or live according to his commandments" (1:15–18). From the time they left Egypt they were disobedient. They did not heed the prophets; they followed other gods (1:19–21). Hence, the Lord brought upon them their calamities, in righteous retribution for their sins (2:1–10), of which Moses had earlier warned them (cf. Deut. 28:15f.).

The exiles now address God, recalling his wonderful saving deeds of the past. They admit their sinfulness and ask for deliverance (2:11–13). Israel's deliverance will bring other nations to recognize that the God of Israel is Lord. Then they too will praise him along with Israel (2:14–18). In failing to submit to the Babylonian yoke as God had commanded, Israel had sinned (2:20–26; cf. Jer. 27:9–14; 29:5–7). Israel, a stiff-necked people, will turn to God in exile. He will give them a new heart, return them to their land, increase their numbers, and make a new covenant with them (2:27–35; cf. Jer. 31:31–34). Another request for mercy follows, along with a confession of past iniquities and a promise to praise God (3:1–8).

A Poem in Praise of Wisdom (3:9 through 4:4): Israel is in exile because she has forsaken God, the fountain of wisdom. Israel is exhorted to seek wisdom, the source of prosperity. True wisdom is hidden from the world; only God can bestow it. God, who knows all things, and whom the sun and stars obey, encompasses all wisdom. He has given wisdom to his people; for he has given them the Law, which is equated with wisdom. Observance of the Law will lead to life.

A Poem of Comfort and Help for Jerusalem (4:5 through 5:9): The exiles, handed over to their enemies on account of their sins, are exhorted to take courage (4:5, 21, 27, 30). Jerusalem, a sorrowing widow bereft of her children, explains to her neighbors and her children the reason for the Exile. She was left desolate because her children turned away from God's law (4:5–16). She exhorts her children in exile to have hope. The eternal God will deliver them; he will soon destroy the enemy (4:17–25). She comforts them with the thought that "the one who brought these calamities upon you will rescue you and bring you everlasting joy" (4:29).

The comforter is now comforted, as Jerusalem is exhorted to "take courage" (4:30). The end of the Exile is imminent. Babylon will be destroyed and become an uninhabited ruin (4:31–35). Jerusalem will be joyful, as her children return home (4:36–37). After her garment of sorrow is removed, she will be clothed in righteousness and peace (5:1–4). The Holy One will accompany her children home. No obstacle will stand in their path as hills will be lowered and valleys filled (5:5–7; cf. Isa. 40:3–4). "They will return with great joy, guided by his mercy and righteousness, surrounded by the light of his glorious presence" (5:9).

OUTLINE OF BARUCH

Historical introduction	1:1–14	In praise of wisdom	3:9–4:4
A prayer of confession and deliverance	1:15–3:8	Comfort and help for Jerusalem	4:5–5:9

FOCUS	PRAYER OF EXILES		PRAISE AND CONSOLATION	
REFERENCE	1.1———————1.15———————		3.9—————————4.5——————————5.9	
DIVISION	MEETING IN BABYLON	CONFESSION AND DELIVERANCE	ADVICE AND TEACHING	COMFORT AND HELP
TOPIC	PRAYER		POEM	
SETTING	BABYLONIAN CAPTIVITY			

BARUCH

THE LETTER OF

JEREMIAH

The Letter of Jeremiah

This work is purported to have been written by Jeremiah to his fellow countrymen as they were about to be deported to Babylon by Nebuchadnezzar. He wrote it, not only to inform the exiles of the length of their stay, but especially to warn them of the dangers of apostasy. He exhorted them to remain faithful to the Lord, and to avoid the worship of idols.

The letter is extant only in Greek, but many scholars hold that it was originally composed in Hebrew or Aramaic. The manuscripts of the Septuagint have Baruch, Lamentations, and the Letter of Jeremiah after the Book of Jeremiah. In the Vulgate the Letter of Jeremiah becomes chapter 6 of Baruch.

The Author of the Letter of Jeremiah

The superscription (v. 1) states that Jeremiah wrote this letter to his fellow countrymen as they were about to be led into exile. This letter was probably attributed to Jeremiah because of its resemblance to an earlier letter which the prophet had sent the exiles in 597 B.C. (Jer. 29:1–23). Modern scholarship holds that the work is a homily, not a letter, and that Jeremiah is not the author. The author, who lived centuries later, is unknown. Influenced by Isaiah 44:9–20 and especially by Jeremiah 10:2–15, he composed this work to warn his fellow Jews of the current dangers of idolatry.

The Time of the Letter of Jeremiah

An exact date for the letter is difficult to determine. Perhaps verse 3 provides a clue. It states that the Babylonian captivity would last for seven generations, thus suggesting a date of about 300 B.C., or later. Many scholars assign the work to the late fourth century B.C., or early third century B.C. Others prefer a second-century B.C. date.

Survey of the Letter of Jeremiah

The Letter of Jeremiah may be divided as follows: the introduction (vv. 1–7), and the ten-part homily (vv. 8–73). Each part of the homily ends with a similarly worded refrain, conveying that idols are not gods.

The Introduction (vv. 1–7): The prophet Jeremiah wrote a letter to his fellow countrymen as they were about to be taken into exile. He informed them that because of their sins they would be taken to Babylon where they would remain for seven generations. There they would witness the worship of false gods, but they must worship only God, whose angel will protect them.

The Ten-Part Homily (vv. 8–73): In verses 8–16 the Babylonian gods are helpless. They can neither speak nor clothe themselves. They cannot protect themselves from rust, termites, dust, war, or thieves. Though they carry scepters, they have no power. "All of this proves that they are not gods—do not worship them" (v. 16). In verses 17–23 the gods are covered with dust and soot from the temples, destroyed by termites, used and abused by unclean animals, and confined like hardened criminals. "All of this proves that they are not gods—do not worship them" (v. 23). In verses 24–29 the idols have neither breath nor feelings. Others have to polish or move them. Sacrifices offered to idols are exploited by priests and their wives, and are defiled by unclean women. "All of this proves that they are not gods—do not worship them" (v. 29).

In verses 30–40a "How can they ever be called gods . . ." (v. 30), since they tolerate defiled sacrifices from women, mourning practices forbidden to priests (Lev. 21:5–6, 10), and dishonesty? Powerless to protect themselves, they cannot protect others. They are unable to raise up or dethrone a king, bestow riches, restore sight, or aid widows or orphans. "How can anyone think that they are gods or call them gods?" (v. 40). In verses 40b–44 worshipers beg a god who cannot speak to grant the gift of speech. It cannot. Yet they continue to worship powerless gods, and cultic prostitution is rampant. "How can anyone think that they are gods or call them gods?" (v. 44). In verses 45–49 idols, the creation of mortal men, are useless in perilous times. "Why can't people realize that these idols are not gods?" (v. 49). In verses 50–52 idols are only wood covered with gold and silver; they are powerless products of men. "Anyone should know they are not really gods" (v. 52). In verses 53–56 these gods are powerless and useless. They cannot make a king, provide rain, nor right wrongdoings. They cannot save themselves or others from ruin. "How can anyone believe that they are gods?" (v. 56).

In verses 57–65 unable to protect themselves from thieves and robbers, idols are useless and powerless. Forces of nature obey God and render blessings and judgment; idols do neither. "You know that they are not gods—do not worship them" (v. 65). In verses 66–73 idols are powerless over kings and nature. They are more helpless than inanimate heavenly bodies and wild animals. They are as helpless and ineffective as a scarecrow, a thorn bush, or a corpse. "The righteous person has an advantage over others; he does not own any idols, and they can never make a fool of him" (v. 73).

OUTLINE OF THE LETTER OF JEREMIAH

| Introduction | 1–7 | Ten-part homily | 8–73 |

FOCUS	CONDEMNATION OF IDOLATRY		
REFERENCE	1————————8————————————————————————73		
DIVISION	INTRODUCTION	HELPLESSNESS OF IDOLS AND FOOLISHNESS OF WORSHIPING IDOLS	
TOPIC	WARNING AND EXHORTATION	HOMILY	
SETTING	JERUSALEM BEFORE BABYLONIAN CAPTIVITY		

LETTER OF JEREMIAH

THE PRAYER OF AZARIAH AND THE SONG OF
THE THREE YOUNG MEN

Greek Additions to the Book of Daniel

These three sections, the Prayer of Azariah and the Song of the Three Young Men, the story of Susanna, and the stories of Bel and the Dragon, are Greek additions to the Aramaic and Hebrew Masoretic Text. According to Catholic practice, which accepts these additions as Scripture, they are inserted with the Book of Daniel and are read as Daniel 3:24–90; 13:1–64; and 14:1–42, respectively.

The Prayer of Azariah

A later author expanded the text of Daniel to include a prayer uttered by Azariah and one of the three young men thrown into the fiery furnace in Daniel 3:23. The prayer, written originally in Hebrew or Aramaic, is now preserved only in a Greek translation which was not a part of the Hebrew Bible, and thus is not accepted by the Jews or Protestant Christians. It is a prayer of praise to God which reflects the situation in which the Jewish people found themselves after the Temple had been destroyed. The prayer is important theologically, since it interprets the disaster of the fall of Jerusalem as the just punishment from God for the refusal of the Jews to obey the laws of the covenant he had made with them. The prayer ends with a petition which expresses the soul of the Jewish faith: "Let them know that you alone are Lord and God . . ." (v. 22).

The Song of the Three Young Men

This addition follows the Prayer of Azariah and is very similar to the hymn of praise in Psalm 148. It consists of two litanies, the first in verses 52–56, which is a pure hymn of praise. It is distinctive because it mentions the heavenly Temple where God is enthroned forever. The second and longer litany invites all of creation to worship the Lord, the God whose "mercy lasts forever" (vv. 67–68).

OUTLINE OF THE PRAYER OF AZARIAH
AND THE SONG OF
THE THREE YOUNG MEN

Prayer of Azariah	1–22	The song of the three young	
Description of the fiery fur-		men	28–68
nace	23–27		

FOCUS	HISTORY OF DANIEL	PLAN FOR GENTILES			PLAN OF ISRAEL	WISDOM TRIUMPHS	FALSENESS OF IDOL WORSHIP
REFERENCE	1.1————2.1————3.23～～～～3.24————7.1————13.1————14.1——14.42						
DIVISION	PERSONAL VISION OF DANIEL AND OTHERS	PRAYER OF AZARIAH AND THREE YOUNG MEN (GREEK)	VISIONS CONTINUED	DANIEL'S VISIONS	SUSANNA (GREEK)	BEL AND THE DRAGON (GREEK)
TOPIC	DANIEL'S BACKGROUND	KING'S DREAM	PRAYER	DREAMS BANQUET LION'S DEN	ANGEL INTERPRETS DANIEL'S DREAMS	JUDGMENT	WISDOM AND COURAGE
SETTING	BABYLON OR PERSIA						

THE BOOK OF

SUSANNA

The Story of Susanna

See "Greek Additions to the Book of Daniel" in the introduction to The Prayer of Azariah and the Song of the Three Young Men. Another addition to the Hebrew-Aramaic Book of Daniel, the episode of Susanna gives yet another indication of the wisdom of Daniel and of God's providence for his faithful people. The Lord's prophet is led to vindicate Susanna, "a Jewish woman" (v. 57), from the false accusation of adultery made against her by some false elders of the people. The innocent Susanna has also been interpreted as a symbol of the faithful people of God. Early Christian art used the figure of Susanna to represent the innocent but persecuted church, ultimately freed from injustice.

OUTLINE OF SUSANNA

Two wicked judges attempt to seduce Susanna	1–27	Daniel rescues Susanna and the judges are condemned to death	42–64
Susanna is condemned to death	28–41		

FOCUS	HISTORY OF DANIEL	PLAN FOR GENTILES			PLAN OF ISRAEL	WISDOM TRIUMPHS	FALSENESS OF IDOL WORSHIP
REFERENCE	1.1————2.1————	3.23———	3.24———	7.1———	13.1———	14.1——14.42
DIVISION	PERSONAL VISION OF DANIEL AND OTHERS	PRAYER OF AZARIAH AND THREE YOUNG MEN (GREEK)	VISIONS CONTINUED	DANIEL'S VISIONS	SUSANNA (GREEK)	BEL AND THE DRAGON (GREEK)
TOPIC	DANIEL'S BACKGROUND	KING'S DREAM	PRAYER	DREAMS BANQUET LION'S DEN	ANGEL INTERPRETS DANIEL'S DREAMS	JUDGMENT	WISDOM AND COURAGE
SETTING	BABYLON OR PERSIA						

BEL AND THE DRAGON

The Story of the Priests of Bel

See "Greek Additions to the Book of Daniel" in the introduction to The Prayer of Azariah and the Song of the Three Young Men. This story, like the other additions, forms part of what has been called the "Daniel Cycle," a collection of stories showing the wisdom of Daniel and how it helped him uncover the corruption of his pagan adversaries. Here, the god Bel is depicted as receiving rich offerings of food from his priests. The king is deceived into thinking that Bel is really alive (v. 6), and that he himself consumes the sacrifices. Actually, the priests remove the food, presumably for their own use. Daniel cleverly exposes the fraud, proving once again the superiority of the God of the Jews over all the gods of the nations.

The Story of the Dragon

This story's plot is similar to the story of Bel: Another Babylonian god, a dragon, is exposed as a false god when Daniel poisons him with food. The people, angry now that Bel and the Dragon have been blasphemed, convince the king to have Daniel thrown to the lions. This famous incident is full of basic Jewish professions of faith. When an angel miraculously brings Habakkuk the prophet to Babylon, with food for Daniel in the lion pit, he exclaims, "God, you did remember me; you never abandon those who love you" (v. 38). The lions do not attack Daniel; and when the king goes to the pit to mourn for Daniel, he finds him alive and praises God saying, "O Lord, the God of Daniel, how great you are. You alone are God" (v. 41).

OUTLINE OF BEL AND THE DRAGON

Daniel's wisdom defeats the
  priests of Bel   1–22
Daniel kills the dragon   23–32

Daniel is rescued from the
  pit of lions   33–42

FOCUS	HISTORY OF DANIEL	PLAN FOR GENTILES			PLAN OF ISRAEL	WISDOM TRIUMPHS	FALSENESS OF IDOL WORSHIP
REFERENCE	1.1———2.1———	3.23——————3.24———		7.1———		13.1———	14.1——14.42
DIVISION	PERSONAL VISION OF DANIEL AND OTHERS		PRAYER OF AZARIAH AND THREE YOUNG MEN (GREEK)	VISIONS CONTINUED	DANIEL'S VISIONS	SUSANNA (GREEK)	BEL AND THE DRAGON (GREEK)
TOPIC	DANIEL'S BACKGROUND	KING'S DREAM	PRAYER	DREAMS BANQUET LION'S DEN	ANGEL INTERPRETS DANIEL'S DREAMS	JUDGMENT	WISDOM AND COURAGE
SETTING	BABYLON OR PERSIA						

DANIEL

THE FIRST BOOK OF THE

MACCABEES

The Book of First Maccabees

The Book of First Maccabees is the first of four books listed in Greek manuscripts under the title "Books of the Maccabees." The first two of these books deal with the Jewish revolt against King Antiochus IV of Syria. The third book is about the persecution of the Jews under the Egyptian Pharaoh, Ptolemy IV (221–204 B.C.). This third book probably was included under the title "Books of the Maccabees" because it treats a situation similar to that in the first two books, namely, the persecution of Jews by a foreign oppressor. The fourth book is about the martyrdom of Eliezar and a mother with her seven sons (cf. 2 Macc. 6:18 through 7:42). Since the subject matter of the fourth book is related in the Book of Second Maccabees, that material is also included under the heading, "Books of the Maccabees."

The name "Maccabee" comes from the first book. The author introduces the five sons of Mattathias (1 Macc. 2:2–5). To each he gave a second name. He introduces the third son as "Judas (also called Maccabeus)" (1 Macc. 2:4). Although three of the five sons figure prominently in the revolt, described in the first book, Judas is the real hero. Actually, the second book is limited to his exploits only.

The Book of First Maccabees is a historical book which narrates the exploits of Mattathias and three of his sons in their revolt against the repressive measures of Antiochus IV of Syria and his successors.

The Author of First Maccabees

The book does not give us any direct information about the identity of the author. Certain aspects of his personality are revealed by his work. It appears that he was an orthodox and very patriotic Jew. He lived and wrote his book in Palestine because he shows a detailed understanding of Palestinian topography and geography. It is very possible that he participated in the events of which he writes. In any case, he shows considerable familiarity with affairs of state, military operations, and intrigues going on in the court. He must then have held a rank that gave him access to official sources and the archives.

He appears to be a zealous partisan of the Hasmonean family (the family name of the "Maccabees") and highlights all they have done for the glory of the Jewish people. He manifests his admiration for all the members of the Hasmonean family. He highlights Judas in his achievement of religious liberty, the role of Jonathan in his expansion of Jewish territory, and the wisdom and diplomacy of Simon in gaining political independence.

Several critics think the author was a Sadducee because of his sympathetic attitude toward the priesthood and his tolerance in the question of the Sabbath. But the author actually does not appear to be a man of any particular sect or party. He is simply one of a party of Jews faithful to the Law. He writes in an epoch in which the deep rupture between John Hyrcanus and the Pharisees, and the deep division between Pharisees and Sadducees, has not yet occurred.

The Time of First Maccabees

In 198 B.C. the Seleucid rulers of Syria, under the leadership of Antiochus III (223–187 B.C.), seized control of Palestine from Egypt.

Antiochus III was favorably disposed toward the Jews and granted them many privileges. His son and successor, Seleucus, at first continued this benevolent policy of his father. But the enormous debt his father left him made him greedy for the Temple treasury in Jerusalem. A certain Jew, Simon, who was intriguing against the pious Jewish High Priest, Onias III, to secure the high priesthood for himself, had drawn the king's attention to it. To obtain the treasury, Antiochus III sent his chancellor, Heliodorus, to Jerusalem. But he was miraculously hindered from entering the Temple (2 Macc. 3). Upon his return to Antioch, the capital of Syria, he assassinated the king and took possession of the throne. But the brother of Seleucus, Antiochus IV, returned suddenly from Rome, expelled the usurper, and began to reign.

With the accession of Antiochus IV, a growing group of Hellenophiles (Jews favoring Greek culture), recruited from among the rich and noble, particularly the priestly aristocracy, thought themselves strong enough to accelerate the hellenization of the nation, with the aid of the Syrian government. A certain Jason, the brother of Onias the High Priest, gave money to Antiochus in exchange for the high priesthood and authorization to build a Greek gymnasium at Jerusalem. Onias was removed from the office of High Priest, and Jason replaced him. Three years later, a certain Jew, Menelaus, offered a larger sum and secured the high priesthood for himself. He then put Onias to death.

Meanwhile, the rumor spread that Antiochus IV had died during an expedition to Egypt. The people of Jerusalem rose against Menelaus and Jason returned to his lost post. But Antiochus IV returned victoriously from Egypt. As he passed through Palestine in 170 B.C., he punished the rebel city.

Two years later Jerusalem was again the scene of horrible massacres. The walls of the city were destroyed, and a strong acropolis built on Mount Zion which was then occupied by the Syrian garrison.

Antiochus went further. He forbade the practice of the Jewish religion under penalty of death, especially the observance of the Sabbath and circumcision. He ordered that all the Jewish religious books be destroyed and that the Jews must offer sacrifice to the pagan gods. In 168 B.C., a sacrifice was offered to Zeus Olympicus in the Temple on the altar of Holocausts.

The scattered Jewish resistance to this attempt to destroy their religion was soon organized by the priest, Mattathias, who began the holy war, which came to be known as the Maccabean war. Mattathias died soon after, around 167 B.C., but his eldest son, Judas, became the leader of the insurgents. The war was subsequently continued by two other sons of Mattathias: Jonathan (161–143 B.C.), and Simon (143–135 B.C.).

The history recounted in the Book of First Maccabees then covers a period of 40 years, 175–135 B.C.—from the accession of Antiochus IV to the throne of Syria until the death of Simon, the last surviving son of Mattathias.

The actual time of writing is much disputed. The narrative after giving the story of the death of Simon (135 B.C.) mentions the first acts of his successor, John Hyrcanus, who ruled from 135–106 B.C.

On the basis of 16:23–24, some critics argue that the reign of John Hyrcanus was well advanced or even past when those verses were written. This argument should not be pressed to an extreme. The author, writing at the beginning of the reign of John Hyrcanus, and not wishing to begin in detail the history of his reign that he cannot finish, refers his readers to the official annals of his reign.

A satisfactory date for the writing of the book would be 140–130 B.C.

Survey of First Maccabees

The history unfolds chronologically. An introduction (chs. 1–2) opens with the death of Alexander the Great (323 B.C.) and the division of his vast kingdom. One of these divisions became the Seleucid kingdom of Syria. The author then passes over about 150 years of history and records the accession of King Antiochus IV of Syria in the year 175 B.C. After a description of the oppressive measures enacted by Antiochus IV, the author recounts the story of the revolt initiated by Mattathias and his sons. These chapters conclude with the account of the death of Mattathias. Chapters 3:1 through 9:22 cover the years 167–161 B.C., and narrate the exploits and achievements of Judas Maccabee. His greatest achievement is the liberation of Jerusalem and the purification and rededication of the Temple.

The revolt continues under the leadership of Jonathan (161–143 B.C.). Through a series of brilliant diplomatic moves, Jonathan secures control of large portions of Syrian territory in Palestine for himself and his brother Simon (cf. 9:23 through 12:53).

After Jonathan, Simon (143–135 B.C.) succeeds in being recognized by Syria as ruler of the Jewish nation. This event marks the beginning of a new era—the era of freedom. The Jewish nation is once again free and sovereign (cf. 13:1 through 16:24).

The book closes with the death of Simon and the succession of his son, John Hyrcanus, to the throne.

OUTLINE OF FIRST MACCABEES

Presecution and the revolt of Mattathias	1:1–2:70	Maccabee	3:1–9:22
The leadership of Judas		The leadership of Jonathan	9:23–12:53
		The leadership of Simon	13:1–16:24

FOCUS	JEWISH HISTORY FROM ANTIOCHUS EPIPHANES TO JOHN HYRCANUS			
REFERENCE	1.1———————3.1—————————9.23———————13.1—————————16.24			
DIVISION	DEATH OF ALEXANDER AND SPLIT OF HIS KINGDOM	EXPLOITS OF JUDAS	EXPLOITS OF JONATHAN	EXPLOITS OF SIMON
TOPIC	THE HASMONEAN FAMILY SAVES ISRAEL			
SETTING	PALESTINE			

1 MACCABEES

THE SECOND BOOK OF THE

MACCABEES

The Book of Second Maccabees

The Book of Second Maccabees tells in further detail the first part of the history covered in the Book of First Maccabees. It covers the period from Seleucus IV (187–175 B.C.) down to Judas' defeat of the Syrian general, Nicanor, about 161–160 B.C.

Like the first book, this book is basically a historical work. The author himself tells us (2:19–32) that his work is a one-volume resume of a work of five volumes composed by a certain Jason of Cyrene.

Different from the first book, it is in a Greek style which authors call "pathetic history"—a history narrated with much emotion, moving the reader to share the emotions of the actors. Each of the five tableaus is written to move and persuade. With Onias the High Priest, the reader tastes the peace enjoyed in the regular service of the Temple. Then the reader shares his agony when the Holy Place is threatened, in order to experience the joy of triumph when Heliodorus, chastised, recognizes the holiness of God who dwells there. In the second tableau, the irreverence of humans and the wrath of God are highlighted, from the time of Jason to the time of Menelaus, from the pillage of the Temple to its profanation. In contrast the death of the martyrs, which calms the wrath of God, leaves the reader with an impression of hope. In the last three tableaus Judas is elevated, while his adversaries Antiochus IV (also called Epiphanes), Lysias, Antiochus V (Eupator), and finally Nicanor perish proclaiming the glory of the Almighty who reveals himself in his temple.

The author, therefore, intends to search out the religious thrust of events and neglects the historian's concern with exact details. He takes much liberty with chronology and detail. Despite the liberties he takes, in view of the religious effect, the book still remains a work of history.

The Author of Second Maccabees

The second book gives us no direct teaching about the person of the author. Reading the book, however, tells us something about him. His competence in the Greek language and the flowery character of his style reveal an Alexandrian Jew, or at least one formed in the schools of the rhetoricians. His pharisaic mentality appears in his zeal for the law and dedication to the Temple, plus his profound piety and affirmed belief in the resurrection.

The whole book is expressed with a profound piety manifested in the author's judgment of events and their causes: God punishes violators of his law and pardons those who repent.

Some critics see the author as a Pharisee and enemy of the Hasmonean (Maccabean) dynasty. They note that he passes over Mattathias and the brothers of Judas in silence. But this is not sufficient evidence. Actually, Judas Maccabee is treated sympathetically by the author, who emphasizes Judas' role in the struggle to save the law. And it is Judas who holds first place in the institution of the two great feasts: Festival of Dedication and the Day of Nicanor, which are central to the whole narrative of the author.

The Time of Second Maccabees

The author ends his book with the statement: "The city of Jerusalem remained in the possession of the Jewish people from that time on" (the defeat of Nicanor). From this we must conclude that the work was completed before 63 B.C. when Jerusalem was conquered by Pompey, who profaned the Temple and dared to enter the Holy of Holies.

The history narrated in the book comes to a close in the year 161 or 160 B.C. It should be noted that the second letter recorded in the book is dated 124 B.C. It is very possible that this letter was written to be sent with the book to Egypt. Then the composition of the book would be shortly before 124 B.C.

If this is not the case, all that can be said is that the author made a resume of the five books of Jason sometime between 125 B.C. and 63 B.C. As for the work of Jason himself, it could have been written anytime after 160 B.C. This does not exclude the date of 125 B.C. or a date as late as 63 B.C.

Survey of Second Maccabees

The book opens with two letters from the Jews in Jerusalem to the Jewish community of Egypt.

The first letter (1:1–10), written in 124 B.C., invites the Jews in Egypt to celebrate, with their brothers and sisters in Jerusalem, the Festival of the Dedication of the Temple in Jerusalem, on the fortieth anniversary of the rededication and purification of the Temple under Judas Macca-bee in 164 B.C.

The second letter (1:10 through 2:18) is older. It was allegedly written on the occasion of the feast celebrating the rededication and purification of the Temple in 164 B.C., under Judas Maccabee. It recounts the death of Antiochus IV in 164 B.C., a short time before the letter was written, and assigns the rebuilding of the Temple to the time of Nehemiah. Actually, the Temple was rebuilt by Zerubbabel (520–516 B.C.), a century before Nehemiah, who actually supervised the rebuilding of the walls of Jerusalem. The review of the marvelous deeds accompanying the rebuilding of the Temple and its history is intended to highlight the importance of the present celebration of the purification and rededica-tion of the Temple under Judas Maccabee.

The proper work of the author begins here with a preface in which he describes his intentions and method. The source for his book is a five-volume work of a certain Jason of Cyrene, whose chronicle the present author resumes in the remainder of the book (2:23). The work then develops in five tableaus. The center of each is the Temple.

Under a pious High Priest, Onias, the Temple is inviolable, as Helio-dorus learns to his sorrow (ch. 3).

When the high priesthood becomes the prize for the two intriguers, Jason and Menelaus, the wrath of God descends on the Temple: the Temple is pillaged and is profaned by the offering of impure sacrifices. Faithful Jews give their lives in an act of expiation which dispels the wrath of the Almighty (chs. 4 through 7).

The wrath of the Lord now changed to mercy, Judas defeats the pagans. Antiochus IV dies while recognizing that it is the hand of God who strikes him. Judas purifies the Temple (8:1 through 10:9).

Under the administration of Lysias, who governs for the king of Syria, Judas leads the battle on all frontiers against the hellenized cities of the pagan population. He then secures liberty of worship. Lysias even offers sacrifices in the Temple and invites the neighboring cities not to trouble the Jews. Menelaus is put to death (10:10 through 13:26).

Under King Demetrius, a new contender for the high priesthood, named Alcimus, gains the support of the king. The general of the royal armies, Nicanor, is appointed governor of Judah and sent to kill Judas. Nicanor blasphemes against the Temple and is killed by Judas. His head is exposed in front of the Temple. A feast recalls each year the memory of this victory (14:1 through 15:36).

The book closes with an epilogue in which the indulgence of the reader is begged in considering the author's work.

OUTLINE OF SECOND MACCABEES

Letters to the Jews in Egypt	1:1–2:18	Victories of Judas and purification of the Temple	8:1–10:9
Author's preface	2:19–32	Judas secures liberty of worship	10:10–13:26
Heliodorus' attempt to profane the Temple	3:1–40	Defeat of Nicanor	14:1–15:36
Profanation and persecution	4:1–7:42	Epilogue	15:37–39

FOCUS	JEWISH HISTORY FROM ONIAS III TO NICANOR						
REFERENCE	1.1————	2.19————	3.1————	4.1————	8.1————	10.1————	14.1————15.39
DIVISION	LETTERS TO JEWS IN EGYPT	AUTHOR'S PREFACE	ATTEMPT TO PROFANE TEMPLE	PROFANATION AND PERSECUTION	VICTORY AND PURIFICATION OF TEMPLE	FREEDOM OF WORSHIP	DEFEAT OF NICANOR AND EPILOGUE
TOPIC	LOYALTY TO LAW AND GOD'S REWARD TO MARTYRS						
SETTING	PALESTINE						

2 MACCABEES

THE FIRST BOOK OF

ESDRAS

The Book of First Esdras

The Book of First Esdras tells the biblical story of Judah from Josiah's Passover (2 Chron. 35) to the reading of the Law by Ezra (Neh. 8). It was known to Josephus, who used it for his account of King Josiah, generally following the order of events found in First Esdras. The book is united by content, language, interest, and outlook with the canonical books of Second Chronicles, Ezra, and Nehemiah. First Esdras is quoted by Tertullian, Clement of Alexandria, and Athanasius, among others. Jerome, however, condemned it because of its dreams and because it did not conform to the Hebrew text of Ezra-Nehemiah. The Council of Florence rejected it from the canonical listing in the fifteenth century. The Council of Trent did likewise in the sixteenth century.

The Author of First Esdras

Nothing definitive can be said of the author or his purpose in writing this book. *"Esdras"* is the Greek and Latin translation of the Hebrew *Ezra*. The author of First Esdras is probably not the famous scribe, Ezra.

Today, some scholars think that the author of First Esdras was a compiler of relevant portions from the Septuagint version of Second Chronicles, Ezra, and Nehemiah. Others think the author translated into Greek the relevant portions of First Chronicles, Ezra, and Nehemiah from an original Hebrew text. Whoever he was, the author obviously was interested in telling the story of the last period of the Temple until its reconstruction. His purpose in writing simply could have been to preserve a record of the past or to make a plea to support the Temple and its cult. He also could have been interested in writing a revision of history, since he obviously magnifies the position of Ezra in the story of the reconstruction.

The Time of First Esdras

The story contained in the book begins in the middle of Josiah's reign (640–609 B.C.). The king is celebrating the Passover shortly after his reform. First Esdras also contains a story not found in canonical Ezra or Nehemiah. In First Esdras 3:1 through 5:6 we are told of a contest among three bodyguards at the Persian court of Darius (540 B.C.). Zerubbabel wins the contest and is awarded the prize of leading the Jews back to Jerusalem.

The vocabulary of this story and that of First Esdras corresponds in general to that of the second-century B.C. books of Sirach, Judith, Esther, and First Maccabees. Most would agree today that First Esdras was written after 333 B.C. and before 100 B.C. The probable date for the literary composition is around 150 B.C.

Survey of First Esdras

First Esdras contains a different view of the events surrounding the return of the exiles and the reconstruction of the Temple than the account contained in the canonical books of Ezra and Nehemiah. The traditions found in these three books represent concurrent forms which have influenced each other. Only First Esdras 3:1 through 5:6 is original and not found in Ezra or Nehemiah. Which tradition is older or more historical is the subject of much debate.

The following is the usual division of the book: the period of Josiah and the last kings of Judah (1:1–58); the decree of Cyrus and responses (2:1–30); the story about Zerubbabel (3:1 through 5:6); preparations for and return from captivity (5:7–73); the reconstruction of the Temple (6:1–7:15); and the Ezra story (8:1–9:55).

The Period of Josiah and the Last Kings of Judah (1:1–58): Josiah celebrates the most notable Passover in Israel since the days of Solomon. The pious Josiah, however, meets with a tragic death. He dies on the plain of Megiddo at the hands of Neco, Pharaoh of Egypt. The history of Judah under Joahaz, Jehoiakim, Jehoiakin, and Zedekiah is briefly told.

The Decree of Cyrus and Responses (2:1–30): The Lord arouses the spirit of Cyrus, king of the Persians. He issues a decree permitting the rebuilding of the Temple in Jerusalem. Cyrus hands over the sacred utensils of the Lord to Sheshbazzar, the governor of Judah. The Samaritans write a letter to King Artaxerxes complaining against the inhabitants of Judah and Jerusalem. They object to the rebuilding of what they call the rebellious and evil city. The rebuilding of the Temple is discovered.

The Story about Zerubbabel (3:1 through 5:6): During a reception held by Darius, the three youthful bodyguards decide to have a contest. Each will write down the one thing he considers the most powerful. The king and three Persian magnates will judge which is the wisest and most clever. A prize of victory will go to the winner. Zerubbabel writes, "Women are the strongest but truth is victorious over everything." He is declared the victor. For his prize he asks Darius to permit the return of exiles to rebuild Jerusalem and the Temple.

Preparations and Return from Captivity (5:7–73): Family heads, according to their tribes, are selected for return. The list of returning captives includes laymen, priests, Levites, Temple singers, gatekeepers, Temple servants, and Solomon's servants, including some who were unable to trace their families or descent in Israel. After the return, an altar is erected and worship services begin.

The Reconstruction of the Temple (6:1 through 7:15): Haggai and Zechariah urge and inspire the work of rebuilding. Some provincial authorities, however, ask by what authority the Temple is being rebuilt. These authorities write to Darius who orders a search of the royal archives in Babylon. The edict of Cyrus is found and work on the Temple is to continue with no opposition. The work is completed and the Passover is celebrated.

The Ezra Story (8:1 through 9:55): Ezra returns during the reign of Artaxerxes. He is to investigate affairs in Jerusalem and Judah to see that all is in harmony with the law of the Lord. All is not well. The people of Israel have not kept themselves apart from defilement with the aliens of the land. The people respond to Ezra's plea and mend their ways.

OUTLINE OF FIRST ESDRAS

Josiah and the fall of Jerusalem	1:1–58	from captivity	5:7–73
The decree of Cyrus and responses	2:1–30	The Temple rebuilt and dedicated	6:1–7:15
The story about Zerubbabel	3:1–5:6	Ezra returns with other exiles	8:1–9:55
Preparations for and return			

FOCUS	RESTORATION OF THE TEMPLE		REFORMATION OF THE PEOPLE	
REFERENCE	1.1————————3.1————		7.1————————9.1————————10.44	
DIVISION	FIRST RETURN TO JERUSALEM	CONSTRUCTION OF THE TEMPLE	SECOND RETURN TO JERUSALEM	RESTORATION OF THE PEOPLE
TOPIC	ZERUBBABEL		EZRA	
	FIRST RETURN OF EXILES		SECOND RETURN OF EXILES	
SETTING	PERSIA TO JERUSALEM		PERSIA TO JERUSALEM	

EZRA

THE SECOND BOOK OF

ESDRAS

The Book of Second Esdras

The Book of Second Esdras generally contains material of two kinds. The first is material dealing with apocalyptic and eschatological mysteries. The second is material dealing with religious problems and speculations. For example, what is the religious significance of the fall of Jerusalem? Why are God's chosen people a prey to the Gentiles? The answers to these problems are related to the author's view of history and the revelation of God's plan of salvation. The book belongs to the pseudepigraphal writings. It was given the name *Esdras* (the Greek and Latin form of the Hebrew *Ezra*) because Ezra the scribe was revered and honored in Jewish and Christian circles. Ezra's name would attach great authority to the book. Second Esdras has some close resemblance to the New Testament. A number of scholars thinks it reflects the influence of the school of Shammai. Second Esdras has been translated into many languages. The Latin, Syriac, Ethopic, Arabic, and Armenian are the most important versions we have. The Latin version is the only one to preserve Second Esdras in its entirety. The oldest and best known Latin manuscripts are the *Codex Sangermanensis* and the *Codex Ambianensis*, both ninth-century manuscripts.

The Author of Second Esdras

Theories abound on the question of the author of Second Esdras. According to some scholars, the author is an editor or redactor who used previously existing sources. The principal sources, according to this theory, are found in the main section of the book, chapters 3 through 14. These sources include: (1) The Shealtiel Apocalypse; (2) The Eagle Vision; (3) The Son of Man Vision; and (4) The Ezra Legend. Each of these sources would have had its own author who had his individual theology and purpose of writing. The final editor or redactor would have edited these and imposed his own theological purpose on the final work. Other scholars, while recognizing the secondary character of chapters 1 and 2, as well as 15 and 16, theorize that chapters 3 through 14 are not a compilation from previously existing sources. They assume that one author may have drawn upon memories and observations but did not use major sources. A single author, according to this theory, produced the fine artistic work. The whole book represents his own concept and handiwork.

The Time of Second Esdras

The first two chapters of Second Esdras purport to be a revelation of God to the scribe, Ezra, who was a captive in the land of the Medes in the reign of Artaxerxes, the king of the Persians. Critical scholarship concludes for the most part that these two chapters are a Christian work, originally composed in Greek in the late first century or early second century A.D.

The first vision (3:1 through 5:19) indicates that Shealtiel received his revelation in the thirtieth year of the downfall of the city (presumably Jerusalem) while he was in Babylon. This would be A.D. 100. Most scholars date the Eagle Vision during A.D. 69–96. The interpretation of the Son of Man Vision presupposes a date before A.D. 70, but the final form is dated at the close of the first century A.D. The Ezra Legend makes no mention of the horrible struggles that took place before Jerusalem fell. It could well have taken on its basic literary form before A.D. 70, even as early as 30 B.C. Most scholars would agree that the material in chapters 3 through 14 are a Jewish work, probably written originally in Hebrew or Aramaic and likely translated into Greek. Both of these versions are lost. Only the Latin version remains. The dates generally agreed upon for chapters 3 through 14 are A.D. 95–120.

Chapters 15 and 16 are a Christian conclusion or appendix. They were originally written in Greek, but only three of fifteen verses remain. The Latin version contains all fifteen verses. Chapters 15 and 16 date from the third century A.D.

Survey of Second Esdras

The Book of Second Esdras acknowledges God as Creator of the universe. God is also the Creator of his covenant people, whose ancestors are Noah, Abraham, Isaac, Jacob, and David. God is actively concerned with his people because of his great mercy and love. No human being can know the ways of God. He is the Lord of history.

Second Esdras discusses the religous problems of the day. Besides being interested in the fall of Jerusalem, the book also ponders the problem and prevalence of sin. Second Esdras laments over the oppression, suffering, and torments of God's people. Yet there is a dominant theme of hope. God will usher in his eternal kingdom. The Messiah will destroy his enemies. The book can be divided in the following way: Ezra's divine commission (1:1 through 2:48); the Ezra apocalypse (3:1 through 14:48); and appendix (15:1 through 16:78).

Ezra's Divine Commission (1:1 through 2:48): God speaks to Ezra and reminds him of how forgetful his people have been. God has delivered them from bondage and provided for their every need. Their forgetfulness will not go unpunished. God will reject them and turn to the Gentiles.

The Ezra Apocalypse (3:1 through 14:48): In this section there is a series of seven visions. The first four contrast the wealth of the Gentiles with the poverty and devastation of God's chosen people. This leads to reflection on the problems of evil and sin. Critical questions are raised. Conclusions are reached: God's ways are inscrutable; the human mind is finite; the course of the present world has been predetermined; God's love for Israel will never cease or fail.

The fifth vision is the eagle vision. Ezra seeks an interpretation of his vision of an eagle with twelve wings and three heads. The eagle is the fourth kingdom that appeared in a vision to Daniel. It represents a most dreadful earthly kingdom. The Lion of Judah, however, will destroy it. When this happens, a theocracy will be set up. God will rule.

The sixth vision concerns a Man who arises from the sea. This Man is God's Son. No power can subdue him for he is the one whom the Supreme God has kept for many ages, through whom to deliver his creation. He will create a new order. In the seventh vision Ezra hears a voice from a bush. He is instructed to go away for forty days and take a good supply of writing tablets with him. Then Ezra and his five assistants wrote ninety-four books in forty days. Twenty-four were to be published. The remaining seventy were to be handed over to the wise men among the people.

Appendix (15:1 through 16:78): Ezra is directed to speak and write down the words the Lord is putting into his mouth. Calamities will come upon the whole earth, but God will deliver his people from Egypt once again. Ezra sees a dreadful vision from the east and storm clouds from various directions. Woes are directed against Babylon, Asia, Egypt, and Syria. God's people are to prepare for combat. Iniquity will be removed from the earth. God delivers the just from persecution. The people are to keep his law.

OUTLINE OF SECOND ESDRAS

Introduction	1:1–2:48	The fifth vision	11:1–12:50
The first vision	3:1–5:19	The sixth vision	12:51–13:56
The second vision	5:20–6:34	The seventh vision	13:57–14:48
The third vision	6:35–9:25	Additional prophecies	15:1–16:78
The fourth vision	9:26–10:59		

FOCUS	GOD IS LORD OF HISTORY		
REFERENCE	1.1————————————3.1————————————15.1————————————16.78		
DIVISION	EZRA'S COMMISSION	EZRA APOCALYPSE	ADDITIONAL PROPHECIES
TOPIC	ISRAEL REJECTED	SEVEN VISIONS	THE END OF ALL THINGS
SETTING	LAND OF MEDES AND PERSIANS		

2 ESDRAS

THE PRAYER OF MANASSEH

The Book of the Prayer of Manasseh

Among the apocryphal literature of the intertestamental period is included this beautiful prayer of King Manasseh on the occasion of his personal repentance. The text is rooted in the events of Second Chronicles 33:10–13, which mentions the prayer of repentance by Manasseh after his many offenses against true worship of the Lord. This noncanonical text has been preserved in the Septuagint and represents a beautiful example of the devotional literature of the time. In some manuscripts the prayer has been added to the Book of Psalms, with which the prayer has many close similarities in style and form.

The Author of the Prayer of Manasseh

Manasseh, son of Hezekiah and father to Amon, ruled Judah from about 687 to 642 B.C. During his long reign in the southern kingdom, the people follow the king's wickedness in idolatry and injustice. The text as it now stands in the apocryphal literature is evidently the product of an unknown Jewish author using the first person form in behalf of King Manasseh, and dates from the period of one hundred years before or after the coming of Christ. Possible sources for the work are cited in Second Chronicles 33:18–19 as the Chronicles of the Kings of Judah and the Chronicles of the Seers, two works which are not available to us. Scholars today generally accept Second Chronicles 33:10 as the inspiration for the Prayer of Manasseh, but do not accept its historical genuineness from that early period.

The Time of the Prayer of Manasseh

During the rule of Manasseh, the kingdom of Judah suffers as a vassal state, paying regular tribute to its Assyrian overlords. The setting for the prayer is a recent Assyrian victory over Judah, which the Bible attributes to God's punishment for the sins of the people and the king. In the prayer Manasseh repents of his evil and pleads for mercy. God responds with mercy and Manasseh continues upon the throne. But this situation will not last long: quickly Manasseh and the people return to the pagan practices and idolatry of their neighbors, and are condemned by the prophets of the time. Thus Manasseh contributes his part to the decline of Judah, which climaxes in the Babylonian Exile in 587 B.C.

Survey of the Prayer of Manasseh

The Prayer of Manasseh is a very short, fifteen-verse prayer which may be broken down into these sections: (1) invocation to God Almighty, the Creator and Lord of all living things (vv. 1–5); (2) praise of God's mercy and compassion (vv. 6–7); (3) confession of sin by Manasseh the king (vv. 8–12); (4) a plea for forgiveness (vv. 13–14); and (5) concluding proclamation of praise for God and his goodness (vv. 14–15).

OUTLINE OF THE PRAYER OF MANASSEH

Invocation to God Almighty	1–5	Sin	8–12
Praise of God's Mercy and		Plea for Forgiveness	13–14
Compassion	6–7	Praise of God	15
Manasseh's Confession of			

FOCUS	PRAISE		CONFESSION		PRAISE
REFERENCE	1————————6	————————8	————————13————————	15————————	
DIVISION	PRAYER TO GOD, CREATOR AND LORD	PRAISE OF GOD, LORD MOST HIGH	CONFESSION TO THE LORD GOD	PLEA FOR FORGIVENESS	GOD'S GOODNESS PROCLAIMED
TOPIC	PRAYER OF REPENTANCE				
SETTING	KINGDOM OF JUDAH				

PRAYER OF MANASSEH

THE GOSPEL ACCORDING TO

MATTHEW

The Book of Matthew

Matthew is a gospel written for a church which consisted of both Jews and Gentiles. Why did Matthew write his gospel? No one can give a definitive answer. A careful reading of the gospel, however, shows that Matthew was responding to several crises in his church. Christianity started out as a Jewish phenomenon. Over the years more and more Gentiles were entering the church. This shift, plus the delay of the Second Coming and the separation of the church from the synagogue necessitated a reinterpretation of the traditions handed on to the church and a new look at the Old Testament.

Matthew documents how Jesus is the Messiah, the son of Abraham and the son of David. More importantly, Matthew shows that Jesus is the Son of God, the New Israel. Jesus is *the* teacher of Christian morality. He calls disciples to follow him and makes a new existence possible for them by his death and resurrection.

The Author of Matthew

In his *Ecclesiastical History* (A.D. 323) Eusebius quoted a statement by Papias (c. A.D. 140) that "Matthew, in Aramaic, grouped in order the sayings of the Lord and each interpreted them as best he could." Scholars have not been able to agree on the meaning of the word "sayings" (*logia* in Greek). For some the word "sayings" means gospel. For others, the word refers to a literary form of the first century in which the sayings of famous men were preserved.

Scholars are agreed that the canonical Gospel of Matthew was written in Greek and is not a translation of an Aramaic original. The question arises as to the identity of Matthew. The unanimous tradition of the early church is that Matthew the apostle wrote sayings (gospel?) of the Lord in Aramaic for Jewish converts in Palestine.

Modern scholars dispute this. They contend that the author of our Gospel of Matthew is either a Gentile Christian or a Greek-speaking Diaspora Jewish Christian. They point to the apparently unrelenting rejection of Israel in the gospel and the withering denunciation of the Pharisees. There are also examples in the gospel which show that the author is not familiar with Jewish matters. All this makes it improbable that the author can be identified with the Matthew-Levi mentioned in the first three gospels.

The Time of Matthew

Like all the gospels, Matthew is not easy to date. If Matthew depended on Mark's gospel as a source, which is a widely accepted view, the date of Mark would determine the earliest date for Matthew. Over the years, scholars have suggested dates as early as A.D. 40 and as late as A.D. 140. The most likely time frame for this book is the last third of the first century, sometime between A.D. 80–90. It may have been written in Palestine, but probably Antioch in Syria was its place of origin.

Survey of Matthew

The Old Testament prophets predicted and longed for the coming of the Anointed One who would enter history to bring redemption and deliverance. The first verse of Matthew briefly announces the fulfillment of Israel's hope in the coming of Christ: "Jesus Christ, a descendant of David, who was a descendant of Abraham." Matthew was placed first in the canon of New Testament books by the early church because it is a natural bridge between the Testaments. This gospel describes the person and work of Israel's messianic King. An important part of Matthew's structure is revealed in the phrase "when Jesus finished" (7:28; 11:1; 13:53; 19:1; 26:1), which is used to conclude the five key discourses of the book: the Sermon on the Mount (5:1 through 7:27); the missionary discourse (10:5–42); the parables discourse (13:3–52); the discourse on church life (18:1–35); and the eschatological discourse (24:4 through 25:46). Matthew can be outlined as follows: the prologue, the birth of the Messiah (1:1 through 2:23); Book One: the proclamation of the kingdom of God (3:1 through 7:29); Book Two: the ministry in Galilee (8:1 through 11:1); Book Three: controversy and parables (11:2 through 13:52); Book Four: the formation of the disciples (13:53 through 18:35); Book Five: the ministry in Jerusalem (19:1 through 25:46); the passion narrative (26:1 through 27:66); the resurrection narrative (28:1–20).

The Prologue, the Birth of the Messiah (1:1 through 2:23): In this carefully constructed narrative, Matthew shows how Jesus of Nazareth is the fulfillment of God's promises to Abraham and David. Jesus, together with Mary and Joseph, follows a divinely guided itinerary which demonstrates that he is the New Israel, the King of the Jews. Gentile participation in God's plan of salvation is present in the genealogy as well as in the Magi episode. The rejection and the suffering of the Messiah is already a reality in the Infancy Narratives.

Book One: The Proclamation of the Kingdom of God (3:1 through 7:29): John the Baptist, the messianic forerunner who breaks four hundred years of prophetic silence, bears witness to Jesus. Jesus overcomes temptation, proving that he has an undivided heart loyal to the will of his Father. The Messiah, the authoritative teacher, proclaims the new law, the new standard of moral living for his disciples and followers. This discourse requires less than fifteen minutes to read, but its brevity has not diminished its profound influence on the world.

Book Two: The Ministry in Galilee (8:1 through 11:1): Having presented Jesus as the Messiah, powerful in word, Matthew now presents Jesus as the Messiah, powerful in deed. Through a series of ten miracles (chs. 8 and 9), Jesus shows his authority over disease, demons, death, and nature. Then the Messiah, powerful in word and in deed, authoritatively sends his disciples to take part in his mission (10:5–42).

Book Three: Controversy and Parables (11:2 through 13:52): Here Matthew presents a series of reactions to Jesus' words and deeds. The opposition mounts a powerful offensive. Jesus makes yet another effort to convince his opponents in a series of parables. He spends more and more time with his disciples, giving them private instruction.

Book Four: The Formation of the Disciples (13:53 through 18:35): Jesus begins to prepare his disciples for his suffering and death. The death of John the Baptist is an ominous sign. At Caesarea Philippi, Simon confesses Jesus as the Messiah, Son of the living God. Jesus changes his name to Peter and gives him "the keys of the Kingdom."

Book Five: The Ministry in Jerusalem (19:1 through 25:46): Jesus emphasizes once again the significance of accepting or rejecting his person and his teaching. Most of his words in this section are directed to those who reject him. He predicts the terrible judgment that will befall Jerusalem and he describes his second coming as judge and Lord of all.

The Passion Narrative (26:1 through 27:66): Jesus' death is portrayed by Matthew as the "turning point of the ages." The tearing of the Temple veil, the earthquake, and the centurion's profession of faith are signs that the day of the Lord has arrived. All barriers, geographical and ethnic, are broken down. The crucified Messiah draws all to himself.

The Resurrection Narrative (28:1–20): The empty tomb, the Resurrection, and the appearances, authenticate the person and the mission of Jesus. He is the Christ, prophesied in the Old Testament, the Son of God. Divine love has overcome human hatred and sin.

OUTLINE OF MATTHEW

The prologue, birth of the Messiah	1:1–2:23
Book One: proclamation of the kingdom	3:1–7:29
Book Two: the ministry in Galilee	8:1–11:1
Book Three: controversy and parables	11:2–13:52
Book Four: formation of the disciples	13:53–18:35
Book Five: ministry in Jerusalem	19:1–25:46
The passion narrative	26:1–27:66
The Resurrection narrative	28:1–20

FOCUS	BIRTH	MINISTRY	DEATH AND RESURRECTION
REFERENCE	1.1————————————3.1——————————————26.1————————————28.20		
DIVISION	JESUS IS SON OF GOD	NARRATIVES AND DISCOURSES	JESUS: SUFFERING, RISEN MESSIAH
TOPIC	JESUS: SON OF ABRAHAM, SON OF DAVID, KING OF JEWS	JESUS: PREACHER, TEACHER, HEALER	ARREST, TRIAL, PASSION, APPEARANCES
SETTING	BETHLEHEM AND NAZARETH	TOWNS AND VILLAGES OF GALILEE	JERUSALEM AND GALILEE

MATTHEW

THE GOSPEL ACCORDING TO

MARK

The Book of Mark

It is possible to capture the message of the Gospel of Mark in a single verse: "For even the Son of Man did not come to be served; he came to serve and to give his life to redeem many people" (10:45). Chapter by chapter, the book unfolds the dual focus of Jesus' life: service and sacrifice, as well as his identity both as Messiah and Son of God.

Mark portrays Jesus as a Servant on the move, instantly responsive to the will of the Father. By preaching, teaching, and healing, he ministers to the needs of others even to the point of death. After the Resurrection, he commissions his followers to continue his work in his power—servants following in the steps of the perfect Servant.

Mark, according to most scholars today, was the first to write a gospel. In fact, he invented this new literary form. Therefore he is the first interpreter of, and commentator on, the tradition of the sayings and deeds of Jesus.

The Author of Mark

The earliest witness to the identity of the author of this gospel is Papias (A.D. 140). He wrote a five-volume work entitled *Explanation of the Lord's Sayings*. Although we do not have copies of this work today, a few sections of it are found in Eusebius' *Church History* (A.D. 323).

Papias identifies the author as Mark, an interpreter of Peter. Mark's gospel is not a biography, nor is it a strict chronological account of Jesus' life. Eusebius quotes Papias on this point: Mark "wrote down accurately, but not however in order, as much as he remembered of the words and deeds of the Lord; for he had neither heard the Lord nor been in his company, but subsequently joined Peter as I said. Now Peter did not intend to give a connected account of the Lord's sayings but delivered his teaching to meet the needs [of his hearers]."

The early church uniformly attested that Mark wrote this gospel. Papias, Irenaeus, Clement of Alexandria, and Origen are among the church writers who affirmed Marcan authorship.

Today, scholars do not think that all Mark's stories came from Peter. There was already in existence a living oral tradition. Mark would have drawn from this source when he wrote his gospel. Also, Mark's gospel relates incidents at which Peter was not present (7:24–30; 14:53–65; 15:1 through 16:8). No one can say definitively whether the author of the gospel should be identified with the John Mark who appears in the Acts of the Apostles.

This much can be said of the author. He was a literary genius. He had theological motives for writing his gospel and was guided by those theological motives, by the tradition he had inherited, and by the problems in his church.

The Time of Mark

There is no certainty about the date of this gospel. Irenaeus in his work, *Against Heresies,* wrote that Mark was writing after the death of Peter and Paul, which occurred in A.D. 64. The so-called Little Apocalypse, (13:5–37) indicates knowledge of events leading up to the Jewish war against Rome (A.D. 66–70) but demonstrates no clear knowledge of the fall of Jerusalem (A.D. 70). Most scholars think the gospel was written slightly before the fall of Jerusalem. The probable range for this gospel is A.D. 65–75.

Early church tradition attests that Mark wrote from Rome. This has been accepted by most scholars today. It would seem that the gospel was written for Gentile Christians. Some scholars suggest Galilee or Antioch in Syria as the place of origin.

Survey of Mark

Mark, the shortest and simplest of the four gospels, gives a crisp and fast-moving look at the life of Christ. With few comments, Mark lets the narrative speak for itself as it tells the story of the Servant who constantly ministers to others through preaching, healing, teaching, and ultimately his own death. Mark traces the steady building of hostility and opposition to Jesus as he resolutely moves toward the fulfillment of his earthly mission. Almost forty percent of this gospel is devoted to a detailed account of the last eight days of Jesus' life, climaxing in his resurrection. Mark can be outlined as follows: prologue (1:1–15); Jesus, Messiah—Teacher, Healer (1:16 through 8:21); Jesus, suffering Messiah—Son of Man (8:22 through 10:52); Jesus in Jerusalem (11:1 through 13:37); the Passion and Resurrection (14:1 through 16:20).

Prologue (1:1–15): The story of Jesus marks a new beginning. All are called to leave their ordinary cares and worries and go out to be baptized by John in the Jordan. Jesus sets the example. After he is baptized by John, the Father and the Spirit are in intimate communication with him. Led by the Spirit, he is tempted in the desert. God is with his Son in every trial and temptation.

Jesus, Messiah—Teacher, Healer (1:16 through 8:21): Jesus calls the first disciples. They hear his "new teaching in authority" and are spellbound with the crowds because he does not teach as the scribes. The disciples also witness Jesus' powerful deeds. Through word and deed Jesus gradually reveals who he is, although the disciples do not yet understand.

Jesus, Suffering Messiah—Son of Man (8:22 through 10:52): This is the central section of Mark's gospel. Here Mark reveals his theology of the Cross. Three times Jesus predicts his suffering, death, and resurrection. Three times the disciples fail to understand how the idea of suffering can be connected with the concept of the Messiah. After each misunderstanding by the disciples, Jesus gives a discourse on the necessity of suffering discipleship. While Jesus can restore sight to the blind man at Bethsaida (8:22–26) and to Bartimaeus (10:46–52), he cannot give insight to his disciples.

Jesus in Jerusalem (11:1 through 13:37): During his last days in Jerusalem, hostility from the chief priests, scribes, elders, Pharisees, Herodians, and Sadducees reaches crisis proportions as Jesus publicly refutes their arguments in the Temple. The fig tree, together with the Temple incident and the "Little Apocalypse," indicates that the end of the old order is near.

The Passion and Resurrection (14:1 through 16:20): The Suffering Servant has his last supper with his disciples. Afterward he offers no resistance to his arrest, abuse, and agonizing crucifixion. A centurion proclaims him Son of God. The Servant is vindicated. The tomb is empty. The only path to glory is participation in the suffering of Jesus.

OUTLINE OF MARK

Prologue	1:1–15	Son of Man	8:22–10:52
Jesus, Messiah—Teacher,		Jesus in Jerusalem	11:1–13:37
Healer	1:16–8:21	Passion and Resurrection	14:1–16:20
Jesus, suffering Messiah–			

FOCUS	JESUS IS MESSIAH		JESUS IS SUFFERING SERVANT	JESUS IS SON OF GOD
REFERENCE	1.1————————1.16————————		8.22————————14.1————————16.20	
DIVISION	PRESENTATION OF MESSIAH	OPPOSITION TO MESSIAH	INSTRUCTION BY SUFFERING SERVANT	REJECTION AND RESURRECTION OF SON OF GOD
TOPIC	BAPTISM AND CONVERSION	SAYINGS AND SIGNS	THEOLOGY OF CROSS	SUFFERING AND GLORY
SETTING	DESERT	GALILEE		JERUSALEM AND GALILEE

MARK

THE GOSPEL ACCORDING TO

LUKE

The Book of Luke

Luke addresses Theophilus in the opening verses of the gospel. He seeks to assure him and all who read his writings that the instruction they have received is indeed reliable. Luke is writing sometime after the public ministry of Jesus. Much has happened in the meantime. Persecutions, doctrinal controversies, internal squabbling, defections from the faith, and the gentile problem were some of the things that caused people to doubt the faith. Luke wants to put an end to the confusion. What Luke teaches is rooted in the earliest Jesus tradition. God's plan of salvation involves both Israel and the Gentiles. The God of Abraham, Isaac, and Jacob glorified Jesus and raised him from the dead. Peter and Paul are the apostles to the Gentiles. If anyone wants to find the path to salvation amid all the confusion of the day, he will find it only within the tradition represented by Peter and Paul. It is this tradition that Luke teaches in his gospel and in his companion work, the Acts of the Apostles.

The Author of Luke

Long-standing church tradition identifies Luke as the author of this gospel. The Muratorian Canon (A.D. 170–180) contains a very early testimony to Lucan authorship. The Muratorian Canon tells us that Luke was a physician and a companion of Paul. The Canon also states that Luke was not an eyewitness to the public ministry of Jesus.

Luke is mentioned several times in the New Testament. In Philemon 24 he is mentioned as one of Paul's fellow workers. In Colossians 4:14 he is called "our dear doctor" and sends greetings to the Colossian community. In Second Timothy 4:11 the author states that he has no one with him but Luke.

Irenaeus, in his *Against Heresies*, says that Luke was a companion of Paul and that he wrote the gospel preached by Paul. Irenaeus' main argument for Lucan authorship is the "We" sections of the Acts of the Apostles (16:10–17; 20:5–15; 21:1–18; 27:1 through 28:16). Many scholars today claim that Irenaeus' testimony is not on solid ground.

They question whether Luke was Paul's inseparable companion and whether Luke even read any of Paul's letters. The most they will claim is that Luke might have been a collaborator with Paul at some time or other.

Scholars cannot agree on Luke's ethnic background. Some claim he is a Gentile Christian, perhaps of Greek origin. Others say he was a convert from Judaism. The anti-Marcionite Prologue (A.D. 160–180) says that Luke was a Syrian of Antioch. There he would have been exposed to, if not well educated in, a Hellenistic atmosphere and culture. Luke is regarded as an excellent writer, acquainted with Old Testament literary traditions and Hellenistic literary techniques. Jerome long ago recognized that Luke, among all the evangelists, was the most skilled writer of Greek.

The Time of Luke

Luke tells us in his brief prologue (1:1–4) that in writing his gospel he is dependent on sources. The events about which he will write have been transmitted to him by the original eyewitnesses and ministers of the Word.

Most scholars today agree that Luke is dependent on the Gospel of Mark. If we date Mark sometime between A.D. 65–75, then Luke's gospel would have to be dated sometime after that. The most likely time for Luke's gospel is A.D. 80–85.

Where was Luke written? Commentators, both ancient and modern, cannot agree. Places suggested are Achaia, Boeotia, Rome, and Asia Minor. To whom did Luke write? The fact that Luke wants to relate his account of Jesus' life, death, and resurrection to the secular history of his time is a strong clue that he is writing for a gentile audience. Also to be noted is how Luke either eliminates Jewish preoccupations from his sources (e.g., Mark and the Sayings source, Q) or adjusts Palestinian traditions to a gentile Hellenistic situation (e.g., 5:19; 6:48–49). It is possible that Luke is writing for Christians who are being harassed by their Jewish neighbors during the beginning of the Jamnia reform. Still, it seems that Luke's audience is predominantly Gentile-Christian.

Survey of Luke

Luke builds his gospel narrative on the platform of historical reliability. His emphasis on chronological and historical details makes this the most comprehensive of the four gospels. This is the longest and most literary of the gospels. Jesus is presented as the fulfillment of Old Testament prophecy. In his person and his preaching a new age has dawned. He brings release, sight, and liberty to all. Luke's gospel can be divided as follows: prologue and infancy narrative (1:1 through 2:52); preparation for the public ministry (3:1 through 4:13); the Galilean ministry (4:14 through 9:50); the journey to Jerusalem (9:51 through 19:27); the Jerusalem ministry (19:28 through 21:38); and the passion-resurrection narratives (22:1 through 24:53).

The Prologue and Infancy Narrative (1:1 through 2:52): Luke places a strong emphasis on the ancestry, birth, and early years of Jesus and his forerunner, John the Baptist. Their infancy stories are intertwined as Luke parallels their announcements of birth, their actual birth, and their presentations. In each instance Jesus and his parents are seen to be superior to John and his parents. God is present in Jesus, not the Temple. Law gives way to grace. Jesus will spend many years preparing for his brief public ministry.

Preparation for the Public Ministry (3:1 through 4:13): The preaching of John the Baptist sets the stage for the dawn of the new age. Before he can baptize Jesus, John is imprisoned by Herod Antipas. This concludes John's ministry and the door opens on Jesus. Jesus is a prayerful man. His ancestry is traced back to the first man, Adam.

The Galilean Ministry (4:14 through 9:50): Jesus' authority over every realm is demonstrated. He has power over demons, disease, nature, sin, and death. In his controversies with the Pharisees, Jesus is a man of powerful words. The reaction to Jesus on the part of the crowds and religious leaders is carefully presented in a series of stories.

The Journey to Jerusalem (9:51 through 19:27): This section is often referred to as the Travel Account. The time has come for Jesus to end his ministry in Galilee. The opening verse of this section is most solemn. God's plan of salvation is moving to a new stage of realization. Jesus knows this. He sets his face resolutely toward Jerusalem and all that awaits him there. Opposition to his ministry intensifies. Knowing all this, Jesus keeps his eyes on his destination and instructs his disciples on many important matters.

The Jerusalem Ministry (19:28 through 21:39): Jesus enters the holy city in triumph. The Temple will be the scene of much of his activity during the days before his arrest. Tension mounts. Jesus purges the Temple and delivers a Jeremiah-like prediction of its fate. Jesus further instructs his disciples. Between the desolation of Jerusalem and the coming of the Son of Man, the disciples must be vigilant, living lives of faith, giving witness daily to their conversion and repentance.

The Passion-Resurrection Narratives (22:1 through 24:53): Jesus is the Messiah who must suffer. This note of suffering with its sacrificial significance is present in the Last Supper account and throughout the Passion Narrative. Forgiveness of sins comes only in the name of Jesus, the suffering Messiah. Jesus conquers death as he promised and appears on a number of occasions to his disciples. Peace, life, and the Spirit are gifts of the risen Jesus to his disciples.

OUTLINE OF LUKE

Prologue and infancy narrative	1:1–2:52	Ministry in Galilee	4:14–9:50
		Journey to Jerusalem	9:51–19:27
Preparation for public ministry	3:1–4:13	Ministry in Jerusalem	19:28–21:38
		Passion and Resurrection	22:1–24:53

FOCUS	JESUS AND JOHN COMPARED	PUBLIC MINISTRY	PASSION AND RESURRECTION
REFERENCE	1.1———————————3.1———————————22.1———————————24.53		
DIVISION	BEGINNING	DEVELOPMENT	END AND NEW BEGINNING
TOPIC	ANNOUNCEMENTS AND BIRTHS OF JOHN AND JESUS	TEACHING, PREACHING, HEALING	SUFFERING AND GLORY
SETTING	JERUSALEM AND GALILEE	GALILEE AND JERUSALEM	JERUSALEM

LUKE

THE GOSPEL ACCORDING TO

JOHN

The Book of John

Christian tradition and doctrine teach that Jesus Christ has two natures, human and divine. Most scholars would agree that the Gospel of John portrays Jesus in his divine nature as Son of God. John's purpose in writing is crystal clear: to set forth a portrait of Jesus Christ in his divinity in order to spark his readers to "believe that Jesus is the Messiah, the Son of God, and that through your faith in him you may have life" (20:31).

John's gospel is not simply history. His theology is what guides the selection and the arrangement of the material found in the gospel. Jesus' discourses and miracles are carefully constructed by the evangelist to emphasize his divinity.

The Author of John

Irenaeus in his *Against Heresies* (c. A.D. 180) writes that after the writing of the other gospels, "John, the disciple of the Lord, who also reclined on his bosom, published his gospel while staying at Ephesus in Asia." In general, the early church tradition confirms that John the apostle, one of Zebedee's sons, wrote the fourth gospel.

There has been much discussion by modern scholars about the authorship of the fourth gospel. They point out that the gospel speaks of a beloved disciple who rested on Jesus' bosom at the Last Supper. Is this beloved disciple to be identified with John, the son of Zebedee, whose brother was James? The story in 21:1–7 is but one clue indicating that such an identification cannot easily be made. Zebedee's sons are listed among those who went fishing with Peter. Others are named as well. Also present, however, are two unnamed disciples. It would seem that one of them is the beloved disciple who in verse 7 cries out to Peter, "It is the Lord." This is consistent with the other references to the beloved disciple in the fourth gospel where he is always unnamed. There is no New Testament evidence that the son of Zebedee ever went to Ephesus. Paul does not seem to know of his presence there when he addresses the Ephesians in Acts 20:18ff. Even in his

Epistle to the Ephesians (A.D. 63) Paul does not know of John's presence at Ephesus. Much later, around A.D. 110, Ignatius wrote a letter to the Ephesians. He does not seem to know that John the apostle stayed at Ephesus either.

Most scholars today believe that John, son of Zebedee, is not the author of the fourth gospel. Opinions vary as to whether the beloved disciple is the author or not.

It is best to say that John, son of Zebedee, could well have been responsible for some of the earliest tradition that went into the fourth gospel. This tradition was then reshaped and reinterpreted by a theologian of consummate skill. He developed his own literary style and patterns. He, not John, son of Zebedee, would have been responsible for the final literary product that we know as the fourth gospel. It seems likely that new material was added later by a final editor who would have been a disciple of the evangelist.

The Time of John

Until recently it was popular to propose a second-century date for this book (e.g., A.D. 140–170). The usual argument in support of a late dating rested on the idea of the development of theology. John represented a high christological synthesis, far beyond that of the first three gospels, or even Paul. The most conclusive argument against such a late dating was the discovery of the John Rylands Papyrus. This was an Egyptian codex fragment containing portions of John 18:31–33 and 18:37–38. Some date this papyrus to about A.D. 135, and a considerable period of time must have been required for John's gospel to be copied and circulated before it reached Egypt.

The historical traditions underlying this gospel are usually dated to A.D. 40–60. There had to be a lapse of time between the formation of this tradition and the actual writing of the gospel with its distinctive literary patterns and developed theology. The gospel was probably written during the last ten years of the first century, most likely between A.D. 95–100.

Survey of John

The content and style of the Gospel of John are quite distinct. It contains material similar to that found in the first three gospels, yet independent of those gospels. It also contains material not found in the three. It is at once a simple, yet most profound, literary work. For many it is the greatest and most powerful gospel. John can be outlined as follows: the prologue (1:1–18); the book of signs (1:19 through 12:50); the book of glory (13:1 through 20:31); and the epilogue (21:1–25).

The Prologue (1:1–18): The evangelist used this early Christian hymn to serve as an introduction to his gospel narrative. The entire gospel is said to be contained in miniature in these eighteen verses. The principal themes of light, life, glory, darkness, and flesh are found here. So too are the themes of rejection, hostility, and struggle. The victory of light over darkness is announced. The eternal Logos, who was face to face with God in the beginning, became flesh and pitched his tent among us.

The Book of Signs (1:19 through 12:50): In this section Jesus is under careful scrutiny and consideration by the leaders of the Jews. He is introduced by "a man named John" who was sent to bear witness to the light. Through a series of seven signs which the evangelist expands into full-length episodes, the portrait of Jesus comes into clear focus. The first sign takes place at Cana in Galilee, where Jesus changes water into wine. This marks a new beginning as Jesus replaces the water of Jewish purifications: law is replaced by grace. The second sign is the healing of the official's son. Jesus' word is life-giving. There is spiritual restoration in the message he brings. The third sign is the healing of the paralytic at Bethesda Pool. Again, Jesus' word is life-giving. This healing occurs on a Sabbath day. The evangelist shows that Jesus performs works that only God can do on the Sabbath. The fourth sign is the multiplication of the loaves. Jesus is the Bread of Life who satisfies all human hunger. The fifth sign is the walking on water. Jesus is "I Am." He transforms fear to faith. The sixth sign is the healing of the man born blind. Jesus is the Light of the World. He is the model shepherd. The seventh sign is the raising of Lazarus. Life conquers death. Jesus' word brings people from death to life. The Lord shows that there is life through death.

The Book of Glory (13:1 through 20:31): The psychological atmosphere of Jesus' last supper with his disciples holds much of this section together. During the meal Jesus washes his disciples' feet. This one act is both a symbol of Jesus' death and an example of humble service. Afterward Jesus begins the farewell discourses. Here the evangelist captures the Lord's words of comfort and assurance to a group of fearful and confused followers. Jesus is in complete control of the situation. He knows the Cross is but hours away. He speaks of all the resources that will be at the disciples' disposal after his departure.

The Paraclete will come and dwell within them. So too will Jesus and the Father. During the arrest scene, Jesus is still in complete command of all that is happening. This serene control is in evidence even when Jesus stands before the representative of imperial Rome. In one sense Jesus is on trial. For the evangelist it is Pilate who is really on trial. On the Cross Jesus is the Lamb of God who takes away the sin of the world. The Resurrection is the ultimate sign pointing to Jesus as the Son of God.

The Epilogue (21:1–25): Chapter 20 closes with the appearance of the risen Jesus to his disciples. Notably absent from this chapter is any word by which Jesus sends forth his disciples on a mission. In chapter 21 Peter is both fisherman and shepherd bringing many to Jesus. Peter's role in relation to that of the beloved disciple is clarified. Also clarified is the relation of the Johannine community to the apostolic church. Jesus provided for the needs of his church by showing his followers how to maintain unity in diversity.

OUTLINE OF JOHN

Prologue	1:1–18	Book of glory	13:1–20:31
Book of signs	1:19–12:50	Epilogue	21:1–25

FOCUS	INCARNATION	PUBLIC MINISTRY	PREPARATION FOR DEPARTURE	PASSION AND RESURRECTION
REFERENCE	1.1	1.19	13.1	18.1 21.25
DIVISION	INTRODUCTION	REVELATION		
TOPIC	THE WORD	SIGNS AND SAYINGS	FAREWELL DISCOURSES	SUFFERING AND GLORY
SETTING	IN THE BEGINNING	GALILEE AND JERUSALEM	JERUSALEM	JERUSALEM AND GALILEE

THE ACTS
OF THE APOSTLES

The Book of Acts

The Book of Acts is the second volume in a two-part work written by the author of the third gospel. The title of "Acts" or "The Acts of the Apostles" is found in all Greek manuscripts but probably the author is not responsible for the title. The longer title, "The Acts of the Apostles," is misleading. The title is not an accurate description of the content, for generally speaking, it records only the acts of the two most important apostles, Peter and Paul; and its account even of their actions is far from complete, especially for Peter. Actually, in the first twelve chapters, Peter is the principal hero; Paul, in the remaining chapters. The latter, although twice called "apostle" was not one of the Twelve. Except for the list in 1:13 most of the other apostles are not named at all. Only Judas, John, and his brother, James, are mentioned by name and made the subject of some small happenings. In ancient times the title often given to a book was determined by the subject matter of the first pages of the book. In the first chapter of Acts a list of the eleven apostles is given, and in the same chapter the choice of Matthias to succeed Judas completes the Twelve. It is very possible then that this first chapter prompted the choice of the title.

The material and the order of the material follow the programmatic commission of the risen Lord to the eleven: "You will be witnesses for me in Jerusalem, in all Judea and Samaria, and to the ends of the earth." The book is the story of the men and women who, following Pentecost, began to spread the news of the risen Savior. It concludes with the account of Paul preaching this good news in Rome, the capital of the civilized world of the day.

Traditionally, the book has been regarded as an historical work written with the intention of giving a detailed history of the early church. Critical studies, however, have shown that the book does not meet the canons for a work of general history—even those of ancient times. This does not mean that much of what is written is not historical. It means that the author had a specific purpose for choosing the data he incorporates into his work. What that purpose was is highly debated. One theory that appears to account for all the data and emphases in the book is that it was written for a gentile audience to convince them that the Christian religion is the one true religion planned from the beginning of time by the one true God, established by him through Jesus Christ for the salvation of humankind. It is an invitation to the Gentiles to recognize this new way as the one way to the salvation for which they yearn. At the same time the narrative is a source of edification and strengthening of the faith of those who have already committed themselves to the way to God and salvation proclaimed by the Lord and his Spirit-filled ministers.

The Author of Acts

There is almost unanimous agreement among scholars that the author of the third gospel is the author of Acts. The third gospel is anonymous. Nowhere in it does the author reveal his identity. The title, "The Gospel According to Luke," is found at the end of the gospel in the oldest extant manuscript. Such manuscript titles date from the end of the second century, when the assignment of the four canonical gospels to their traditional authors was already a common heritage.

The "Luke" who is mentioned here is mentioned three times in the New Testament. In Philemon 24 he is Paul's fellow worker who sends greetings. In Colossians 4:14, he is referred to as the "dear doctor" and sends greetings to the church in Colossae. In Second Timothy 4:11, he is named as Paul's only companion.

The identification of Luke, a doctor and companion of Paul, as the author of the third gospel and Acts is based on an unbroken tradition going back to the last quarter of the second century, and has found support in the "We" sections of Acts (16:10–17; 20:5–15; 21:1–18; 27:1 through 28:16).

In recent times, however, particularly in the last three or four decades, critical scholars have seriously questioned Lucan authorship for a variety of reasons—one of the principal ones being the differences between the picture and teaching of Paul in Acts and that in the Pauline Epistles. Authors argue from these differences that the author could not have been Luke, a companion of Paul. Today, a reaction has set in against the negatively critical position. It can be said that most of the arguments recently brought forth to substantiate the distance of Luke from Paul do not disprove the traditional identification of the author of the third gospel and Acts with Luke the Syrian from Antioch, who quite probably was a doctor and a collaborator with the apostle Paul.

The Time of Acts

The date of the material as presented in the Book of Acts would run from a few weeks after Christ's death to Paul's imprisonment in Rome awaiting trial around the year A.D. 62.

The time of writing is another question. Suggested dates for the writing of the book have extended from A.D. 62 to the middle of the second century. When one considers all the arguments, the best solution for the writing of Luke through the Book of Acts is about A.D. 80–85. A date shortly before or after those years would not be out of line.

Survey of Acts

Luke begins the Book of Acts where he left off in his gospel. Acts records the initial fulfillment of the Great Commission of Matthew 28:19 and 20 as it traces the beginning and growth of the New Testament church (this growth pattern can be seen in 1:15; 2:41, 47; 4:4; 5:14; 6:7; 9:31; 12:24; 13:49; 16:5; 19:20). Acts traces important events in the early history of Christianity, from the ascension of Christ to the outpouring of the Holy Spirit, to the rapid progress of the gospel, beginning in Jerusalem and spreading throughout the Roman Empire. The Book of Acts may be divided as follows: witness in Jerusalem (1:1 through 8:4); witness in Judea and Samaria (8:5 through 12:25); witness to the ends of the earth (chs. 13 through 28).

Witness in Jerusalem (1:1 through 8:4): After appearing to his disciples for "forty days" (1:3), the Lord tells them to wait in Jerusalem for the fulfillment of his promise concerning the Holy Spirit. Ten days after his ascension, this promise is significantly fulfilled as the disciples are suddenly empowered and filled with the Holy Spirit. The disciples are transformed and filled with courage to proclaim the brand new message of the resurrected Savior. Peter's powerful sermon, like all the sermons in Acts, is built upon the Resurrection, and 3,000 persons respond with saving faith. After dramatically healing a man who was lame from birth, Peter delivers a second crucial message to the people of Israel resulting in thousands of additional responses. The religious leaders arrest the apostles, and this gives Peter an opportunity to preach a special sermon to them.

The enthusiasm and joy of the infant church are marred by internal and external problems. Ananias and Sapphira receive the ultimate form of discipline because of their treachery, and the apostles are imprisoned and persecuted because of their witness. Seven men, including Stephen and Philip, are selected to assist the apostles. Stephen is brought before the Council; in his defense, Stephen surveys the Scriptures to prove that the man they condemned and killed was the Messiah himself. The members of the Council react to Stephen's words by dragging him out of the city and making him the first Christian martyr.

Witness in Judea and Samaria (8:5 through 12:25): Philip goes to the province of Samaria and successfully proclaims the new message to a people hated by the Jews. Peter and John confirm his work and exercise their apostolic authority by imparting the Holy Spirit to these new members of the body of Christ. God sovereignly transforms Saul the persecutor into Paul the apostle to the Gentiles, but he uses Peter to introduce the gospel to the Gentiles. In a special vision Peter realizes that Christ has broken down the barrier between Jew and Gentile. After Cornelius and other Gentiles come to Christ through his preaching, Peter convinces the Jewish believers in Jerusalem that "the Gentiles also had received the word of God" (11:1). Even while experiencing more and more persecution, the church continues to increase, spreading throughout the Roman Empire.

Witness to the Ends of the Earth (chs. 13 through 28): Beginning with chapter 13, Luke switches the focus of Acts from Peter to Paul. Antioch in Syria gradually replaces Jerusalem as the headquarters of the church, and all three of Paul's missionary journeys originate from that city. The first journey (A.D. 48–49) concentrates on the Galatian cities of Antioch in Pisidia, Iconium, Lystra, and Derbe. After this journey, a council is held among the apostles and elders of the church in Jerusalem to determine that the gentile converts need not submit to the law of Moses.

The second missionary journey (A.D. 50–52) brings Paul to the Galatian churches, and then for the first time on to Macedonia and Greece. Paul spends much of his time in the cities of Philippi, Thessalonica, and Corinth, and later returns to Jerusalem and Antioch. In his third missionary journey (A.D. 53–57), Paul spends almost three years in the Asian city of Ephesus before visiting Macedonia and Greece for the second time. Although he is warned not to go to Jerusalem, Paul cannot be dissuaded.

It is not long before Paul is falsely accused of bringing Gentiles into the Temple. Only the Roman commander's intervention prevents his being killed by the mob. Paul's defense before the people and before the Council evokes violent reactions. When the commander learns of a conspiracy to assassinate Paul, he sends his prisoner to

Felix, the governor in Caesarea. During his two-year imprisonment there (A.D. 57–59), Paul defends the Christian faith before Felix, Festus, and Agrippa. His appeal to Caesar requires a long voyage to Rome, where he is placed under house arrest until his trial.

OUTLINE OF THE ACTS

Preparation for the witness	1:1–26	b. The conference in Jerusalem	15:1–35
a. Jesus' last command and promise	1:1–14	c. The second missionary journey	15:36–18:22
b. The successor of Judas	1:15–26	d. The third missionary journey	18:23–21:16
The witness in Jerusalem	2:1–8:3	e. Paul a prisoner in Jerusalem, Caesarea, and Rome	21:17–28:31
The witness in Judea and Samaria	8:4–12:25		
The ministry of Paul	13:1–28:31		
a. The first missionary journey	13:1–14:28		

FOCUS	WITNESS IN JERUSALEM		WITNESS IN JUDEA AND SAMARIA	WITNESS TO THE REMOTEST PART OF THE EARTH	
REFERENCE	1.1———————3.1———		—8.5———————13.1—	——————21.17————28.31	
DIVISION	POWER OF THE CHURCH	PROGRESS OF THE CHURCH	EXPANSION OF THE CHURCH	PAUL'S THREE JOURNEYS	PAUL'S TRIALS
TOPIC	JEWS		SAMARITANS	GENTILES	
	PETER		PHILIP	PAUL	
SETTING	JERUSALEM		JUDEA AND SAMARIA	UTTERMOST PART	

PAUL'S LETTER TO THE

ROMANS

The Book of Romans

Romans, Paul's greatest work, is placed first among the fourteen epistles which the Council of Trent referred to as the "Corpus Paulinum," that is, the Pauline body of epistles. The Letter to the Romans is the most systematically developed book of the New Testament. It is a theological treatise rather than a personal letter. The first eleven chapters logically defend and develop the thesis expressed in 1:16, namely, "the gospel; it is God's power to save all who believe." Chapters 12 through 15 offer practical suggestions for Christian living based on the teaching elucidated in the first eleven chapters. The final chapter contains a list of greetings to various persons living in Rome.

The Author of Romans

All critical scholars agree on the Pauline authorship of this book. The vocabulary, style, logic, and theological development are consistent with Paul's other epistles.

A problem arises, not with the authorship, but with the possible disunity of the epistle. Some Latin (but no Greek) manuscripts omit 15:1 through 16:24, and the closing doxology (16:25–27) is placed at the end of chapter 14 in some manuscripts and at the end of chapter 15 in others. These variations have led some scholars to conclude that the last two chapters were not originally part of the epistle, or that Paul issued it in two editions. Most scholars, however, believe that chapter 15 fits in logically with the rest of the epistle. There is more debate over chapter 16 because there Paul greets by name twenty-six persons in a church he has never visited. Some scholars contend that it was a separate letter, perhaps written to Ephesus, that was appended to the letter. Others contend that the people addressed were Christians who had been expelled from Rome under Claudius and who had fled to Ephesus and other cities of the province of Asia where Paul met them. They had recently returned to Rome. That would explain Paul's acquaintance with them. Several reputable scholars reject the closing doxology (16:25–27), not on the basis of manuscript evidence but on the basis of vocabulary and style which they judge foreign to Paul.

The Time of Romans

Rome was founded in 753 B.C. By the time of Paul it was the greatest city in the world, with over one million inhabitants (one inscription says over four million). It was full of magnificent buildings, gave resplendent evidence of wealth, culture, prosperity, and power, but the majority of the inhabitants were slaves: opulence and squalor coexisted in the Imperial City. The church in Rome was well known (1:8), and it had been established for several years by the time of this letter (see 15:23). These latter facts are confirmed by the data of Acts (Acts 28:15). The believers there were probably numerous, and if chapter 16 is authentic, they apparently met in several places (16:1–16). The historian, Tacitus, referred to the Christians who were persecuted under Nero in A.D. 64 as an "immense multitude."

The exact date for the writing of the letter and its chronological relationship to Galatians and the two Corinthian letters are much debated questions among scholars. One acceptable theory would allege that Paul wrote Romans in A.D. 57, near the end of his third missionary journey (Acts 18:23 through 21:14; cf. Rom. 15:19). He wrote it during his three-month stay in Greece (Acts 20:3–6), more specifically in Corinth. If the data of chapter 16 can be trusted, then it can be said that Paul was staying with Gaius of Corinth (16:23; cf. 1 Cor. 1:14). Paul's collection from the churches of Macedonia and Achaia for the poor Christians in Jerusalem was complete (15:26) and he was ready to deliver it (15:25). Instead of sailing directly to Jerusalem, Paul avoided a plot by the Jews by first going north to Philippi. He evidently gave this letter to Phoebe from the church at Cenchreae, near Corinth, and she carried it to Rome (16:1–2).

Survey of Romans

The Letter to the Romans is the most systematically developed work of the New Testament. Paul states his thesis: "the gospel; it is God's power to save all who believe" (1:16). He develops this thesis up to and including chapter 11 through two themes: In it (the gospel) the justice of God is revealed (1:17 through 4:25) and the love of God assures our salvation (5:1 through 11:36). The subsequent section, 12:1 through 15:14, deals with the duties of Christians based on the teaching unfolded in chapters 1 through 11. The conclusion of the book (15:15 through 16:27) deals with personal notices of Paul. Romans can be divided as follows: prologue and thesis (1:1–16); the justice of God revealed (1:17 through 4:25); the love of God assures our salvation (5:1 through 11:36); moral duties of the Christian (12:1 through 15:14); and conclusion (15:15 through 16:27).

Prologue and Thesis (1:1–16): The prologue (1:1–16) consists of a salutation (1:1–7), a statement of Paul's desire to minister in Rome (1:8–15), and the thesis of the book (1:16) which he develops through chapter 11.

The Justice of God Revealed (1:17 through 4:25): The development of his first theme supporting his thesis is that in the gospel the justice of God is revealed (1:17). Paul develops this theme first by developing a solid case for the condemnation of all people under the holy God. Gentiles are without excuse because they have suppressed the knowledge of God they received from nature and their conscience (1:18–32). Their seven-step regression is traced (1:21–31). The Jews are also under the condemnation of God, and Paul overcomes every objection they could raise to this conclusion (2:1 through 3:8). God judges according to truth (2:2–5), works (2:6–10), and impartiality (2:11–16). The moral and religious Jews fail to meet his standard. Paul concluded his discussion of the reasons for the guilt of the Jews by reminding them they do not obey the Law (2:17–29) nor believe the message of God (3:1–8). The divine verdict (3:9–20) is universal: "Everyone has sinned and is far away from God's saving presence" (3:23). Paul then develops positively the theme that the justice of God is revealed in the gospel by focusing on the work and role of Jesus in salvation and redemption. These eleven verses (3:21–31) are the core of the book revealing that, in Christ, God is both Judge and Savior. Justification is by grace (3:21–24), by blood (3:25–26), and by faith (3:27–31).

Chapter 4 illustrates the principle that justification was by faith apart from works as seen in the life of Abraham. Thus, Paul completes his first theme by showing that his doctrine of justification by faith is in accord with the Old Testament.

The Love of God Assures Our Salvation (5:1 through 11:36): In chapter 5 Paul begins to develop this second theme. The theme will continue through chapter 11. First, he states his theme (5:1–11). The one justified has been reconciled to God. If Christ died for humans when they were enemies of God, how much more now that they have been reconciled are they assured of salvation.

Paul then discusses the work of Jesus which brought about this reconciliation with God. First, he shows how Jesus delivered humans from sin and death. In so doing he contrasts the two Adams and the result of their two acts. One brought all men acquittal and life; the other condemnation to all (5:12–21). In chapter 6 he shows how Jesus delivers humans from self. He describes the believer's relationship to sin: the believer through baptism is dead to the principle of sin (6:1–14) and the practice of sin (6:15–23). The reality of identification with Christ is the basis for the sanctified Christian life. Paul then describes how Christ freed us from the law (ch. 7).

Chapter 8 resumes the theme of chapter 5:1–11, namely, the love of God assures our salvation. Here Paul looks at the work of the Holy Spirit who indwells and empowers every believer (8:1–17). The next step is glorification. The glory which the believer is destined to share with Christ far exceeds the sufferings of the present life. As creation shares in humanity's penalty for sin, so also will creation share in the benefits of redemption and future glory. At present, both must suffer until they achieve through hope and patience the full harvest of the Spirit's presence, of which they now possess only the firstfruits or guarantee (8:18–27).

The final verses of this chapter make clear that the love of God assures the salvation of the Christian (8:28–39).

The three following chapters (9 through 11), as in chapter 4, strengthen through Scripture the theme Paul is developing. Some may object to Paul's assurances by pointing to the failure and present state of Israel. They, too, were once God's chosen people and had many promises and assurances. Could their fate become that of the Christian? In chapters 9 through 11, Paul responds: God has not rejected his people. It is they who have rejected him. God's rejection is only partial (there is a spiritual remnant that has trusted in Christ) and temporary (they will be restored; 11:23–27). Paul appropriately quotes frequently the Old Testament in this section, and he emphasizes that God will be faithful to his covenant promise to restore Israel.

Moral Duties of the Christian (12:1 through 15:14): Paul recognizes that behavior must be built on belief, and this is why the practical exhortations of this epistle appear after his teaching on the believer's position in Christ. The salvation described in the first eleven chapters should transform a Christian's life in relation to God (12:1–2), society (12:3–21), higher powers (13:1–7), and one's neighbor (13:8–14). In chapters 14 and 15 the apostle discusses the whole concept of Christian liberty and the obligations of Christian charity in relation to one's liberty.

Conclusion (15:15 through 16:27): The epistle closes with Paul's statement of his plans (15:14–33), a long series of personal greetings (16:1–16), and an admonition followed by a doxology (16:17–27).

OUTLINE OF ROMANS

Introduction and theme	1:1–17	Israel in the plan of God	9:1–11:36
Man's need of salvation	1:18–3:20	Christian conduct	12:1–15:13
God's way of salvation	3:21–4:25	Conclusions and personal	
The new life in Christ	5:1–8:39	greetings	15:14–16:27

FOCUS	REVELATION OF GOD'S RIGHTEOUSNESS			VINDICATION OF GOD'S RIGHTEOUSNESS			APPLICATION OF GOD'S RIGHTEOUSNESS	
REFERENCE	1.1————3.21————6.1———————9.1————9.30————11.1————12.1————14.1—16.27							
DIVISION	NEED FOR GOD'S RIGHTEOUSNESS	IMPUTATION OF GOD'S RIGHTEOUSNESS	DEMONSTRATION OF GOD'S RIGHTEOUSNESS	ISRAEL'S PAST: ELECTION	ISRAEL'S PRESENT: REJECTION	ISRAEL'S FUTURE: RESTORATION	CHRISTIAN DUTIES	CHRISTIAN LIBERTIES
TOPIC	SIN	SALVATION	SANCTIFICATION	SOVEREIGNTY			SERVICE	
	DOCTRINAL						BEHAVIORAL	
SETTING	PROBABLY WRITTEN IN CORINTH							

PAUL'S FIRST LETTER TO THE

CORINTHIANS

The Book of First Corinthians

The first Letter to the Corinthians is one of the richest books of the New Testament.

The immediate occasion of First Corinthians was a letter from the community asking for directions about various matters. This letter of inquiry was evidently delivered by certain Corinthians: Stephanas, Fortunatus, and Achaicus, who were with Paul when First Corinthians was written (1 Cor. 16:15ff.). Further, he had learned by word of mouth from "some people from Chloe's family" (1:11) (apparently the slaves of a well-to-do Christian) that the church had been divided into factions. He had also been informed about other abuses in the community.

The purpose of the letter is to address certain problems in the church: to correct the existence of factions; to correct abuses (a case of incest, taking fellow Christians before pagan courts, and abuses in the liturgical assemblies); questions regarding marriage and celibacy; questions regarding the legitimacy of eating meats sacrificed to idols; questions regarding the charismata (spiritual gifts); and questions relative to the resurrection of the body.

The emphasis in the epistle is on moral or ethical matters. In treating these matters, however, Paul gives us many insights to several areas of systematic theology.

The Author of First Corinthians

Pauline authorship of First Corinthians is almost universally accepted. Instances of this widely held belief can be found as early as A.D. 95, when Clement of Rome wrote to the Corinthian church and cited this epistle in regard to their continuing problem of factions among themselves.

The Time of First Corinthians

Corinth was a key city in ancient Greece until it was destroyed by the Romans in 146 B.C. Julius Caesar rebuilt it as a Roman colony in 46 B.C. and it grew and prospered, becoming the capital of the province of Achaia. Its official language was Latin, but the common language remained Greek. In Paul's day Corinth was the metropolis of the Peloponnesus, since it was strategically located on a narrow isthmus between the Aegean Sea and the Adriatic Sea that connects the Peloponnesus with northern Greece. Because of its two seaports it became a commercial center, and many small ships were rolled or dragged across the Corinthian isthmus to avoid the dangerous 200-mile voyage around southern Greece. Nero and others attempted to build a canal at the narrowest point, but this was not achieved until 1893. The city was filled with shrines and temples, but the most prominent was the Temple of Aphrodite on top of a 1,800-foot promontory called the Acrocorinthus. Worshipers of the "goddess of love" made free use of the 1,000 Hieroduli (consecrated prostitutes). This cosmopolitan center thrived on commerce, entertainment, vice, and corruption; pleasure-seekers came there to spend money on a holiday from morality. Corinth became so notorious for its evils that the term *Korinthiazomai* ("to act like a Corinthian") became a synonym for debauchery and prostitution.

In Paul's day the population of Corinth was approximately 700,000, about two-thirds of whom were slaves. The diverse population produced no philosophers, but Greek philosophy influenced any speculative thought that was there. In spite of these obstacles to the gospel, Paul was able to establish a church in Corinth on his second missionary journey (3:6, 10; 4:15; Acts 18:1–7). Persecution in Macedonia drove him south to Athens, and from there he proceeded to Corinth. He made tents with Aquila and Priscilla and reasoned with the Jews in the synagogue. Silas and Timothy joined him (they evidently brought a gift from Philippi; 2 Cor. 11:8–9; Phil. 4:15), and Paul began to devote all his time to spreading the gospel. Paul wrote First and Second Thessalonians, moved his ministry from the synagogue to the house of Titius Justus because of opposition, and converted Crispus, the leader of the synagogue. Paul taught the word of God in Corinth for eighteen months in A.D. 51 and 52. After Paul's departure, Apollos came from Ephesus to minister in the Corinthian church (3:6; Acts 18:24-28).

It was while Paul was teaching and preaching in Ephesus during his third journey that certain members of Chloe's household brought him information about the factions (1:11). Three men from Corinth brought him the inquiries. At the same time, he learned of the other abuses. It may be that the men who had come from Corinth took this letter back with them. Paul was planning to leave Ephesus (16:5-8). A possible date for the letter is about A.D. 56.

Survey of First Corinthians

Through the missionary efforts of Paul and others, the church had been established in Corinth. The pagan life-style of Corinth exerted a profound influence upon Christians in that corrupt city—problems of every kind plagued them. In this disciplinary letter, Paul is forced to exercise his apostolic authority as he deals firmly with problems of divisiveness, immorality, lawsuits, selfishness, abuses in the liturgy, and spiritual gifts, and possibly denials of the Resurrection. We are not clear on precisely what Paul is dealing with in chapter 15: Is it a denial of the resurrection of bodies or merely a question of the "how" or "manner" of the Resurrection? The epistle is quite orderly in its approach as it sequentially addresses the problems that have come to Paul's attention. Paul also gives a series of perspectives on the various questions and issues raised by the Corinthians in the letter he received. He uses the introductory words "Now, concerning" or "Now" to delineate these topics (7:1, 25; 8:1; 12:1; 15:1).

The Answer to Chloe's Report of Divisions and Factions in the Church (chs. 1 through 4): Personality cults centering around Paul, Apollos, Peter, and a mysterious group which he refers to as "of Christ" (some argue that the latter is not a group but an insert of a copyist) have led to division and false pride among the Corinthians (ch. 1). It is not their wisdom or cleverness that has brought them to Christ, because divine wisdom is contrary to human wisdom. The truth of the gospel is spiritually apprehended (ch. 2). Factions that exist among the saints at Corinth are indications of their spiritual immaturity (ch. 3). They should pride themselves in Christ, not in human leaders who are merely his servants (ch. 4).

Answer to Report of Incest, use of Pagan Courts, and Fornication (chs. 5 and 6): The next problem Paul addresses is that of incest between a member of the church and his stepmother (ch. 5). The Corinthians have experienced no church discipline in this matter and Paul orders them to remove the offender from their fellowship until he repents. He then warns them against the impropriety of one Christian taking another to court before a pagan judge. They should rather be willing to lose all (6:1–11). Paul then writes very strongly against the vice of fornication.

Answer to Letter of Questions (7:1 through 11:1): Paul now considers some questions about marriage, celibacy, and virginity (ch. 7), and the legitimacy of eating meat sacrificed to idols (8:1 through 11:1). Within this letter he takes up the right of the apostle to financial support, his renunciation of that right, and his adaptation for the sake of the mission. In this same section, prompted by the question of eating meat sacrificed to idols, which in itself is a morally neutral action, he cautions them against falling into idolatry, which is an ever-present danger in a pagan society (10:1–22).

Directives for Worship (11:1 through 14:40): The function of each part of this section is not clear, that is, whether he is answering questions or correcting abuses—the problems of covering women's heads in worship (11:3–16), and the correct celebration of the Lord's Supper (11:17–34). (It would seem that in these two latter areas he is correcting abuses, especially in the second.) Also, the role of spiritual gifts in the assembly of the church (12:1 through 14:40) is discussed. He then inserts a hymn-like description of love (*agape*) (13:1–13), which is not a digression but an extension of his discussion of spiritual gifts.

The Bodily Resurrection of Christians (15:1–58): The Corinthians also have problems with the resurrection of bodies which Paul seeks to correct. They have probably presented some questions to him which he seeks to answer. His historical and theological defense of the resurrection includes teaching on the nature of the resurrected body. The Corinthians have probably been struggling over this issue because the idea of a resurrected body is repugnant to their native religious thought.

Conclusion (ch. 16): The epistle closes with Paul's instruction for the collection he will make for the saints in Jerusalem (16:1–4), followed by miscellaneous exhortations and greetings (16:5–24).

OUTLINE OF FIRST CORINTHIANS

Introduction   1:1–9

Factions in the church   1:10–4:21

Sexual morality and family
life   5:1–7:40

Christians and pagans   8:1–11:1

Church life and worship   11:2–14:40

The resurrection of Christ
and of believers   15:1–58

The offering for the Chris-
tians in Judea   16:1–4

Personal matters and con-
clusion   16:5–24

FOCUS	ANSWER TO CHLOE'S REPORT OF DIVISIONS		ANSWER TO REPORT OF ABUSES			ANSWER TO LETTER OF QUESTIONS				
REFERENCE	1.1——1.18		5.1——6.1——6.12			——7.1——8.1——11.2——15.1——16.1——16.24				
DIVISION	REPORT OF DIVISIONS	REASON FOR DIVISIONS	INCEST	LITIGATION	IMMORALITY	MARRIAGE	OFFERINGS TO IDOLS	PUBLIC WORSHIP	RESUR-RECTION	COLLECTION FOR JERUSALEM
TOPIC	DIVISIONS IN THE CHURCH		DISORDER IN THE CHURCH			DIFFICULTIES IN THE CHURCH				
	CONCERN		CONDEMNATION			COUNSEL				
SETTING	WRITTEN IN EPHESUS									

PAUL'S SECOND LETTER TO THE

CORINTHIANS

The Book of Second Corinthians

Since Paul's first letter, the Corinthian church had been swayed by false teachers who stirred the people against Paul. They claimed he was fickle, proud, unimpressive in appearance and speech, dishonest, and unqualified as an apostle of Jesus Christ. Paul sent Titus to Corinth to deal with these difficulties, and upon his return, rejoiced to hear of the Corinthians' change of heart. Paul wrote this letter to express his thanksgiving for the repentant majority and to appeal to the rebellious minority to accept his authority. Throughout the book he defends his conduct, character, and calling as an apostle of Jesus Christ.

To distinguish this epistle from First Corinthians, it was given the title *Pros Korinthious B*, the "Second to the Corinthians." The *A* and *B* were probably later additions to *Pros Korinthious*.

The Author of Second Corinthians

External and internal evidence amply support the Pauline authorship of this letter. As with Romans, the problem of Second Corinthians is with its alleged lack of unity, not with its authorship. Many critics theorize that chapters 10 through 13 were not a part of this letter in its original form because their tone contrasts with that of chapters 1 through 9. It is held that the sudden change from a spirit of joy and comfort to a spirit of concern and self-defense points to a "seam" between two different letters. Many hypotheses have been offered to explain the problem, but the most popular is that chapters 10 through 13 belong to a lost letter referred to in 2:4. This theory has much to support it. The first seven chapters congratulate the Corinthians for heeding the admonition of Paul, and for correcting the difficulties in Corinth. Chapters 8 and 9 deal with the collection of gifts for the needy in the church of Jerusalem. It would appear that the plans for this collection were suspended because of the difficulties. Now that they have been remedied, the collection can be resumed. Then the tone in chapters 10 through 13 completely changes. Paul goes on the attack and begins a defense of himself. It is possible that the redactor had a copy of the sorrowful letter (2 Cor. 2:4—the letter written in much sorrow) and appended it to Second Corinthians. In time it became a part of the letter.

Another problem of unity concerns 2:14 through 7:4. This appears to be an insertion. Paul is talking of his journey to Macedonia. Suddenly, he goes into a discourse on ministry. The latter appears to be in Paul's style and could be something he wrote on another occasion and inserted here. On the other hand, Paul could have merely introduced a digression on ministry here.

Although the two passages raise questions, most are agreed that they are Pauline.

The Time of Second Corinthians

Part of the background of Second Corinthians can be found in "The Time of First Corinthians." Paul was in Ephesus when he wrote First Corinthians and expected Timothy to visit Corinth and return to him (1 Cor. 16:10–11). Timothy apparently brought Paul a report of the opposition that had developed against him in Corinth, and Paul made a brief and painful visit to the Corinthians—not mentioned in Acts, but it can be inferred from Second Corinthians 2:1; 12:14; 13:1–2. Upon returning to Ephesus, Paul regretfully wrote his sorrowful letter to urge the church to discipline the leader of the opposition (2:1–11; 7:8). Titus carried this letter. Paul, anxious to learn the results, went to Troas and then to Macedonia to meet Titus on his return trip (2:12–13; 7:5–16). Paul was greatly relieved by Titus' report that the majority of the Corinthians had repented of their rebellion against Paul's apostolic authority.

Authors who opt for the inclusion of chapters 10 through 13 as originally a part of this epistle would argue that a minority opposition still persisted, evidently led by a group of Judaizers (chs. 10 through 13).

In any event, there in Macedonia, Paul wrote Second Corinthians and sent it with Titus and another brother (8:16–24). This took place late in A.D. 56 or 57, and the Macedonian city from which it was written may have been Philippi. Paul then made his third trip to Corinth (12:14; 13:1–2; Acts 20:1–3). Some say that he wrote his letter to the Romans from there.

Survey of Second Corinthians

Second Corinthians describes the anatomy of an apostle. The Corinthian church has been swayed by false teachers who have stirred the people against Paul, possibly in response to First Corinthians, Paul's disciplinary letter. Throughout this letter (Second Corinthians) Paul praises them for their response to his "sorrowful letter" and defends his apostolic conduct, character, and call. The three major sections are: Paul's explanation of his ministry (chs. 1 through 7); Paul's collection for the saints (chs. 8 and 9); and Paul's vindication of his apostleship (chs. 10 through 13).

Paul's Explanation of His Ministry (chs. 1 through 7): After his salutation and thanksgiving for God's comfort in his afflictions and perils (1:1–11), Paul explains why he had delayed his planned visit to Corinth. It is not a matter of vacillation: the apostle wants them to have enough time to repent (1:12 through 2:4). Paul graciously asks them to restore the repentant offender to fellowship (2:5–13). At this point, Paul embarks on an extended defense of his ministry in terms of his message, circumstances, motives, and conduct (2:14 through 6:10). He then admonishes the believers to separate themselves from defilement (6:11

through 7:1), and expresses his comfort at Titus' news of their change of heart (7:2–16).

Paul's Collection for the Saints (chs. 8 and 9): This is the longest discussion of the principles and practice of giving in the New Testament. The example of the Macedonians' liberal giving for the needy brethren in Jerusalem (8:1–6) is followed by an appeal to the Corinthians to keep their promise by doing the same (8:7 through 9:15). In this connection, Paul commends the messengers he has sent to Corinth to make arrangements for the large gift they have promised. Their generosity will be more than amply rewarded by God.

Paul's Vindication of His Apostleship (chs. 10 through 13): Paul concludes this epistle with a defense of his apostolic authority and credentials that is directed to the still rebellious minority in the Corinthian church. His meekness in their presence in no way diminishes his authority as an apostle (ch. 10). To demonstrate his apostolic credentials, Paul is forced to boast about his knowledge, integrity, accomplishments, sufferings, visions, and miracles (11:1 through 12:13). He reveals his plans to visit them for the third time and urges them to repent so that he will not have to use severity when he comes (12:14 through 13:10). The letter ends with an exhortation, greetings, and a benediction (13:11–14).

OUTLINE OF SECOND CORINTHIANS

Introduction	1:1–11	tians in Judea	8:1–9:15
Paul and the church at Corinth	1:12–7:16	Paul's defense of his authority as an apostle	10:1–13:10
The offering for the Chris-		Conclusion	13:11–14

FOCUS	EXPLANATION OF PAUL'S MINISTRY			COLLECTION FOR THE SAINTS		VINDICATION OF PAUL'S APOSTLESHIP		
REFERENCE	1.1————2.14————6.11————8.1			————8.7————		10.1————11.1————12.14—13.14		
DIVISION	HIS CHANGE OF PLANS	PHILOSOPHY OF MINISTRY	EXHORTATIONS TO THE CORINTHIANS	EXAMPLE OF THE MACEDONIANS	EXHORTATION TO THE CORINTHIANS	ANSWERS HIS ACCUSERS	DEFENDS HIS APOSTLESHIP	ANNOUNCES HIS UPCOMING VISIT
TOPIC	CHARACTER OF PAUL			COLLECTION FOR SAINTS		CREDENTIALS OF PAUL		
	EPHESUS TO MACEDONIA: CHANGE OF ITINERARY			MACEDONIA: PREPARATION FOR VISIT		TO CORINTH: IMMINENT VISIT		
SETTING	WRITTEN IN MACEDONIA							

PAUL'S LETTER TO THE

GALATIANS

The Book of Galatians

The Galatians, having launched their Christian experience by faith, seemed content to leave their voyage of faith and chart a new course based on works—a course Paul found disturbing. This direction was planted in the minds of the Galatians by the Judaizers, a group of Christian converts from Judaism who insisted on circumcision and the observance of the law as the requisites for salvation. In propagating their doctrine, they attacked the authority of Paul by denying him equal status with the apostles. His letter to the Galatians is a strong defense of the authenticity of his apostolate, a vigorous attack on the belief in justification by works, and a defense of justification through faith in Jesus Christ.

Paul begins by setting forth his credentials as an apostle with a message from God: blessing comes from God on the basis of faith, not law. The law declares men guilty and imprisons them; faith sets men free to enjoy freedom in Christ. But liberty is not license. Freedom in Christ means freedom to produce the fruits of righteousness through a Spirit-led life-style.

The book is called *Pros Galatas*, "To the Galatians," and it is the only letter of Paul that is specifically addressed to a number of churches ("To the churches of Galatia," 1:2). The name "Galatians" was given to this Celtic people because they originally lived in Gaul before their migration to Asia Minor.

The Author of Galatians

The Pauline authorship and the unity of this epistle are virtually unchallenged. The first verse clearly identifies the author as "Paul . . . an apostle." Also in 5:2 we read, "I, Paul, tell you. . . ." In fact, Paul actually wrote Galatians (6:11), instead of his usual practice of dictating it to a secretary.

The Time of Galatians

The term *Galatia* was used in an ethnographic sense (that is cultural and geographic origin) and in a political sense. The original ethnographic sense refers to the central part of Asia Minor where these Celtic tribes eventually settled after their conflicts with the Romans and Macedonians. Later, in 189 B.C. Galatia came under Roman domination, and in 25 B.C. Augustus declared it a Roman province. The political or provincial Galatia included territory to the south that was not originally considered part of Galatia (for example, the cities of Antioch in Pisidia, Iconium, Lystra, and Derbe). There are two theories regarding the date and setting of Galatians.

The *North Galatian Theory* holds that Paul was speaking of Galatia in its earlier, more restricted sense. According to this theory, the churches of Galatia were north of the cities Paul visited on his first missionary journey. Paul visited the ethnographic Galatia (the smaller region to the North) for the first time on his second missionary journey, probably while he was on his way to Troas (Acts 16:6). On his third missionary journey, Paul revisited the Galatian churches he had established (Acts 18:23) and wrote this epistle either in Ephesus (A.D. 53–56) or in Macedonia (A.D. 56).

According to the *South Galatian Theory*, Paul was referring to Galatia in its wider political sense as a province of Rome. This means that the churches he had in mind in this epistle were in the cities he evangelized during his first missionary journey with Barnabas (Acts 13:13 through 14:23). This was just prior to the Jerusalem Council (Acts 15), so the Jerusalem visit in Galatians 2:1–10 must have been the Acts 11:27–30 famine-relief visit. Galatians was probably written in Syrian Antioch in A.D. 49 just before Paul went to the Council in Jerusalem.

Paul wrote this epistle in response to a report that the Galatian churches were suddenly taken over by the false teaching of certain Judaizers who professed Jesus yet sought to place gentile converts under the requirements of the Mosaic Law (1:7; 4:17, 21; 5:2–12; 6:12–13).

Thus, authors are divided. There are two possible dates: A.D. 53–56 or A.D. 49. Those who hold the latter date conclude that it was written before First Thessalonians, and thus is the oldest written work of the New Testament.

Survey of Galatians

The Epistle to the Galatians has been called "the Magna Carta of Christian liberty." It is Paul's manifesto of justification by faith, and the resulting freedom. Paul directs this great charter of Christian freedom to a people who are willing to give up the priceless liberty they possess in Christ. The oppressive theology of certain Jewish legalizers has been causing the believers in Galatia to trade their freedom in Christ for bondage to the law. Paul writes this forceful epistle to do away with the false gospel of works and demonstrate the superiority of justification by faith. This carefully written polemic approaches the problem from three directions: the gospel of grace defended (chs. 1 and 2), the gospel of grace explained (chs. 3 and 4), and the gospel of grace applied (chs. 5 and 6).

The Gospel of Grace Defended (chs. 1 and 2): Paul affirms his divinely given apostleship and presents the gospel (1:1–5) because it has been distorted by false teachers among the Galatians (1:6–10). Paul launches into his biographical argument for the true gospel of justification by faith in showing that he received his message not from men but directly from God (1:11–24). When he submits his teaching of Christian freedom to the apostles in Jerusalem, they all acknowledge the validity and authority of his message (2:1–10). Paul also must correct Peter on the matter of freedom from the law (2:11–21).

The Gospel of Grace Explained (chs. 3 and 4): In this section Paul uses eight lines of reasoning to develop his theological defense of justification by faith: (1) The Galatians began by faith, and their growth in Christ must continue to be by faith (3:1–5). (2) Abraham was justified by faith, and the same principle applies today (3:6–9). (3) Christ has redeemed all who trust in him from the curse of the law (3:10–14). (4) The promise made to Abraham was not nullified by the law (3:15–18). (5) The law was given to drive men to faith, not to save them (3:19–22). (6) Believers in Christ are adopted sons of God and are no longer bound by the law (3:23 through 4:7). (7) The Galatians must recognize their inconsistency and regain their original freedom in Christ (4:8–20). (8) Abraham's two sons allegorically reveal the superiority of the Abrahamic promise to the Mosaic Law (4:21–31).

The Gospel of Grace Applied (chs. 5 and 6): The Judaizers seek to place the Galatians under bondage to their perverted gospel of justification by law, but Paul warns them that law and grace are two contrary principles (5:1–12). So far, Paul has been contrasting the freedom of faith with the legalism of law, but at this point he warns the Galatians of the opposite extreme of license or antinomianism (5:13 through 6:10). The Christian is not only set free from bondage of law, but he is also free of the bondage of sin because of the power of the indwelling Spirit. Freedom is not an excuse to indulge in the deeds of the flesh;

rather, it provides the privilege of bearing the fruit of the Spirit by walking in dependence upon him. This letter closes with a contrast between the Judaizers—who are motivated by pride and a desire to avoid persecution—and Paul, who has suffered for the true gospel, but boasts only in Christ (6:11–18).

OUTLINE OF GALATIANS

Introduction	1:1–10	Christian freedom and responsibility	5:1–6:10
Paul's authority as an apostle	1:11–2:21	Conclusion	6:11–18
The gospel of God's grace	3:1–4:31		

FOCUS	GOSPEL OF GRACE DEFENDED		GOSPEL OF GRACE EXPLAINED		GOSPEL OF GRACE APPLIED	
REFERENCE	1.1————2.1————3.1————4.1————5.1————6.1————6.18					
DIVISION	PAUL'S APOSTLESHIP	PAUL'S AUTHORITY	BONDAGE OF LAW	FREEDOM OF GRACE	FRUIT OF THE SPIRIT	FRUITS OF THE SPIRIT
TOPIC	BIOGRAPHICAL EXPLANATION		DOCTRINAL EXPOSITION		PRACTICAL EXHORTATION	
	AUTHENTICATION OF LIBERTY		ARGUMENTATION FOR LIBERTY		APPLICATION OF LIBERTY	
SETTING	SOUTH GALATIAN THEORY: SYRIAN ANTIOCH NORTH GALATIAN THEORY: EPHESUS OR MACEDONIA					

PAUL'S LETTER TO THE

EPHESIANS

The Book of Ephesians

Ephesians is one of the captivity epistles along with Philippians, Colossians, and Philemon. The author of all four indicates that he is writing from prison.

The letter is among the most doctrinal of all the Pauline letters. It is a remarkable synthesis and development of theological concepts found in earlier epistles ascribed to Paul. The letter itself, however, contains no indication of the occasion which elicited this letter.

The relation of Ephesians to Colossians suggests that the occasion was the rise of gnostic syncretism. It is probable that this new problem needed not only a refutation as given in Colossians, but a positive exposition precisely to meet the new errors.

In the earlier epistles ascribed to Paul, the emphasis was on the justification and salvation of the individual. However, this epistle emphasizes the union and reconciliation in Christ of two groups: the Jews and Gentiles.

The themes developed in this epistle are different from those of earlier epistles, but the individual concepts and ideas are germinally found in Paul.

The traditional title of this epistle is *Pros Ephesious*, "To the Ephesians." Many ancient manuscripts, however, omit *en Ephesōi*, "in Ephesus," in 1:1. This has led a number of scholars to challenge the traditional view that this message was directed specifically to the Ephesians. The encyclical theory proposes that it was a circular letter sent by Paul to the churches of Asia. It is argued that Ephesians is really a Christian treatise designed for general use: it involves no controversy and deals with no specific problems in any particular church. This is also supported by the formal tone (no terms of endearment) and distant phraseology ("ever since I heard of your faith," 1:15; if they "have heard" of his message, 3:2). These things seem inconsistent with the relationship Paul must have had with the Ephesians after a ministry of almost three years among them. The only letters that greet specific people are Romans and Colossians, and they were addressed to churches Paul had not visited. Some scholars accept an ancient tradition that Ephesians is Paul's letter to the Laodiceans (Col. 4:16), but there is no way to be sure. If Ephesians began as a circular letter, it eventually became associated with Ephesus, the foremost of the Asian churches.

The Author of Ephesians

When the church defined the Canon of Sacred Scripture at the Council of Trent, the decree spoke of the "Pauline corpus" and listed fourteen epistles embraced by that phrase.

Today, however, an ever-growing number of scholars accept seven epistles only as written by Paul, namely, Romans, First and Second Corinthians, Galatians, Philippians, First Thessalonians, and Philemon. Scholars are presently questioning, in varying degrees, the Pauline authorship of the remaining epistles of the traditional "Pauline corpus."

Although scholars are disagreed, several list Ephesians among the deutero-Pauline letters, that is, letters written by a Pauline disciple.

The arguments against Pauline authorship of the letter can be grouped under three headings: language and style; its relationship to Colossians; and its theology.

The strongest arguments against Pauline authorship are in the realm of theology. There is definitely development in this epistle in the areas of christology and ecclesiology over against the earlier Pauline Epistles. Authorship then boils down to the question: Could these developments have taken place in the time and mind of Paul himself or did they require more time for development, and hence, represent a further development within the later church and within the thought of Paul's disciple? It must be noted that the dependence of Ephesians on Colossians moves several, but not all, authors to postulate pseudonymity for the author. Although several authors still defend Pauline authorship and attempt to answer all the arguments against it, the weight of scholarship is moving toward pseudonymity and authorship by a disciple of Paul.

The Time of Ephesians

This question is naturally related to the question of authorship and that of the destination of the epistle.

Those who defend Pauline authorship and Ephesus as the destination of the epistle would create this scenario: At the end of his second missionary journey, Paul visited Ephesus where he left Priscilla and Aquila (Acts 18:18–21). This strategic city was the commercial center of Asia Minor, but heavy silting required a special canal to be maintained so that ships could reach the harbor. Ephesus was a religious center as well, famous especially for its magnificent temple of *Diana* (Roman name) or *Artemis* (Greek name), a structure considered to be one of the seven wonders of the ancient world (cf. Acts 19:35). The practice of magic and the local economy were clearly related to this temple. Paul remained in Ephesus for nearly three years on his third missionary journey (Acts 18:23 through 19:41); the word of God was spread throughout the province of Asia. Paul's effective ministry began to seriously hurt the traffic in magic and images, leading to an uproar in the huge Ephesian theater. Paul then left for Macedonia, but afterward he met with the Ephesian elders while on his way to Jerusalem (Acts 20:17–38).

Paul probably wrote the "Prison Epistles" (Ephesians, Philippians, Colossians, and Philemon) during his first Roman imprisonment in A.D. 60–62. These epistles all refer to his imprisonment (Eph. 3:1; 4:1; 6:20; Phil. 1:7, 13–14; Col. 4:3, 10, 18; Philem. 9–10, 13, 23), and fit well against the background in Acts 28:16–31. This is especially true of Paul's references to the palace guard (governor's official palace guard, Phil. 1:13) and "the Emperor's palace" (Phil. 4:22). Some commentators believe that the imprisonment in one or more of these epistles refers to Paul's Caesarean imprisonment or to a hypothetical Ephesian imprisonment.

Authors who argue against direct Pauline authorship are not in agreement on the occasion or the date of its writing. One theory popular among English-speaking scholars is based on the fact that while Ephesians depends mainly on Colossians, it shows familiarity with all the other letters attributed to Paul. On the basis of this, some scholars believe that Ephesians was written as a prologue to accompany the Pauline collection of letters when it was being circulated as a distinct body of literature. This must have happened in the last quarter of the first century.

Survey of Ephesians

The author of this epistle wants to make Christians more aware of their position in Christ and to motivate them to draw upon their spiritual source in daily living: "live a life that measures up to the standard God set when he called you" (4:1; see 2:10). The first half of Ephesians lists the believer's heavenly possessions: adoption, redemption, inheritance, power, life, grace, citizenship, and the love of Christ. There are no imperatives in chapters 1 through 3, which focus only on divine gifts. But chapters 4 through 6 include thirty-five directives in the last half of Ephesians that speak of the believer's responsibility to conduct himself according to his individual calling. So Ephesians begins in heaven, but concludes in the home and in all other relationships of daily life. The two divisions are: the position of the Christian (1:1 through 3:21) and the practice of the Christian (4:1 through 6:20).

The Position of the Christian (1:1 through 3:21): After a two-verse prologue, in one long Greek sentence the author extols the triune God for the riches of redemption (1:3–14). This hymn to God's grace praises the Father for choosing us (1:3–6), the Son for redeeming us (1:7–12), and the Spirit for sealing us (1:13–14). The saving work of each divine person is to the praise of the glory of his grace (1:6, 12, 14). Before continuing, the author offers the first of two very significant prayers (1:15–23; cf. 3:14–21). Here he asks that the readers receive spiritual illumination so that they may come to perceive what is, in fact, true. Next, the author describes the power of God's grace by contrasting their former condition with their present spiritual life in Christ, a salvation attained not by human works but by the divine grace (2:1–10). This redemption includes Jews, yet also extends to those Gentiles "who call themselves the circumcised" (2:11–22). In Christ, the two for the first time have become members of one body (2:11–22). The truth that Gentiles would become "members of the same body" (3:6) was formerly a secret that has now been revealed (3:1–13). The author's second prayer (3:14–21) expresses his desire that the readers be strengthened with the power of the Spirit and fully apprehend the love of Christ.

The Practice of the Christian (4:1 through 6:20): The pivotal verse of Ephesians is 4:1, because it draws a sharp line between the doctrinal and the practical divisions of this book. There is a cause-and-effect relationship between chapters 1 through 3 and 4 through 6 because the spiritual walk of a Christian must be rooted in his spiritual wealth. As Paul emphasized in Romans, behavior does not determine blessing; instead, blessing should determine behavior.

Because of the unity of all believers in the body of Christ, growth and maturity come "when each separate part works as it should" (4:16). This involves the exercise of spiritual gifts in love. The author exhorts the readers to "get rid of your old self" (4:22) and "put on the new self" (4:24) that will be manifested by a walk of integrity in the midst of all people. They are also to maintain a walk of holiness as children of light (5:1–21). Every relationship (wives, husbands, children, parents, slaves, masters) must be transformed by their new life in Christ (5:22 through 6:9). The author's colorful description of the spiritual warfare and the armor of God (6:10–20) is followed by a word about Tychicus and then a benediction (6:21–24).

OUTLINE OF EPHESIANS

Introduction	1:1–2	The new life in Christ	4:1–6:20
Christ and the church	1:3–3:21	Conclusion	6:21–24

FOCUS	THE POSITION OF THE CHRISTIAN				THE PRACTICE OF THE CHRISTIAN			
REFERENCE	1.1————1.15————1.24————3.14————4.1————4.17————5.22————————6.10——6.24							
DIVISION	PRAISE FOR REDEMPTION	PRAYER FOR REVELATION	POSITION OF THE CHRISTIAN	PRAYER FOR REALIZATION	UNITY IN THE CHURCH	HOLINESS IN LIFE	RESPONSIBILITIES AT HOME AND WORK	CONDUCT IN THE CONFLICT
TOPIC	BELIEF				BEHAVIOR			
	PRIVILEGES OF THE CHRISTIAN				RESPONSIBILITIES OF THE CHRISTIAN			
SETTING	UNCERTAIN							

PAUL'S LETTER TO THE

PHILIPPIANS

The Book of Philippians

Paul writes a thank-you note to the believers at Philippi for their help in his hour of need, and he uses the occasion to send along some instruction on Christian unity. His central thought is simple: Only in Christ are real unity and joy possible. With Christ as your model of humility and service, you can enjoy a oneness of purpose, attitude, goal, and labor—a truth which Paul illustrates from his own life, and one the Philippians desperately need to hear. Within their own ranks, fellow workers in the Philippian church are at odds, hindering the work in proclaiming new life in Christ. Because of this, Paul exhorts the church to "stand firm . . . try to agree . . . always be joyful in your union with the Lord . . . but in all your prayers ask God for what you need, always asking him with a thankful heart. And God's peace, which is far beyond human understanding, will keep your hearts and minds safe in union with Christ Jesus" (4:1–2, 4, 6–7).

This epistle is called *Pros Philippēsious*, "To the Philippians." The church at Philippi was the first church Paul founded in Macedonia.

The Epistle to the Philippians is one of the four captivity epistles, that is, the epistles written from prison. Two of these epistles, Ephesians and Colossians, are very much related one to the other in language and theological concepts. Philemon is related to Colossians through personal notices. These facts link together the three mentioned epistles. Philippians, on the other hand, except for its having been written from prison, has nothing striking in common with the other three. It is much closer to the Great Epistles in theology.

The Author of Philippians

The external and internal evidence for the Pauline authorship of Philippians is very strong, and there is scarcely any doubt that anyone but Paul wrote it.

Although Pauline authorship is not in question, the unity of the epistle is. Some authors argue that our present epistle is made up of three separate epistles, each following chronologically one after the other. Authors disagree on exactly which verses open and close each letter. Here we offer one example of one author's reconstruction: first letter 4:10–20; second letter 1:1 through 3:1; 4:2–9, 21–23; third letter 3:2 through 4:1.

These scholars all agree that Paul is the author of each letter. It must be said, too, that not all scholars agree with these attempts at dissecting the letter. They argue that the letter as written makes good sense and as it is strongly defend the unity of the letter.

The Time of Philippians

In 356 B.C., King Philip of Macedonia (the father of Alexander the Great) took this town and expanded it, renaming it Philippi. The Romans captured it in 168 B.C. and in 42 B.C. the defeat of the forces of Brutus and Cassius by those of Anthony and Octavian (later Augustus) took place outside the city. Octavian turned Philippi into a Roman colony (cf. Acts 16:12) and a military outpost. The citizens of this colony were regarded as citizens of Rome and given a number of special privileges. Because Philippi was a military city and not a commercial center, there were not enough Jews for a synagogue when Paul came (Acts 16:13).

Paul's "Macedonian Call" in Troas during his second missionary journey led to his ministry in Philippi with the conversion of Lydia and others. Paul and Silas were beaten and imprisoned, but this resulted in the conversion of the Philippian jailer. The magistrates were placed in a dangerous position by beating Roman citizens without a trial (Acts 16:37–40), and that embarrassment may have prevented future reprisals against the new Christians in Philippi. Paul visited the Philippians again on his third missionary journey (Acts 20:1, 6). When they heard of his Roman imprisonment, the Philippian church sent Epaphroditus with financial help (4:18); they had helped Paul in this way on at least two other occasions (4:16). Epaphroditus almost died of an illness, yet remained with Paul long enough for the Philippians to receive word of his malady. Upon his recovery, Paul sent this letter back with him to Philippi (2:25–30).

Silas, Timothy, Luke, and Paul first came to Philippi in A.D. 51, probably eleven years before Paul wrote this letter. Philippians 1:13 and 4:22 suggest that it was written from Rome.

Because of its close relationship with the letter to the Romans, some authors suggest a date nearer to that of Romans (Rom.; 1 and 2 Cor.; Gal.). They thus hold that it was written from Caesarea or Ephesus. Caesarea, however, is too far from Philippi to admit the easy coming and going between the two cities reflected in the letter. Thus several defend Ephesus as the place of origin. Acts has no record of an Ephesus imprisonment of Paul. Nonetheless, Paul spent three years in Ephesus and speaks of his sufferings in the province of Asia. So there is a strong possibility that there was a period of imprisonment in Ephesus of which we have no record.

Survey of Philippians

Philippians is the epistle of joy and encouragement in the midst of adverse circumstances. Paul freely expresses his fond affection for the Philippians, appreciates their consistent testimony and support, and lovingly urges them to center their actions and thoughts on the pursuit of the person and power of Christ. Paul also seeks to correct the problems of disunity and rivalry (2:2–4) and to prevent the problems of legalism, license, and immorality (3:1–19). Philippians focuses on: Paul's account of his present circumstances (ch. 1); Paul's appeal to have the mind of Christ (ch. 2); Paul's appeal to have the knowledge of Christ (ch. 3); Paul's appeal to have the peace of Christ (ch. 4).

Paul's Account of His Present Circumstances (ch. 1): Paul's usual salutation (1:1–2) is followed by his thanksgiving, warm regard, and prayer on behalf of the Philippians (1:3–11). For years, they have participated in the apostle's ministry, and he prays for their continued growth in the real knowledge of Christ. Paul shares the circumstances of his imprisonment and rejoices in the spread of the gospel in spite of and because of his situation (1:12–26). As he considers the outcome of his approaching trial, he expresses his willingness to "leave this life and be with Christ" (1:23) or to continue in ministry. Paul encourages the Philippians to remain steadfast in the face of opposition and coming persecution (1:27–30).

Paul's Appeal to Have the Mind of Christ (ch. 2): Paul exhorts the Philippians to have a spirit of unity and mutual concern by embracing the attitude of humility (2:1–4), the greatest example of which is the incarnation and crucifixion of Christ (2:5–11). The *kenōsis*, or "emptying," of Christ does not mean that he divested himself of his deity, but that he withheld his preincarnate glory and voluntarily restricted his use of certain attributes (e.g., omnipresence and omniscience). Paul asks the Philippians to apply this attitude to their lives (2:12–18), and he gives two more examples of sacrifice, the ministries of Timothy and Epaphroditus (2:19–30).

Paul's Appeal to Have the Knowledge of Christ (ch. 3): It appears that Paul is about to close his letter ("In conclusion, my brothers," 3:1) when he launches into a warning about the continuing problem of legalism (3:1–9). Paul refutes this teaching with revealing autobiographical details about his previous attainments in Judaism. Compared to the goal of knowing Christ, those pursuits are as nothing. True righteousness is received through faith, not by mechanical obedience to any law. Paul yearns for the promised attainment of the resurrected body.

Paul's Appeal to Have the Peace of Christ (ch. 4): In a series of exhortations, Paul urges the Philippians to have peace with the brethren by living a life-style of unity, prayerful dependence, and holiness (4:13). In 4:4–9, Paul describes the secrets of having the peace of God as well as peace with God. He then rejoices over their gift, but explains that the power of Christ enables him to live above his circumstances (4:10–20). This joyous letter from prison closes with greetings and a benediction (4:21–23).

OUTLINE OF PHILIPPIANS

Introduction	1:1–11	Warnings against enemies and dangers	3:1–4:9
Paul's personal circumstances	1:12–26	Paul and his Philippian friends	4:10–20
The life of Christ	1:27–2:18	Conclusion	4:21–23
Plans for Timothy and Epaphroditus	2:19–30		

FOCUS	ACCOUNT OF CIRCUMSTANCES	THE MIND OF CHRIST	THE KNOWLEDGE OF CHRIST	THE PEACE OF CHRIST
REFERENCE	1.1—————————	2.1—————————	3.1—————————	4.1—————————4.23
DIVISION	PARTAKE OF CHRIST	PEOPLE OF CHRIST	PURSUIT OF CHRIST	POWER OF CHRIST
TOPIC	SUFFERING	SUBMISSION	SALVATION	SANCTIFICATION
	EXPERIENCE	EXAMPLES	EXHORTATION	
SETTING	POSSIBLY ROME, BUT NOT CERTAIN			

PAUL'S LETTER TO THE

COLOSSIANS

The Book of Colossians

If Ephesians can be labeled the epistle portraying the "Church of Christ," then Colossians must surely be the "Christ of the Church." Ephesians focuses on the body; Colossians focuses on the head. Like Ephesians, the little Book of Colossians divides neatly in half with the first portion doctrinal (chs. 1 and 2) and the second practical (chs. 3 and 4). Paul's purpose is to show that Christ is preeminent—first and foremost in everything—and the Christian's life should reflect that priority. Because believers are rooted in him, alive in him, hidden in him, and complete in him, it is utterly inconsistent for them to live life without him. Clothed in his love, with his peace ruling in their hearts, they are equipped to make Christ first in every area of life.

This epistle became known as *Pros Kolossaeis*, "To God's people in Colossae," because of 1:2. Paul also wanted it to be read in the neighboring church at Laodicea (4:16).

The Author of Colossians

The testimony to the Pauline authorship of Colossians is ancient and consistent. It not only claims to be written by Paul (1:1, 23; 4:18), but the personal details and close parallels with Philemon make the case even stronger. Nevertheless, a growing number of scholars place it among the deutero-Pauline epistles. The authenticity of the letter has been challenged on the internal grounds of vocabulary and particularly theological development. Scholars offer three categories of arguments against Pauline authorship: language and style; the absence of Pauline concepts; and the presence of concepts not found in the earlier letters.

Despite all these arguments, the majority of exegetes still support the Pauline authorship of Colossians. Studies have shown a remarkable agreement with earlier epistles. The agreement is so widespread that one author who argues against Pauline authorship states just as strongly that the pseudonymous writer must have been a close disciple of Paul's and one thoroughly steeped in Pauline theology. So the questions are: Could the additional concepts have been developed by Paul in his own lifetime, or did the development require the distance of another generation? Could the changed situation explain the absence of concepts common in the earlier epistles? Authors are divided on the answers to these questions. For example, the high christology in Colossians has been compared to John's later statement that Christ is the *Logos* (cf. Col. 1:5, 23 and John 1:1–18), with the conclusion that this high christology was too late for Paul's time. On the other hand, the agreement between the personal notices in Philemon and Colossians is another factor that influences those who claim Pauline authorship.

As has been said, most scholars who review the evidence and arguments do in fact decide in favor of authenticity. The data on which authenticity or pseudonymity has to be decided are not in dispute in the letter to the Colossians. The dispute is in the interpretation of the data.

The Time of Colossians

Colossae was a minor city about one hundred miles east of Ephesus in the region of the seven Asian churches of Revelation 1 through 3. Located in the fertile Lycus Valley by a mountain pass on the road from Ephesus to the East, Colossae once was a populous center of commerce, famous for its glossy black wool. By the time of Paul, it had been eclipsed by its neighboring cities, Laodicea and Hierapolis (cf. 4:13), and was on the decline. Apart from this letter, Colossae exerted almost no influence on early church history. It is evident from 1:4–8 and 2:1 that Paul had never visited the church at Colossae, which was founded by Epaphras. On his third missionary journey, Paul devoted almost three years to an Asian ministry centered in Ephesus (cf. Acts 19:10; 20:31), and Epaphras probably came to Christ during this time. He carried the gospel to the cities in the Lycus Valley and years later came to visit Paul in his imprisonment (4:12–13; Philem. 23).

Those who hold that Paul is the author of Colossians and Ephesians would argue that Colossians, Philemon, and Ephesians were evidently written about the same time and under the same circumstances, judging by the overlapping themes and personal names (cf. Col. 4:9–17 and Philem. 2, 10, 23–24). Although Caesarea and Ephesus have been suggested as the location of authorship, the bulk of the evidence indicates that Paul wrote all four Prison Epistles during his first Roman imprisonment (see "The Time of Ephesians" and "The Time of Philippians"). If so, Paul wrote it before A.D. 63 and sent it with Tychicus and the converted slave Onesimus to Colossae (4:7–9; see Eph. 6:21; Philem. 10–12).

Epaphroditus' visit and report about the conditions in Colossae prompted this letter. Although the Colossians had not yet succumbed (2:1–5), an encroaching heresy was threatening the predominantly gentile (1:21, 27; 2:13) Colossian church. The nature of this heresy can only be deduced from Paul's incidental references to it in his refutation in 2:8–23. It was apparently a religious system that combined elements from Greek speculation (2:4, 8–10), Jewish legalism (2:11–17), and Oriental mysticism (2:18–23). It involved a low view of the body (2:20–23) and probably nature as a whole. Circumcision, dietary regulations, and ritual observances were included in this system, which utilized asceticism, worship of angels as intermediaries, and mystical experiences as an approach to the spiritual realm. Any attempt to fit Christ into such a system would undermine his person and redemptive work.

Those who argue against Pauline authorship would date it in the last quarter of the first century.

Survey of Colossians

Colossians is perhaps the most Christ-centered book in the Bible. In it the author stresses the preeminence of the person of Christ and the completeness of the salvation he provides, in order to combat a growing heresy that is threatening the church at Colossae. This heresy seeks to devaluate Christ by elevating speculation, ritualism, mysticism, and asceticism. But Christ, the Lord of creation and Head of the Body, is completely sufficient for every spiritual and practical need of the believer. The last half of this epistle explores the application of these principles to daily life, because doctrinal truth (chs. 1 and 2) must bear fruit in practical conduct (chs. 3 and 4). The two major topics are: supremacy of Christ (chs. 1 and 2) and submission to Christ (chs. 3 and 4).

Supremacy of Christ (chs. 1 and 2): Paul's greeting (1:1–2) is followed by an unusually extended thanksgiving (1:3–8) and prayer (1:9–14) on behalf of the believers at Colossae. Paul expresses his concern that the Colossians come to a deeper understanding of the person and power of Christ. Even here Paul begins to develop his major theme of the preeminence of Christ, but the most potent statement of this theme is in 1:15–23. He is supreme both in creation (1:15–18) and in redemption (1:19–23), and this majestic passage builds a positive case for Christ as the most effective refutation of the heresy that will be exposed in chapter 2. Paul describes his own ministry of proclaiming the secret of "Christ is in you, which means that you will share in the glory of God" (1:27) to the Gentiles and assures his readers that although he has not personally met them, he strongly desires that they become deeply rooted in Christ alone, who is preeminent in the church (1:24 through 2:3). This is especially important in view of false teachers who would defraud them through enticing rationalism (2:4–7), vain philosophy (2:8–10), legalistic rituals (2:11–17), improper mysticism (2:18–19), and useless asceticism (2:20–23). In each case, Paul contrasts the error with the corresponding truth about Christ.

Submission to Christ (chs. 3 and 4): The believer's union with Christ in his death, resurrection, and exaltation is the foundation upon which his earthly life must be built (3:1–4). Because of his death with Christ, the Christian must regard himself as dead to the old sins and put them aside (3:5–11); because of his resurrection with Christ, the believer must regard himself as alive to him in righteousness and put on the new qualities that are prompted by Christian love (3:12–17). Turning from the inward life (3:1–17) to the outward life (3:18 through 4:6), Paul outlines the transformation that faith in Christ should make in relationships inside and outside the home. This epistle concludes with a statement concerning its bearers (Tychicus and Onesimus), greetings and instructions, and a farewell note (4:7–18).

OUTLINE OF COLOSSIANS

Introduction	1:1–8	The new life in Christ	2:20–4:6
The nature and work of		Conclusion	4:7–18
Christ	1:9–2:19		

FOCUS	SUPREMACY OF CHRIST			SUBMISSION TO CHRIST		
REFERENCE	1.1————1.15—————2.4			————3.1—————3.5————4.7————4.18		
DIVISION	INTRODUCTION	PREEMINENCE OF CHRIST	FREEDOM IN CHRIST	POSITION OF THE BELIEVER	PRACTICE OF THE BELIEVER	CONCLUSION
TOPIC	DOCTRINAL			PRACTICAL		
	WHAT CHRIST DID FOR US			WHAT CHRIST DOES THROUGH US		
SETTING	UNCERTAIN					

PAUL'S FIRST LETTER TO THE
THESSALONIANS

The Book of First Thessalonians

Paul has many pleasant memories of the days he spent with the infant Thessalonian church. Their faith, hope, love, and perseverance in the face of persecution are exemplary. Paul's labors as a spiritual parent to the fledgling church have been richly rewarded, and his affection is visible in every line of his letter.

Paul encourages them to excel in their newfound faith, to increase in their love for one another, and to rejoice, pray, and give thanks always. He closes his letter with instruction regarding the return of the Lord, whose advent signifies hope and comfort for believers both living and dead.

Because this is the first of Paul's two canonical letters to the church at Thessalonica, it received the title *Pros Thessalonikeis A*, the "First to the Thessalonians."

The Author of First Thessalonians

First Thessalonians went unchallenged as a Pauline epistle until the nineteenth century, when critics claimed that its dearth of doctrinal content made its authenticity suspect. But this is a weak objection on two counts: (1) the proportion of doctrinal teaching in Paul's epistles varies widely, and (2) 4:13 through 5:11 is a foundational passage for New Testament eschatology (future events). Paul had quickly grounded the Thessalonians in Christian doctrine, and the only problematic issue when this epistle was written concerned the matter of Christ's return.

New Testament scholars today, almost without exception, accept the Pauline authorship of this epistle. If one accepts the *North Galatian Theory* (cf. Introduction to the Letter to the Galatians), it is the oldest New Testament writing.

The Time of First Thessalonians

In Paul's time, Thessalonica was the prominent seaport and the capital of the Roman province of Macedonia. This prosperous city was located on the *Via Egnatia*, the main road from Rome to the East, within sight of Mount Olympus, legendary home of the Greek pantheon. Cassander expanded and strengthened this site around 315 B.C. and renamed it after his wife, the half-sister of Alexander the Great. The Romans conquered Macedonia in 168 B.C. and organized it into a single province twenty-two years later with Thessalonica as the capital city. It became a "free city" under Augustus with its own authority to appont a governing board of magistrates who were called "politarchs." The strategic location assured Thessalonica of commercial success, and it boasted a population of perhaps 200,000 in the first century. Thessalonica survives under the shortened name Salonika.

Thessalonica had a sizeable Jewish population, and the ethical monotheism of Judaism attracted many Gentiles who had become disenchanted with Greek paganism. These God-fearers quickly responded to Paul's reasoning in the synagogue when he ministered there on his second missionary journey (Acts 17:10). The Jews became jealous of Paul's success and organized a mob to oppose the Christian missionaries. Not finding Paul and Silas, they dragged Jason, Paul and Silas' host, before the politarchs and accused him of harboring traitors of Rome. The politarchs extracted a pledge guaranteeing the departure of Paul and Silas, who left that night for Berea. After a time, the Thessalonian Jews raised an uproar in Berea so that Paul departed for Athens, leaving orders for Silas and Timothy to join him there (Acts 17:11–16). Because of Luke's account in Acts some scholars have reasoned that Paul was in Thessalonica for less than a month ("three Sabbaths," Acts 17:2), but other evidence suggests a longer stay: (1) Paul received two separate offerings from Philippi, 100 miles away, while he was in Thessalonica (Phil. 4:15–16). (2) According to 1:9 and 2:14–16, most of the Thessalonian converts were Gentiles who came out of idolatry. This would imply an extensive ministry directed to the Gentiles after Paul's initial work with the Jews and gentile God-fearers. (3) Paul worked "day and night" (2:9; 2 Thess. 3:7–9) during his time there. He may have begun to work immediately, but Paul supported himself by tentmaking, which took many hours away from his ministry, requiring a longer stay to accomplish the extensive ministry of evangelism and teaching that took place in that city. After Silas and Timothy met Paul in Athens (3:1–2), he sent Timothy to Thessalonica (Silas also went back to Macedonia, probably Philippi), and his assistants later rejoined him in Corinth (Acts 18:5; cf. 1 Thess. 1:1). There he may have written this epistle in A.D. 51 as his response to Timothy's good report.

The purpose of the epistle is (1) to congratulate the Thessalonians and encourage them on their faithful response to their Christian vocation; (2) to correct some difficulties, warning them against heathen vices of unchastity and dishonesty, to defending his own mode of acting from attack; and (3) to answer their questions about the fate of those who have died when Jesus returns.

Survey of First Thessalonians

After Paul's forced separation from the Thessalonians, he grows increasingly concerned about the progress of their faith. His great relief upon hearing Timothy's positive report prompts him to write this warm epistle of commendation, exhortation, and consolation. They are commended for remaining steadfast under afflictions, exhorted to excel still more in their Christian walk, and consoled concerning their loved ones who have died in Christ. The theme of the coming of the Lord recurs throughout this epistle, and 4:13 through 5:11 is one of the fullest New Testament developments of this crucial truth. The two major sections of First Thessalonians are: Paul's personal reflections on the Thessalonians (chs. 1 through 3) and Paul's instructions for the Thessalonians (chs. 4 and 5).

Paul's Personal Reflections on the Thessalonians (chs. 1 through 3): Paul's typical salutation in the first verse combines the customary Greek ("grace") and Hebrew ("peace") greetings of his day and enriches them with Christian content. The opening chapter is a declaration of thanksgiving for the Thessalonians' metamorphosis from heathenism to Christian hope. Faith, love, and hope (1:3) properly characterize the new lives of these believers. In 2:1–16, Paul reviews his brief ministry in Thessalonica and defends his conduct and motives, apparently to answer enemies who are trying to impugn his character and message. He sends Timothy to minister to them and is greatly relieved when Timothy reports the stability of their faith and love (2:17 through 3:10). Paul therefore closes this historical section with a prayer that their faith may continue to deepen (3:11–13).

Paul's Instructions for the Thessalonians (chs. 4 and 5): The apostle deftly moves into a series of exhortations and instructions by encouraging the Thessalonians to continue progressing. He reminds them of his previous teaching on sexual and social matters (4:1–12), since these gentile believers lack the moral upbringing in the Mosaic Law provided in the Jewish community. Now rooted in the word of God (2:13), the readers must resist the constant pressures of a pagan society.

Paul has taught them about the return of Christ, and they have become distressed over the deaths of some among them. In 4:13–18,

Paul comforts them with the assurance that all who die in Christ will be resurrected at his *Parousia* ("presence, coming, advent"). The apostle continues his discourse on eschatology (future events) by describing the coming Day of the Lord (5:1–11). In anticipation of this day, believers are to "be awake and sober" as people who "belong to the light" who are destined for salvation, not wrath. Paul requests the readers to deal with integrity toward one another and to continue growing spiritually (5:12–22). The epistle closes with a wish for their santification, three requests, and a benediction (5:23–28).

OUTLINE OF FIRST THESSALONIANS

Introduction	1:1	Instructions about the coming of Christ	4:13–5:11
Gratitude and praise	1:2–3:13	Final exhortations	5:12–22
Exhortation to Christian conduct	4:1–12	Conclusion	5:23–28

FOCUS	REFLECTIONS ON THE THESSALONIANS			INSTRUCTIONS TO THE THESSALONIANS			
REFERENCE	1.1——————2.1——————2.17————			4.1—————— 4.13———— 5.1————			—5.12——5.28
DIVISION	COMMENDATION FOR GROWTH	FOUNDING OF THE CHURCH	STRENGTHENING OF THE CHURCH	DIRECTION FOR GROWTH	THE DEAD IN CHRIST	THE DAY OF THE LORD	HOLY LIVING
TOPIC	PERSONAL EXPERIENCE			PRACTICAL EXHORTATION			
	LOOKING BACK			LOOKING FORWARD			
SETTING	WRITTEN IN CORINTH						

I THESSALONIANS

PAUL'S SECOND LETTER TO THE

THESSALONIANS

The Book of Second Thessalonians

The core of this letter is chapter 2. There the author begs the recipients not to be so easily agitated or terrified, whether by an utterance, or rumor, or a letter alleged to be the author's, into believing that the Day of the Lord has come. The writer then recalls the teaching in which they were instructed about certain events that must happen before the end, namely, the revelation of the man of lawlessness and the mass apostasy. The author argues that these have not yet occurred.

In the first chapter, which is an introduction to the epistle, the author begins by commending the believers on their faithfulness in the midst of persecution and encouraging them that present suffering will be repaid with future glory.

The purpose and thrust of this epistle is to allay the tensions and anxieties created by speculation on the imminence of the *Parousia* (Second Coming). This may prompt the warnings in chapter 3 to avoid idleness and to continue working for their daily needs.

The Author of Second Thessalonians

The vocabulary and style support the claim in 1:1 and 3:17 that it was written by Paul. Since the early nineteenth century some scholars have doubted Pauline authorship. Today, scholars are very much divided on this question. Some list it among the deutero-Pauline epistles.

The arguments for this latter position are: (1) differing views on the imminence of the *Parousia;* (2) a developed christology with aspects different from the earlier letters; and (3) the verbal similarities with the First Letter to the Thessalonians. From this they argue that Second Thessalonians is so like First Thessalonians and yet so different that it must be an imitation of First Thessalonians written to meet a later situation. Scholars who debate the question are agreed that to opt for either position poses unanswerable questions and creates insurmountable problems. One author accepts the Pauline authorship on the basis that it creates less problems than the theory of pseudonymity.

The Time of Second Thessalonians

Those who accept Pauline authorship argue that this letter was probably written a few months after First Thessalonians (cf. "The Time of First Thessalonians"), while Paul was still in Corinth with Silas and Timothy (1:1; cf. Acts 18:5). The bearer of the first epistle may have brought Paul an update on the new developments, prompting him to write this letter. They were still undergoing persecution, and the false teaching about the Day of the Lord led some of them to overreact by giving up their jobs. The problem of idleness recorded in First Thessalonians 4:11–12 had become more serious (3:6–15). By this time, Paul was beginning to see the opposition he would face in his ministry at Corinth (3:2; see Acts 18:5–10).

Those who opt for pseudonymity would date it in the last decades of the first century near the time of the Book of Revelation. The *Parousia* has been delayed beyond anything Paul himself envisaged. The problem of persecution and the response to it are reaching a stage known from the Book of Revelation, which was written at the end of the first century. Also, doctrine about Christ is significantly advanced from, though clearly related to, that in First Thessalonians. The letter, therefore, they would say, represents the church coming to terms with the problems of the generation following Paul's, though still consciously and immensely indebted to the apostle.

Survey of Second Thessalonians

This epistle is the theological sequel to First Thessalonians, which developed the theme of the coming Day of the Lord (1 Thess. 5:1–11). However, not long after the Thessalonians receive that letter, they fall prey to false teaching or outright deception, thinking the Day of the Lord has already begun. The author writes this brief letter to correct the error and also to encourage those believers whose faith is being tested by the difficulties presented by persecution. He also reproves those who have decided to cease working because they believe the coming of Christ is near. Second Thessalonians deals with the author's encouragement in persecution (ch. 1); his explanation of the Day of Lord (ch. 2); and his exhortation to the church (ch. 3).

The Author's Encouragement in Persecution (ch. 1): After his two-verse salutation, the author gives thanks for the growing faith and love of the Thessalonians and assures them of their ultimate deliverance from those who are persecuting them (1:3–10). They are encouraged to patiently endure their afflictions, knowing that the Lord Jesus will judge their persecutors when he "appears from heaven with his mighty angels, with a flaming fire" (1:7–8). Before the author moves to the next topic, he concludes this section with a prayer for the spiritual welfare of his readers (1:11–12).

The Author's Explanation of the Day of the Lord (ch. 2): Because of the severity of their afflictions, the Thessalonians have become susceptible to false teaching (and possibly a fraudulent letter in the name of Paul), claiming that they are already in the Day of the Lord (2:1–2). This was particularly disturbing because Paul's previous letter had given them the comforting hope that they were not destined for the wrath of that day (1 Thess. 5:9). The author therefore assures them that the Day of the Lord is yet in the future and will not arrive unannounced (2:3–12). He then concludes with a word of encouragement and a benedictory prayer of comfort before moving to his next topic.

The Author's Exhortation to the Church (3:1–18): The author requests the Thessalonian church to pray on his behalf and to wait patiently for the Lord (3:1–5). Having thus commended, corrected, and comforted his readers, the tactful author closes his letter with a sharp word of command to those who have been using the truth of Christ's return as an excuse for disorderly conduct (3:6–15; cf. 1 Thess. 4:11–12). The doctrine of the Lord's return requires a balance between waiting and working. It is a perspective that should encourage holiness, not idleness. This final section, like the first two, closes on a benedictory note (3:16–18).

OUTLINE OF SECOND THESSALONIANS

Introduction	1:1–2	Exhortation to Christian	
Praise and commendation	1:3–12	conduct	3:1–16
Instructions about the coming of Christ	2:1–17	Conclusion	3:17–18

FOCUS	ENCOURAGEMENT IN PERSECUTION			EXPLANATION OF THE DAY OF THE LORD		EXHORTATION TO THE CHURCH	
REFERENCE	1.1————1.5————1.11——			2.1————2.13————		3.1————3.6——3.18	
DIVISION	THANKSGIVING FOR GROWTH	ENCOURAGEMENT IN PERSECUTION	PRAYER FOR BLESSING	EVENTS PRECEDING	COMFORT OF THE BELIEVER	WAIT PATIENTLY	WITHDRAW
TOPIC	DISCOURAGED BELIEVERS			DISTURBED BELIEVERS		DISOBEDIENT BELIEVERS	
	THANKSGIVING FOR THEIR LIFE			INSTRUCTION OF THEIR DOCTRINE		CORRECTION OF THEIR BEHAVIOR	
SETTING	POSSIBLY WRITTEN IN CORINTH						

2 THESSALONIANS

PAUL'S FIRST LETTER TO THE
TIMOTHY

The Book of First Timothy

The First Letter to Timothy is the first of three epistles—two addressed to Timothy and one to Titus—known as the "Pastoral Epistles" because of the author's obvious pastoral concern for the churches and the ministry.

The three are closely related in matter and form. They are devoted principally to advice about the exercise of the pastoral office. They are not private letters primarily, but official documents with comprehensive instructions about combating heresy, organization of the church, and the pastoral care of particular classes. Second Timothy, written as the testament of Paul on his way to face martyrdom, is the only one of them which in form and matter resembles a private letter.

Being official documents, at least First Timothy and Titus are intended for the communities as much as for their leaders.

In the first letter, the setting is that Paul, pictured as the aged and experienced apostle, writes to the young pastor, Timothy, who is facing a heavy burden of responsibility in the church at Ephesus. The task is challenging: false doctrine must be erased, public worship safeguarded, and mature leadership developed. In addition to the conduct of the church, Paul talks pointedly about the conduct of the minister. Timothy must be on his guard, lest his youthfulness become a liability rather than an asset to the gospel. He must be careful to avoid false teachers and greedy motives, pursuing instead righteousness, godliness, faith, love, perseverance, and the gentleness that befits a man of God.

The Author of First Timothy

Since the early nineteenth century, the authenticity of the Pastoral Epistles has been questioned more than any other epistle ascribed to Paul. The similarity of these epistles requires that they be treated as a unit in terms of authorship because they stand or fall together.

The arguments against Pauline authorship are: (1) There seems to be no incontestable attestation of the pastorals as Pauline letters until the latter part of the second century. (2) the style and especially the language of the pastorals differ from those of the acknowledged letters of Paul as a whole by a factor of about two to three times the variation found in any one, or in any group, of the other letters. The pastorals themselves represent a singular stylistic and linguistic group over against the other letters. (3) The pastorals presuppose a historical setting found in neither Acts nor the other letters. (4) The church situation is peculiar in two respects. First, the danger of heresy is not acute. Second, a regular ministry and system of ordination seem to exist. Ministry and laity are now distinguished within the church. (5) A certain theological difference is implied, especially by ascribing different meanings to Pauline words.

These authors agree that all these arguments, taken together, suggest that the letters were written fifty years or so after Paul by one attempting to speak a genuine word of Paul to his own day.

The Time of First Timothy

Those who accept Pauline authorship argue that Paul was acquitted and released from the Roman imprisonment narrated in Acts 28. He then continued his missionary labors and again was imprisoned. Tradition holds one date for his execution as A.D. 67. These authors believe that First Timothy was written sometime between his release (A.D. 63) and his execution after his second Roman imprisonment (A.D. 67). There is some (but not irrefutable) evidence for the two Roman imprisonments on which this theory is based.

Those who argue for pseudonymity differ widely when it comes to dating. Some argue for the first decade of the second century; others claim a much later date in the second century.

Survey of First Timothy

In the eighteenth century, the letters to Timothy and Titus came to be known as the Pastoral Epistles even though they do not use any terms such as shepherd, pastor, flock, or sheep. Still, this title is appropriate for First Timothy and Titus, since they focus on the oversight of church life. It is less appropriate in the case of Second Timothy, which is a more personal than church-oriented letter. The Pastoral Epistles abound with principles for leadership and righteous living.

In his first letter to Timothy, Paul is portrayed as seeking to guide his younger and less experienced assistant in his weighty responsibility as the overseer of the the work at Ephesus and other Asian cities.

The author writes, in effect, a challenge to Timothy to fulfill the task before him: combating false teaching with sound doctrine, developing qualified leadership, teaching God's word, and encouraging Christian conduct. Because of the personal and conversational character of this letter, it is loosely structured around five clear charges that end each section (1:18–20; 3:14–16; 4:11–20; 5:21–25; 6:20–21): charge concerning doctrine (ch. 1); charge concerning public worship (chs. 2 and 3); charge concerning false teachers (ch. 4); charge concerning church discipline (ch. 5); and charge concerning pastoral motives (ch. 6).

Charge Concerning Doctrine (ch. 1): After his greetings (1:1–2), the author warns Timothy about the growing problem of false doctrines, particularly as they relate to the misuse of the Mosaic Law (1:3–11). The writer then recounts his radical conversion to Christ and subsequent calling to the ministry (1:12–17). Timothy, too, has received a divine calling, and the author charges him to fulfill it without wavering in doctrine or conduct (1:18–20).

Charge Concerning Public Worship (chs. 2 and 3): Turning his attention to the church at large, the author addresses the issues of church worship and leadership. Efficacious public prayer should be a part of worship, and he associates this with the role of men in the church (2:1–8). He then turns to the role of women (2:9–15), wherein he emphasizes the importance of the inner quality of godliness. In 3:1–17, the author lists several qualifications for church leaders (overseers) or bishops. The word for "overseer" (*episkopos*) is used synonymously with the word for "elder" (*presbuteros*) in the New Testament. The qualifications for the office of deacon (*diakonos*, "servant") are listed in 3:8–13.

Charge Concerning False Teachers (ch. 4): Timothy obviously had difficulties with some of the older men (5:1) who had left the faith. The author carefully advises on the issues of marriage, food, and exercise. The closing charge exhorts Timothy not to neglect the spiritual gift given to him.

Charge Concerning Church Discipline (ch. 5): One of the most difficult pastoral duties for the young minister is to lead in the exercise of church discipline. Commencing with the general advice of treating all members of the church as family (5:1–2), the author concentrates on the two special areas of widows and elders, focusing on Timothy's responsibility and providing practical instruction.

Charge Concerning Pastoral Duties (ch. 6): In addition, the insidious doctrine was being taught that godliness will eventually result in material blessing. The book closes with an extended charge (6:11–21), which is supplemented by an additional charge that Timothy is to give to the wealthy of this age (6:17–19).

OUTLINE OF FIRST TIMOTHY

Introduction	1:1–2	Instructions to Timothy	
Instructions concerning the church and its officers	1:3–3:16	about his work	4:1–6:21

FOCUS	DOCTRINE	PUBLIC WORSHIP	FALSE TEACHERS	CHURCH DISCIPLINE	PASTORAL MOTIVES
REFERENCE	1.1 ——————	2.1 ——————	4.1 ——————	5.1 ——————	6.1 —————— 6.21
DIVISION	PROBLEM OF FALSE DOCTRINE	PUBLIC WORSHIP AND LEADERSHIP	PRESERVE TRUE DOCTRINE	PRESCRIPTIONS FOR WIDOWS AND ELDERS	PASTORAL MOTIVATIONS
TOPIC	WARNING	WORSHIP	WISDOM	WIDOWS	WEALTH
	DANGERS OF FALSE DOCTRINE	DIRECTIONS FOR WORSHIP	DEFENSE AGAINST FALSE TEACHERS	DUTIES TOWARD OTHERS	DEALINGS WITH RICHES
SETTING	UNCERTAIN				

1 TIMOTHY

PAUL'S SECOND LETTER TO

TIMOTHY

The Book of Second Timothy

As a literary entity, the Second Letter to Timothy differs from the other two pastorals. In essence, the two other epistles treat ecclesiastical order. On the other hand, Second Timothy consists of an admonition of Paul, who is going to his death, to his pupil to stand firm and fight heresy. That is, the epistle has the form of a literary testament. In all three epistles, Paul appears as the author. It is only in Second Timothy that we find personal correspondence to a considerable extent.

He begins by assuring Timothy of his continuing love and prayers, and reminds him of his spiritual heritage and responsibilities. Only the one who perseveres, whether as a soldier, athlete, farmer, or minister of Jesus Christ, will reap the reward. Paul warns Timothy that his teaching will come under attack as men desert the truth for what they are itching to hear (4:3). But Timothy has Paul's example to guide him and God's word to fortify him as he faces growing opposition and glowing opportunities.

The Author of Second Timothy

Since the Pastoral Epistles have to be treated as a unit on the matter of authorship, see "The Author of First Timothy" for comments on the origin of Second Timothy.

Those who defend Pauline authorship give the following details on the relationship of Timothy to Paul from their initial meeting up to the relationship expressed in the Second Letter to Timothy.

Timothy's name is found more often in the salutations of the Pauline Epistles than any other (2 Cor.; Phil.; Col.; 1 and 2 Thess.; 1 and 2 Tim.; Philem.). His father was a Greek (Acts 16:1), but his Jewish mother Eunice and grandmother Lois reared him in the knowledge of the Hebrew Scriptures (1:5; 3:15). Timothy evidently became a convert of Paul (1 Cor. 4:17; 1 Tim. 1:2; 2 Tim. 1:2) when the apostle was in Lystra on his first missionary journey (Acts 14:8–20). When he visited Lystra on his second missionary journey, Paul decided to take Timothy along with him and circumcised him because of the Jews (Acts 16:1–3). Timothy was ordained to the ministry (1 Tim. 4:14; 2 Tim. 1:6) and served as a devoted companion and assistant to Paul in Troas, Berea, Thessalonica, and Corinth (Acts 16 through 18; 1 Thess. 3:1–2). During the third missionary journey, Timothy labored with Paul and ministered for him as his representative in Ephesus, Macedonia, and Corinth. He was with Paul during his first Roman imprisonment and evidently went to Philippi (2:19–23) after Paul's release. Paul left him in Ephesus to supervise the work there (1 Tim. 1:3) and years later summoned him to Rome (4:9, 21). According to Hebrews 13:23, Timothy was imprisoned and released, but the passage does not say where. Timothy was sickly (1 Tim. 5:23), timid (1:7), and youthful (1 Tim. 4:12), but he was a gifted teacher who was trustworthy and diligent.

Those who claim pseudonymity would have no difficulty with many of the details given above. They would, however, say that the details given in the second epistle have been inserted by the author, a disciple of Paul, to give the authority of Paul to the letter he has composed in his name.

The Time of Second Timothy

Those who defend Pauline authorship set up the following sequence of events: The cruel and unbalanced Nero, emperor of Rome from A.D. 54 to 68, was responsible for the beginning of the Roman persecution of Christians. Half of Rome was destroyed in July A.D. 64 by a fire, and mounting suspicion that Nero was responsible for the conflagration caused him to use the unpopular Christians as his scapegoat. Christianity thus became a *religio illicita*, and persecution of those who professed Christ became severe. By the time of Paul's return from Spain to Asia in A.D. 66, his enemies were able to use the official Roman position against Christianity to their advantage. Fearing for their own lives, the Asian believers failed to support Paul after his arrest (1:15), and no one supported him at his first defense before the Imperial Court (4:16). Abandoned by almost everyone (4:10–11), the apostle found himself in circumstances very different from those of his first Roman imprisonment (Acts 28:16–31). At that time he was merely under house arrest, people could freely visit him, and he had the hope of release. Now he was in a cold Roman cell (4:13), regarded "like a criminal" (2:9), and without hope of acquittal in spite of the success of his initial defense (4:6–8, 17–18). Timothy evidently was in Ephesus at the time of this letter (see 1:18; 4:19), and on his way to Rome he would go through Troas (4:13) and Macedonia. Priscilla and Aquila (4:19) probably returned from Rome (Rom. 16:3) to Ephesus after the burning of Rome and the beginning of the persecution. Tychicus may have been the bearer of this letter (4:12).

As can be noted, the above scenario holds the position that Paul was released after his first imprisonment described in Acts 28. He then visited Spain, returned to Rome, and was arrested again. It was while in prison that he wrote the Second Letter to Timothy. This would date the letter around A.D. 66 or 67 shortly before the death of Paul.

Those who claim pseudonymity date the letter around the turn of the second century. Some would make it as late as A.D. 125.

Survey of Second Timothy

As Paul presents himself, or is presented by the author, he knows as he writes this epistle that his days on earth are quickly drawing to a close. About to relinquish his heavy burdens, the godly apostle seeks to challenge and strengthen his somewhat timid but faithful associate, Timothy, in his difficult ministry in Ephesus. In spite of Paul's bleak circumstances, this is a letter of encouragement that urges Timothy on to steadfastness in the fulfillment of his divinely appointed task. Paul calls Timothy a "loyal soldier of Christ Jesus" (2:3), and it is clear from the sharp imperatives that this letter is really a combat manual for use in the spiritual warfare: "keep alive" (1:6); "Do not be ashamed" (1:8); "Hold firmly . . . true words" (1:13); "keep the good things" (1:14); "be strong" (2:1); "Take your part in suffering" (2:3); "Do your best to win full approval in God's sight" (2:15); "Avoid . . . strive" (2:22); "keep away" (2:23); "Be on your guard" (4:15). Central to everything in Second Timothy is the sure foundation of the word of God. Paul focuses on the need to persevere in present testing (chs. 1 and 2), and to endure in future testing (chs. 3 and 4).

Persevere in Present Testing (chs. 1 and 2): After his salutation to his "dear son" (1:2), Paul expresses his thanksgiving for Timothy's "sincere faith" (1:5). He then encourages Timothy to stand firm in the power of the gospel and to overcome any fear in the face of opposition. At personal risk, Onesiphorus boldly seeks out Paul in Rome, but most of the Asian Christians fail to stand behind Paul at the time of his arrest. Timothy must remain faithful and not fear possible persecution. Paul then exhorts his spiritual son to reproduce in the lives of others what he has received in Christ (four generations are mentioned in 2:2). He is responsible to work hard and discipline himself like a teacher, a soldier, a farmer, a workman, a vessel, and a servant, following the example of Paul's perseverance (2:1–13). In his dealings with others, Timothy must not become entangled in false speculation, foolish quarrels, or youthful lusts, which would hamper his effectiveness. As he pursues "righteousness, faith, love, and peace" (2:22), he must know how to overcome error graciously.

Endure in Future Testing (chs. 3 and 4): Paul anticipates a time of growing apostasy and wickedness when men and women will be increasingly susceptible to empty religiosity and false teaching (3:1–9). Arrogance and godlessness will breed further deception and persecution, but Timothy must not waver in using the Scripture to combat doctrinal error and moral evil (3:10–17). The Scriptures are inspired (God-breathed) and with them Timothy is equipped to carry out the ministry to which he was called. Paul's final exhortation to Timothy (4:1–5) is a classic summary of the task of the man of God to proclaim the gospel in spite of opposing circumstances. This very personal letter closes with an update of Paul's situation in Rome along with certain requests (4:6–22). Paul longs to see Timothy before the end, and he also needs certain articles, especially "the ones made of parchment" (probably portions of the Old Testament Scriptures).

OUTLINE OF SECOND TIMOTHY

Introduction	1:1–2	Paul's own situation	4:6–18
Praise and exhortation	1:3–2:13	Conclusion	4:19–22
Counsel and warning	2:14–4:5		

FOCUS	PERSEVERE IN PRESENT TESTINGS			ENDURE IN FUTURE TESTINGS		
REFERENCE	1.1————1.6————2.1————			3.1————4.1————4.6————4.22		
DIVISION	THANKSGIVING FOR TIMOTHY'S FAITH	REMINDER OF TIMOTHY'S RESPONSIBILITY	CHARACTERISTICS OF A FAITHFUL MINISTER	APPROACHING DAY OF APOSTASY	CHARGE TO PREACH THE WORD	APPROACHING DEATH OF PAUL
TOPIC	POWER OF THE GOSPEL		PERSEVERANCE OF THE GOSPEL	PROTECTOR OF THE GOSPEL	PROCLAMATION OF THE GOSPEL	
	REMINDER		REQUIREMENTS	RESISTANCE	REQUESTS	
SETTING	UNCERTAIN					

2 TIMOTHY

PAUL'S LETTER TO
TITUS

The Book of Titus

The Letter to Titus is the third of the Pastoral Epistles. Whereas Timothy is overseeing the church organization at Ephesus, Titus is assigned to carry out the same task on Crete. This letter is more in the style of First Timothy. Like First Timothy, it is concerned with church organization and less personal than the style of Second Timothy. Paul writes advising him to appoint elders, men of proven spiritual character in their homes and businesses, to oversee the work of the church. But elders are not the only individuals in the church who are required to excel spiritually. Men and women, young and old, all have vital functions to fulfill in the church if they are to be living examples of the doctrine they profess. Throughout his letter to Titus, Paul stresses the necessary, practical working out of salvation in the daily lives of both the elders and the congregation. Good works are desirable and profitable for all believers.

This third Pastoral Epistle is simply titled *Pros Titon*, "To Titus." Ironically, this was also the name of the Roman general who destroyed Jerusalem in A.D. 70 and succeeded his father Vespasian as emperor.

The Author of Titus

Since the Pastoral Epistles have to be treated as a unit on the matter of authorship, see "The Author of First Timothy" for the authorship of Titus.

Titus is not mentioned in Acts, but the references to him in the Pauline Letters make it clear that he was one of Paul's closest and most trusted companions. Titus was probably from Syrian Antioch, if he was one of the disciples of Acts 11:26. Paul brought this uncircumcised Greek believer to Jerusalem (Gal. 2:3) where he became a test case on the matter of Gentiles and liberty from the law. Years later, when Paul set out from Antioch on his third missionary journey (Acts 18:22), Titus must have accompanied him because he was sent by the apostle to Corinth on three occasions during that time (2 Cor. 2:12–13; 7:5–7, 13–15; 8:6, 16–24).

Those who hold for Pauline authorship of Titus note that Titus is not mentioned again until Paul leaves him in Crete to carry on the work (Titus 1:5). Paul speaks of him as "my true son in the faith" (Titus 1:4). They note that Titus was with Paul during his second Roman imprisonment but left to go to Dalmatia (2 Tim. 4:10), possibly on an evangelistic mission. They argue that Paul's confidence in Titus is evidenced in Second Corinthians, where he speaks of him as his "brother" (2 Cor. 2:13), his "partner" (2 Cor. 8:23), and his "son" (1:4). He lauded Titus' character and conduct in Second Corinthians 7:13–15 and 8:16–17. This would justify Paul's confidence in him— enough confidence to put him in charge of the church at Crete.

Those who claim pseudonymity of the letter, as in the case of the other pastorals, would see all these references to Paul in Titus as inserted by the pseudonymous author to gain authority for the epistle by highlighting Paul's relationship to Titus.

The Time of Titus

The Mediterranean island of Crete is 156 miles long and up to 30 miles wide. Its first-century inhabitants were notorious for untruthfulness and immorality (1:12–13). "To act like a Cretan" became an idiom meaning "to play the liar." A number of Jews from Crete were present in Jerusalem at the time of Peter's sermon on the Day of Pentecost (Acts 2:11), and some of them may have believed in Christ and introduced the gospel to their countrymen. Certainly, Paul would not have had the opportunity to do evangelistic work during his brief sojourn in Crete while he was en route to Rome (Acts 27:7–13).

Those who defend Pauline authorship would argue that the apostle spread the gospel in the cities of Crete after his release from his first Roman imprisonment and left Titus there to finish organizing the churches (1:5). Because of the problem of immorality among the Cretans, it was important for Titus to stress the need for righteousness in Christian living. False teachers, "especially the converts from Judaism" (1:10), were misleading and divisive. This construction, as in the other pastorals, would affirm Paul's release from his first Roman captivity and a second Roman captivity prior to his death in presumably A.D. 67.

Again, those who claim pseudonymity of the letter argue that the epistle was written at the turn of the century or, according to some, further into the second century.

Survey of Titus

This letter was written to encourage and assist Titus in his task. It stresses sound doctrine and warns against those who distort the truth, but it also is a conduct manual that emphasizes good deeds and the proper conduct of various groups within the churches. This epistle falls into two major sections: appoint elders (ch. 1); put things in order (chs. 2 and 3).

Appoint Elders (ch. 1): The salutation to Titus is actually a compact doctrinal statement, which lifts up his word as the source of the truth that reveals the way to eternal life (1:1–4). Paul reminds Titus of his responsibility to organize the churches of Crete by appointing elders (also called church leaders; see 1:7) and rehearses the qualifications these spiritual leaders must meet (1:5–9). This is especially important in view of the disturbances that are being caused by false teachers who are upsetting a number of the believers with their Judaic myths and commandments (1:10–16). The natural tendency toward moral laxity among the Cretans coupled with that kind of deception is a dangerous force that must be overcome by godly leadership and sound doctrine.

Put Things in Order (chs. 2 and 3): Titus is given the charge to "teach what agrees with sound doctrine" (2:1), and Paul delineates Titus' role with regard to various groups in the church, including older men, older women, young women, young men, and servants (2:2–10). The knowledge of Christ must effect a transformation in each of these groups so that their testimony will "bring credit to the teaching about God our Savior" (2:10). The second doctrinal statement of Titus (2:11–14) gives the basis for the appeals Paul has just made for righteous living. God in his grace redeems believers from being slaves of sin, assuring them the "blessed Day" of the coming of Christ that will eventually be realized. Paul urges Titus to proclaim these truths authoritatively (2:15).

In chapter 3, Paul moves from conduct in groups (2:1–10) to conduct in general (3:1–11). The behavior of believers as citizens must be different from the behavior of unbelievers because of their regeneration and renewal by the Holy Spirit. The third doctrinal statement in this book (3:4–7) emphasizes the kindness and love of God who saves us "not because of any good deeds that we ourselves had done" (3:5). Nevertheless, the need for good deeds as a result of salvation is stressed six times in the three chapters of Titus (1:16; 2:7, 14; 3:1, 8, 14). Paul exhorts Titus to deal firmly with dissenters who would cause factions and controversies (3:9–11) and closes the letter with three instructions, a greeting, and a benediction (3:12–15).

OUTLINE OF TITUS

Introduction	1:1–4	the church	2:1–15
Church officers	1:5–16	Exhortations and warning	3:1–11
Duties of various groups in		Conclusion	3:12–15

FOCUS	APPOINT ELDERS		SET THINGS IN ORDER	
REFERENCE	1.1————————1.10————————		2.1————————————3.1————————3.15	
DIVISION	ORDAIN QUALIFIED ELDERS	REBUKE FALSE TEACHERS	SPEAK SOUND DOCTRINE	MAINTAIN GOOD WORKS
TOPIC	PROTECTION OF SOUND DOCTRINE		PRACTICE OF SOUND DOCTRINE	
	ORGANIZATION	OFFENDERS	OPERATION	OBEDIENCE
SETTING	UNCERTAIN			

TITUS

PAUL'S LETTER TO

PHILEMON

The Book of Philemon

Does Christian brotherly love really work, even in situations of extraordinary tension and difficulty? Will it work for example, between a prominent slave owner and one of his runaway slaves? Paul has no doubt! He writes a "postcard" to Philemon, his beloved brother and fellow worker, on behalf of Onesimus—a deserter, thief, and formerly worthless slave, but now Philemon's brother in Christ. With much tact and tenderness, Paul asks Philemon to receive Onesimus back with the same gentleness with which he would receive Paul himself. Any debt Onesimus owes, Paul promises to make good. Knowing Philemon, Paul is confident that brotherly love and forgiveness will carry the day.

Since this letter is addressed to Philemon in verse 1, it becomes known as *Pros Philēmona*, "To Philemon." Like First and Second Timothy and Titus, it is addressed to an individual, but unlike the Pastoral Epistles, Philemon is also addressed to a family and a church (v. 2).

The Author of Philemon

The authenticity of Philemon was not called into question until the fourth century, when certain theologians concluded that its lack of doctrinal content made it unworthy of the apostle Paul. But men like Jerome and Chrysostom soon vindicated this epistle, and it was not challenged again until the nineteenth century. Some who denied the authenticity of Colossians also denied the Pauline authorship of Philemon because of the close connection between the two epistles (e.g., the same people are associated with Paul in both letters: cf. Col. 4:9–10, 12, 14, with Philem. 10, 23–24). The general consensus of scholarship, however, recognized Philemon as Paul's work.

The Time of Philemon

Reconstructing the background of this letter, it appears that a slave named Onesimus had robbed or in some other way wronged his master Philemon and had escaped. He had made his way from Colossae to Rome where he had found relative safety among the masses in the Imperial City. Somehow Onesimus had come into contact with Paul; it is possible that he had even sought out the apostle for help (Onesimus no doubt had heard Philemon speak of Paul). Paul had led him to Christ (v. 10), and although Onesimus had become a real asset to Paul, both knew that as a Christian, Onesimus had a responsibility to return to Philemon. That day came when Paul wrote his epistle to the Colossians. Tychicus was the bearer of that letter. Paul decided to send Onesimus along with Tychicus to Colossae (Col. 4:7–9; Philem. 12), knowing that it would be safer, in view of slave catchers, to send Onesimus with a companion.

Philemon was written and dispatched at the same time as Colossians, during Paul's first Roman imprisonment (see vv. 1, 9–10, 13, 23). Philemon 22 reflects Paul's confident hope of release: "get a room ready for me, because I hope that God will answer the prayers of all of you and give me back to you."

Philemon was a resident of Colossae (Col. 4:9, 17; Philem. 1–2) and a convert of Paul's (v. 19), perhaps through an encounter with Paul in Ephesus during Paul's third missionary journey. Philemon's house was large enough to serve as the meeting place for the church there (v. 2). He was benevolent to other believers (vv. 5–7), and his son Archippus evidently held a position of leadership in the church (Col. 4:17; Philem. 2). Philemon may have had other slaves in addition to Onesimus, and he was not alone as a slave owner among the Colossian believers (Col. 4:1). Thus this letter and his response would provide guidelines for other master-slave relationships.

According to Roman law, runaway slaves such as Onesimus could be severely punished or condemned to a violent death. It is doubtful that Onesimus would have returned to Philemon even with this letter if he had not become a believer in Christ.

It should be noted that this treatment presumes the authenticity of the letter to the Colossians. A growing number of critics are questioning the authenticity of the latter. Nonetheless, it should further be pointed out that a good number of scholars still defend Pauline authorship of Colossians.

Rome as the place of origin is widely contested. Several have proposed Caesarea; others have suggested Ephesus. There are problems with each of these views. Caesarea creates fewer problems but Roman origin is defensible.

Survey of Philemon

This briefest of Paul's epistles (only 334 words in the Greek text) is a model of courtesy, discretion, and loving concern for the forgiveness of one who would otherwise face the sentence of death. This tactful and highly personal letter can be divided into three components: prayer of thanksgiving for Philemon (vv. 1–7); petition for Onesimus (vv. 8–16); promise to Philemon (vv. 17–25).

Prayer of Thanksgiving for Philemon (vv. 1–7): Writing this letter as a "prisoner for the sake of Christ Jesus," Paul addresses it personally to Philemon (a Christian leader in Colossae), to Apphia and Archippus (evidently Philemon's wife and son), as well as to the church that meets in Philemon's house. The main body of this compact letter begins with a prayer of thanksgiving for Philemon's faith and love.

Petition for Onesimus (vv. 8–16): Basing his appeal on Philemon's character, Paul refuses to command Philemon to pardon and receive Onesimus. Instead, Paul seeks to persuade his friend of his Christian responsibility to forgive even as he was forgiven by Christ. Paul urges Philemon not to punish Onesimus but to receive him as "not just a slave" but as "a dear brother in Christ" (v. 16).

Promise to Philemon (vv. 17–25): Paul places Onesimus' debt on his account, but then reminds Philemon of the greater spiritual debt which Philemon himself owes as a convert to Christ (vv. 17–19).

Paul closes this effective epistle with a hopeful request (v. 22), greetings from his companions (vv. 23–24), and a benediction (v. 25). The fact that it was preserved indicates Philemon's favorable response to Paul's pleas.

OUTLINE OF PHILEMON

Introduction	1–3	Appeal for Onesimus	8–22
Praise for Philemon	4–7	Conclusion	23–25

FOCUS	PRAYER OF THANKSGIVING	PETITION FOR ONESIMUS	PROMISE TO PHILEMON
REFERENCE	1————————8	————————17	————————25
DIVISION	COMMENDATION OF PHILEMON'S LOVE	INTERCESSION FOR ONESIMUS	CONFIDENCE IN PHILEMON'S OBEDIENCE
TOPIC	PRAISE OF PHILEMON	PLEA OF PAUL	PLEDGE OF PAUL
	CHARACTER OF PHILEMON	CONVERSION OF ONESIMUS	CONFIDENCE OF PAUL
SETTING	UNCERTAIN		

THE LETTER TO THE

HEBREWS

The Book of Hebrews

Many Jewish believers, having stepped out of Judaism into Christianity, want to reverse their course in order to escape persecution by their countrymen. The writer of Hebrews exhorts them to "go forward, then, to mature teaching" (6:1). His appeal is based on the superiority of Christ over the Judaic system. Christ is better than the angels, for they worship him. He is better than Moses, for he created him. He is better than the Aaronic priesthood, for his sacrifice was once for all time. He is better than the law, for he mediates a better covenant. In short, there is more to be gained in Christ than to be lost in Judaism. Pressing on in Christ produces tested faith, self-discipline, and a visible love seen in good works.

Although several versions use the title "The Epistle of Paul the Apostle to the Hebrews," there is no early manuscript evidence to support this. The oldest and most reliable title is simply *Pros Ebraious*, "To the Hebrews."

The Author of Hebrews

Like the ancestry of Melchizedek, the origin of Hebrews is unknown. Uncertainty plagues not only its authorship, but also where it was written, its date, and its readership. The question of authorship delayed its recognition in the West as part of the New Testament canon in spite of early support by Clement of Rome. Not until the fourth century was it generally accepted as authoritative in the western church, when the testimonies of Jerome and Augustine settled the issue. In the eastern church, there was no problem of canonical acceptance because it was regarded as one of the "fourteen" epistles of Paul. The issue of its canonicity was again raised during the Reformation, but the spiritual depth and quality of Hebrews bore witness to its inspiration, despite its anonymity.

Hebrews 13:18–24 tells us that this book was not anonymous to the original readers; they evidently knew the author. For some reason, however, early church tradition is divided over the identity of the author. Part of the church attributed it to Paul; others preferred Barnabas, Luke, or Clement; and some chose anonymity. Thus, external evidence will not help determine the author.

Internal evidence must be the final court of appeal, but here, too, the results are ambiguous. Some aspects of the language, style, and theology of Hebrews are very similar to Paul's epistles, and the author also refers to Timothy (13:23). However, significant differences have led the majority of biblical scholars to reject Pauline authorship of this book. Hebrews appears not to have been written by Paul although the writer shows a Pauline influence. The authority of Hebrews in no way depends upon Pauline authorship, especially since it does not claim to have been written by Paul.

Tertullian referred to Barnabas as the author of Hebrews, but it is unlikely that this resident of Jerusalem (Acts 4:36–37) would include himself as one of those who relied on others for eyewitness testimony about Jesus (2:3). Other suggestions include Luke, Clement of Rome, Apollos, Silvanus (Silas), Philip, and even Priscilla. Some of these are possibilities, but we must agree with the third-century theologian Origen who wrote: "Who it was that really wrote the Epistle, God only knows."

The Time of Hebrews

Because of the exclusive use of the Septuagint (Greek translation of the Hebrew Old Testament) and the elegant Greek style found in Hebrews, some recent scholars have argued that this book was written to a gentile readership. However, the bulk of the evidence favors the traditional view that the original recipients of this letter were Jewish Christians. In addition to the ancient title "To Hebrews," there is also the frequent use of the Old Testament as an unquestioned authority, the assumed knowledge of the sacrificial ritual, and the many contrasts between Christianity and Judaism, which are designed to prevent the readers from lapsing into Judaism.

Many places have been suggested for the locality of the readers, but this letter's destination cannot be determined with any certainty. In the past, Jerusalem was most frequently suggested. The majority view today is that the recipients of Hebrews probably lived in Rome. The statement "The brothers from Italy send you their greetings" in 13:24 seems to suggest that Italians away from Italy are sending their greetings home.

The recipients of this letter were believers (3:1) who had come to faith through the testimony of the eyewitnesses of Christ (2:3). They were not novices (5:12), and they had successfully endured hardships because of their stand for the gospel (10:32–34). Unfortunately, they had become "so slow to understand" (5:11) and were in danger of drifting away (2:1; 3:12). This made them particularly susceptible to the renewed persecutions that were coming upon them (12:4–12), and the author found it necessary to check the downward spiral with "this message of encouragement" (13:22). While there is disagreement over the specific danger involved, the classic position that the readers were on the verge of lapsing into Judaism to avoid persecution directed at Christians seems to be supported by the whole tenor of the book. Hebrews' repeated emphasis on the superiority of Christianity over Judaism would have been pointless if the readers were about to return to Gnosticism or heathenism.

The place of writing is unknown, but a reasonable estimate of the date can be made. Hebrews was quoted in A.D. 96 by Clement of Rome. Timothy was still alive (13:23), persecution was mounting, and the old Jewish system was about to be removed (12:26–27). All this suggests a date possibly before A.D. 70 and certainly before A.D. 96.

Survey of Hebrews

Hebrews stands alone among the New Testament epistles in its style and approach. This profound work builds a case for the superiority of Christ through a cumulative argument in which Christ is presented as "better" in every respect. In his person he is better than the angels, Moses, and Joshua; and in his performance he provided a better priesthood, covenant, sanctuary, and sacrifice. Evidently, the readers are in danger of reverting to Judaism because of the suffering they are beginning to experience for their faith in Christ. However, by doing so, they would be retreating from the substance back into the shadow. In addition to his positive presentation of the supremacy of Christ, the writer intersperses five solemn warnings about the peril of turning away from Christ (2:1–4; 3:7 through 4:13; 5:11 through 6:20; 10:19–39; 12:25–29). These parenthetical warnings include cautions against neglect (2:1–4) and refusal (12:25–29). After using the Old Testament to demonstrate the superiority of Christ's person (1:1 through 4:13) and the superiority of Christ's work (4:14 through 10:18), the writer applies these truths in a practical way to show the superiority of the Christian's walk of faith (10:19 through 13:25).

The Superiority of Christ's Person (1:1 through 4:13): Instead of the usual salutation, this epistle immediately launches into its theme— the supremacy of Christ even over the Old Testament prophets (1:1–3). Christianity is built upon the highest form of divine disclosure:

the personal revelation of God through his incarnate Son. Christ is therefore greater than the prophets, and he is also greater than the angels, the mediators of the Mosaic Law (1:4 through 2:18; see Acts 7:53; Heb. 2:2). This is seen in his name, his position, his worship by the angels, and his incarnation. The Son of God partook of flesh and blood and "had to become like his brothers in every way" (2:17) "in order to bring many sons to share his glory" (2:10). Christ is also superior to Moses (3:1–6), for Moses was a servant in the house of God, but Christ is the Son over God's household. Because of these truths, the readers are exhorted to avoid the divine judgment that is visited upon unbelief (3:7 through 4:13). Their disbelief had prevented the generation of the Exodus from becoming the generation of the conquest, and the rest that Christ offers is so much greater than what was provided by Joshua. The readers are therefore urged to enter the eternal rest that is possessed by faith in Christ.

The Superiority of Christ's Work (4:14 through 10:18): The high priesthood of Christ is superior to the Aaronic priesthood (4:14 through 7:28). Because of his incarnation, Christ can "feel sympathy for our weaknesses," having been "tempted in every way that we are, but did not sin" (4:15). Christ was not a Levite, but he qualified for a higher priesthood according to the order of Melchizedek. The superiority of Melchizedek to Levi is seen in the fact that Levi, in effect, paid tithes through Abraham to Melchizedek (7:9–10). Abraham was blessed by Melchizedek, and "the one who blesses is greater than the one who is blessed" (7:7). The parenthetical warning in 5:11 through 6:20 exhorts the readers to "go forward, then, to mature teaching" by moving beyond the basics of salvation and repentance.

By divine oath (7:21), Christ has become a permanent and perfect High Priest "as the covenant which he arranged between God and his people is a better one" (8:6). The new covenant has made the old covenant obsolete (8:6–13). Our Great High Priest similarly ministers in a "tent . . . greater and more perfect; it is not a man-made tent, that is, it is not a part of this created world" (9:11). And unlike the former priests, he offers himself as a sinless and voluntary sacrifice once and for all (9:1 through 10:18).

The Superiority of the Christian's Walk of Faith (10:19 through 13:25): The author applies what he has been saying about the superiority of Christ by warning his readers of the danger of discarding their faith in Christ (10:19–39). The faith that the readers must maintain is defined in 11:1–3 and illustrated in 11:4–40. The triumphs and accomplishments of faith in the lives of Old Testament believers should encourage the recipients of "an even better plan" (11:40) in Christ to "keep our eyes fixed on Jesus, on whom our faith depends from beginning to end" (12:2). Just as Jesus endured great hostility, those who believe in him will sometimes have to endure divine discipline for the sake of holiness (12:1–29). The readers are warned not to turn away from Christ during such times, but to place their hope in him. The character of their lives must be shaped by their dedication to Christ (13:1–19), and this will be manifested in their love of each other through their hospitality, concern, purity, contentment, and obedience. The author concludes this epistle with one of the finest benedictions in Scripture (13:20–21) and some personal words (13:22–25).

OUTLINE OF HEBREWS

Introduction: Christ the complete revelation of God — 1:1–3

Christ's superiority over the angels — 1:4–2:18

Christ's superiority over Moses and Joshua — 3:1–4:13

The superiority of Christ's priesthood — 4:14–7:28

The superiority of Christ's covenant — 8:1–9:28

The superiority of Christ's sacrifice — 10:1–31

The primacy of faith — 11:1–12:25

Final exhortations and conclusions — 13:1–25

FOCUS	CHRIST'S PERSON			CHRIST'S WORK			THE WALK OF FAITH		
REFERENCE	1.1———1.4———3.1———4.14———8.1———9.1———————10.19———12.1———————13.1———13.25								
DIVISION	CHRIST OVER PROPHETS	CHRIST OVER ANGELS	CHRIST OVER MOSES	PRIEST-HOOD	COVENANT	SANCTUARY AND SACRIFICE	ASSURANCE OF FAITH	ENDURANCE OF FAITH	EXHORTATION TO LOVE
TOPIC	MAJESTY OF CHRIST			MINISTRY OF CHRIST			MINISTERS FOR CHRIST		
	DOCTRINE						DISCIPLINE		
SETTING	PLACE OF WRITING UNKNOWN								

HEBREWS

THE LETTER FROM
JAMES

The Book of James

Faith without works cannot be called faith. Faith without works is dead, and a dead faith is worse than no faith at all. Faith must work; it must produce; it must be visible. Verbal faith is not enough; mental faith is insufficient. Faith must be there, but it must be more. It must inspire action. Throughout his epistle to Jewish believers, James integrates true faith and everyday practical experience by stressing that true faith must manifest itself in works of faith.

Faith endures trials. Trials come and go, but a strong faith will face them head-on and develop endurance. Faith understands temptations. It will not allow us to consent to our lust and slide into sin. Faith obeys the word. It will not merely hear and not do. Faith produces doers. Faith harbors no prejudice. For James, faith and favoritism cannot coexist. Faith displays itself in works. Faith is more than mere words; it is more than knowledge; it is demonstrated by obedience; and it overtly responds to the promises of God. Faith controls the tongue. This small but immensely powerful part of the body must be held in check. Faith can do it. Faith acts wisely. It gives us the ability to choose wisdom that is heavenly and to shun wisdom that is earthly. Faith produces separation from the world and submission to God. It provides us with the ability to resist the Devil and humbly to draw near to God. Finally, faith waits patiently for the coming of the Lord. Through trouble and trial it stifles complaining.

The name *Jakōbos* (James) in 1:1 is the basis for the early title *Jakōbou Epistolē*, "Epistle of James." *Jakōbos* is the Greek form of the Hebrew name Jacob, a Jewish name common in the first century.

The Author of James

Four men are named James in the New Testament: (1) James, the father of Judas (not Iscariot), is mentioned twice (Luke 6:16; Acts 1:13) as the father of one of the twelve disciples, but is otherwise completely unknown. (2) James, the son of Alphaeus (Matt. 10:3; Mark 3:18; Luke 6:15; Acts 1:13), elsewhere called the younger James (Mark 15:40), was one of the twelve disciples. Apart from being listed with the other disciples, this James is completely obscure, and it is doubtful that he is the authoritative figure behind the epistle. Some attempts have been made to identify this James with the Lord's brother (Gal. 1:19), but this view is difficult to reconcile with the gospel accounts. (3) James, the son of Zebedee and brother of John (Matt. 4:21; 10:2; 17:1; Mark 3:17; 10:35; 13:3; Luke 9:54; Acts 1:13), was one of Jesus' intimate disciples, but his martyrdom by A.D. 44 (Acts 12:2) makes it very unlikely that he wrote this epistle. (4) James, the Lord's brother (Matt. 13:55; Mark 6:3; Gal. 1:19), was one of the "pillars" in the church in Jerusalem (Acts 12:17; 15:13–21; 21:18; Gal. 2:9, 12). Tradition points to this prominent figure as the author of the epistle, and this best fits the evidence of Scripture. There are several clear parallels between the language of the letter drafted under his leadership in Acts 15:23–29 and the Epistle of James (e.g., the unusual word *chairein*, "greeting," is found only in Acts 15:23; 23:26; and James 1:1). The Jewish character of this epistle with its stress upon the law, along with the evident influence by the Sermon on the Mount (e.g., 4:11–12; 5:12), complement what we know about James "the Just" from Scripture and early tradition.

The brevity and limited doctrinal emphasis of James kept it from wide circulation; and by the time it became known in the church as a whole, there was uncertainty about the identity of the James in 1:1. Growing recognition that it was written by the Lord's brother led to its acceptance as a canonical book.

The Time of James

James is addressed "to all God's people scattered over the whole world" (1:1), and it is apparent from verses like 1:19 and 2:1, 7 that this greeting refers to Hebrew Christians, outside of Palestine. Their place of meeting is called a "synagogue" in the Greek text of 2:2, and the whole epistle reflects Jewish thought and expressions (e.g., 2:19, 21; 4:11–12; 5:4, 12). There are no references to slavery or idolatry, and this also fits an originally Jewish readership.

These Jewish believers were beset with problems that were testing their faith, and James was concerned that they were succumbing to impatience, bitterness, materialism, disunity, and spiritual apathy. As a resident of Jerusalem and a leader of the church, James no doubt had frequent contact with Jewish Christians from a number of Roman provinces. He therefore felt a responsibility to exhort and encourage them in their struggles of faith.

According to Josephus, James was martyred in A.D. 62 (Hegesippus, quoted in Eusebius, fixed the date of James' death at A.D. 66). Those who accept him as the author of this epistle have proposed a date of writing ranging from A.D. 45 to the end of his life.

Survey of James

James is the Proverbs of the New Testament because it is written in the terse moralistic style of Wisdom Literature. It is evident that James was profoundly influenced by the Old Testament (especially by its Wisdom Literature) and by the Sermon on the Mount. But James' impassioned preaching against inequity and social injustice also earns him the title of the Amos of the New Testament. Because of the many subjects in this epistle, it is difficult to outline; suggestions have ranged from no connection between the various topics to a unified scheme. The outline used here is: the test of faith (1:1–18); the characteristics of faith (1:19 through 5:6); and the triumph of faith (5:7–20).

The Test of Faith (1:1–18): The first part of this epistle develops the qualities of genuine faith in regard to trials and temptations. After a one-verse salutation to geographically dispersed Hebrew Christians (1:1), James quickly introduces his first subject, outward tests of faith (1:2–12). These trials are designed to produce mature endurance and a sense of dependence upon God, to whom the believer turns for wisdom and enablement. Inward temptations (1:13–18) do not come from the One who bestows "every good gift" (1:17). These solicitations to evil must be checked at an early stage or they may result in disastrous consequences.

The Characteristics of Faith (1:19 through 5:6): A righteous response to testing requires that one be "quick to listen, but slow to speak and slow to become angry" (1:19), and this broadly summarizes the remainder of the epistle. Quickness of hearing involves an obedient response to God's word (1:19–27). True hearing means more than mere listening; the word must be received and applied. After stating this principle (1:21–22), James develops it with an illustration (1:23–25) and an application (1:26–27). A genuine faith should produce a change in attitude from partiality to the rich to a love for the poor as well as the rich (2:1–13). True faith should also result in actions (2:14–26). In Romans 4, Paul used the example of Abraham to show that justification is by faith, not by works. But James says that Abraham was justified by works (2:21). In spite of the apparent contradiction, Romans 4 and James 2 are really two sides of the same coin. In context,

Paul is writing about justification before God while James writes of the evidence of justification before men. A faith that produces no change is not saving faith.

Moving from works to words, James shows how a living faith controls the tongue ("slow to speak," 1:19). The tongue is small, but it has the power to accomplish great good or equally great evil. Only the power of God applied by an active faith can tame the tongue (3:1–12). Just as there are wicked and righteous uses of the tongue, so there are demonic and divine manifestations of wisdom (3:13–18). James contrasts characteristics of human wisdom with qualities of divine wisdom.

The strong pulls of worldliness (4:1–12) and wealth (4:13 through 5:6) create conflicts that are harmful to the growth of faith. The world system is at enmity with God, and the pursuit of its pleasures produces covetousness, envy, fighting, and arrogance (4:1–6). The believer's only alternative is submission to God out of a humble and repentant spirit. This will produce a transformed attitude toward others as well (4:7–12). This spirit of submission and humility should be applied to any attempts to accrue wealth (4:13–17), especially because wealth can lead to pride, injustice, and selfishness (5:1–6).

The Triumph of Faith (5:7–20): James encourages his readers to endure the sufferings of the present life patiently in view of the future prospect of the coming of the Lord (5:7–12). They may be oppressed by the rich or by other circumstances, but as the example of Job teaches, believers can be sure that God has a gracious purpose in his dealings with them. James concludes his epistle with some practical words on prayer and restoration (5:13–20). James makes mention of *Presbyteroi* or "elders" in 5:14–15, and recommends that they be invited to pray over and anoint the sick of the community.

OUTLINE OF JAMES

Faith and testing	1:1–18	Triumph of faith	5:7–20
Characteristics of faith	1:19–5:6		

FOCUS	TEST OF FAITH		CHARACTERISTICS OF FAITH	TRIUMPH OF FAITH		
REFERENCE	1.1———1.13———		1.19———————————	5.7————	5.13———	5.19———5.20
DIVISION	PURPOSE OF TESTS	SOURCE OF TEMPTATION	OUTWARD DEMONSTRATION OF INNER FAITH	ENDURES WAITING	PRAYS FOR AFFLICTED	CONFRONTS SIN
TOPIC	DEVELOPMENT OF FAITH		WORKS OF FAITH	POWER OF FAITH		
	RESPONSE OF FAITH		REALITY OF FAITH	REASSURANCE OF FAITH		
SETTING	PROBABLY JERUSALEM					

JAMES

THE FIRST LETTER FROM

PETER

The Book of First Peter

The four gospels are unanimous in the view that Christianity was born in persecution. Jesus is opposed throughout his public ministry and finally killed. Acts describes the persecution suffered by Peter, Paul, and Stephen, showing that "persecution" was a way of life for the infant church. When we read First Peter, it is impossible to be very concrete as to the agents responsible for the suffering of his readers. It is probably not yet the official empire-wide persecution of the second and third centuries. But First Peter is convinced that persecution can cause either growth or bitterness in the Christian life. Response determines the result. In writing to Jewish believers struggling in the midst of persecution, First Peter encourages them to conduct themselves courageously for the person and program of Christ. Both their character and conduct must be above reproach. Having been born again to a living hope, they are to imitate the Holy One who has called them. The fruit of that character will be conduct rooted in submission: citizens to government, servants to masters, wives to husbands, husbands to wives, and Christians to one another. Only after submission is fully understood does First Peter deal with the difficult area of suffering. The Christians are not to be surprised "at the painful test you are suffering, as though something unusual were happening to you" (4:12), but are to "be glad that you are sharing Christ's sufferings" (4:13). That response to life is truly the climax of one's submission to the good hand of God.

This epistle begins with the phrase *Petros apostolos Iēsou Christou*, "Peter, apostle of Jesus Christ." This is the basis of the early title *Petrou A*, the "First of Peter."

The Author of First Peter

The early church universally acknowledged the authenticity and authority of First Peter. The apostle Peter's name is given in 1:1, and there are definite similarities between certain phrases in this letter and Peter's sermons as recorded in the Book of Acts (cf. 1 Peter 1:20

and Acts 2:23; 1 Peter 4:5 and Acts 10:42). The epistle contains a number of allusions to events in the life of Christ that held special significance for Peter (e.g., 2:23; 3:18; 4:1; 5:1; cf. 5:5 and John 13:4).

Since the nineteenth century, scholars have challenged the authenticity of First Peter on several grounds. Some claim that 1:1–2 and 4:12 through 5:14 were later additions that turned an anonymous address or a baptismal sermon into a Petrine epistle. Others argue that the sufferings experienced by readers of this letter must refer to the persecution of Christians that took place after the time of Peter in the reigns of the emperors Domitian (A.D. 81–96) and Trajan (A.D. 98–117). Another challenge asserts that the quality of the Greek of this epistle is too high for a Galilean like Peter. But Galileans were bilingual and some were skillful in their use of Greek. However, it is unlikely that Peter the apostle wrote this letter.

The Time of First Peter

This letter is addressed to "God's chosen people who live as refugees" (1:1). This, coupled with the injunction to keep their "conduct among the heathen . . . so good" (2:12), gives the initial appearance that the bulk of the readers are Hebrew Christians. The opposite view that most of these believers were Gentiles may be true. They were called "out of darkness" (2:9), and they at "one time . . . were not God's people, but now . . . are his people" (2:10). Their former "worthless manner of life handed down by [their] ancestors" was characterized by ignorance and futility (1:14, 18; cf. Eph. 4:17). Because they no longer engage in debauchery and idolatry, they are maligned by their countrymen (4:3–4). These descriptions do not fit a predominantly Hebrew Christian readership. Although Peter the apostle is probably not the author, this letter was written close to the time period in which he lived. First Peter was written sometime between A.D. 70 to 80.

This epistle is described as being written in Babylon (5:13), probably a symbolic reference to Rome. The pagan identity of the empire would suggest to the epistle's Jewish readers the ancient pagan Babylon, where Israel was held in exile.

Survey of First Peter

The author addresses this epistle to "refugees" in a world that is growing increasingly hostile to Christians. These believers are beginning to suffer because of their stand for Christ, and the author uses this letter to give them counsel and comfort by stressing the reality of their living hope in the Lord. By standing firm in the grace of God (5:12) they will be able to endure their "painful test" (4:12), knowing that there is a divine purpose behind their pain. This letter logically proceeds through the themes of the salvation of the believer (1:1 through 2:12); the submission of the believer (2:13 through 3:12); and the suffering of the believer (3:13 through 5:14).

The Salvation of the Believer (1:1 through 2:12): Addressing his letter to believers in several Roman provinces, the author briefly describes the saving work of the triune Godhead in his salutation (1:1–2). He then extols God for the riches of this salvation by looking in three temporal directions (1:3–12). First, the author anticipates the future realization of the Christian's manifold inheritance (1:3–5). Second, he looks at the present joy that this living hope produces in spite of various trials (1:6–9). Third, he reflects upon the prophets of the past who predicted the gospel of God's grace in Christ (1:1–12).

The proper response to this salvation is the pursuit of sanctification or holiness (1:13 through 2:10). This involves a purifying departure from conformity with the world to godliness in behavior and love. With this in mind, the author exhorts his readers to always thirst "for the pure spiritual milk, so that by drinking it [they] may grow" (2:2) by applying "the living and eternal word of God" (1:23).

The Submission of the Believer (2:13 through 3:12): The author turns to the believer's relationships in the world and appeals for an attitude of submission as the Christlike way to harmony and true freedom. Submission for the Lord's sake to those in governmental (2:13–17) and social (2:18–20) authority will foster a good testimony to outsiders. Before moving on to submission in marital relationships (3:1–7), the author again picks up the theme of Christian suffering (mentioned in 1:6–7 and 2:12, 18–20) and uses Christ as the supreme model: He suffered sinlessly, silently, and as a substitute for the salvation of others (2:21–25; cf. Isa. 52:13 through 53:12). The author summarizes his appeal for Christlike submission and humility in 3:8–11.

The Suffering of the Believer (3:13 through 5:14): Anticipating that growing opposition to Christianity will require a number of his readers to defend their faith and conduct, the author encourages them to be ready to do so with gentleness and respect (3:13–16). Three times he tells them that if they must suffer, it should be for righteousness' sake and not as a result of sinful behavior (3:17; see 2:20; 4:15–16).

As believers in Christ, the readers are no longer to pursue the lusts of the flesh as they did formerly, but rather the will of God (4:1–6). In view of the hardships that they may suffer, the author exhorts them to be strong in their mutual love and to exercise their spiritual gifts in the power of God so that they will be built up (4:7–11). They should not be surprised when they are slandered and reviled for their faith because the sovereign God has a purpose in all things, and the time of judgment will come when his name and all who trust in him will be vindicated (4:12–19). They must therefore "by their good actions trust themselves completely to their Creator" (4:19).

In a special word to the elders of the churches in these Roman provinces, the author urges them to be diligent but gentle shepherds over the flocks that have been divinely placed under their care (5:1–4). The readers as a whole are told to clothe themselves with humility toward one another and toward God who will exalt them at the proper time (5:5–7). They are to resist the adversary in the sure knowledge that their calling to God's eternal glory in Christ will be realized (5:8–11). The author ends his epistle by stating his theme ("the true grace of God") and conveying greetings and a benediction (5:12–14).

OUTLINE OF FIRST PETER

Salvation of the believer   1:1–2:12   Suffering of the believer   3:13–5:14
Submission of the believer   2:13–3:12

FOCUS	SALVATION OF THE BELIEVER		SUBMISSION OF THE BELIEVER	SUFFERING OF THE BELIEVER			
REFERENCE	1.1———————1.13———————2.13—————————————3.13————————3.18—————4.7——————————5.1————5.14						
DIVISION	SALVATION OF THE BELIEVER	SANCTIFICA-TION OF THE BELIEVER	GOVERNMENT, BUSINESS, MARRIAGE, AND ALL OF LIFE	CONDUCT IN SUFFERING	CHRIST'S EXAMPLE OF SUFFERING	COMMANDS IN SUFFERING	MINISTER IN SUFFERING
TOPIC	BELIEF OF CHRISTIANS		BEHAVIOR OF CHRISTIANS	BUFFETING OF CHRISTIANS			
	HOLINESS		HARMONY	HUMILITY			
SETTING	EITHER ROME OR BABYLON						

I PETER

THE SECOND LETTER FROM
PETER

The Book of Second Peter

First Peter deals with problems from the outside; Second Peter deals with problems from the inside. The author writes to warn the believers about the false teachers who are peddling damaging doctrine. He begins by urging them to keep close watch on their personal lives. The Christian life demands diligence in pursuing moral excellence, knowledge, self-control, perseverance, godliness, brotherly kindness, and selfless love. By contrast, the false teachers are sensual, arrogant, greedy, and covetous. They scoff at the thought of future judgment and live their lives as if the present would be the pattern for the future. The author reminds them that although God may be long-suffering in sending judgment, ultimately it will come. In view of that fact, believers should live lives of godliness, blamelessness, and steadfastness.

The Author of Second Peter

No other book in the New Testament poses as many problems of authenticity as does Second Peter. Unlike First Peter, this letter has very weak external testimony, and its genuineness is hurt by internal difficulties as well. Because of these obstacles, many scholars reject the Petrine authorship of this epistle, even though a statement of authorship in 1:1 is very clear: "Simon Peter, a servant and apostle of Jesus Christ."

There are no undisputed second-century quotations from Second Peter, but in the third century it is quoted in the writings of several church fathers, notably Origen and Clement of Alexandria. Third-century writers were generally aware of Second Peter and respected its contents, but it was still cataloged as a disputed book. The fourth century saw the official acknowledgment of the authority of Second Peter in spite of some lingering doubts.

Second Peter bears testimony to its apostolic origin. It claims to be by "Simon Peter" (1:1), and 3:1 says "My dear friends, this is now the second letter." The writer refers to the Lord's prediction about the apostle's death in 1:14 (cf. John 21:18–19) and says he was an

355

eyewitness of the Transfiguration (1:16–18). As an apostle (1:1), he places himself on an equal level with Paul (3:15).

A number of troublesome areas challenge the traditional position: differences between the style and vocabulary of First and Second Peter, similarity to Jude, and reference to the collection of Paul's letters (3:15–16).

Second Peter was written by the apostle Peter, by a disciple of his, or by a believer who lived later and wanted the material attached to Peter's name. In any case, the book is now accepted as Scripture by all authorities and is useful for correction and teaching.

The Time of Second Peter

This epistle was written in response to the spread of heretical teachings which were all the more insidious because they emerged from within the churches. These false teachers perverted the doctrine of justification and promoted a rebellious and immoral way of life. It was probably written during the period A.D. 100 to A.D. 125.

Survey of Second Peter

This epistle focuses on internal opposition caused by false teachers whose "destructive, untrue doctrines" (2:1) can seduce believers into error and immorality. Second Peter stresses the need for growth in the grace and knowledge of Christ. The best antidote for error is a mature understanding of the truth. Second Peter divides into three parts: cultivation of Christian character (ch. 1); condemnation of false teachers (ch. 2): and confidence in Christ's return (ch. 3).

Cultivation of Christian Character (ch. 1): The salutation (1:1–2) is an introduction to the major theme of chapter 1, that is, the true knowledge of Jesus Christ. The readers are reminded of the "great and precious gifts" that are theirs because of their calling to faith in Christ (1:3–4). They have been called away from the corruption of the world to conformity with Christ, and the author urges them to progress by forging a chain of eight Christian virtues from faith to love (1:5–7). If a believer does not transform profession into practice, he becomes spiritually useless, perverting the purpose for which he was called (1:8–11).

As an eyewitness of the life of Christ (he illustrates this with a portrait of the Transfiguration in 1:16–18), the author affirms the authority and reliability of the prophetic word. The clearest biblical description of the divine-human process of inspiration is found in 1:21: "but men were under the control of the Holy Spirit as they spoke the message that came from God."

Condemnation of False Teachers (ch. 2): The discussion of true prophecy leads to an extended denunciation of false prophecy in the churches. These false teachers were especially dangerous because they arose within the church and undermined the confidence of believers (2:1–3). The extended description of the characteristics of these false teachers (2:10–22) exposes the futility and corruption of their strategies. Their teachings and life-styles reek of arrogance and selfishness, but their crafty words are capable of enticing immature believers.

Confidence in Christ's Return (ch. 3): Again it is stated that this letter is designed to stir up the minds of the readers "by reminding you" (3:1; cf. 1:13). This very timely chapter is designed to remind them of the certain truth of the imminent *Parousia* (this Greek word, used in 3:4, 12, refers to the second coming or advent of Christ) and to refute those mockers who will deny this doctrine in the last days. These scoffers will claim that God does not powerfully intervene in world affairs, but attention is called to two past and one future divinely induced catastrophic events: the Creation, the Flood, and the dissolution of the present heavens and earth (3:1–7). It may appear that the promise of Christ's return will not be fulfilled, but this is untrue for two reasons: God's perspective on the passing of time is quite unlike that of men, and the apparent delay in the *Parousia* is due to his patience in waiting for more individuals to come to a knowledge of Christ (3:8–9). Nevertheless, the day of consummation will come, and all the matter of this universe will evidently be transformed into energy from which God will fashion a new cosmos (3:10–13).

In light of this coming Day of the Lord, the readers are exhorted to live lives of holiness, steadfastness, and growth (3:14–18). Mention is made of the letters of "our dear brother Paul" and significantly places them on a level with the Old Testament Scriptures (3:15–16). After a final warning about the danger of false teachers, the epistle closes with an appeal to growth, and a doxology.

OUTLINE OF SECOND PETER

Cultivation of Christian character	1:1–21	teachers	2:1–22
Condemnation of false		Confidence in Christ's return	3:1–18

FOCUS	CULTIVATION OF CHRISTIAN CHARACTER		CONDEMNATION OF FALSE TEACHERS			CONFIDENCE IN CHRIST'S RETURN	
REFERENCE	1.1————1.15		2.1————2.4————2.10			3.1————3.8————3.18	
DIVISION	GROWTH IN CHRIST	GROUNDS OF BELIEF	DANGER	DESTRUCTION	DESCRIPTION	MOCKERY IN THE LAST DAYS	DAY OF THE LORD
TOPIC	TRUE PROPHECY		FALSE PROPHETS			PROPHECY: DAY OF THE LORD	
	HOLINESS		HERESY			HOPE	
SETTING	PROBABLY ROME						

2 PETER

THE FIRST LETTER OF

JOHN

The Book of First John

While it does not conform to the classical structure of the epistle exemplified by the epistles of Paul, there is no question that the present work is a letter written to a particular unnamed community for a particular occasion. It is not a narrative about Jesus' life and teachings (a gospel), but presumes that those addressed are already very familiar with that basic teaching. It is obviously written to a community of people who were already believers, but who are in need of the reminders about key beliefs of Christian faith and its warnings about others, presumably former members of the community, who have meanwhile accepted different interpretations of the importance and meaning of Jesus. The author writes to build up the community with whom he has had a close relationship, and to prevent divisions which would occur if the members were to adopt the positions of those who had already fallen away. Most scholars see a real relationship between this epistle and the Gospel of John, at least to the extent that both the author and the community members knew that version of the gospel in some form.

The Author of First John

Technically, the work is anonymous since the text itself does not say who wrote it. The author, probably "the Elder" of Second and Third John, is clearly someone who feels responsible for the community to whom he is writing. He expects to be heeded, though his tone toward his readers is quite affectionate, addressing them variously as "my children" or "my brethren." While modern scholarship distinguishes between the author of the Gospel of John and the author of these epistles, the literary connection between all these works was noted very early and probably resulted in the naming of these epistles "According to" John, which in turn may have been an early argument for including them in the canon, or official list of Scripture. Still, it is more plausible to maintain that the author of the Johannine epistles is not the evangelist, nor the "beloved disciple" himself. He is a "presbyter," an elder of the community, and asserts that his interpretation of the gospel is the authentic one.

The Time of First John

Since the work is undated, one must be satisfied with conjecture regarding the exact time of its composition. There is wide agreement that the Gospel according to John was written in the nineties of the first century. Since this epistle, as well as Second and Third John appear to know of the gospel, it is reasonable to date the work during the last years of the first century, or early in the second century.

Survey of First John

The author writes his first epistle at a time when apostolic doctrine is being challenged by a proliferation of false teachings. Like Second Peter and Jude, First John has a negative and a positive thrust: it refutes erroneous doctrine and encourages its readership to walk in the knowledge of the truth. John lists the criteria and characteristics of fellowship with God and shows that those who abide in Christ can have confidence and assurance before him. This simply written but profound work develops the meaning of fellowship in the basis of fellowship (1:1 through 2:27) and the behavior of fellowship (2:28 through 5:21).

The Basis of Fellowship (1:1 through 2:27): The prologue (1:1–4) recalls the beginning of apostolic contact with Christ. It relates the author's desire to transmit this apostolic witness to his readers so that they may share the same fellowship with Jesus Christ, the personification of life. This proclamation is followed by a description of the conditions of fellowship (1:5 through 2:14).

The readers' sins have been forgiven and they enjoy fellowship with God. As a result, they know "him who has existed from the beginning" and are strengthened to overcome the temptations of the Evil One (2:12–14). The cautions to fellowship are both practical (the lusts of the corrupt world system which opposes God, 2:15–17) and doctrinal (the teachings of those who differentiate between Jesus and the Christ, 2:18–23). In contrast to these antichrists, the readers have the knowledge of the truth and an anointing from the Holy One. Therefore, it would be foolish for them to turn away from the teachings of the apostles to the innovations of the antichrists. The antidote to these heretical teachings is abiding in the apostolic truths that they "heard from the beginning," which are authenticated by the anointing they have received (2:24–27).

The Behavior of Fellowship (2:28 through 5:21): The basic theme of First John is summarized in 2:28—assurance through abiding in Christ. The next verse introduces the motif of regeneration, and 2:29 through 3:10 argues that regeneration is manifested in the practice of righteousness. Because we are children of God through faith in Christ, we have a firm hope of being fully conformed to him when he appears (3:1–3). Our present likeness to Christ places us in a position of incompatibility with sin, because sin is contrary to the person and work of Christ (3:4–6). The concept in 3:6 does not contradict 1:8 because it is saying that the abider, insofar as he abides, does not sin. When the believer sins, he does not reflect the regenerate new man but Satan, the original sinner (3:7–10).

Regeneration is shown in righteousness (2:29 through 3:10), and righteousness is manifested in love (3:10–23). The author uses the example of Cain to illustrate what love is not: hatred is murdering in spirit, and it arises from the worldly sphere of death. The author then uses the example of Christ to illustrate what love is: love is practiced in self-sacrifice, not mere profession. This practical expression of love results in assurance before God and answered prayers because the believer is walking in obedience to God's commands to believe in Christ and love one another.

In 3:24 the author introduces two important motifs, which are developed in 4:1–16: the indwelling God, and the Spirit as a mark of this indwelling. The Spirit of God confesses the incarnate Christ and confirms apostolic doctrine (4:1–6). The mutual abiding of the believer in

God and God in the believer is manifested in love for others, and this love produces a divine and human fellowship that testifies to and reflects the reality of the Incarnation (4:7–16). It also anticipates the perfect fellowship to come and creates a readiness to face the One from whom all love is derived (4:17–19).

The author joins the concepts he has presented into a circular chain of six links that begins with love for the brethren (4:20 through 5:17): (1) Love for believers is the inseparable product of love for God (4:20 through 5:1). (2) Love for God arises out of obedience to his commandments (5:2–3). (3) Obedience to God is the result of faith in his Son (5:4–5). (4) This faith is in Jesus, who was the Christ not only at his baptism (the water), but also at his death (the blood; 5:6–8). (5) The divine witness to the person of Christ is worthy of complete belief (5:9–13). (6) This belief produces confident access to God in prayer (5:14–17). Since intercessory prayer is a manifestation of love for others, the chain has come full circle.

The epilogue (5:18–21) summarizes the conclusions of the epistle in a series of three certainties: (1) Sin is a threat to fellowship, and it should be regarded as foreign to the believer's position in Christ (cf. Rom. 6). (2) The believer stands with God against the satanic world system. (3) The Incarnation produces true knowledge and communion with Christ. Since he is the true God and eternal life, the one who knows him should avoid the lure of any substitute.

OUTLINE OF FIRST JOHN

The basis of fellowship   1:1–2:27   The behavior of fellowship   2:28–5:21

FOCUS	BASIS OF FELLOWSHIP		BEHAVIOR OF FELLOWSHIP	
REFERENCE	1.1————————2.15————		——2.28————————5.4————————5.21	
DIVISION	CONDITIONS FOR FELLOWSHIP	CAUTIONS TO FELLOWSHIP	CHARACTERISTICS OF FELLOWSHIP	CONSEQUENCES OF FELLOWSHIP
TOPIC	MEANING OF FELLOWSHIP		MANIFESTATIONS OF FELLOWSHIP	
	ABIDING IN GOD'S LIGHT		ABIDING IN GOD'S LOVE	
SETTING	PROBABLY EPHESUS			

1 JOHN

THE SECOND LETTER OF
JOHN

The Book of Second John

This work conforms more closely to the classical form of an epistle. The author is "the Elder" and the addressee is "the dear Lady." The Elder is presumably the same as the author of First John (see "The Author of First John"). The "dear Lady" is probably the personification of the community to whom he is writing. The epistle is extremely brief, probably a single piece of papyrus. Its purpose was to warn the community against some teachers who were spreading false doctrines about who Jesus was, and about the proper way to live the Christian life.

The Author of Second John

Because of the similarity of the contents and circumstances of Second and Third John, the authorship of both will be considered here. These letters were not widely circulated at the beginning because of their brevity and their specific address to a small number of people. This limited circulation, combined with the fact that they have few distinctive ideas to add that are not found in First John, meant that they were seldom quoted in the patristic writings of the early church. Their place in the canon of New Testament books was disputed for a time, but it is significant that there was no question in the minds of the early church fathers that these two epistles were written by the apostle John. The second-century writers Irenaeus and Clement of Alexandria entertained no other view. Only as the details of their origin were forgotten did doubts arise, but the positive evidence in their favor eventually won for them the official recognition of the whole church.

It is obvious that the recipients of Second and Third John well knew the author's identity, although he did not use his name. Instead, he designated himself in the first verse of both letters as "the Elder."

The similarity of style, vocabulary, structure, and mood between Second and Third John makes it clear that these letters were written by the same author.

The Time of Second John

For comments on the time of Second John, turn to the discussion under "The Time of First John."

Survey of Second John

This brief letter has much in common with First John, including a warning about the danger of false teachers who deny the incarnation of Jesus Christ. The Elder encourages the readers to continue walking in love but exhorts them to be discerning in their expression of love. Second John breaks with two parts: primacy of love (vv. 1–6) and warning against false doctrine (vv. 7–13).

Primacy of Love (vv. 1–6): The salutation (vv. 1–3) centers on the concept of abiding in the truth. The recipients are loved for their adherence to the truth by "all who know the truth." The Elder commends his readers on their walk in truth in obedience to God's commandment (v. 4), and reminds them that this commandment entails the practice of love for one another (vv. 5–6). The divine command is given in verse 5 and the human response follows in verse 6.

Warning Against False Doctrine (vv. 7–13): Moving from the basic test of Christian behavior (love for the brethren) to the basic test of Christian belief (the person of Christ), the Elder admonishes the readers to beware of deceivers "who do not acknowledge that Jesus Christ came as a human being" (vv. 7–9). In no uncertain terms, the Elder enjoins the readers to deny even the slightest assistance or encouragement to itinerant teachers who promote an erroneous view of Christ (and hence of salvation; vv. 10–11).

This letter closes with the Elder's explanation of its brevity: he anticipates a future visit during which he will be able to "talk with you personally" with his readers (v. 12). The meaning of the greeting in verse 13 relates to the interpretation of verse 1.

OUTLINE OF SECOND JOHN

Primacy of love	1–6
Warning against false doctrine	7–13

FOCUS	PRIMACY OF LOVE			WARNING AGAINST FALSE DOCTRINE		
REFERENCE	1————————4————————5————————			7————————10————————11————————13		
DIVISION	SALUTATION	WALK IN TRUTH	WALK IN LOVE	DOCTRINE OF FALSE TEACHERS	AVOID THE FALSE TEACHERS	BENEDICTION
TOPIC	WALK IN COMMANDMENTS			WATCH FOR COUNTERFEITS		
	PRACTICE THE TRUTH			PROTECT THE TRUTH		
SETTING	PROBABLY EPHESUS					

2 JOHN

THE THIRD LETTER OF

JOHN

The Book of Third John

First John discusses fellowship with God; Second John forbids fellowship with false teachers; and Third John encourages fellowship with Christian brothers. This third epistle from John the Elder is very similar to Second John in style, but has a particular occasion for its composition. It is addressed to a certain Gaius, not simply to encourage him to continue to live faithfully in the community, but also to warn him of a certain Diotrephes, who pays no attention to the Elder, and in addition has caused problems for other Christian missionaries. Following his expression of love for Gaius, the Elder assures him of his prayers for his health and voices his joy over Gaius' persistent walk in truth and for the manner in which he shows hospitality and support for missionaries who have come to his church.

The Author of Third John

For a discussion of the author of Third John, see "The Author of First John."

The Time of Third John

For a discussion of the time of Third John, see "The Time of First John."

Survey of Third John

Third John is the shortest book in the Bible, but it is very personal and vivid. It offers a stark contrast between two men who respond in opposite ways to the itinerant teachers who have been sent out by the apostle. The faithful Gaius responds with generosity and hospitality, but the faithless Diotrephes responds with arrogance and opposition. Thus, the Elder writes this letter to commend Gaius for walking in the truth (vv. 1–8) and to condemn Diotrephes for walking in error (vv. 9–14).

Introduction and Commendation of Gaius (vv. 1–8): The Elder writes to a "dear friend" whose godly behavior has given the Elder great joy (vv. 1–4). The "Christian brothers," upon returning to the Elder, have informed him of Gaius' faithfulness, love, and generosity in their behalf. The Elder acknowledges these actions and urges Gaius to continue supporting traveling teachers and missionaries who go out "in the service of Christ" (vv. 5–8).

Diotrephes Condemned and Demetrius Commended (vv. 9–15): The epistle suddenly shifts to a negative note as the Elder describes a man whose actions are diametrically opposed to those of Gaius (vv. 9–11). Diotrephes boldly rejects the Elder's authority and refuses to receive the itinerant teachers sent out by the Elder. Diotrephes evidently has been orthodox in his doctrine, but his evil actions indicate a blindness to God in his practice.

By contrast, the Elder gives his full recommendation to Demetrius, another emissary and probably the bearer of this letter to Gaius (v. 12). He expresses his hope of a personal visit in the closing remarks (vv. 13–14), as he does in Second John.

OUTLINE OF THIRD JOHN

Introduction and commendation of Gaius	1–8	demned and Demetrius commended	9–15
Diotrephes con-			

FOCUS	INTRODUCTION AND COMMENDATION OF GAIUS			DIOTREPHES CONDEMNED AND DEMETRIUS COMMENDED		
REFERENCE	1————————2————————5————————9————————12————————13————————15					
DIVISION	SALUTATION	GODLINESS OF GAIUS	GENEROSITY OF GAIUS	PRIDE OF DIOTREPHES	PRAISE FOR DEMETRIUS	BENEDICTION
TOPIC	SERVANTHOOD			SELFISHNESS		
	DUTY OF HOSPITALITY			DANGER OF HAUGHTINESS		
SETTING	PROBABLY EPHESUS					

3 JOHN

THE LETTER FROM

JUDE

The Book of Jude

Fight! Contend! Do battle! When apostasy arises, when false teachers emerge, when the truth of God is attacked, it is time to fight for the faith. Only believers who are spiritually "in shape" can answer the summons. At the beginning of his letter Jude focuses on the believers' common salvation, but then feels compelled to challenge them to contend for the faith. The danger is real. False teachers have slipped into the church, turning God's grace into unbounded license to do as they please. Jude reminds such men of God's past dealings with unbelieving Israel, disobedient angels, and wicked Sodom and Gomorrah. In the face of such danger Christians should not be caught off guard. The challenge is great, but so is the God who is able to keep them from stumbling.

The Greek title *Iouda*, "Of Jude," comes from the name *Ioudas* which appears in verse 1. This name, which can be translated Jude or Judas, was popular in the first century because of Judas Maccabee (died 160 B.C.), a leader of the Jewish resistance against Syria during the Maccabean revolt.

The Author of Jude

In spite of its limited subject matter and size, Jude was accepted as authentic and quoted by early church fathers. There may be some older allusions, but undisputed references to this epistle appear in the last quarter of the second century. It was included in the Muratorian Canon (c. A.D. 170) and accepted as part of Scripture by early leaders, such as Tertullian and Origen. Nevertheless, doubts arose concerning the place of Jude in the canon because of its use of the apocryphal Book of Enoch. It was a disputed book in some parts of the church, but it eventually won universal recognition.

The author identifies himself as "servant of Jesus Christ, and brother of James" (v. 1). This designation, combined with the reference in verse 17 to the apostles, makes it unlikely that this is the apostle Jude, called "Judas son of James" in Luke 6:16 and in Acts 1:13. This leaves the traditional view that Jude was one of the Lord's brothers, called Judas in Matthew 13:55 and Mark 6:3 (see "The Author of James"). His older brother James (note his position on the two lists) was the famous leader of the Jerusalem church (Acts 15:13–21) and author of the epistle that bears his name. Like his brothers, Jude did not believe in Jesus before the Resurrection (John 7:1–9; Acts 1:14). An increasing number of scholars are content to call Jude an anonymous writing.

The Time of Jude

Jude's general address does not mark out any particular circle of readers, and there are no geographical restrictions. Nevertheless, he probably had in mind a specific region that was being troubled by false teachers. There is not enough information in the epistle to settle the question of whether his readers were predominately Jewish or Gentile Christians (there is probably a mixture of both). In any case, the progress of the faith in their region was threatened by a number of apostates who rejected Christ in practice and principle. These proud libertines were especially dangerous because of their deceptive flattery (v. 16) and infiltration of Christian meetings (v. 12). They perverted the grace of God (v. 4) and caused divisions in the church (v. 19).

Jude's description of these heretics is reminiscent of that found in Second Peter and leads to the issue of the relationship between the two epistles. The strong similarity between Second Peter 2:1 through 3:4 and Jude 4–18 can hardly be coincidental, but the equally obvious differences rule out the possibility that one is a mere copy of the other. It is also doubtful that both authors independently drew from an unknown third source, so the two remaining options are that Peter used Jude or Jude used Peter.

Because of the silence of the New Testament and tradition concerning Jude's later years, we cannot know where this epistle was written. Nor is there any way to be certain of its date.

Survey of Jude

A surprisingly large number of the Pauline and non-Pauline epistles confront the problem of false teachers, and almost all of them allude to it. But Jude goes beyond all other New Testament epistles in its relentless and passionate denunciation of the apostate teachers who have "slipped in unnoticed." With the exception of its salutation (vv. 1–2) and doxology (vv. 24–25), the entire epistle revolves around this alarming problem. This urgent letter has four major sections: purpose of Jude (vv. 1–4); description of false teachers (vv. 5–16); defense against false teachers (vv. 17–23); and doxology of Jude (vv. 24–25).

Purpose of Jude (vv. 1–4): Jude addresses his letter to believers and wishes for them the threefold blessing of mercy, peace, and love (vv. 1–2). Grim news about the encroachment of false teachers in the churches has impelled Jude to put aside his commentary on salvation to write this timely word of rebuke and warning (vv. 3–4). In view of apostates who "distort the message about the grace of our God in order to excuse their immoral ways" and deny Christ, it is crucial that believers "fight on for the faith."

Description of False Teachers (vv. 5–16): Jude begins by illustrating their ultimate doom with three examples of divine judgment from the Pentateuch (vv. 5–7). Like unreasoning animals, these apostates are ruled by the things they revile, and they are destroyed by the things they practice (vv. 8–10). Even the chief angel Michael is more careful in his dealings with superhuman powers than are these arrogant men. He compares these men to three spiritually rebellious men from Genesis (Cain) and Numbers (Balaam and Korah) who incurred the condemnation of God (v. 11). Verses 12 and 13 succinctly summarize their character with five highly descriptive metaphors taken from nature. After affirming the judgment of God upon such ungodly men with a quote from the Book of Enoch (vv. 14–15), Jude catalogs some of their practices (v. 16).

Defense Against False Teachers (vv. 17–23): This letter has been exposing apostate teachers (vv. 8, 10, 12, 14, 16), but now Jude directly addresses his readers ("But remember, my friends" v. 17). He reminds them of the apostolic warning that such men would come (vv. 17–19) and encourages them to protect themselves against the onslaught of apostasy (vv. 20–21). The readers must become mature in their own faith so that they will be able to rescue those who are enticed or already ensnared by error (vv. 22–23).

Doxology of Jude (vv. 24–25): Jude closes with one of the greatest doxologies in the Bible. It emphasizes the power of Christ to keep those who trust in him from being overthrown by error.

OUTLINE OF JUDE

Purpose of Jude	1–4	ers	17–23
Description of false teachers	5–16	Doxology	24–25
Defense against false teach-			

FOCUS	PURPOSE	DESCRIPTION OF FALSE TEACHERS			DEFENSE AGAINST FALSE TEACHERS	DOXOLOGY
REFERENCE	1————5————8————14————17————24————25					
DIVISION	INTRODUCTION	PAST JUDGMENT	PRESENT CHARACTERISTICS	FUTURE JUDGMENT	DUTY OF BELIEVERS	CONCLUSION
TOPIC	REASON TO CONTEND				HOW TO CONTEND	
	ANATOMY OF APOSTASY				ANTIDOTE FOR APOSTASY	
SETTING	UNKNOWN					

JUDE

THE REVELATION
TO JOHN

The Book of Revelation

Jewish apocalyptic literature flourished when prophecy ceased in Israel. Yet this literature adopted many of the symbols found in the prophetic tradition. Apocalyptic literature circulated widely in Judaism from 200 B.C. to A.D. 200. It borrowed many images and concepts from Persian (Zoroastrian) sources. Apocalyptic literature deals with the final period of world history. It contains many revelations about the future. These revelations were usually given to some famous figure of the past (a patriarch or prophet), but for some reason were kept sealed until their discovery at a later time.

The title of this book in the Greek text is *Apokalypsis Joannou*. The usual translation is "The Revelation of John." It is also known as the Apocalypse, a transliteration of the word *Apokalypsis*, meaning "unveiling" or "disclosure."

The book contains a number of visions received by the seer, John. These visions concern the future, but are meant to illuminate the present experience of the author and his contemporaries.

The Author of Revelation

The Book of Revelation is one of a few books in the New Testament that supplies us with information concerning the name of the author. In chapter 1:9 the book purports to have been written at Patmos near Ephesus by a person named John. Was this John the apostle, the son of Zebedee, one of the Twelve? Early Christian tradition answers in the affirmative. Justin Martyr in his *Dialogue with Trypho* declared, "A man of our number, by name John, one of the apostles of Christ, prophesied in a revelation granted to him that those who believe in our Christ will dwell for a thousand years in Jerusalem" (cf. Rev. 20:4–6). That John the apostle wrote the Book of Revelation was also held by Irenaeus, Clement of Alexandria, Tertullian, and others.

In the third century Denis of Alexandria (A.D. 265) questioned whether the apostle John wrote the Book of Revelation. He made a careful analysis of the language, style, and thought of the gospel, the First Letter of John, and the Book of Revelation. He concluded that only the gospel and the epistle were written by the apostle. The school of Antioch refused to accept Revelation as apostolic and called into question its canonicity.

Today, scholars are agreed that there existed in the early church a Johannine community. This school produced the Gospel of John and the Johannine epistles. Few today would hold that Revelation came from the Johannine school. It is thus unlikely that the same author, or authors, who wrote the gospel and the epistles, also wrote Revelation.

While the presence of some words or phrases seem to bring the Gospel of John and Revelation together, it must be acknowledged that numerous details separate them. The most that can be said about the author of Revelation is that he is an unknown Christian prophet named John.

The Time of Revelation

John directed this prophetic word to seven selected churches in the Roman province of Asia (1:3–4). The messages to these churches in chapters 2 and 3 begin with Ephesus, the most prominent church, and continue in a clockwise direction until Laodicea is reached. It is likely that this book was initially carried along this circular route. While these messages had particular significance for the churches, they were also relevant for the church as a whole ("If you have ears, then, listen to what the Spirit says to the churches!").

John's effective testimony for Christ led the Roman authorities to exile him to the small, desolate island of Patmos in the Aegean Sea (1:9). This island of volcanic rock was one of several places to which the Romans banished criminals and political offenders.

Revelation was written at a time when Roman hostility to Christianity was erupting into overt persecution (1:9; 2:10, 13). Some scholars believe that it should be given an early date during the persecution of Christians under Nero after the A.D. 64 burning of Rome. The Hebrew letters for Nero Caesar *(Neron Kesar)* add up to 666, the number of the beast (13:18), and there was a legend that Nero would reappear in the East after his apparent death (cf. Rev. 13:3, 12, 14). This kind of evidence is weak, and a later date near the end of the reign of the Emperor Domitian (A.D. 81–96) is preferable. Irenaeus dates Revelation to this period, "at the end of Domitian's reign." Eusebius dates the book during the fourteenth year of Domitian. It is possible, of course, that

Revelation was written in stages or that it underwent a series of editions. It could well have spanned the time between Nero and Domitian (A.D. 54–96). Also, the churches of Asia appear to have been in existence for a number of years, long enough for some to reach a point of complacency and decline (cf. 2:4; 3:1, 15–18). The deeds of Domitian are more relevant than those of Nero to the themes of the Apocalypse. Worship of deceased emperors had been practiced for years, but Domitian was the first emperor to demand worship while he was alive. This led to a greater clash between the state and the church, especially in Asia, where the worship of Caesar was widely practiced. The persecution under Domitian was a preview of the more severe persecutions to follow. Thus, it is likely that John wrote this book in the form in which it has come to us in A.D. 95–96.

Survey of Revelation

In reading any book of the Bible it is important to remember that the meaning intended by ancient authors of the East is not always as obvious as it might be in the works of writers of our own time. The authors of Scripture did not always use the forms and kinds of speech we use today. To read and study Scripture we must determine what literary forms each author uses. We also must determine to what extent the manner of expression or the literary form used by the author leads to a correct and genuine understanding of what he intended to say.

The Book of Revelation speaks of mystery. Who can explain a mystery? Human language is certainly inadequate for the task. The best we can do is capture some of the depth and complexity of mystery by the use of symbols and vivid, imaginative language. God's plan of salvation is a mystery. So, too, is the existence of suffering and pain, persecution and martyrdom, sin, and death. How all these are related to God's plan of salvation is also a mystery.

Only God can unravel these mysteries, because there is something transcendent in them. To do this, God communicates with man. In the case of the Book of Revelation, God grants his servant, John, a vision to help him understand the mystery of God's plan of salvation. John writes down the vision by using symbolic language. The intention of the author is to offer encouragement and strength to the Christian communities who face peril and threat of extinction at the hands of powerful forces. John wants his readers to come to terms with powerlessness, suffering, and death. Jesus Christ is their model. He has shown that suffering, pain, sin, and death can be overcome. They are not the final word. Christians must make choices in the world. They, too, can live in the world as Jesus did, and transform it as Jesus did. They will do this by being completely dedicated to God's will and by living courageously, full of faith and hope, in the midst of persecution and trial. The Book of Revelation can be divided as follows: prologue and opening vision (1:1–20); letters to the seven churches (2:1 through 3:22); visions (4:1 through 22:5); and epilogue (22:6–21).

Prologue and Opening Vision (1:1–20): The Revelation was received by Christ from the Father and communicated by an angel to John. This is the only biblical book that specifically promises happiness to those who read it (1:3), but it also warns those who add to or detract from it (22:18–19). The salutation and closing benediction show that it was probably written as an epistle to seven Asian churches.

A rich theological portrait of the triune God (1:4–8) is followed by an overwhelming theophany (visible manifestation of God) in 1:9–20. The omnipotent and omniscient Christ, who will subjugate all things under his authority, is the central figure in this book.

Letters to the Seven Churches (2:1 through 3:22): Jesus Christ has something to say to the churches at Ephesus, Smyrna, Pergamum, Thyatira, Sardis, Philadelphia, and Laodicea. Jesus knows what is taking place in each church. He mentions their good points as well as their bad ones. There is more danger from forces inside these churches than from outside. Each church is to keep its eye on the promised, glorious future.

Visions (4:1 through 22:5): John is taken up to heaven, where he is given a vision of divine majesty. In it the Father ("a throne with some-one sitting on it") and the Son (the Lion/Lamb) are worshiped by the twenty-four elders, the four living creatures, and the angelic host, because of who they are and what they have done (creation and redemption; chs. 4 and 5).

Three cycles of seven judgments in chapters 6 through 16 consist of seven seals, seven trumpets, and seven bowls. There is a prophetic insert between the sixth and seventh seal judgments and between the sixth and seventh trumpet judgments. There is also an extended insert between the trumpet and bowl judgments. Because of the similarity of the seventh judgment in each series, it is possible that the three sets of judgments take place concurrently or with some overlap, so that they all terminate with the return of Christ. An alternate approach views them as three consecutive series of judgments, so that the seventh seal is the seven trumpets and the seventh trumpet is the seven bowls.

The seven seals (6:1 through 8:5) include war, famine, and death that are associated with war and persecution. The prophetic insert between the sixth and seventh seals (ch. 7) describes the protective sealing of 144,000 "of Israel," 12,000 from every tribe. It also looks ahead to the multitudes from every part of the earth "who have come safely through the terrible persecution." The catastrophic events in most of the trumpet judgments are called "horrors" (8:2 through 11:19). The prophetic interlude between the sixth and seventh trumpets (10:1 through 11:14) adds more details about the nature of the persecution period and mentions a fourth set of seven judgments (the "seven thunders"), which would have extended it if they had not been withdrawn. Two unnamed witnesses minister during three-and-a-half years of the persecution (42 months or 1,260 days). At the end of their ministry they are overcome by the beast, but their resurrection and ascension confound their enemies.

Chapters 12 through 14 contain a number of miscellaneous prophecies that are inserted between the trumpet and bowl judgments to give further background on the time of persecution. In chapter 12 a woman gives birth to a male child, who is caught up to God. The woman flees into the wilderness and is pursued by a dragon who is cast down to earth. Chapter 13 gives a graphic description of the beast and his false prophet, both empowered by the dragon. The first beast is given political, economic, and religious authority. Because of his power and the lying miracles performed by the second beast, he is worshiped as the ruler of the earth. Chapter 14 contains a series of visions, including the 144,000 at the end of the persecution, the fate of those who follow the beast, and the outpouring of the wrath of God.

The seven bowl judgments of chapter 16 are prefaced by a heavenly vision of the power, holiness, and glory of God in chapter 15. Chapters 17 and 18 anticipate the final downfall of Babylon, the great prostitute sitting upon a scarlet-colored beast.

The marriage banquet of the Lamb is ready; the King of kings and Lord of lords leads the armies of heaven into battle against the beast and his false prophet. The beast and false prophet are cast into a lake of fire (ch. 19).

In chapter 20 the dragon—Satan—is bound for a thousand years. He is cast into a bottomless pit. During this thousand-year period Christ reigns over the earth with his resurrected saints, but by the end of this millennium, many have been born who refuse to submit their hearts to Christ. At the end of the thousand years, Satan is released and a final battle ensues. This is followed by the judgment at the great white throne.

A new universe is created, this time unspoiled by sin, death, pain, or sorrow. The New Jerusalem, described in 21:9 through 22:5, is shaped like a gigantic cube, 1,500 miles in length, width, and height (the Most Holy Place in the Old Testament sacred Tent and the Temple was also a perfect cube). Its multicolored stones will reflect the glory of God, and it will continually be filled with light. But the greatest thing of all is that believers will be in the presence of God and "they will see his face."

Epilogue (22:6–21): The Revelation concludes with an epilogue (22:6–21), which reassures the readers that Christ is coming soon (22:7, 12, 20) and invites all who wish to "accept the water of life as a gift" (22:17).

OUTLINE OF REVELATION

Prologue and opening vi-sion	1:1–20	churches	2:1–3:22
Letters to the seven		Visions	4:1–22:5
		Epilogue	22:6–21

FOCUS	PROLOGUE AND OPENING VISION	LETTERS	VISIONS					EPILOGUE
REFERENCE	1.1——————2.1——————4.1————6.1————19.7————20.1————22.6—22.21							
DIVISION	THE LORD JESUS CHRIST	SEVEN CHURCHES	THE JUDGE	TRIBULATION	SECOND COMING	MILLENNIUM	ETERNAL STATE
TOPIC	VISION OF CHRIST		VISION OF CONSUMMATION					
SETTING	WRITTEN ON THE ISLAND OF PATMOS							

REVELATION

PART IV

ADDITIONAL
STUDY
HELPS

JEWISH CALENDAR, FEASTS

The Jewish Calendar

The Jews used two kinds of calendars:

Civil Calendar—official calendar of kings, childbirth, and contracts.

Sacred Calendar—from which festivals were computed.

NAMES OF MONTHS	CORRESPONDS WITH	NO. OF DAYS	MONTH OF CIVIL YEAR	MONTH OF SACRED YEAR	
TISHRI	Sept.–Oct.	30 days	1st	7th	The Jewish day was from sunset to sunset, in 8 equal parts:
HESHVAN	Oct.–Nov.	29 or 30	2nd	8th	
CHISLEV	Nov.–Dec.	29 or 30	3rd	9th	FIRST WATCH........ SUNSET TO 9 P.M.
TEBETH	Dec.–Jan.	29	4th	10th	SECOND WATCH ...... 9 P.M. TO MIDNIGHT
SHEBAT	Jan.–Feb.	30	5th	11th	THIRD WATCH .... MIDNIGHT TO 3 A.M.
ADAR	Feb.–Mar.	29 or 30	6th	12th	FOURTH WATCH ..... 3 A.M. TO SUNRISE
NISAN	Mar.–Apr.	30	7th	1st	
IYAR	Apr.–May	29	8th	2nd	
SIVAN	May–June	30	9th	3rd	FIRST WATCH........ SUNRISE TO 9 A.M.
TAMMUZ	June–July	29	10th	4th	SECOND WATCH ..... 9 A.M. TO NOON
AB	July–Aug.	30	11th	5th	THIRD WATCH....... NOON TO 3 P.M.
*ELUL	Aug.–Sept.	29	12th	6th	FOURTH WATCH ..... 3 P.M. TO SUNSET

* Hebrew months were alternately 30 and 29 days long. Their year, shorter than ours, had 354 days. Therefore, about every 3 years (7 times in 19 years) an extra 29-day-month, VEADAR, was added between ADAR and NISAN.

Jewish Feasts

Feast of	Month on Jewish Calendar	Day	Corresponding Month	References
*Passover (Unleavened Bread)	Nisan	14–21	Mar.–Apr.	Ex. 12:43—13:10; Matt. 26:17–20
*Pentecost (Firstfruits or Weeks)	Sivan	6 (50 days after Passover)	May–June	Deut. 16:9–12; Acts 2:1
Trumpets, *Rosh Hashanah*	Tishri	1, 2	Sept.–Oct.	Num. 29:1-6
Day of Atonement, *Yom Kippur*	Tishri	10	Sept.–Oct.	Lev. 23:26–32; Heb. 9:7
*Tabernacles (Booths or Ingathering)	Rishri	15–22	Sept.–Oct.	Neh. 8:13–18; John 7:2
Dedication (Lights), *Hanukkah*	Chislev	25 (8 days)	Nov.–Dec.	John 10:22
Purim (Lots)	Adar	14, 15	Feb.–Mar.	Est. 9:18–32

* The three major feasts for which all males of Israel were required to travel to the Temple in Jerusalem (Ex. 23:14-19).

CHRONOLOGY OF THE BIBLE

B.C. = Before Christ
c. = circa (around)*

DATE   Time scales represented varied number of years.

DATE	
Prehistory	**THE BEGINNINGS: EVENTS IN PREHISTORY** Creation Adam and Eve in the Garden Cain and Abel Noah and the Flood The Tower of Babel
2000 B.C.	**THE ANCESTORS OF THE ISRAELITES** Abraham comes to Palestine. *c.* 1900 Isaac is born to Abraham Jacob is born to Isaac.
1800 B.C.	Jacob has twelve sons, who become the ancestors of the twelve tribes of Israel. The most prominent of these sons is Joseph, who becomes adviser to the King of Egypt. **THE ISRAELITES IN EGYPT** The descendants of Jacob are enslaved in Egypt. *c.* 1700–*c.* 1250
1600 B.C.	
1250 B.C.	Moses leads the Israelites out of Egypt. *c.* 1250 The Israelites wander in the wilderness. During this time Moses receives the Law on Mount Sinai. *c.* 1250–*c.* 1210 **THE CONQUEST AND SETTLEMENT OF CANAAN** Joshua leads the first stage of the invasion of Canaan. *c.* 1210 Israel remains a loose confederation of tribes, and leadership is exercised by heroic figures known as the Judges. **THE UNITED ISRAELITE KINGDOM**
1000 B.C.	Reign of Saul *c.* 1030–*c.* 1010 Reign of David *c.* 1010–*c.* 970 Reign of Solomon *c.* 970–931

* A circa date is only an approximation. Generally speaking, the earlier the time, the less precise is the dating. From the time of the death of Solomon in 931 B.C. to the Edict of Cyrus in 538 B.C., the dates given are fairly accurate, but even in this epoch a possible error of a year or two must be allowed for.

CHRONOLOGY OF THE BIBLE

DATE

930 B.C.

THE TWO ISRAELITE KINGDOMS

JUDAH (Southern Kingdom)   ISRAEL (Northern Kingdom)

Kings   *Kings*

Rehoboam 931–913   Jeroboam 931–910

Abijam 913–911   Nadab 910–909

900 B.C.

Asa 911–870   Baasha 909–886

     Elah 886–885

Jehoshaphat 870–848   *Prophets*   Zimri 7 days in 885

     Omri 885–874

     Elijah

     Ahab 874–853

850 B.C.

Jehoram 848–841

Ahaziah 841   Ahaziah 853–852

Queen Athaliah   Elisha   Joram 852–841

   841–835   Jehu 841–814

Joash 835–796   Jehoahaz 814–798

800 B.C.

Amaziah 796–781   Jehoash 798–783

Uzziah 781–740

     Jeroboam II 783–743

   Amos

750 B.C.

Jotham 740–736   Zechariah 6 mo. in 743

     Shallum 1 mo. in 743

Ahaz 736–716   Hosea   Menahem 743–738

   Micah   Pekahiah 738–737

     Pekah 737–732

Hezekiah 716–687   Isaiah   Hoshea 732–723

     Fall of Samaria 722

700 B.C.

THE LAST YEARS OF THE KINGDOM OF JUDAH

Manasseh 687–642

650 B.C.

Amon 642–640

     Prophets

Josiah 640–609

     Zephaniah

Joahaz 3 mo. in 609

     Nahum

Jehoiakim 609–598

Jeremiah   Habakkuk?

600 B.C.

Jehoiakin 3 mo. in 598

Zedekiah 598–587

     Ezekiel

   Fall of Jerusalem July 587 or 586

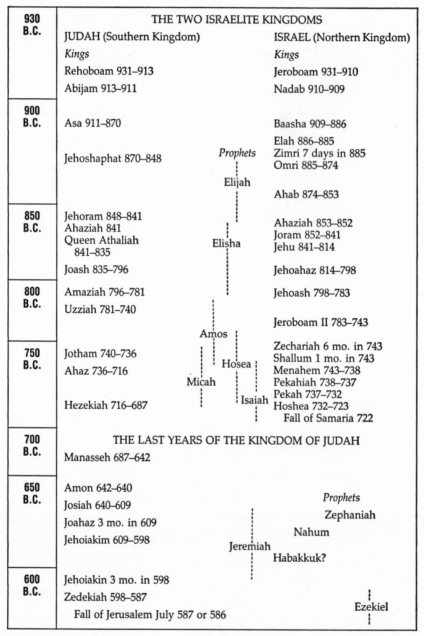

CHRONOLOGY OF THE BIBLE

DATE

580 B.C.	**THE EXILE AND THE RESTORATION**

The Jews taken into exile in Babylonia after the fall of Jerusalem

Persian rule begins. 539
Edict of Cyrus allows Jews to return. 538
Foundations of New Temple laid. 520
Restoration of the walls of Jerusalem 445–443

Prophets
Haggai   Zechariah
Obadiah
Malachi
Joel?

400 B.C.	**THE TIME BETWEEN THE TESTAMENTS**

Alexander the Great establishes Greek rule in Palestine. 333

Palestine is ruled by the Ptolemies, descendants of one of Alexander's generals who had been given the position of ruler over Egypt. 323 to 198

200 B.C.	Palestine is ruled by the Seleucids, descendants of one of Alexander's generals who had acquired the rule of Syria. 198 to 166

Jewish revolt under Judas Maccabee reestablishes Jewish independence. Palestine is ruled by Judas' family and descendants, the Hasmoneans. 166 to 63

The Roman general Pompey takes Jerusalem 63 B.C. Palestine is ruled by puppet kings appointed by Rome. One of these is Herod the Great, who rules from 37 B.C. to 4 B.C.

THE TIME OF THE NEW TESTAMENT

A.D. 1	Birth of Jesus

Ministry of John the Baptist; baptism of Jesus and beginning of his public ministry

Death and resurrection of Jesus

A.D. 30	Conversion of Paul (Saul of Tarsus) *c.* A.D. 37

Ministry of Paul *c.* A.D. 41 to A.D. 65

Final imprisonment of Paul *c.* A.D. 65

HARMONY OF THE GOSPELS

Date	Event	Location	Matthew	Mark	Luke	John	Related References
	Luke's Introduction				1:1-4		Acts 1:1
	Pre-fleshly state of Christ					1:1-18	Heb. 1:1-14
	Genealogy of Jesus Christ		1:1-17		3:23-38		Ruth 4:18-22 1 Chr. 1:1-4

BIRTH, INFANCY, AND ADOLESCENCE OF JESUS AND JOHN THE BAPTIST IN 17 EVENTS

Date	Event	Location	Matthew	Mark	Luke	John	Related References
7 B.C.	(1) Announcement of Birth of John	Jerusalem (Temple)			1:5-25		Num. 6:3
7 or 6 B.C.	(2) Announcement of Birth of Jesus to the Virgin	Nazareth			1:26-38		Isa. 7:14
c. 5 B.C.	(3) Song of Elizabeth to Mary	{Hill Country of Judah			1:39-45		
	(4) Mary's Song of Praise				1:46-56		Ps. 103:17
5 B.C.	(5) Birth, Infancy, and Purpose for Future of John the Baptist	Judea			1:57-80		Mal. 3:1
	(6) Announcement of Jesus' Birth to Joseph	Nazareth	1:18-25				Isa. 9:6, 7
5-4 B.C.	(7) Birth of Jesus Christ	Bethlehem	1:24, 25		2:1-7		Isa. 7:14
	(8) Proclamation by the Angels	{Near Bethlehem			2:8-14		1 Tim. 3:16

Date	Event	Location	Matthew	Luke	O.T. References
	(9) The Visit of Homage by Shepherds	Bethlehem		2:15–20	Lev. 12:3
	(10) Jesus' Circumcision	Bethlehem		2:21	
4 B.C.	(11) First Temple Visit with Acknowledgments by Simeon and Anna	Jerusalem		2:22–38	Ex. 13:2 / Lev. 12
	(12) Visit of the Wise Men	Jerusalem & Bethlehem	2:1–12		Num. 24:17
	(13) Flight into Egypt and Massacre of Innocents	Bethlehem, Jerusalem, & Egypt	2:13–18		Jer. 31:15
	(14) From Egypt to Nazareth with Jesus	Nazareth	2:19–23	2:39	
Afterward A.D 7–8	(15) Childhood of Jesus	Nazareth		2:40, 51	
	(16) Jesus, 12 Years Old, Visits the Temple	Jerusalem		2:41–50	Deut. 16:1–8
Afterward	(17) 18-Year Account of Jesus' Adolescence and Adulthood	Nazareth		2:51, 52	1 Sam. 2:26

TRUTHS ABOUT JOHN THE BAPTIST

Date		Location	Matthew	Mark	Luke	John	O.T. References
c. A.D. 25–27	John's Ministry Begins	Judean Wilderness	3:1	1:1–4	3:1, 2	1:19–28	Mal. 3:1
	Man and Message		3:2–12	1:2–8	3:3–14		Isa. 40:3
	His Picture of Jesus		3:11, 12	1:7, 8	3:15–18	1:26, 27	Acts 2:38
	His Courage		14:4–12		3:19, 20		

385

BEGINNING OF JESUS' MINISTRY IN 12 EVENTS

Date	Event	Location	Matthew	Mark	Luke	John	Related References
c. A.D. 27	(1) Jesus Baptized	Jordan River	3:13–17	1:9–11	3:21–23	1:29–34	Ps. 2:7
	(2) Jesus Tempted	Wilderness	4:1–11	1:12, 13	4:1–13		Ps. 91:11
	(3) Calls First Disciples	Beyond Jordan				1:35–51	
	(4) The First Miracle	Cana in Galilee				2:1–11	
	(5) First Stay in Capernaum	(Capernaum is "His" city)				2:12	
A.D. 27	(6) First Cleansing of the Temple	Jerusalem				2:13–22	Ps. 69:9
	(7) Received at Jerusalem	Judea				2:23–25	
	(8) Teaches Nicodemus about Second Birth	Judea				3:1–21	Num. 21:8, 9
	(9) Co-Ministry with John	Judea				3:22–30	
A.D. 27	(10) Leaves for Galilee	Judea	4:12	1:14	4:14	4:1–4	
	(11) Samaritan Woman at Jacob's Well	Samaria				4:5–42	Josh. 24:32
	(12) Returns to Galilee			1:15	4:15	4:43–45	

THE GALILEAN MINISTRY OF JESUS IN 55 EVENTS

Date	Event	Location	Matthew	Mark	Luke	John	Related References
A.D. 27–29							
A.D. 27	(1) Healing of the Nobleman's Son	Cana				4:46–54	
	(2) Rejected at Nazareth	Nazareth			4:16–30		Isa. 61:1, 2

Date	Event	Location	Matthew	Mark	Luke	John	References
	(3) Moved to Capernaum	Capernaum	4:13–17				Isa. 9:1, 2
	(4) Four Become Fishers of Men	Sea of Galilee	4:18–22	1:16–20	5:1–11		Ps. 33:9
	(5) Demoniac Healed on the Sabbath Day	Capernaum		1:21–28	4:31–37		
c. A.D. 27	(6) Peter's Mother-in-Law Cured. Plus Others	Capernaum	8:14–17	1:29–34	4:38–41		Isa. 53:4
	(7) First Preaching Tour of Galilee	Galilee	4:23–25	1:35–39	4:42–44		
	(8) Leper Healed and Response Recorded	Galilee	8:1–4	1:40–45	5:12–16		Lev. 13:49
	(9) Paralytic Healed	Capernaum	9:1–8	2:1–12	5:17–26		Rom. 3:23
	(10) Matthew's Call and Reception Held	Capernaum	9:9–13	2:13–17	5:27–32		Hos. 6:6
	(11) Disciples Defended via a Parable	Capernaum	9:14–17	2:18–22	5:33–39		
A.D. 28	(12) Goes to Jerusalem for Second Passover; Heals Lame Man	Jerusalem				5:1–47	Ex. 20:10
	(13) Plucked Grain Precipitates Sabbath Controversy	En Route to Galilee	12:1–8	2:23–28	6:1–5		Deut. 5:14
	(14) Withered Hand Healed Causes Another Sabbath Controversy	Galilee	12:9–14	3:1–6	6:6–11		
	(15) Multitudes Healed	Sea of Galilee	12:15–21	3:7–12	6:17–19		

Date	Event	Location	Matthew	Mark	Luke	John	Related References
	(16) Twelve Apostles Selected After a Night of Prayer	Near Capernaum		3:13-19	6:12-16		
	(17) Sermon on the Mt.	Near Capernaum	5:1-7:29		6:20-49		
	(18) Centurion's Servant Healed	Capernaum	8:5-13		7:1-10		Isa. 49:12, 13
	(19) Raises Widow's Son from Dead	Nain			7:11-17		Job 19:25
	(20) Jesus Allays John's Doubts	Galilee	11:2-19		7:18-35		Mal. 3:1
	(21) Woes Upon the Privileged		11:20-30				Gen. 19:24
	(22) A Sinful Woman Anoints Jesus	Simon's House, Capernaum			7:36-50		
	(23) Another Tour of Galilee	Galilee			8:1-3		
	(24) Jesus Accused of Blasphemy	Capernaum	12:22-37	3:20-30	11:14-23		
	(25) Jesus' Answer to a Demand for a Sign	Capernaum	12:38-45		{11:24-26, 29-36		
	(26) Mother, Brothers Seek Audience	Capernaum	12:46-50	3:31-35	8:19-21		
	(27) Famous Parables of Sower, Seed, Tares, Mustard Seed, Leaven, Treasure, Pearl, Dragnet, Lamp Told	By Sea of Galilee	13:1-52	4:1-34	8:4-18		Joel 3:13

Date	Event	Location	Matthew	Mark	Luke	John	Other
	(28) Sea Made Serene	Sea of Galilee	8:23-27	4:35-41	8:22-25		
	(29) Gadarene Demoniac Healed	{ E. Shore of Galilee	8:28-34	5:1-20	8:26-39		
	(30) Jairus' Daughter Raised and Woman with Hemorrhage Healed		9:18-26	5:21-43	8:40-56		
	(31) Two Blind Men's Sight Restored		9:27-31				
A.D. 28	(32) Mute Demoniac Healed		9:32-34				
	(33) Nazareth's Second Rejection of Christ	Nazareth	13:53-58	6:1-6			
	(34) Twelve Sent Out		9:35-11:1	6:6-13	9:1-6		1 Cor. 9:14
	(35) Fearful Herod Beheads John	Galilee	14:1-12	6:14-29	9:7-9		
Spring A.D. 29	(36) Return of 12, Jesus Withdraws, 5000 Fed	{ Near Bethsaida	14:13-21	6:30-44	9:10-17	6:1-14	
	(37) Walks on the Water	Sea of Galilee	14:22-33	6:45-52		6:15-21	
	(38) Sick of Gennesaret Healed	Gennesaret	14:34-36	6:53-56			
	(39) Peak of Popularity Passes in Galilee	Capernaum				{ 6:22-71 7:1	Isa. 54:13
	(40) Traditions Attacked		15:1-20	7:1-23			Ex. 21:17
A.D. 29	(41) Aborted Retirement in Phoenicia: Syro-Phoenician Healed	Phoenicia	15:21-28	7:24-30			
	(42) Afflicted Healed	Decapolis	15:29-31	7:31-37			
	(43) 4000 Fed	Decapolis	15:32-39	8:1-9			

389

Date	Event	Location	Matthew	Mark	Luke	John	Related References
	(44) Pharisees Increase Attack	Magdala	16:1-4	8:10-13			
	(45) Disciples' Carelessness Condemned: Blind Man Healed	{Near Caesarea Philippi	16:5-12	8:14-26			Jer. 5:21
	(46) Peter Confesses Jesus Is the Christ	{Caesarea Philippi	16:13-20	8:27-30	9:18-21		
	(47) Jesus Foretells His Death		16:21-26	8:31-37	9:22-25		
	(48) Kingdom Promised	{Mountain Unnamed	16:27, 28	9:1	9:26, 27		Prov. 24:12
	(49) The Transfiguration	{Mt. of Transfiguration	17:1-13	9:2-13	9:28-36		Isa. 42:1
	(50) Epileptic Healed		17:14-21	9:14-29	9:37-42		
	(51) Again Tells of Death, Resurrection	Galilee	17:22, 23	9:30-32	9:43-45		
	(52) Taxes Paid	Capernaum	17:24-27				Ex. 30:11-15
	(53) Disciples Contend About Greatness; Jesus Defines; also Patience, Loyalty, Forgiveness	Capernaum	18:1-35	9:33-50	9:46-62		
	(54) Jesus Rejects Brothers' Advice	Galilee				7:2-9	
c. Sept. A.D. 29	(55) Galilee Departure and Samaritan Rejection		19:1		9:51-56	7:10	

390

LAST JUDEAN AND PEREAN MINISTRY OF JESUS IN 42 EVENTS

Date	Event	Place			Luke	John	OT
Oct. A.D. 29	(1) Feast of Tablernacles	Jerusalem				7:2, 11–52	
	(2) Forgiveness of Adulteress	Jerusalem				7:53–8:11	Lev. 20:10
A.D. 29	(3) Christ—the Light of the World	Jerusalem				8:12–20	
	(4) Pharisees Can't Meet the Prophecy Thus Try to Destroy the Prophet	{Jerusalem— {Temple				8:12–59	Isa. 6:9
	(5) Man Born Blind Healed; Following Consequences	Jerusalem				9:1–41	
	(6) Parable of the Good Shepherd	Jerusalem				10:1–21	
	(7) The Service of the Seventy	{Probably {Judea			10:1–24		
	(8) Lawyer Hears the Story of the Good Samaritan	Judea (?)			10:25–37		
	(9) The Hospitality of Martha and Mary	Bethany			10:38–42		
	(10) Another Lesson on Prayer	Judea (?)			11:1–13		
A.D. 29	(11) Accused of Connection with Beelzebub				11:14–36		
	(12) Judgment Against Lawyers and Pharisees				11:37–54		Mic. 6:8
	(13) Jesus Deals with Hypocrisy, Covetousness, Worry, and Alertness				12:1–59		Mic. 7:6

Date	Event	Location	Matthew	Mark	Luke	John	Related References
	(14) Repent or Perish				13:1–5		
	(15) Barren Fig Tree				13:6–9		
	(16) Crippled Woman Healed on Sabbath	Probably Perea			13:10–17		Deut. 5:12–15
	(17) Parables of Mustard Seed and Leaven				13:18–21		
Winter A.D. 29	(18) Feast of Dedication	Jerusalem				10:22–39	Ps. 82:6
	(19) Withdrawal Beyond Jordan					10:40–42	
	(20) Begins Teaching Return to Jerusalem with Special Words About Herod						
	(21) Meal with a Pharisee Ruler Occasions Healing Man with Dropsy; Parables of Ox, Best Places, and Great Supper	Perea			13:22–35		Ps. 6:8
	(22) Demands of Discipleship				14:1–24		
	(23) Parables of Lost Sheep, Coin, Son	Perea			14:25–35		1 Pet. 2:25
	(24) Parables of Unjust Steward, Rich Man and Lazarus				15:1–32		
	(25) Lessons on Service, Faith, Influence				16:1–31		
					17:1–10		

	Event	Place	Matthew	Mark	Luke	John	OT Reference
A.D. 30	(26) Resurrection of Lazarus	{Perea to Bethany				11:1-44	
	(27) Reaction to It: Withdrawal of Jesus					11:45-54	
	(28) Begins Last Journey to Jerusalem via Samaria & Galilee	{Samaria, Galilee			17:11		
	(29) Heals Ten Lepers				17:12-19		Lev. 13:45, 46
	(30) Lessons on the Coming Kingdom				17:20-37		Gen. 6-7
	(31) Parables: Persistent Widow, Pharisee and Tax Collector				18:1-14		
	(32) Doctrine on Divorce		19:1-12	10:1-12			Deut. 24:1-4 Gen. 2:23-25
	(33) Jesus Blesses Children: Objections		19:13-15	10:13-16	18:15-17		
	(34) Rich Young Ruler	Perea	19:16-30	10:17-31	18:18-30		Ps. 131:2 Ex. 20:1-17
	(35) Laborers of the 11th Hour	Perea	20:1-16				
	(36) Foretells Death and Resurrection	{Near Jordan	20:17-19	10:32-34	18:31-34		Ps. 22
	(37) Ambition of James and John		20:20-28	10:35-45			
	(38) Blind Bartimaeus Healed	Jericho		10:46-52	18:35-43		
	(39) Interview with Zacchaeus	Jericho			19:1-10		
	(40) Parable: the Minas	Jericho			19:11-27		
	(41) Returns to Home of Mary and Martha	Bethany				{11:55-12:1	
	(42) Plot to Kill Lazarus	Bethany				12:9-11	

393

JESUS' FINAL WEEK OF WORK AT JERUSALEM IN 41 EVENTS

Date	Event	Location	Matthew	Mark	Luke	John	Related References
Spring A.D. 30							
Sunday	(1) Triumphal Entry	Bethany, Jerusalem, Bethany	21:1-9	11:1-11	19:28-44	12:12-19	Zech. 9:9
Monday	(2) Fig Tree Cursed and Temple Cleansed	{ Bethany to Jerusalem	21:10-19	11:12-18	19:45-48		Jer. 7:11
	(3) The Attraction of Sacrifice	Jerusalem				12:20-50	Isa. 6:10
Tuesday	(4) Withered Fig Tree Testifies	{ Bethany to Jerusalem	21:20-22	11:19-26			
	(5) Sanhedrin Challenges Jesus. Answered by Parables: Two Sons, Wicked Vinedressers, and Marriage Feast	Jerusalem	{ 21:23–22:14	{ 11:27–12:12	20:1-19		Isa. 5:1, 2
	(6) Tribute to Caesar	Jerusalem	22:15-22	12:13-17	20:20-26		
	(7) Sadducees Question the Resurrection	Jerusalem	22:23-33	12:18-27	20:27-40		Ex. 3:6
	(8) Pharisees Question Commandments	Jerusalem	22:34-40	12:28-34	20:41-44		
	(9) Jesus and David	Jerusalem	22:41-46	12:35-37	20:45-47		Ps. 110:1
	(10) Jesus' Last Sermon	Jerusalem	23:1-39	12:38-40	21:1-4		
	(11) Widow's Mite	Jerusalem		12:41-44			Lev. 27:30

	Location	Matthew	Mark	Luke	John	Reference
(12) Jesus Tells of the Future	Mt. Olives	24:1-51	13:1-37	21:5-36		Dan. 12:1
(13) Parables: Ten Virgins, Talents. The Day of Judgment	Mt. Olives	25:1-46				Zech. 14:5
(14) Jesus Tells Date of Crucifixion		26:1-5	14:1, 2	22:1, 2		
(15) Anointing by Mary at Simon's Feast	Bethany	26:6-13	14:3-9		12:2-8	
(16) Judas Contracts the Betrayal		26:14-16	14:10, 11	22:3-6		Zech. 11:12
Thursday (17) Preparation for the Passover	Jerusalem	26:17-19	14:12-16	22:7-13		Ex. 12:14-28
Thursday P.M. (18) Passover Eaten. Jealousy Rebuked	Jerusalem	26:20	14:17	{ 22:14-16, 24-30		
(19) Feet Washed	Upper Room				13:1-20	
(20) Judas Revealed, Defects	Upper Room	26:21-25	14:18-21	22:21-23	13:21-30	Ps. 41:9
(21) Jesus Warns About Further Desertion; Cries of Loyalty	Upper Room	26:31-35	14:27-31	22:31-38	13:31-38	Zech. 13:7
(22) Institution of the Lord's Supper	Upper Room	26:26-29	14:22-25	22:17-20		1 Cor. 11:23-34
(23) Last Speech to the Apostles and Intercessory Prayer	Jerusalem				{ 14:1- 17:26	Ps. 35:19

Date	Event	Location	Matthew	Mark	Luke	John	Related References
Thursday-Friday Friday	(24) The Grief of Gethsemane	Mt. Olives	26:30, 36–46	14:26, 32–42	22:39–46	18:1	Ps. 42:6
	(25) Betrayal, Arrest, Desertion	Gethsemane	26:47–56	14:43–52	22:47–53	18:2–12	
	(26) First Examined by Annas	Jerusalem				18:12–14, 19–23	
	(27) Trial by Caiaphas and Council; Following Indignities	Jerusalem	26:57, 59–68	14:53, 55–65	22:54, 63–65	18:24	Lev. 24:16
	(28) Peter's Triple Denial	Jerusalem	26:58, 69–75	14:54, 66–72	22:54–62	18:15–18, 25–27	
	(29) Condemnation by the Council	Jerusalem	27:1	15:1	22:66–71		Ps. 110:1 Acts 1:18, 19
	(30) Suicide of Judas	Jerusalem	27:3–10				
	(31) First Appearance Before Pilate	Jerusalem	27:2, 11–14	15:1–5	23:1–7	18:28–38	
	(32) Jesus Before Herod	Jerusalem			23:6–12		
	(33) Second Appearance Before Pilate	Jerusalem	27:15–26	15:6–15	23:13–25	18:39– 19:16	Deut. 21:6–9
	(34) Mockery by Roman Soldiers	Jerusalem	27:27–30	15:16–19		19:16, 17	Ps. 69:21
	(35) Led to Golgotha	Jerusalem	27:31–34	15:20–23	23:26–33		
	(36) 6 Events of First 3 Hours on Cross	Calvary	27:35–44	15:24–32	23:33–43	19:18–27	Ps. 22:18
	(37) Last 3 Hours on Cross	Calvary	27:45–50	15:33–37	23:44–46	19:28–30	Ps. 22:1
	(38) Events Attending Jesus' Death	Calvary	27:51–56	15:38–41	23:45, 47–49		
	(39) Burial of Jesus	Jerusalem	27:57–60	15:42–46	23:50–54	19:31–37	Ex. 12:46

Friday-Saturday	(40) Tomb Sealed / (41) Women Watch	Jerusalem / Jerusalem	27:61-66	15:47	23:55, 56		Ex. 20:8-11

THE RESURRECTION THROUGH THE ASCENSION IN 12 EVENTS

Time	Event	Location	Matthew	Mark	Luke	John	Other
Dawn of First Day (Sunday, "Lord's Day")	(1) Women Visit the Tomb	Near Jerusalem	28:1-10	16:1-8	24:1-11		
	(2) Peter and John See the Empty Tomb				24:12	20:1-10	
	(3) Jesus' Appearance to Mary Magdalene	Jerusalem		16:9-11		20:11-18	
	(4) Jesus' Appearance to the Other Women	Jerusalem	28:9, 10				
	(5) Guards' Report of the Resurrection		28:11-15				
Sunday Afternoon	(6) Jesus' Appearance to Two Disciples on Way to Emmaus			16:12, 13	24:13-35		1 Cor. 15:5
Late Sunday	(7) Jesus' Appearance to Ten Disciples Without Thomas	Jerusalem		16:14	24:36-43	20:19-25	
One Week Later	(8) Appearance to Disciples with Thomas	Jerusalem				20:26-31	
During 40 Days until Ascension	(9) Jesus' Appearance to Seven Disciples by Sea of Galilee	Galilee				21:1-25	
	(10) Appearance to 500	Mt. in Galilee					1 Cor. 15:6
	(11) Great Commission	Mt. in Galilee	28:16-20	16:15-18	24:44-49		
Ascension	(12) The Ascension	Mt. Olivet		16:19, 20	24:50-53		Acts 1:4-11

397

THE PARABLES OF JESUS CHRIST

Parable	Matthew	Mark	Luke
1. Lamp Under a Basket	5:14–16	4:21, 22	8:16, 17
			11:33–36
2. A Wise Man Builds on Rock and a Foolish Man Builds on Sand	7:24–27		6:47–49
3. Unshrunk (New) Cloth on an Old Garment	9:16	2:21	5:36
4. New Wine in Old Wineskins	9:17	2:22	5:37, 38
5. The Sower	13:3–23	4:2–20	8:4–15
6. The Tares (Weeds)	13:24–30		
7. The Mustard Seed	13:31, 32	4:30–32	13:18, 19
8. The Leaven	13:33		13:20, 21
9. The Hidden Treasure	13:44		
10. The Pearl of Great Price	13:45, 46		
11. The Dragnet	13:47–50		
12. The Lost Sheep	18:12–14		15:3–7
13. The Unforgiving Servant	18:23–35		
14. The Workers in the Vineyard	20:1–16		
15. The Two Sons	21:28–32		
16. The Wicked Vinedressers	21:33–45	12:1–12	20:9–19
17. The Wedding Feast	22:2–14		
18. The Fig Tree	24:32–44	13:28–32	21:29–33
19. The Wise and Foolish Virgins	25:1–13		
20. The Talents	25:14–30		
21. The Growing Seed		4:26–29	
22. The Absent Householder		13:33–37	
23. The Creditor and Two Debtors			7:41–43
24. The Good Samaritan			10:30–37
25. A Friend in Need			11:5–13
26. The Rich Fool			12:16–21
27. The Faithful Servant and the Evil Servant			12:35–40
28. Faithful and Wise Steward			12:42–48
29. The Barren Fig Tree			13:6–9
30. The Great Supper			14:16–24
31. Building a Tower and a King Making War			14:25–35
32. The Lost Coin			15:8–10
33. The Lost Son			15:11–32
34. The Unjust Steward			16:1–13
35. The Rich Man and Lazarus			16:19–31
36. Unprofitable Servants			17:7–10
37. The Persistent Widow			18:1–8
38. The Pharisee and the Tax Collector			18:9–14
39. The Minas (Pounds)			19:11–27

THE MIRACLES OF JESUS CHRIST

Miracle	Matthew	Mark	Luke	John
1. Cleansing a Leper	8:2	1:40	5:12	
2. Healing a Centurion's Servant (of paralysis)	8:5		7:1	
3. Healing Peter's Mother-in-law	8:14	1:30	4:38	
4. Healing the Sick at Evening	8:16	1:32	4:40	
5. Stilling the Storm	8:23	4:35	8:22	
6. Demons Entering a Herd of Swine	8:28	5:1	8:26	
7. Healing a Paralytic	9:2	2:3	5:18	
8. Raising the Ruler's Daughter	9:18, 23	5:22, 35	8:40, 49	
9. Healing the Hemorrhaging Woman	9:20	5:25	8:43	
10. Healing Two Blind Men	9:27			
11. Curing a Demon-possessed, Mute Man	9:32			
12. Healing a Man's Withered Hand	12:9	3:1	6:6	
13. Curing a Demon-possessed, Blind and Mute Man	12:22		11:14	
14. Feeding the Five Thousand	14:13	6:30	9:10	6:1
15. Walking on the Sea	14:25	6:48		6:19
16. Healing the Gentile Woman's Daughter	15:21	7:24		
17. Feeding the Four Thousand	15:32	8:1		
18. Healing the Epileptic Boy	17:14	9:17	9:38	
19. Temple Tax in the Fish's Mouth	17:24			
20. Healing Two Blind Men	20:30	10:46	18:35	
21. Withering the Fig Tree	21:18	11:12		
22. Casting Out an Unclean Spirit		1:23	4:33	
23. Healing a Deaf Mute		7:31		
24. Healing a Blind Paralytic at Bethsaida		8:22		
25. Escape from the Hostile Multitude			4:30	
26. Draught of Fish			5:1	
27. Raising of a Widow's Son at Nain			7:11	
28. Healing the Infirm, Bent Woman			13:11	
29. Healing the Man with Dropsy			14:1	
30. Cleansing the Ten Lepers			17:11	
31. Restoring a Servant's Ear			22:51	
32. Turning Water into Wine				2:1
33. Healing the Nobleman's Son (of fever)				4:46
34. Healing an Infirm Man at Bethesda				5:1
35. Healing the Man Born Blind				9:1
36. Raising of Lazarus				11:43
37. Second Draught of Fish				21.1

medieval explanations of Bible

p 20

"Jahist" + "Elohist"

p 40

page 312 *